SWEET ROBI

No HAMLET in index

X rehab

O/p 266, 301 (TILBURY).

Does he quote anyone re Leicester's
ever smiling face etc?

- In his rehab of L., Wilson at the same
time describes his contemporary reputation
for intrigue, murder, adultery, (etc.)
(X, 306)
- Use 306 - 09 - 312329 etc 37
84

NOTHING re poisonings, except 325

L. hated by many 192, 3 per Cecil. 321

Death 303 - 4

DEREK WILSON

SWEET ROBIN

A Biography of
Robert Dudley, Earl of Leicester
1533-1588

a&b

This edition published in Great Britain in 1997 by
Allison & Busby Ltd
114 New Cavendish Street
London W1M 7FD

First published in Great Britain in 1981 by Hamish Hamilton Ltd

A catalogue record for this book is available from the
British Library

ISBN 0 74900 360 X

Typeset by N-J Design Associates
Romsey, Hampshire
Printed and bound in Great Britain by
Hartnolls Ltd
Bodmin, Cornwall

For Ruth
without whom . . .

. . . Robert Dudley, the Duke of Northumberland's younger Son, who was restored in bloud by Queen Mary, a man of flourishing age, and comely Feature of body and lims; whose Father and Grand-father were not so much hated of the people, but he was as much favoured by Queen Elizabeth, through her rare and Royal Clemency, who heaped Honours upon him, saving his life, whose Father would have had Her destroyed. Whether this proceeded from any Vertue of his, whereof he gave some shadowed tokens, or from their common condition of Imprisonment under Queen Mary, or from his Nativity, and the hidden consent of the Stars at the hour of their Birth, and thereby a most strait conjunction of their Minds, a man cannot easily say . . .

William Camden, 1615

CONTENTS

ILLUSTRATIONS

Between pages 148 and 149

We are grateful to the following for permission to reproduce illustrations: National Portrait Gallery, London, 1a, 2b; National Monuments Record, 1b; copyright the College of Arms (MS.C M6, f.416), 2a; National Trust, photograph courtesy of the Courtauld Institute of Art, 4a; The Marquess of Bath, Longleat House, Wiltshire, 3b 4b; Essex Record Office, 6b; Koninklijk Penningkabinet, The Hague, 8a, 8b; Rijkmuseum, Amsterdam, 7b; The Collection at Parham Park, Pulborough, West Sussex, 7a; Public Record Office, (Document SP12/215, no. 65) 8c; illustrations 1c and 5 are Crown copyright reproduced with the permission of the Controller of Her Majesty"s Stationery Office.

The map was drawn by Patrick Leeson.

INTRODUCTION

When a man has been the subject of no serious biography in four hundred years* it might reasonably be assumed either that he is of no lasting importance or that adequate material for a life does not exist. In the case of Robert Dudley, Earl of Leicester, neither assumption would be correct. He was a colourful and lively personality who, through his political activity, his patronage and, above all, his influence with his sovereign, made a considerable mark upon his age. A sizeable corpus of correspondence and personal papers has been preserved in the Marquess of Bath's library at Longleat and there are numerous letters written to or by Dudley in various other public and private collections. In addition, references to his activities abound in the foreign and domestic state papers of the period.

The reasons for four centuries of neglect are not, however, elusive. Contemporaries, especially jealous contemporaries who resented Leicester's hold on the Queen's affections, were wont to judge by appearances and to dismiss Robert Dudley as an extravagant, licentious and, therefore, shallow man. He was a royal favourite and such creatures are never popular. Add to this that both his father and grandfather had been executed for treason and it begins to become clear why it was difficult for many Tudor Englishmen to regard Robert Dudley as a positive, let alone a wholesome, influence in affairs of state. He was an easy target for libellers and gossip-mongers. Many leading figures in history have had their vilifiers but probably no piece of gross and obvious calumny has achieved such lasting success as that usually known as *Leicester's Commonwealth*. This chronicle of murders, adulteries, treasons, plots and deceptions was inspired by immediate political and religious motives but achieved a longer and separate life as a 'classic' of scurrility, being reprinted in every century from the sixteenth to the twentieth. It seems to have been generally assumed, doubtless on the dubious ground that there is 'no smoke without fire', that there must be a core of truth in the rotten fruit of lies and rumour. Even serious historians have allowed themselves to be deceived into dismissing Leicester as at best an irrelevance and at worst a bad influence on Elizabeth I.

*The studies by Waldman and Chamberlin, both entitled *Elizabeth and Leicester*, were not, as the titles suggest, full studies of Robert Dudley.

Fortunately, the tide has begun to turn in the last decade or two.Elizabeth Rosenberg has indicated the enormous importance of Leicester as a patron. Professor Collinson has demonstrated clearly Dudley's close involvement with the Puritan cause. Professors MacCaffrey, Pulman and others have pulled into sharper focus the political landscape of Elizabethan England and drawn attention to Dudley's contribution as an activist motivated, partly at least, by principle rather than by personal ambition. More work, however, needs to be done if Leicester's career and, indeed, Elizabeth's reign are to be seen in truer perspective.

What I have attempted in the present study is a general biography of Dudley which would illustrate as many aspects of his life as possible and provide a sound argument for that rehabilitation of Leicester which is clearly long overdue. In deliberately choosing a large canvas I have had to inhibit myself over some matters of detail. It would have been possible to devote more time and study to many aspects of my subject - an analysis of Dudley's household accounts, a closer examination of the position he occupied in the royal court, his network of agents and protégés, his day to day handling of affairs in the Netherlands during his governorship, etc., etc. In avoiding such minutiae I have been motivated by my own limitations, the stipulations of my long-suffering publishers as to the length of the book, and the hope that abler scholars than I will fill the gaps and make good the shortcomings of the present narrative.

Having said all that, there is one area in which I have felt it necessary to 'spread' myself in the present book, a decision which some readers may believe should be justified. If a re-evaluation of Robert Dudley's place in history is vitally necessary, a fresh appreciation of his father's character and importance is more so. For too long John Dudley has been regarded as one of the foremost English villains; the schemer who deliberately wrought the downfall of Somerset and sought to divert the royal succession into his own family; a man whose only loyalty was to himself; a politique who sought power for its own sake. This verdict is such an absurd distortion that to accept it is to misread completely the story of England in the years 1547-1553. These were the years of Robert Dudley's adolescence. This highly impressionable period of his life was spent in the royal court as companion to the young king while his father and elder brothers were involved in a prolonged and ever-changing power struggle. Since it is important to understand the background to Robert's early life and particularly his father's place in it, and since these events need reinterpreting, I have felt it necessary to cover them in more detail than I would otherwise have done. Anyone who remains unconvinced by this line of argument I can only advise to begin reading at Chapter 4.

This book has been several years in the writing and during my research I have run up heavy debts of obligation to many people. The Marquess of Bath gave permission for me to study the Dudley Papers at Longleat, and his librarian, Miss Austin, was the epitome of courtesy and helpfulness to a student who made great demands on her already full timetable. Viscount de L'Isle and Dudley allowed me access to his family papers. I am grateful to the staff of the following institutions for information and assistance of many kinds: Wiltshire Library and Museum Service, the Public Record Office, the British Library, Cambridge University Library, Clwyd Record Office, Norfolk County Archives Office, the University of Bristol Library, Exeter University Library, Liverpool University Library, Kent County Archive Office, Essex Records Office and the National Registry of Archives. Mrs John Stephens and her colleagues in the West Somerset Library Service have once again provided a magnificent book-finding service. Mrs W Stubbings helped me to obtain information about Robert's house at Wanstead.

A very special 'thank you' is due to Professor Patrick Collinson who read my first draft and made many very helpful suggestions for improvements. For encouragement and advice I am also indebted to Dr Claire Cross and Dame Daphne de Maurier. My English and American publishers were alike patient about the length of time taken to deliver the typescript and to make the necessary revisions. Miss Caroline Tonson Rye handled both script and author with tact and efficiency. My wife did so much more than just type the various drafts, though that was no simple task. To all who have made this book possible I offer my profound thanks. I hope they find *Sweet Robin* worthy of their endeavours.

CHAPTER ONE

'DROIT ET LOYAL'

> I am a Dudley in blood . . . and do acknowledge . . . that
> my chiefest honour is to be a Dudley, and truly am glad to
> have cause to set forth the nobility of that blood whereof I
> am descended.[1]

The words were written by Sir Philip Sidney, one of the most popular and gifted Elizabethans, in defence of one of the most widely
disliked and misunderstood. The soldier-poet was writing to refute
a scurrilous attack* upon his uncle, Robert Dudley, Earl of Leicester.
Sidney's work remained in manuscript for over a century and a half.
The original libel was published and re-published, translated and
re-translated, until it had achieved total success in its attempt to
transform a living man into a legendary monster.[2] Leicester's
detractors have held the field ever since.

Not content with accusing his victim of sorcery, murder and a
Pandora's box of other crimes, the anonymous author of *Leicester's
Commonwealth* reached back into Dudley's ancestry to strip his progenitors of their nobility. The story was soon current that Robert's
'upstart' father was the son of a Staffordshire carpenter.

In fact, the blood which flowed in Leicester's veins could scarcely
have been bluer, as Philip Sidney was at pains to point out in his
defence. It is true that in the male line Robert was descended from
a mere cadet branch of the baronial Dudley family but his ancestry
was embellished with such ancient and prestigious names as Talbot,
Beauchamp and Neville.

The Elizabethan experts in all matters genealogical and armorial
were in no doubt about Leicester's origins. Robert Glover, Somerset
Herald, wrote:

> The origin of this family is to be sought either in the most illustri-
> ous race of the Suttons of Holderness, in the province of York, or
> rather from the origin of the ancient family of the same name
> which formerly was settled in the county of Nottingham, near
> Worksop.
>
> Some of these enrolled in the list of barons derived their titles of
> dignity from Malpas and Shocklachen in the county of Chester,
> and from the very ancient castle of Dudley, in the country of

*Leicester's Commonwealth, discussed in full on pp. 252-70 below.

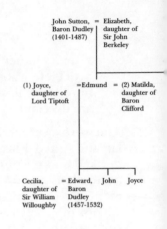
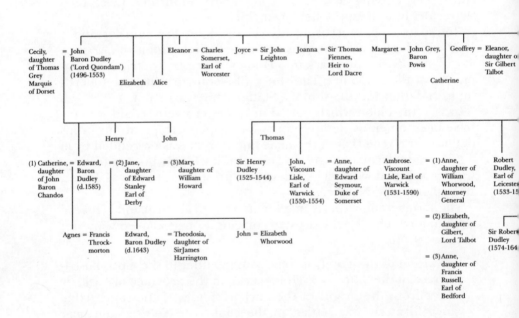

John Sutton, = Elizabeth,
Baron Dudley | daughter of
(1401-1487) | Sir John
Berkeley

(1) Joyce, = Edmund = (2) Matilda,
daughter of | daughter of
Lord Tiptoft | Baron
Clifford

Cecilia, = Edward,   John   Joyce
daughter of   Baron
Sir William   Dudley
Willoughby   (1457-1532)

Cecily, = John   Eleanor = Charles   Joyce = Sir John   Joanna = Sir Thomas   Margaret = John Grey,   Geoffrey = Eleanor,
daughter   Baron Dudley   Somerset,   Leighton   Fiennes,   Baron   daughter of
of Thomas   ('Lord Quondam')   Earl of   Heir to   Powis   Sir Gilbert
Grey   (1496-1553)   Worcester   Lord Dacre   Talbot
Marquis   Elizabeth   Alice
of Dorset   Catherine

Henry   John   Thomas

(1) Catherine, = Edward, = (2) Jane, = (3) Mary,   Sir Henry   John,   = Anne,   Ambrose.   = (1) Anne,   Robert
daughter   Baron   daughter   daughter of   Dudley   Viscount   daughter of   Viscount   daughter of   Dudley,
of John   Dudley   of Edward   William   (1525-1544)   Lisle,   Edward   Lisle, Earl of   William   Earl of
Baron   (d.1585)   Stanley   Howard   Earl of   Seymour,   Warwick   Whorwood,   Leicester
Chandos   Earl of   Warwick   Duke of   (1531-1590)   Attorney   (1533-15...)
Derby   (1530-1554)   Somerset   General

Agnes = Francis   Edward,   = Theodosia,   John = Elizabeth   = (2) Elizabeth,
Throck-   Baron Dudley   daughter of   Whorwood   daughter of
morton   (d.1643)   Sir James   Gilbert,   Sir Robert
Harrington   Lord Talbot   Dudley
(1574-164...)
= (3) Anne,
daughter of
Francis
Russell,
Earl of
Bedford

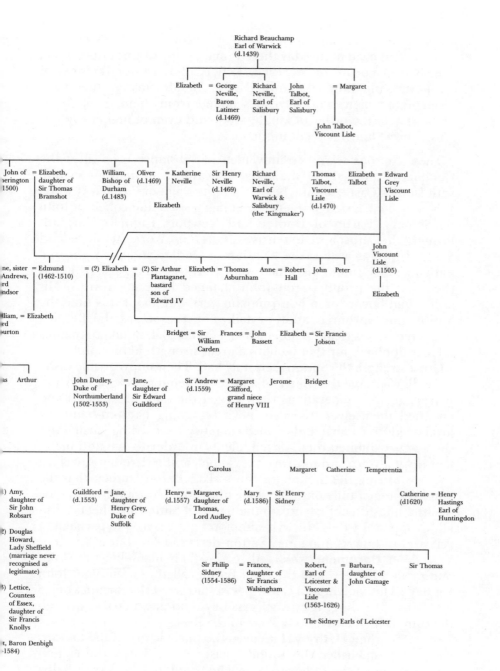

Richard Beauchamp
Earl of Warwick
(d.1439)

Elizabeth = George Neville, Baron Latimer (d.1469)   Richard Neville, Earl of Salisbury   John Talbot, Earl of Salisbury = Margaret

John Talbot, Viscount Lisle

John of ...erington ...500) = Elizabeth, daughter of Sir Thomas Bramshot

William, Bishop of Durham (d.1483)   Oliver (d.1469) = Katherine Neville   Sir Henry Neville (d.1469)

Elizabeth

Richard Neville, Earl of Warwick & Salisbury (the 'Kingmaker')

Thomas Talbot, Viscount Lisle (d.1470)   Elizabeth Talbot   Elizabeth = Edward Grey Viscount Lisle

John Viscount Lisle (d.1505)

Elizabeth

ne, sister = Edmund Andrews, (1462-1510) rd ndsor

lliam, = Elizabeth rd urton

= (2) Elizabeth = (2) Sir Arthur Plantaganet, bastard son of Edward IV   Elizabeth = Thomas Asburnham   Anne = Robert Hall   John   Peter

Bridget = Sir William Carden   Frances = John Bassett   Elizabeth = Sir Francis Jobson

as   Arthur

John Dudley, Duke of Northumberland (1502-1553) = Jane, daughter of Sir Edward Guildford   Sir Andrew = Margaret (d.1559) Clifford, grand niece of Henry VIII   Jerome   Bridget

Carolus   Margaret   Catherine   Temperentia

.) Amy, daughter of Sir John Robsart

2) Douglas Howard, Lady Sheffield (marriage never recognised as legitimate)

) Lettice, Countess of Essex, daughter of Sir Francis Knollys

t, Baron Denbigh -1584)

Guildford (d.1553) = Jane, daughter of Henry Grey, Duke of Suffolk

Henry = Margaret, (d.1557) daughter of Thomas, Lord Audley   Mary = Sir Henry (d.1586) Sidney

Catherine = Henry (d1620) Hastings Earl of Huntingdon

Sir Philip Sidney (1554-1586) = Frances, daughter of Sir Francis Walsingham

Robert, Earl of Leicester & Viscount Lisle (1563-1626) = Barbara, daughter of John Gamage   Sir Thomas

The Sidney Earls of Leicester

Worcester – domains formerly of no inconsiderable extent and value; and even to this day there remain some distinguished men, such as Ambrose of Warwick, Robert of Leicester (knights of renown) and Edward Baron Dudley, besides many other most celebrated men, who have descended from them through an ancestry of the order of knighthood, and even of higher dignity, by a direct lineal descent in the male line.[3]

These Suttons were certainly men of substance soon after the Conqueror studded the Midlands with castles, but their association with Dudley Castle did not begin until the reign of Edward II when John Sutton married Margaret de Somery, sister and coheir of John de Somery, Baron of Dudley and Newport Pagnell. Margaret brought her husband extensive estates in Worcestershire and Staffordshire as well as the lordship of Dudley and the right to a parliamentary summons which went with the title. Perhaps it was then that the proud Baron John changed his coat of arms. His father had borne 'or, a lion rampant vert' but about this time the Sutton lion sprouted another tail. The reason, as the heralds pointed out, was clear: 'A lion having a double tail, signifieth that his force is doubled, for that he hath a great strength in his tail.'[4]

Great strength the Suttons certainly had. Their impregnable castle at Dudley became the centre of an ever-widening circle of land and patronage. For generations they served the king of England and enriched themselves (the two inevitably going hand-in-hand) by loyal deeds in combat and council chamber. Succeeding barons and their sons exploited their varied talents in order to win and maintain royal favour, and to prove the family motto: 'Droit et Loyal'.

It was during the lifetime of John, sixth Baron Dudley, that the family emerged fully onto the stage of national history. By this time (i.e. the mid-fifteenth century) the name of Sutton had been virtually dropped. In 1342 the writ summoning the Baron to parliament referred to him as 'Johannes Sutton de Duddeley' but a hundred years later documents referred to the then incumbent as 'John Sutton alias Dudley' and the sixth Baron called himself plain John Dudley.[5] This violent and canny peer established the fortunes of his family by threading his way successfully – no mean task – through the complicated and bloody Wars of the Roses.

By 1485, when Henry VII secured the final victory of the Lancastrians and established the Tudor dynasty, Baron Dudley, at eighty-four, was one of the few great men who could look back over half a century of civil strife with a degree of cynical detachment. The old man had outlived all his sons except John Dudley of Atherington.

Both men accepted the new regime and were accepted by it. Within months of Henry's accession the younger John was pricked sheriff of Sussex and, with Sir Reginald Bray, was nominated to enquire into the King's possessions in the county and this was but the first of many capacities in which the lord of Atherington served the Tudor regime in the field of local government.

Baron Dudley remained in full possession of his faculties until near the end of his remarkably long life. He died on 30 September 1487 and was succeeded by his thirty-year-old grandson, Edward (heir of his eldest son, Edmund). From this point onward the senior line of the baronial family has only peripheral interest to our story, which is primarily concerned with John of Atherington and his descendants.

As far as we know, five of the children born to John and Elizabeth, his wife, survived infancy. Their first son, Edmund, was born about 1462. He was the child of a new generation. His grandfather and father were fighting men. His Uncle William was Bishop of Durham. But Edmund's education was dominated neither by martial arts nor theology. He passed his most impressionable years at Oxford and Gray's Inn in company with the scions of many other noble houses, the sons of prosperous merchants and the poor scholars whose gentle or yeoman fathers had pawned their meagre lands to put them to the common law.[6]

Edmund learned well and by 1485 his talent had already marked him out as an up and coming lawyer of considerable promise. He also enjoyed the patronage of Sir Reginald Bray, one of the most influential of Henry VII's confidential advisers known as 'the King's Council Learned in the Law', which acted as a special court for trying cases of a financial nature and as a royal debt collecting agency. Edmund became Under-Sheriff of London about 1499 and Speaker of the House of Commons in 1504, a sure sign that Henry Tudor had taken notice of him. That fact was confirmed before the year was out when Edmund Dudley's name appeared among the members of the royal Council. Before long he was a member of the Council Learned in the Law. The perquisites of office brought him the wherewithal to extend his Sussex and Hampshire estates and to buy extensive acreages in Lincolnshire, Cambridgeshire, Oxfordshire, Wiltshire, Dorset and Surrey. He now had a fine house at the heart of the capital in Candlewick Street, close by the ancient London Stone, one of the sights of the City. Next door lived the Council colleague with whom Dudley's name has always been bracketed, Sir Richard Empson.

Empson and Dudley were the principal agents in devising and executing those rapacious policies which put financial pressure on the King's wealthier subjects. With their colleagues they ferreted among private papers to discover lands and other sources of revenue which had been concealed. They prosecuted in the prerogative courts those who had offended the King. They devised ways to exploit long defunct feudal laws to the advantage of the exchequer.[7] Not only were they well rewarded by a grateful sovereign, they also received bribes from anxious suitors and defendants. Inevitably they were accused of perverting justice for their own ends. In the popular imagination Empson and Dudley represented a grasping and despotic king, and, since it was treason to grumble against the head of state, men grumbled at his agents instead.

When, in 1509, Henry VII lay dying, Empson and Dudley were obliged to take measures for their own protection. At their petition, the Council entered into a recognizance to hold no individual member guilty of crimes committed in pursuance of royal policy, and they seem to have taken the precaution of preparing harness and arranging for friends and dependants to muster in Candlewick Street in the event of trouble. When the time came either their resolve failed or their enemies acted too quickly. One of Henry VIII's first orders was for the arrest of the two ministers.

The recent recognizance was set aside on the ground that it had been 'made without any cause reasonable or lawful [by] certain of the learned Council of our late father, contrary to law, reason and good conscience'.[8] On 16 July 1509 Edmund Dudley was taken from the Tower to Guildhall and there arraigned on a charge of constructive treason in that he did conspire 'to seize the King and his Council by force and to govern according to his will'.[9] It was an absurd accusation designed to disembarrass the government of unpopular members. The two lawyers were both convicted of treason and confined to the Tower pending attainder and possible execution.

Edmund lay in the Tower for sixteen months. Apart from one abortive attempt to escape, he devoted most of his energies to writing, his principal accomplishment being an allegorical political treatise entitled *The Tree of Commonwealth*. This book, remarkable not so much for its originality as for its breadth and wisdom, was conceived as a vade-mecum for the new ruler. It reveals a humane man who had thought deeply about the affairs of kings and subjects, a brilliant lawyer capable of marshalling his thoughts to achieve the utmost clarity and impact, and a faithful servant impelled by 'a hearty good will and love towards the prosperous estate of my natural country'.[10] Loyalty to king and loyalty to country could not always be combined. Dudley was fully aware of his old master's faults and, if he was not prepared to challenge Henry VII in life, he certainly advised his successor to avoid the avarice and the manipulation of the law which had been his father's weaknesses.

If Henry VIII had read and taken note of Dudley's words England might have been spared a great deal of bloodshed and turbulence.

He did not. *The Tree of Commonwealth* remained in manuscript form in the royal archives and was destined not to be printed for centuries, though transcripts were made for the financier's famous son and grandson. The long delay in despatching Empson and Dudley may suggest a certain reluctance on the part of the government to exact the ultimate penalty. Their attainders were complete in January 1510 but it was 17 August before the two men were led out to their execution on Tower Hill. Even in death many privileges were extended to them, a further indication that their persecutors had little confidence in the justice of their actions. The normal barbarous sentence for traitors was commuted to simple beheading. Their bodies were not interred unceremoniously in the Chapel of St Peter ad Vincula at the Tower; permission was given for burial according to their own wishes. Dudley was, accordingly, laid to rest in the Church of the Black Friars in the south-west corner of the City. The severed heads of the 'traitors' were also treated with seemly reverence and not stuck on poles for prominent display as was the custom.

Edmund Dudley left a widow and five children. Of these only the eldest, Elizabeth, was already married to William, Lord Stourton. Within fifteen months the children's mother married again. Henceforth she bore a far more illustrious name, for her new husband was Arthur Plantagenet, thirty-year-old illegitimate son of Edward IV. The Tudors liked to keep a close watch on all would-be Yorkist claimants to the crown, and bastards were no exception. Arthur Plantagenet was kept at court as an esquire on Henry VIII's bodyguard with a quarterly salary of £6. 13s. 4d. Marriage to Elizabeth Dudley enabled him to set himself up in a more becoming style, for the attainder on the late minister was reversed in his favour and he received, with his wife, most of Edmund's lands.

But it was to Kent that nine-year-old John Dudley, Edmund's heir, was despatched. His wardship was purchased by Sir Edward Guildford, an old friend of his father.* Guildford was Master of the Ordnance and (later) Warden of the Cinque Ports and Marshal of Calais. He was one of the three major landowners in Kent and

---

*By feudal law when a man died leaving his estates to a minor the heir became a ward of the Crown until he became of age, when he paid the appropriate fee (*relief*) and entered on his inheritance. In practice, these wardships were usually sold to prominent courtiers or magnates who could then administer the lands during the minority and arrange for the marriage of the heir to a member of their own family. This was one of the principal ways of building up estates in the sixteenth century.

Sussex, the heart of his extensive lands being around Tenterden and his principal residence at High Halden. He was the ideal man to give his young ward a solid grounding both in estate management and also the accomplishments of a courtier.

It was thanks to his guardian that John Dudley's family fortunes were restored and his own career established. Guildford had no sons of his own and a really close bond was established between the man and the boy. At an early age John was betrothed to Sir Edward's daughter, Jane, and when they were old enough they were married. Here again a deep and lasting affection was established and the union was much more successful than were many arranged marriages. Through over thirty years John was faithful to his wife. She, for her part, bore him thirteen children and revered her husband's memory to the last, even though she may have had cause to blame him for the straitened circumstances in which she found herself at the end. Her will contains many references to 'my lord, my dear husband'. She leaves to her daughter Mary a clock 'that was the lord her father's, praying her to keep it as a jewel'.

John Dudley was a young man of only modest means when he began to make his mark at court. In 1521 he was a member of Cardinal Wolsey's entourage on a diplomatic mission to France. Two years later he was back in that country as an officer in the Duke of Suffolk's army. He had scarcely come of age when he was knighted by the Duke following a battle at the crossing of the Somme.[11] It was as a soldier and an exponent of the martial arts that John made his name. In 1524 he excelled himself in the tourney which formed part of the Christmas celebrations at Greenwich. Probably this was not his first performance in the lists. Certainly from henceforth he was one of the great champions of the tilt-yard and frequently rode in the royal team against foreign challengers.

At this stage of his career John Dudley was only one young hopeful in a court full to overflowing with ambitious young men seeking wealth and employment in the royal service. Nor did his prospects appear very bright when compared with those of his colleagues who were related to Henry's leading noblemen and ministers. His patrimony was small. The shadow of his father's attainder lay across his path. His patron, Edward Guildford, though an important official, certainly lacked the prestige to advance Dudley to the topmost rungs of royal service. Yet the young knight gained the support of first Wolsey, then Thomas Cromwell, and the favour of the King. He received titles, lands and important offices and by the end of the reign he was one of the leading men in the country.

Henry Tudor, like his father before him and Elizabeth after him, was a shrewd judge of character. He surrounded himself with men of talent and had no room for fools or incompetents. In John Dudley he saw a man after his own heart, a man who embodied all the virtues of medieval chivalry. Guildford's protégé was tall, darkly handsome, full of charm and recklessly brave. He was never happier than when on campaign against his country's enemies and was early marked out as a commander whom foes respected and soldiers happily followed. He was the King's man through and through; a favourite companion of Henry in the tilt-yard and in the hunting field; an unquestioning supporter of royal policy who proved his loyalty in combat of arms and (later) in House of Commons debate.

He also inherited his father's subtle mind. A contemporary averred that Dudley 'had such a head that he seldom went about anything, but he conceived first three or four purposes beforehand'.[12] Dudley the soldier was no empty-headed swashbuckler but a strategist and tactician of the front rank. He also applied his incisive intelligence to the achievement of personal wealth and power. He was very ambitious. Faithful service to the King could bring the most magnificent rewards and Dudley was no more indifferent to those rewards than any of his contemporaries. Initially his energies were directed towards acquiring the ancient Midlands estates of his family.

In January 1532 Edward, Baron Dudley, died. He had been but a shadow of his warlike, Midlands ancestors, spending most of his time at his rented house in Tothill Street, Westminster, and pawning many parcels of land in order to maintain an impressive style at court. The situation became worse when his son, John, inherited. The eighth Baron was a simpleton who proceeded with alarming rapidity to dispose of his entire patrimony in order to obtain ready cash. The situation presented Sir John Dudley with an unexpected opportunity and also a responsibility. If he could somehow find several thousand pounds, Dudley Castle and all the family's Midlands estates were his for the buying. He turned to his wealthy friends for aid and, on 3 July 1532, George Talbot, Earl of Shrewsbury, Thomas West, Baron de la Warr, Thomas Fitzalan, Lord Maltravers, William Whorwood, Attorney-General, Sir Thomas Arundell, Sir George Carew, Sir Thomas Wyatt and Sir Andrew Dudley (Sir John's brother) purchased the bulk of the baronial estates on behalf of Sir John Dudley for £4,200.

Whatever Sir John's motives, his actions were not such as to promote goodwill within the family. The Baron's closest relatives besieged him with visits and letters bitterly blaming him for allowing himself to be cheated out of his inheritance. He had, they insisted, made himself a laughing stock; all London was calling him 'Lord

Quondam' ('Lord Once-upon-a-time') and he had irretrievably impoverished his children and grandchildren. Neither these nor appeals to the King's most powerful minister, Thomas Cromwell, availed the Baron's family anything.[13] John Dudley was too secure in his Prince's favour. As he prospered, relatives and acquaintances swallowed their pride and clamoured for his patronage. Even Arthur, Lord Quondam's brother, made his peace with his cousin and, as a result of John's influence, was appointed Prebendary of Worcester.

By 1533 Sir Edward Guildford had become too infirm to carry out all his duties. John now succeeded him as Master of the Tower Armoury. In the following year the aged knight died and Sir John inherited, through his wife, all the Guildford lands in Kent and Sussex (though not without having to fight a long law suit with Sir Edward's nephew). He was also elected to fill the Commons seat made vacant by his guardian's death. Thus he took his place for the last few sessions of what history would call the Reformation Parliament. Amidst his many duties and his enthusiastic furthering of his own career he found time for some family life. Jane was sometimes at court with him, although she probably spent most of her time with the children in the country (or at Ely Place, Holborn, which John acquired at about this time). John's wife had borne him almost one child a year. The eldest was Henry, who was about eight. After him came Mary, John, Margaret, Ambrose and Catherine. And in the summer of that eventful year, 1533, Jane Dudley was brought to bed of yet another son, probably in her favourite house at Halden in Kent. He was born on John the Baptist's Day (24 June) but the Dudleys already had one son John. The new baby was christened Robert.[14]

CHAPTER TWO

CHILDHOOD

Robert was born into a family which was close-knit despite the strains imposed upon it by the demands of public life. As a father John Dudley was kind to the point of over-indulgence. His wife and children meant much to him, the more so as he emerged into greater prominence. The passing years brought increased public responsibilities, declining health and widespread unpopularity. Under these circumstances it was always to his family that he turned for comfort and appreciation. A few months before his death he wrote: 'What should I wish any longer this life, that seeth such frailty in it? Surely, but for a few children, which God has sent me, which also helps to pluck me on my knees, I have no great cause to desire to tarry much longer here'.[1]

In 1534 a sixth son was born to John and Jane and named Guildford, in memory of his grandfather. There followed another boy and four girls. Of the thirteen children Jane Dudley brought into the world, nine survived infancy, a high score for the sixteenth century. Contemporaries who were generous in the abuse they heaped upon the name of John Dudley never accused him of inconstancy or sexual debauchery. The few extant letters referring to family matters support this negative evidence. They reveal a genuine warmth between husband and wife, father and children. John's official reports from abroad contain messages to be passed on to Jane and promises of gifts on his return for her and the children. As late as 1552 when the troubled state of the border detained him in the north his despatch to Secretary Cecil concluded with the words 'I pray you keep this from my wife'.[2] In the same year his eldest son John, was on a diplomatic mission to France. It was the 22-year old lad's first experience of such responsibility and probably his first time abroad. A lack of savoir faire and the company of dishonest men ready to take advantage of him soon drove John into financial difficulties but he was too ashamed to send home for more money. When his father heard of John's plight he hastened to write and his mother appended a brief note in her own hand:

I had thought you had more discretion than to hurt yourself thorough fantasies or care, specially for such things as may be remedied or holpen. Well enough you must understand that I know you cannot live under great charges. And therefore you should not hide from me your debts whatsoever it be, for I would be loth but you should keep your credit with all men. And therefore send me word in any wise of the whole sum of your debts, for I and your mother will see them forthwith paid and whatsoever you do spend in honest service of our master and for his honour, so long as you do not let wild and wanton men consume it, as I have been served in my days, you must think all is spent as it should be, and all that I have must be yours and that you spend before, you may with God's grace help it hereafter by good and faithful service, wherein I trust you will never be found slack and then you may be sure you cannot lack, serving such a master as you have . . . whom the living God preserve and restore you to perfect health. And so with my blessing I commit you to his tuition. Your loving father,

Northumberland
P.S. Your loving mother that wishes you health daily,
Jane Northumberland.[3]

No serious rifts ever divided John from his family. His sons, when they grew to manhood, supported him loyally. Sir Andrew Dudley, himself a soldier of distinction, was content to follow his elder brother's lead. Even Lord Quondam's sons sought service with the man who had become de facto head of the family. Doubtless, this was in part an acknowledgement of John's growing prestige and power but there is plenty of evidence that John inspired deep devotion among many of his close associates. When we consider that such 'tribal solidarity' was by no means the norm in the upper ranks of Tudor society we can begin to put a true value on Dudley cohesiveness. The ideological conflicts of the Reformation era divided many families. Competing ambitions split others. The mighty Howard clan, for example, almost destroyed itself more than once by its internecine strife, and Edward Seymour, Duke of Somerset, might well have survived but for the jealousy of his brother, Thomas, and the intolerable arrogance of his wife.

The Dudley household spent most of the winter months at Ely Place, a magnificent fourteenth-century house near the City's western wall which was very convenient for a courtier eager to spend with his family the little free time his duties left him. The sprawling residence, once the London home of the bishops of Ely, was entered from Holborn via a massive gatehouse on which the gilded arms of Bishop Arundell, the builder, glowed in polychrome and gilt. Around its courtyards and cloister were ranged a great hall, chapel, numerous state rooms, chambers and domestic offices. The sergeants-at-law had often held their feasts there and, only a few years before the Dudleys took up residence they had entertained Henry VIII and Queen Catherine. The year was 1531 and the royal couple were already estranged so that it is no surprise to read that they dined in separate chambers. The numbers present on this occasion give a very good idea of the size of John Dudley's town house. Besides those who ate at the royal tables, there were the foreign ambassadors who were entertained in a third chamber.

> In the hall at the high table sat Sir Nicholas Lambard, Mayor of London, the judges, the barons of the Exchequer, with certain aldermen of the city. At the board on the south side sat the Master of the Rolls, the Master of the Chancery, and worshipful citizens. On the north side of the hall certain aldermen began the board, and then followed merchants of the city. In the cloister, chapel and gallery knights, esquires and gentlemen were placed. In the halls the crafts of London. The sergeants of law and their wives kept in their own chambers.[4]

The opportunities offered by all the dark corners of passageways for hide-and-go-seek and other games must have been endless and in fine weather there were the gardens. These stretched over ten acres and ran northwards from the house towards the open fields, watered by Turnmill Brook, the village of Islington and Highgate Hill on the skyline. Here Robert and his brothers and sisters must have enjoyed all the popular children's games of the time such as prisoners' bars and skittles. Here, too, the boys will have practised archery and sword play, and perhaps first flown a hawk and learned to sit a horse.

Ely place was not the only Dudley residence and every summer the family joined the exodus of wealthier citizens who moved to the country to escape the plague. There were the estates in Sussex and Kent to be visited and, as the years passed, John bought and sold property in many other parts of the country. Like most men close to the king, he profited from the dissolution of the monasteries gaining the priory of St James, Dudley, the Premonstratensian house at Halesowen and sundry other fragments of the confiscated lands. In 1545 the manor of Birmingham was among those which came his way. In all John's territorial negotiations a clear pattern emerges: steadily he was shifting his power base from the south-east to the Midlands and making Dudley Castle the centre of a much-augmented barony.

The new owner completely transformed the ancient de Sutton stronghold. The twelfth-century walls ringing the summit of the steep escarpment were retained, as were the impressive fourteenth-century gatehouse and keep. But the accommodation block along the eastern side of the courtyard was completely rebuilt as a compact but far from modest manor house in which every attention was paid to the comfort and convenience of the occupants. Dudley was able to acquire the services of no less a person than Sir William Sharington to plan and supervise the new work. In this age before the emergence of professional architects, Sharington was one of the most talented owner-designers in England. His great house at Lacock, converted from an Augustinian nunnery, was the envy of the Tudor aristocracy, most of whom were vying with each other in the creation of splendid mansions in this great epoch of English domestic building. Thirty or forty years after their construction the great hall and private chambers at Dudley were sufficiently grand for Queen Elizabeth to honour the owner with a visit.

The England of Robert's childhood was a profoundly disturbed land. The monasteries fell to decay. Land changed hands with astonishing rapidity as speculators rushed to take part in the property boom. Farms were consolidated. The open field system vanished from many areas. Arable land became pasture. Rural unemployment emptied hamlets and villages. Prices and rents (except for copyhold and longterm leases) rose. Wages fell. Old holy days were abolished. Religious discord was everywhere, severing established friendships and turning 'papist' fathers against 'heretic' sons. The power of central government reached deeper than before into men's lives. The people (and population was rising steadily in these years) were bewildered and resentful; some were in deep distress, driven to vagabondage, crime or destitution. And beneath all this disturbing social change were the revolutionary ideas of the Reformation. Scholars were questioning the age-old dogmas and practices of the Church. Lawyers and ministers were affirming the complete independence of the crown from papal control. Students and courtiers, merchants and peasants met in secret groups to study Tyndale's New Testament and other banned books. From time to time mistrust of religious innovation and resentment at economic uncertainty erupted into revolt. There were major outbreaks throughout the north in the winter of 1536-7. In 1549 Norfolk and the south-west were aflame with rebellion. The years between were far from quiescent.

Men at the centre of affairs had to choose whether they supported the forces of change or of conservatism. John Dudley was no scholar, a fact which he often lamented, but his sympathies were all with the

New Leaning. He lacked both the theologian's subtlety and the peasant's blind devotion to priest or Bible. He was a practical royal servant. The King's cause was his cause, the King's enemies his enemies.

One conviction that John fully shared with the humanist and reforming scholars was a belief in the importance of learning. As a boy he had been entered at the Inner Temple but, for some reason, he seems never to have followed either a legal training or the course of instruction offered to the sons of gentlemen at the inns of court. His practical education fitted him well for life as a soldier and courtier but he was no Latin scholar, he had an indifferent grasp of French and, as far as we know, mastered no other foreign language. Like many men conscious that they have missed out on book learning, John had a great respect for others with outstanding intellectual gifts. He loved to talk and correspond with theologians such as Cranmer and Hooper. He was the patron of eminent scholars like Thomas Wilson, Walter Haddon and John Cheke. He was particularly interested in the burgeoning sciences of mathematics, cosmography and astronomy, for these bore directly on maritime navigation with which he became closely concerned on his appointment as Lord High Admiral in 1543. Walter Haddon, writing in later years to Robert Dudley, extolled the attitude of the latter's father to scholars. Though we must make allowance for flattery there is no reason to doubt Haddon's veracity. 'You have certainly inherited a love of scholarship, for your father, although he acknowledged himself uneducated, was yet most devoted to learning. This was certainly apparent in his patronage of me, for, although he received no formal education, he valued highly one able to make a modest display of academic ability'.[5]

The scholarly gifts lacked by John were, to a certain extent, made up for by his wife. Jane Dudley had come under the influence of brilliant intellects at an early age. As a girl she had studied, together with Henry VIII's daughter Mary and the young Catherine Parr, in the royal school, where her instructor had been the great Spanish humanist, Juan Luys Vives. Vives' pioneer work, *The Education of a Christian Woman*, had a deep influence in England, its principles helping to produce that remarkable coterie of devout and learned ladies which included Catherine Parr, Margaret More, Elizabeth Tudor, Jane Grey, Anne Bacon and Mildred Cecil, some of whom were among Jane's friends.

With such parents it is not surprising that very close attention was paid to the education of the Dudley children: not only were they taught the traditional pursuits of the ancient families – feats of arms, horsemanship and the chase – but also more academic subjects. The result was that each of the children developed his or her own talents and interests. Henry, the eldest, showed an aptitude for military matters, John was the scholar and artist of the family,[6] and Ambrose, too, was a serious-minded young man. Sermons and theological debate probably attracted him from an early age. Certainly he would later become a major patron of Puritans and, as, the good Lord Warwick', a byword for charity and kindliness, Catherine, too, was a devout Christian and would later become the pious wife of Henry Hastings, the Calvinist Earl of Huntingdon.[7]

Robert had little natural aptitude for book learning. He was tall, handsome and athletic and loved most sports, but was never happier than when astride a horse in the hunting field. Only in one area of scholarship does his interest seem to have been seriously aroused: he was fascinated by mathematics and the new sciences. In this he was almost certainly influenced by John Dee, one of the most remarkable men of the English Renaissance, who was employed for a time as a tutor to the Dudley children. In 1564 Roger Ascham wrote to Robert deprecating his lack of fluency in Latin and his neglect of other languages, accomplishment in which was vital to a courtier-diplomat. He was scornful of Robert's preference for geometry rather than rhetoric: 'I think you did yourself injury in changing Tully's wisdom with Euclid's pricks and lines'.

Scholars were divided on the value of mathematical studies, or perhaps it would be truer to say they were concerned that such studies should be directed towards useful ends. Geometrical and arithmetical abstractions, according to Vives, 'withdraw the mind from the practical concerns of life and render it less fit to face concrete and mundane realities' and were only to be followed if they led to the understanding of 'measurement, proportion, movement and [the] position of heavy weights'. Astronomy also should not be studied for its own sake but

> should be applied to descriptions and determinations of time and seasons, without which rustic toil, on which all life is dependent, could not be carried on; then to the positions of places, showing what is the longitude and latitude of each, and to questions of distance. All this is very useful for cosmography and absolutely necessary to the general theory of navigation; without this knowledge the sailor would wander in uncertainty amidst the greatest and most grievous dangers.[8]

Yet, however much the educationalists might pontificate, minds like Robert Dudley's, which revelled in the divine mysteries of harmony, symmetry and pattern, were captivated by the rediscovered works of Euclid, Strabo, Pliny and Ptolemy. Nor need Ascham and Vives have worried: it was interest in the new sciences, coupled with a love of adventure, which inspired Robert's generation of young gentle-men to be the patrons and captains of the great era of Elizabethan maritime expansion. Indeed, one of the most important English works on navigation was dedicated to Robert Dudley as early at 1559. This was William Cunningham's *The Cosmographical Glass, containing the pleasant Principles of Cosmography, Geography, Hydrography, or Navigation.* In it the author thanks his patron for 'your Lordship's encouragement of me to knowledge, both in words and most liberal rewards' and praises him as one 'which doth not only favour Science, but also [has] given her within your breast a resting place.'[9]

On 12 July 1543 an event occurred which was to change the course of English history and which certainly had far reaching results for Robert Dudley. In a quiet ceremony at Hampton Court Henry VIII married Catherine Parr. Among the small gathering which witnessed Henry's last marriage was the new Queen's old friend and colleague, Jane Dudley. John would certainly have been present if he had not been at sea engaged in naval operations against the French. The couple's position at court scarcely needed strengthen-ing but additional security was always welcome in the household of the capricious Henry VIII. The real importance of Catherine Parr's elevation to the royal bed was that it established a moderate Protestant clique in the King's immediate circle, a clique which the forces of reaction were powerless to remove. Henry had only three and a half more years to live. During those years the radical party remained strong in court and Council. It was in an unassailable position at the King's death and ready to lead England farther along the road of Reformation during the reign of Edward VI. The importance of Catherine Parr's elevation for Robert Dudley was that it brought him into close contact with Princess Elizabeth.

Kindly, gentle, devout, twice-widowed Queen Catherine made it one of her objectives to bring together the children of Henry's vari-ous marriages and to attempt to create a family atmosphere around her sick husband. It was no easy matter to overcome the suspicions of Mary and Elizabeth, the bastardized and neglected princesses, but Catherine not only succeeded, she won their genuine affection. Within six weeks of her wedding she had brought the King and his children together at the royal manor of Ashridge. Throughout the rest of the reign the family was seldom under one roof but children and stepmother maintained contact through a continual inter-change of letters and gifts.

Catherine paid close attention to the education of Elizabeth and Edward. The prince and princess had their own households, of course, and their own tutors but there was an interchange of personnel and the same principles governed both establishments. The teachers, the men who, more than any others, shaped the minds of the royal children, were all of the humanist persuasion and most of them were from Cambridge, the academic home of the English Reformation. Richard Coxe was in charge of Edward's household and Sir John Cheke was his tutor-in-chief. William Grindal was Elizabeth's principal instructor and he was succeeded in 1548 by the greatest educationalist of them all, Roger Ascham. In 1545 William Buckley was brought to court to teach mathematics and related subjects. He was a captivating mentor who believed passionately that every possible means should be used to make learning a delight and pleasure to the young. His *Arithmetica Memorativa* was a translation of the rules of arithmetic into Latin verses so that they might be the more readily committed to memory.[10]

The royal schools were open to the children of leading courtiers and Jane Dudley lost little time in placing the younger members of her family in the classroom alongside the prince and princess. Robert was now frequently in the company of Elizabeth. They were of an age and, though the precociously brilliant girl far outstripped her companion academically, they had sufficient in common to become friends. They both especially enjoyed riding, the chase and dancing.

The friendship of a princess was valuable but the friendship of the heir to the throne was more so. Sometime in the mid 1540s Robert was placed in the household of Prince Edward.[11] By the time of his thirteenth birthday he must have become aware of the tense political background to all his games and lessons with the royal children; must have known that his parents had their own reasons for urging him to be on the best possible terms with the prince. These were precarious days. King Henry was ill and prematurely aged: his ulcerated legs gave him continual pain and brought on occasional fevers. More than once he came close to death and passed well beyond the limited competence of his band of physicians. Those near to the throne began to face the inevitability of the accession of a minor. They laid their plots and made their plans accordingly. Among the handful of men in the very top echelon of power John Dudley now found himself.

His promotion had been as steady and dramatic as it was well deserved. During the 1530s he had fulfilled a number of important and varied functions in court and county: MP for his late guardian's Kentish seat; Sheriff of Staffordshire; Master of the Horse to Anne of Cleves; enthusiastic propagandist of the Reformation in all areas where he had authority. But it was the renewed warfare of the 1540s which gave him the opportunity to prove his worth. When the King decided, after a decade or more, to return to an aggressive policy towards the alliance of France and Scotland he needed a new generation of generals. Two of the younger courtiers were obvious choices. One was the King's brother-in-law, Edward Seymour, Earl of Hertford. The other was his comrade in arms, John Dudley.

John was raised to the peerage in 1542. On the death of his step-father, Arthur Plantagenet Viscount Lisle, the title was recreated in favour of Dudley. He served on the northern border in the autumn and when, in November, Hertford, unwilling to be stationed far from court, sought to be released from his post as Lord Warden and Keeper of His Grace's Marches Towards Scotland it was Dudley who was appointed to succeed him. Two months later he again followed Seymour in a position hastily relinquished by the latter. It was one he would hold for the remainder of the reign, give up very reluctantly in 1547 and resume again in 1549 as soon as he had the power to do so. The title of Lord High Admiral was often conferred as an honour and reward upon a leading courtier or soldier. It was not considered necessary for the leader of the navy to have specialised knowledge. Naval warfare was traditionally a mere extension of land warfare and consisted largely of conveying troops and occasionally grappling with enemy vessels in order to engage in hand-to-hand fighting. But times were changing. The increasing fire power of ships ushered in a new era of naval tactics. All the major powers were experimenting with designs of sailing vessels and galleys. The golden accomplishments of Spanish and Portuguese conquistadors inspired captains of other nations to venture farther on to unknown seas. Scientific and mathematical discoveries promised important innovations for navigators.

John Dudley was aware of all this when he accepted the post of Lord High Admiral in January 1543. He was aware of his sovereign's care for and pride in the English navy. He was aware, above all, of his own inadequacy for the task. All this is evident from the detailed and frequent letters he was soon writing concerning the day-to-day administration of maritime affairs.

> . . . and where your lordships writeth unto me that the King's Majesty's pleasure is, that when Baldwin Willoughby, and the other three captains do come unto me I should instruct every of them, after my discretion and wisdom, for the execution of such charge as shall be committed unto them, my lords, it shall be most requisite that the King's Majesty's instructions for Sir Rice Mansfield (who is appointed for this time Vice Admiral) be devised by your lordships, and to be signed by the King's Majesty, and to be sent hither with speed; and that done I shall endeavour myself, as far as my poor wit

and discretion will serve, to give them the best advice that I can, albeit that I know it right well I had more need to be instructed in such like cause by some of them, than they by me.[12]

In this post, as in all others he undertook, John Dudley applied himself with enormous industry and creative effort. Letters flowed from his pen. He seldom slept before all the day's business had been concluded. Nor was this activity simply directed towards keeping the existing organisation in motion. It was during his tenure of office that the Navy Board was founded – the first regular government department to cater for the needs of ships and sailors. He established the first floating academy for English captains under the greatest living expert, Sebastian Cabot. He patronised scientific scholars such as John Dee and William Cunningham. He encouraged and backed enterprising captains and it was during his period in supreme power (1549-1553) that the first official English expeditions began to explore the farther reaches of the Atlantic, the Levant and the coast of Africa. This stage of maritime expansion culminated in the departure of Sir Hugh Willoughby's fleet questing for the north-east passage.[13]

The Dudley home was certainly a bustling and intellectually lively place during those years. When Viscount Lisle was not at sea or on campaign he conducted much of his official business from Ely Place. Here he presided over sessions of the High Court of Admiralty, hearing complaints about piracy, evasions of harbour dues and plundering of wrecks. Here he planned military and mercantile expeditions with members of the Navy Board, captains and merchants from London, Bristol, Southampton. Here he increased his own knowledge of practical seamanship and theoretical navigation in discussion with Cabot, Dee, Chancellor and others of that new intelligentsia who had a vision of their country as a leading maritime power. It is little wonder that John, Ambrose and Robert all shared their father's enthusiasm for overseas adventure or that Ambrose and Robert, the only boys to survive the collapse of the family fortunes in 1553, became prime movers in the expansion of Elizabethan England.

In April 1543 Lisle received the supreme accolade: he was admitted to the Order of the Garter and appointed a member of the Council. It had taken thirty-four years, but the son of the disgraced Edmund Dudley had, at last, regained his father's place at his sovereign's right hand. Both men had followed the same path to recognition and fortune. It was the one most succinctly described in the family motto, 'Droit et Loyal'. Edmund and John had devoted themselves wholeheartedly to their royal masters. Although this unquestioning devotion had ultimately destroyed his father, John religiously brought

t the siege of Boulogne. On this campaign he took with him
t son, Henry. The action lasted for two months and on 18
er the Tudor monarch, who still styled himself king of
and France, entered the town in high spirits at the head of
rious forces.

a hollow triumph. English losses were few but the campaign
ously expensive. Boulogne had little value and would remain
cial and diplomatic millstone until the government (then
ed by Dudley) restored it to the French six years later.
t Lisle came in for his share of praise from an ebullient King
him, also, Boulogne had been taken at too great a cost. Among
illed in the preliminary skirmishing was his son and heir.

e Henry's body was sent home for interment his father was
ted Governor of Boulogne, charged with the task of rebuild-
d strengthening the fortifications. At his own petition he was
ted to keep the post of Lord High Admiral. In both functions
s extremely and vitally busy during the following critical
s. He put Boulogne in a state of defence. He harried French
ng and harbours. He warded off a massive invasion attempt in
mmer of 1545. Soon his wide responsibilities were subsumed
r the grand title of Lieutenant General of the Army and
da upon the Sea in Outward Parts against the French.

n Dudley was now propelled into the forefront of public notice
esteem. He was England's greatest general. The king recog-
it, the Duke of Suffolk recognised it.[16] His French opposite
ber, Admiral d'Annebault, recognised it. Wherever he went the
le acclaimed him as a hero. The failures and comparatively
est successes of other commanders served only to highlight
ley's achievements. After Charles Brandon's death in August
Lisle to some extent filled the large gap made in Henry's life
he loss of his old friend. On his visits to court he was seldom out
he King's company. Frequently the two played cards together
o into Henry's sleepless nights. By the late summer of 1546 it
becoming obvious to the Imperial ambassador that a radical
ty had emerged which dominated court and Council and that
n Dudley was one of its leaders.

the King favours these stirrers of heresy, the Earl of Hertford and
he Lord Admiral, which is to be feared both for the reasons that I
ave already given and because the Queen, instigated by the
Duchess of Suffolk, the Countess of Hertford and the Lord Admiral's
wife, shows herself infected, words and exhortations, even in the
name of your Majesty, would only make the king more obstinate.[17]

up his own children to place duty to th

His military and naval duties, howe
be absent from Council meetings. In
fleet which carried Seymour and the a
rode at his friend's side on a fearsom
Leith and the Lowlands. After a few
Lisle rode southwards to bear the news
to King Henry, carrying in his purse a le
which began:

Pleasith Your Highness to be advertise
Lord Admiral repaireth unto your Ma
to recommend him unto your Highne
you hardly, wisely, diligently, painfully,
that I have seen, most (humbly) beseech
may perceive by Your Highness that I ha

John Dudley always needed assurance. T
the competition fierce; for years he had ha
and colleague as a potential rival. Even no
what he must have regarded as the summit
to be sure that his services were being fa
others were not taking all the credit. Suspicio
constant bedfellows to the very end.

Lisle had more cause than most to be appr
and, increasingly, as a sailor he was in his own
enjoyed administration. He was not happy or
desk and he was only too aware of his shortco

Your lordships doth know my bringing up
practised nor experimented in no matters o
time. At my first coming hither [i.e. to Scotla
written early in 1543] it was open war; it was
conduce those affairs than these which be
Therefore knowing mine own infirmity and t
me in day and night, lest anything should pass
gence contrary to the King's majesty's pleasure,
bounden duty and for mine own discharge, b
your lordships herewith.[15]

Lisle was recalled to London in order to comp
for one of the most grandiose expeditions of the re
himself was going on campaign to France. The L
the king and his army of over 40,000 men safely acr
and then took up his position as second in comman

Suffolk a
his eldes
Septemb
Englanc
his vict

It was
was rui
a finan
control
Viscou
but for
those k

Whil
appoii
ing an
permi
he wa
month
shipp
the s
unde
Arma

Joh
and
nisec
num
peop
mo
Duc
154
by t
of t
dee
wa
pai
Jol

I
t
l

Seymour and Dudley, they were the leaders at Court during the last months of Henry VIII's reign. They were still there when the king died. As late as 29 January 1547 (two days before Henry VIII's death was announced) Eustace Chapuys wrote, 'If (which God forbid) the king should die . . . it is probable that these two men, Seymour and Dudley, will have the management of affairs, because apart from the king's affection for them, and other reasons, there are no other nobles of a fit age and ability for the task.'[18]

Robert, now entering his teens, had an honoured place at court. He was able to attend banquets (probably as cup-bearer to his father or his Uncle Andrew) and other festivities. Perhaps he was present in July 1545 when the king went to Portsmouth with his household and was entertained to dinner by his Lord Admiral aboard the flag-ship *Henri Grâce à Dieu*. Furthermore, with two older brothers to be trained for the serious work of politics and the management of the Dudleys' increasing territorial empire, Robert was relatively free to indulge more congenial pursuits. John Dudley liked to see all his sons well practised in the martial arts and in Robert he had a boy eager and able to emulate his own exploits in the tilt-yard. Almost certainly Robert had his first suit of armour before his age was reckoned in double figures, although he would only have worn it for ceremonial purposes and for short periods of time. Outfits of padded canvas and leather were more regularly worn for practising the various aspects of mounted and foot combat. Under expert tuition Robert, together with his brothers and friends, ran at the quoit and the quintain, and fought with sword, pike and staff. He paid particular attention to the science of 'defence' or fencing, for his father was a patron of this increasingly popular craft and one of the first schools in London was set up in Ely Place. There, favoured and wealthy pupils, including the Dudley boys, were instructed into the elaborate mysteries of combat with estoc, rapier, buckler and left-handed dagger by Spanish and Italian masters who chalked out intricate moves on the floor and were notorious for the strange oaths with which their instructions were salted.

Contemporary records speak of two groups of young men in the princely court: the 'henchmen' and the 'young lords attendant upon the Prince'. It is not clear whether or not there was, in fact, a distinction between different categories of Edward's attendants or whether the two terms describe the same body of young men.[19] Possibly the titles indicate a social distinction which was of small importance in the day-to-day working of the household. Prince Edward's companions were boys (for the most part older than their royal master) who attended lessons with him, played with him, attended him on formal occasions and sometimes stood proxy for him. It seems to have been a large group, a fact which undoubtedly reflects the successful endeavours of place hunters. It is significant that by September 1552 so many young lords were eating at court that their table had to be 'stopped'.[20]

Apart from the royal tutors, the young attendants had their own mentors. In overall charge was the Master of the Henchmen and his deputy was the Yeoman. In addition there was a schoolmaster. For example, in July 1550 William Buckley M. A. was appointed instructor of the 'adolescentulos nostros vocatos *henchmen*' – 'our young men called *henchmen*' at £40 per annum.[21] The schoolmaster was a kind of tutor responsible for the all-round education of his charges and co-ordinating the efforts of his colleagues. Buckley had been some time on the royal teaching staff. His knowledge of mathematics and his novel method of teaching impressed Edward deeply and made their mark on his companions, and not least upon Robert Dudley.

As well as the regular routine of lessons, the Prince and his companions were urged to hear sermons on Sundays and the important Christian festivals. Hugh Latimer, Archbishop Cranmer Nicholas Ridley, Thomas Becon, John Taylor and other reformist theologians were among the frequent visitors to the royal chapel. Edward paid close attention to these devout and earnest men, taking copious notes of their sermons and discussing them with his teachers and fellow pupils. Powerful sermons they were too. The impact of a man like Latimer on the minds and hearts (especially the young minds and hearts) of his fashionable congregations was dramatic. No respecter of persons, the fiery zealot lashed the corruption and greed of court life and exposed dishonest practices. So conscience-smitten were Latimer's hearers that, over a spell of two years, the preacher received more than £500 brought to him secretly by men who had defrauded the government and who now begged him to make restitution on their behalf.

Young Edward, as observers frequently noted, was pious and zealous beyond his years and co-operated fervently with his mentors in ensuring that his household was a godly one.

> Believe me, my much esteemed friend, you have never seen in the world for these thousand years so much erudition united with piety and sweetness of disposition. Should he live and grow up with these virtues he will be a terror to all the sovereigns of the earth. He receives with his own hand a copy of every sermon he hears, and most diligently requires an account of them after dinner from those who study with him. Many of the boys and

youths who are his companions in study are well and faithfully instructed in the fear of God and in good learning.[22]

Thus, despite his extrovert temperament and his inaptitude for learning, Robert gained a profound and precise grounding in Protestant theology. In the court of a boy-prince and, later a boy-king he learned Reformed doctrine and absorbed those teachings which would enable him in later years to become the leading patron of Puritans.

Yet there must have been times when he rebelled. At least one observer complained that members of Edward's household 'neither feared to rail against the Word of God, and against the true preachers of the same'.[23] There is one story told by a foreign ambassador which rings very true and which it is hard to imagine Robert Dudley not being involved in. It dates from 1547 when Edward was ten and Robert scarcely fourteen.

King Edward, by the bad advice of one of his juvenile companions, was induced to adopt the use of such thundering oaths as he was told were appropriate to his sovereign dignity. On this being observed, an inquiry was made as to the origin of such a change in his behaviour; whereupon he ingenuously confessed that one of his playfellows had given him instructions in the right royal accomplishment. When this had been ascertained, his masters took care to give the guilty boy a sharp whipping in the king's view, and to admonish the latter that he witnessed the appropriate recompense of such presumption, bidding him to remember that he also had deserved the same punishment, and must therefore abstain from that excess for the future.[24]

Fortunately, the contrast between Edward and his more boisterous companions was not absolute and, as time went by, it became less marked. The Prince did have a more jovial and relaxed side to his nature and in fairness to his mentors it must be said that they fully appreciated that he needed some relaxation. When he became king and as he began to demonstrate his Tudor self-will, he paid increasing attention to sports, recreations and court revels. These tendencies, and particularly an interest in the martial arts, were encouraged by John Dudley when he came to power. Under these circumstances young Robert came into greater prominence. In fact, a great deal changed as soon as Henry VIII's gargantuan struggle with death came to an end.

CHAPTER THREE

MAN'S ESTATE

As soon as Henry VIII died the Earl of Hertford rode urgently through the night to Ashridge accompanied by Sir Anthony Browne, the Master of the Horse. He ordered the immediate withdrawal of the Prince's household to Enfield, so Robert and his colleagues were busy for several hours supervising the packing of chests and carts for the twenty-mile journey to Princess Elizabeth's winter residence.

It was not until the next day – 29 January 1547 – that the two children were told of the death of their father. Edward sobbed in his sister's arms while Seymour, Browne and all others present knelt in homage to their new King in the panelled presence chamber of Enfield Palace. Men and women, as well as boys and girls, showed their emotions more readily four hundred years ago but the young sovereign and those closest to him might well feel grief and apprehension. The death of so totally commanding a figure as Henry VIII left an enormous gap in their lives and in the life of the nation. The atmosphere at Enfield was heavy, subdued, the youthful household uncharacteristically quiet: all games, sports, lessons and music suspended.

But the political leaders could not afford to indulge in shocked inertia: they had to make careful arrangements for the future. It was Seymour who now took command. The old King had placed power in the hands of a committee of equals but common sense dictated the necessity for a strong individual at the helm. Seymour, thus, became Lord Protector, and no member of the Council opposed his assumption of power. Dudley supported his old comrade-in-arms fully. He was not jealous, had never thought in terms of supreme rule for himself. Ambitious he certainly was, but for land and wealth, not political power. If fresh spoils were to come his way, they would come as rewards for continued loyalty and friendship to the Protector.[1] Indeed, titles and lands began to flow immediately. The leaders of the new regime possessed themselves of fresh dignities and higher rank, ostensibly in accordance with the late King's wishes. Seymour became Duke of Somerset and Dudley Earl of Warwick.

John both gained and lost in this reshuffling of honours. The title originally proposed for him was the earldom of Leicester or that of Coventry, both of which had long since been incorporated in the crown. Lisle, however, urged that as a descendant of Richard

Beauchamp through the female line the earldom of Warwick should be revived in his favour.[2] This somewhat tortuous claim was recognised and Dudley became possessed of the most prestigious name in the Midlands. It was, however, some months before he received adequate lands to maintain his new estate, and he had to press hard for the grant of Warwick Castle which now became the magnificent focal point of Dudley territory in Staffordshire, Warwickshire, Worcestershire, Leicestershire and Northamptonshire.[3] In addition to this dignity John was also granted the high and ancient (though by now purely ceremonial) office of Lord Great Chamberlain.

Significant as all these grand titles were, the position which John now lost was more so. He was obliged to resign as Lord High Admiral. It was a bitter blow because the office was a profitable one, because Dudley enjoyed his work with the navy and had devoted considerable energy to it, but above all because he had to vacate it in favour of Thomas Seymour. The Protector's younger brother, for whom impressive titles and perquisites had to be found, was a restless, ambitious ne'er-do-well. He had served under Dudley as a vice-admiral and had caused his superior considerable trouble by inadequate performance of his duties and scandalous patronage of pirates. It is not difficult to understand Somerset's motive for handing such an important job to an incompetent. Apart from his desire to placate his brother, the Protector wanted to deprive his old friend of military power. In his mind Dudley had now become a potential rival and he acted swiftly to restrict that rival's sphere of activity. Perhaps we may see the same thinking behind his reluctance to make over Warwick Castle and large Midlands estates to the new earl. Dudley has always been blamed for sowing the seed of enmity between himself and Edward Seymour. It is much more likely that it first took root and flourished in the fear and suspicion of the Protector's mind as that nervous and isolated man strove to make himself secure.

The King and his adolescent companions were at the centre of the political tempest which was now boiling up and yet they were partially sheltered from it. Robert and his friends knew little of the day-to-day clashes of personalities and factions in the Council chamber but the general drift of affairs was something that affected them all. Each one of them was expected to use his influence with Edward on behalf of his family and patrons. Robert, for his part, was an important strand in the cord which Warwick used to secure his hold on political power. The fact that his name occurs little in official documents should not deceive us into dismissing him as merely a courtier and royal playfellow. He was a part, and an increasingly important part, of the Dudley interest. Now that the companion whose affection he had been set to cultivate was titular head of state there was, in theory, almost no limit to the favours he might win. Already his family had reached the summit of social and political prestige. His father was the second man in the kingdom, popular with the people for his fine military record and for the splendour and liberality with which he comported himself in public. The future was bright with promise though the present was seldom void of anxiety.

In accordance with tradition the court spent the first few days of the reign in the Tower of London. The royal suite occupied hastily prepared buildings in the south-east corner of the inner ward – old, neglected buildings unvisited by royalty since the coronation of Anne Boleyn nearly fourteen years before. There Robert and his colleagues made themselves as comfortable as they could in chambers hurriedly equipped with furniture and tapestries brought from the adjacent Wardrobe Tower. There they witnessed the well-rehearsed Edward make his first official speech. On 17 February Robert stood in the thirteenth-century great hall of the Tower and watched as, one by one, the members of the Council, each still dressed in solemn but sumptuous mourning, came forward to receive their new titles from the King.

Two days later Robert took his place in the coronation procession which, in accordance with tradition made its way from the Tower to Westminster through City streets decked with bunting and thronged with cheering Londoners. All the dignitaries of the land had their appointed place in the long train of richly dressed lords, ladies, bishops, knights, ambassadors and officers of state. Robert may have ridden near the front of the procession in that space allotted to 'Earls' sons' or he may have claimed a much more important and exciting position among the henchmen who immediately followed the King and the Master of the Horse 'on nine goodly horses, with saddles of estate and riding bare headed, every of them apparelled in cassocks parted in the midst, one half cloth of gold the other cloth of silver, and their horses trapped with like trappers of the same.'[4]

It was a heady experience for a thirteen-year-old courtier but the day held one more momentous event for Robert. It was customary for the king to make several knights of the Bath at his coronation. The ceremonies attendant upon this were long and exacting so it was decided that young Edward should not follow the ancient custom. He could, however, confer ordinary knighthoods and this he did. Of the six young men so honoured one was the elder Dudley boy, John, who had now taken his father's old title of Viscount Lisle.

The elaborate festivities continued at court for several days, but afterwards life settled back into a routine not dissimilar to that which had prevailed in Edward's household before. Lessons, games and sermons were resumed. The earnest Duke of Somerset kept his nephew on a tight rein but now that Edward was King, and not just a king in training, he began in a modest way to keep court. That meant that he and his companions were involved in festivities and entertainments. The serious boy emerged gradually from his shell. In February of 1548 or 1549 an order was placed for 'garments to be made for six masques, whereof the King's Majesty shall be one, and the residue of his stature, and six other garments of like bigness for torch bearers, with convenient diligence, so as the same may be in readiness against Sunday next at the uttermost . . .'[5] These festal garments were obviously for the use of Edward and his young hench-men in the Shrovetide revels, and there must have been other royal performances for which no records have survived. By 1551 the King's household boasted eighteen trumpeters, two lutanists, one harpist, one rebec player, seven viol players, four sackbut players, one bagpiper, eight minstrels and several singing men. Edward himself learned to perform on the lute and virginals. He kept bulls, bears and mastiffs for baiting. He practised with the bow and enjoyed hunting and tennis. Restraints were, of course, placed on the King: his tender years, his indifferent health and the Protector's natural desire to shield him from injury prevented Edward from participating fully in all the sports and pastimes permitted to his more expendable companions. He had to be content to watch and to note in his journal the contests in the tilt-yard between various members of his suite.

The role of Robert and his colleagues was an ambiguous one. The boisterous activities of the young household were increasingly punc-tuated by solemn ceremonial. Edward had to preside over banquets, investitures, receptions of foreign diplomats. The boy King had to carry on his shoulders the public show of sovereignty. This made for a certain ambivalence in his attitude towards his play-fellows. When playing tennis, shooting at the mark or running at the ring they were boys together. Then they would go in to dinner and everything would change. Now the King sat on a cushioned chair of state while his erstwhile colleagues knelt to proffer the flagons and the golden dishes which came hot from the kitchen. Yet it must have been an amiable existence in the pleasant, privileged little cosmos of the royal household. Whether it was at Whitehall, Greenwich, Hampton Court, St James's, Oatlands or Windsor, the pattern of life of the court was little changed and always remained effectively shielded from the real world.

Life in that real world was far from amiable. The country was in a state of unprecedented social and economic turmoil. The government was bankrupt and its attempts to deal with the national ills were almost universally unsuccessful. Furthermore, the move by Somerset and Archbishop Cranmer to carry the English church firmly into the Protestant camp was widely resented. As inflation, changing land use and continuing property speculation caused ever greater hardships discontent grew. Here and there, groups of impoverished and unemployed farm workers took the law into their own hands, breaking down hedges and ploughing up pasture. At first the Protector did nothing. Then, when the problem had grown too large to ignore, he listened to the muddle-headed and simplistic theories of zealous social and religious reformers like John Hales, who persuaded him that the greed of wealthy landowners was the sole root cause of economic decline. Somerset espoused anti-enclosure policies and let it be widely known that he was the poor man's friend. This won him the support of the masses but did nothing whatsoever to relieve their distress. Indeed, half-hearted, libertarian measures only encouraged disorder and set the propertied classes, led by the Council, firmly against the government. For months Seymour ignored the demand of his colleagues that he should make a show of strength before law and order broke down totally. Events at last forced him into action. He was nearly too late. By the spring of 1549 almost the whole of southern England was in revolt. The worst affected areas were the south-west and Norfolk.

Somerset had forced himself into an impossible situation. He was so confused in his own mind that he was unable to pursue a consistent policy. Quick military success was needed but he wanted to avoid bloodshed. He had to put able generals in the field but hesitated to give the members of the Council (which now opposed him almost to a man) command of troops. The situation called for his personal presence at the head of an army but he dared not leave London and the King. Eventually he authorised Lord Russell, Sir William Herbert, Lord Grey de Wilton and the Marquess of Northampton to proceed against the insurgents.

Northampton was sent to East Anglia to regain control of Norwich, the second city in the kingdom, which was in the hands of Robert Kett and his rebel army. He bungled the job largely because he underestimated his enemy. The motley assembly of peasants and tradesmen might look like a badly disciplined, ill-equipped rabble: in fact they were men made desperate by suffering; men so bitter, so indifferent to punishment that, as an eye-witness reported, they would crawl through their own blood, 'the sinews of their legs cut asunder . . . yet creeping on their knees, were moved with such fury, as they wounded our soldiers, lying amongst the slain . . .'[6] These determined men routed Northampton, slaughtered a hundred or more of his soldiers, and sent him scurrying back to London on 1 August. It was at that point – and even then only after he had toyed with the prospect of taking the field himself – that Somerset appointed John Dudley to assume command of the Norfolk campaign.

Warwick, though unwell, had for weeks been ready to 'live and die' wherever the Protector should send him[7] and had already sent messages into the Midlands requiring all his friends and tenants to repair to Warwick Castle. But, while he and the other men of action either chafed at the bit awaiting instructions or did their best to combat insurrection with inadequate forces, Somerset dithered. Warwick was to go to Devon, then he was to go north, then he was destined for East Anglia. He would serve under the Protector; then the orders were changed and he was given supreme command. When, at last, he was allowed to proceed with clear instructions he moved quickly. His first objective was to gather as large an army as possible. He needed every man he could find able to bear arms. That included two of his sons.

Some time in early August Robert found himself riding at speed along the Oxford road with Ambrose, their father and a large body of Dudley servants. He was just sixteen and the prospect of seeing real action must have thrilled him. He had been promised command of a company of foot soldiers in the forthcoming campaign, and, though he would certainly have experienced captains at his side to make the important decisions, the mantle of command would be on his shoulders, as befitted the son of a peer. Robert helped in the mustering of troops throughout the West Midlands and the border. He watched as the 6,000 foot soldiers and 1,500 horse assembled in and around Warwick Castle. He took his place among the commanders as the army moved eastwards through Northampton, St Neots, Cambridge (here the contingent was joined by fresh levies from Essex, Suffolk and Cambridgeshire) and Newmarket to reach Wymondham on 22 August.

The gentlemen of the shire, who hurried to join Warwick with such retainers as they could rely on, were worried men. Their barns and granaries had been pillaged by foraging rebels. Many of their servants and tenants had been seduced into joining Kett's host. Some of their colleagues had been captured and were even now being held prisoner in Norwich. They had seen one royal emissary sent packing and it was with considerable relief, probably tinged with apprehension, that they now welcomed England's greatest general. The situation was not a simple one of loyal gentry versus rebellious peasantry. Kett, himself, was a man of substance and related to some of those who were now in arms against him. Indeed, the conflict had its catalyst in rivalries between members of the closely interrelated county families. There were few Norfolk gentlemen who did not find themselves involved with combatants on both sides.

Take Sir John Robsart of Syderstone, for example. In about 1530 he married Elizabeth, widow of Roger Appleyard, who was, like himself, of an ancient and distinguished Norfolk family. The union brought him Stanfield Hall, near Wymondham, and, since this was much more conveniently situated than his own estates in the north-west of the county, he made it his principal residence. There he cared for his new wife and her four children by her previous marriage, and there his only daughter, Amy, was born in 1532 or 1533. The union also brought him a fresh crop of relatives. They were all people he knew, gentlemen of the shire like himself and of ancient families. They included Robert Kett, married to his wife's sister-in-law. When his step-children grew up he made suitable marriages for them with other respectable Norfolk clans – the Hugans, Sheltons and Bigots. Young Frances was betrothed to William, eldest son of Sir John Flowerdew of Hethersett, landowner, lawyer and steward of the Robsart estates in Norfolk.

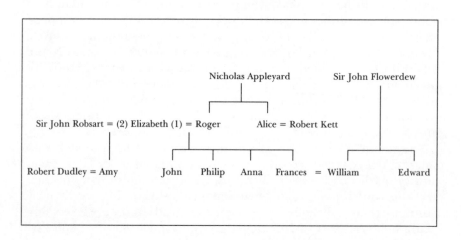

There had been bad blood between the Flowerdews and Ketts for more than a decade, and when, in July 1549, a group of malcontents threw down some of Flowerdew's fences, the lawyer assumed Kett to be behind the raid. He retaliated by offering money to some peasants to attack his rival's farmland. Robert Kett turned the tables by putting himself at the head of the rioters, helping them to uproot his own enclosures and then marching with them to Hethersett for a more complete devastation of Flowerdew's land. From then on Kett's Rebellion ceased to be a local dispute and became a national issue. Vagabonds, tenant farmers and yeomen flocked to the champion who had set himself against the greedy self-interest of the big landowners. The sheriff ordered the mob to disperse – and barely escaped with his life. The insurgents moved on Norwich, pressing whatever gentlemen they could find to join their ranks. Some resisted, some fled, some were captured. Among the latter were Kett's own nephews, John and Philip Appleyard, stepsons of Sir John Robsart.

It was to Sir John's house at Stanfield that the Earl of Warwick and his retinue came late on a summer's afternoon. The general and his captains were entertained in the Hall while their men camped outside in the level parkland which extended almost to the houses of Wymondham.[8] It was here that Robert met, probably for the first time, the girl he was to marry.

We have no means of knowing whether Robert and Amy already knew each other. It is possible, for Sir John Robsart, like most Norfolk gentry, enjoyed the patronage of the Howards, and in the halcyon days before the Duke's downfall a place may have been found for the Robsart girl in the nobleman's household. Though the Howard children were reared principally at nearby Kenninghall they certainly visited the family's other houses in and around London and they were always attended by their chosen companions. Since early 1548 they had been assigned to the guardianship of the Duchess of Richmond and divided their time between Reigate Castle and Mountjoy House, London. Robert may well have seen Amy on visits to the Duchess or at court functions.

Whatever the facts about their former acquaintance, Robert now rode into Amy's life in a dashing and romantic manner. Mounted on a fine steed and wearing part armour, plumed helmet and scarlet sash, he cut a fine figure. The daughter of a country squire could hardly fail to be impressed.

There was no immediate opportunity to cement their relationship: the next day the army was on the move again, making the short five-mile march to Sir Thomas Gresham's house at Intwood.

The army, now poised for the final confrontation with Kett's followers, was impressive. At its head were five peers of the realm (Warwick, Northampton, Lord Grey of Powis, Lord Willoughby of Parham and Lord Bray) and a group of gentlemen many of whom were distinguished for past military service or administrative expertise. In addition there were a number of young men of high birth, like Ambrose and Robert, out to win their spurs. They commanded a force variously estimated at between 7,500 and 14,000 men; about 10,000 seems to be the most likely figure.[9] They had a few pieces of artillery and, although most of their men were scantily-trained levies, there was a hard core of veterans and mercenaries. Yet the rebel host against which they were moving was scarcely less formidable. Kett commanded over 12,000 men who made up in desperation what they lacked in military experience. Moreover, they had achieved one victory, were in control of a great city, and many of them (though possibly not Kett) rated highly their chances of further success.

Warwick resolved first of all to try conciliation. When this failed he was committed to the unwelcome task of slaughtering his own countrymen. There is no evidence that he relished the job but he executed it with despatch and efficiency. He moved his army along the Wymondham road to the south-west wall of the city. Norwich now lay before him, barred and barricaded by the rebels whose main camp lay beyond the river to the north-east on Mousehold Heath. He ordered a force under Northampton's command to attack St Stephen's Gate. The decision to send Northampton first into the city he had so ignominiously left was obviously deliberate. It won Warwick a firm supporter and revealed once more his understanding of men and his ability to handle them. Parr's artillery battered down the portcullis and a group of pioneers simultaneously overran the nearby postern known as Brazen Doors. Then the Marquess and a local hero called Captain Drury led the charge through the breach, scattering defenders and cutting down many of them in the narrow streets beyond. According to an eye-witness Ambrose acquitted himself well in the assault being 'one with the first that entered the gate upon the rebels.'[10]

Within minutes St Benedict's Gate on the Dereham road had been thrown open and the Lord Lieutenant entered with the rest of his army. He marched to the Market Square where forty-nine captured rebels were summarily hanged and the wavering populace harangued into co-operation with the King's army. But the day was far from won. Kett's followers still controlled the area north of the river and the eastern part of the city. It was in the latter quarter that the party bringing up some of Warwick's artillery found themselves after taking a wrong turning. The enemy swooped down on them and triumphantly trundled the guns away over Bishop Bridge to Mousehold Heath. Savage street-fighting continued throughout the afternoon and evening. Nightfall found weary soldiers stationed all round the walls and regularly patrolling every ward. The rebels gave them no respite. They launched fresh attacks. At one stage they crossed the Wensum and set fire to several houses and warehouses in the south-east quarter between the river and King Street. Despite the entreaties of citizens whose property was going up in flame, Warwick refused to send men to fight the blaze, suspecting, probably correctly, that it was a diversionary tactic designed to draw defenders from the gates and walls. Neither captains nor men got much sleep that night. The Lord Lieutenant himself toured the ramparts and the hastily prepared breaches. Where he led, Robert and the other commanders had to follow, conscientiously performing their tedious duties throughout the night.

Dawn found the situation little changed. The defenders were drooping at their posts. The attitude of the citizens was ambivalent. Norwich was in a poor state to withstand a siege. Yet if Warwick were to lead his men out, he would have to offer the rebels battle on their own terrain and they were strategically well established on the high ground of Mousehold Heath. The city fathers sent a deputation. They suggested that their streets and houses were not the best battleground on which to face the rebels and asked the Lord Lieutenant to withdraw his army outside the walls. Their self-interest and lack of confidence in the government forces were obvious. Warwick was on the spot. These wavering burghers had to be won over. If they were antagonized or if they decided that the King's cause was lost, some of them might well betray the city into Kett's hands. John Dudley rose to the occasion with one of those gestures that mark the truly great man of action. Young Robert was there to witness it and the next few minutes must have remained forever fixed in his memory. Warwick summoned all his captains. Before them and the elders of Norwich he announced his reaction to the suggestion that he should leave the city: 'I will first suffer fire, sword, finally all extremity before I will bring such a stain of infamy and shame either on myself or you.' He commanded his officers to draw their swords, to 'kiss one another's swords, making the sign of the holy cross' and then to swear that they would not desert Norwich before they had 'utterly banished the enemy or else, fighting manfully, had bestowed their lives cheerfully for the King's majesty'.[11] This chivalrous panache was a quality that Robert inherited from his father in full measure without, unfortunately, the military brilliance to go with it.

Dudley's words heartened the Norwich merchants and brought a measure of calm to the inhabitants of the beleaguered city.

And now for that the Lord Lieutenant had taken up Mr Austen [the] steward's house and set his arms on the gate did other lords, squires, and gentlemen the like and for the time took each man's house as their own till their departure whom then for joy of the victory every man set up the ragged staff upon their gates and doors in the Lord Lieutenant's honour which so continued many years after . . .[12]

Warwick's judgement was vindicated on 26 August when, at midday, 1,100 German mercenary reinforcements clattered into the city, boisterously firing their handguns. In fact, while the Lord Lieutenant had given every impression of being besieged by the rebels he had been turning the tables on them. Cavalry forays into the surrounding countryside had cut off Kett's supplies and, by the 26th, the Mousehold camp was desperately short of food. The royal forces had beaten off all raids, their morale was excellent and, now that their numbers were augmented with more professionals, they were ready to move on to the offensive. On 27 August Warwick rode out of Norwich by St Martin's Gate with all his cavalry, leaving the foot soldiers to guard the city. Robert, who commanded an infantry company, must therefore have remained behind and have missed the carnage of Dussindale which brought the Norfolk rebellion to a tragic end.

The relief felt by the men of substance in and around Norwich can be guessed at rather than fully appreciated. Some of the prisoners in rebel hands had been killed during the battle but the majority, including Sir John Robsart's stepsons, were safely restored to their families. Peace and order could now be re-established – something that had seemed impossible days before. The bells of the city pealed out their rejoicing. Dudley and his men were hailed as heroes. The Lieutenant General stayed another two weeks dispensing justice, hearing claims for restitution of stolen or damaged property, helping the mayor and corporation rebuild ruined walls. Robert's duties were light in the aftermath of battle. He had plenty of time to enjoy the hospitality of merchants and local gentlemen and, above all, to renew and deepen his friendship with Sir John Robsart's daughter.

His father had little opportunity for such pleasant pastimes. Apart from the many duties that had to be performed he had much to occupy his mind. The sight of 3,500 dead Englishmen at Dussindale was an appalling comment on Protector Somerset's mistaken policies and inept rule. If the local leaders had had their way, drastic retribution would have added hundreds more victims to the list of the slain. Warwick had had to restrain their sense of outrage and their demand for unlimited vengeance:

> There must be measure kept, and above all things in punishment men must not exceed. He knew [he said] their wickedness to be such as deserved to be grievously punished and with the severest judgement that might be. But how far would [the gentlemen] go? Will they ever show themselves discontented and never pleased? Would they have no place for humble petition; none for pardon and mercy? Would they be ploughmen themselves and harrow their own land?[13]

It had to come to this – all Seymour's fine words and ill-conceived policies – gentlemen and peasants at each other's throats, the breakdown of the social order, the stirring up of class hatred. Perhaps it was then, in the shocked aftermath of Dussindale, that Warwick decided that Somerset's personal rule must come to an end.

A contemporary partisan of the Protector, being wise – or malicious – after the event, affirmed that as Warwick returned from East Anglia, he,

> began to move the whole nobility and gentlemen that was with him in that journey against the Duke of Somerset, calling him secretly, to such of his acquaintance as he might trust, a coward, a breaker of promises, a niggard, covetous and ambitious, and such a one as never none of service could hope to have any good by, except they would flatter, lie, and play the knave as Fisher did; by which means the Duke of Somerset was deadly hated among the whole camp . . . and so at their departure . . . every gentleman there fell in a great liking of [the Earl of Warwick] and in a great praising of him [and] in the despising, dispraising and hatred of the Duke of Somerset . . .[14]

This assessment, which has contributed to the popular representation of Warwick as a Machiavellian schemer, not only misrepresents Dudley's motivation, it oversimplifies the confused and confusing events of the next few months. The key to understanding the political dislocation is not the ruthless ambition and preconceived manoeuvres of one man but the continuing entropy within the Council. The settlement of January 1547 had only brought about a temporary truce. This body, rent by personal rivalries, personality clashes and disagreements over foreign and religious policy, had, by the summer of 1549, reached a united conviction that the arrangements for the regency must be renegotiated but this was merely the precursor to a further round of power broking. Dudley and his colleagues were adamant that the arrogant Somerset must be toppled from his perch. Even Seymour's friend, William Paget, warned the Protector to stop alienating his colleagues and return to a semblance of conciliar government. Yet the very concept of rule by committee was naïve. With a child king on the throne and two bastardised half-sisters next in succession, England needed a strong man to hold the reins of power and control the direction of policy until Edward was able to take on these responsibilities for himself. Nor was it simply a question of maintaining security at home. On the continent persecution of confessional minorities was spreading, exiles were crossing state borders in growing numbers to find sanc-tuary, and international conflicts were increasingly assuming a religious nature. England had to decide which alliances she might be obliged by principle or self-interest to enter into.

There is no evidence that Warwick saw himself, before the East Anglian campaign, as the nation's political saviour[15] but the rebel-lion must have made him listen more attentively to friends and false friends who were urging such a role upon him. Added to this was his growing alienation from Somerset who seemed to be going out of his way to create fresh causes of grievance. Dudley had decided to reward young Ambrose for his valiant service and had made arrangements accordingly with his old friend and comrade-in-arms, Sir Andrew Flammock. Flammock was elderly and had, perhaps, sustained some injury during the campaign (he made his will on 6 September and died within a few months). Warwick sought the reversion to Ambrose of certain offices held by Flammock on the latter's death. From Norwich he wrote to Somerset with his request. The reply, when it came, was not only a refusal, it was an arrogant insult to the man who had just saved the country from insurrection. The Protector told his one-time friend that he had decided to bestow the reversion of the offices in question on Thomas Fisher. Fisher had once been Warwick's steward but had since left him to become one of Somerset's secretaries.

The gulf between the erstwhile colleagues widened in the immedi-ate aftermath of the campaign. The Dudleys returned to London about 8 September to the cheers of a relieved populace. At West-minster Warwick received the congratulations of his fellow councillors, but there was no welcome from the Protector. As if he could not bring himself to face up to Warwick's success, Seymour retired to his Hampshire estates and spent the next few weeks hunt-ing. Messages sent from the capital received curt, unsympathetic replies.[16] By his absence and hubris the Protector made the task of the palace revolutionaries very much easier.

The coup which followed was by no means a simple *bouleversement* whereby Warwick replaced Somerset as leader of the realm: it was a complex series of plots and counter-plots in the course of which both men came close to losing their heads.[17] Every major player had his own agenda made up of ideology and ambition. The black and white pieces on the Westminster chess board were still the evangelical and Catholic factions but those pieces were quite capable of changing colour when self-interest required it.

Dudley's political objectives were to maintain or accelerate the process of religious change and to engineer those foreign alliances necessary to the security of a Protestant nation. Thomas Wriothesley (now Earl of Southampton) who became his joint leader in the conspiracy, had other ideas. With the backing of the Earl of Arundel and (from the Tower) Bishop Gardiner he projected a Catholic coup which involved packing the Council with adherents of the old religion and establishing Princess Mary as Protector. He and his associates were quickened in their resolve by the very public fate of the Bishop of London. In September this outspoken critic of the reforming regime was tried by an ecclesiastical commission, deprived of his see and thrown into prison. From the Catholic point of view an effective counter-attack was desperately required. Wriothesley needed Warwick for the overthrow of Somerset because of Warwick's obvious stature and the support he commanded, and because the coup could only succeed if a wedge were driven between the two old friends. That achieved, Wriothesley's plan was to 'dispose' of Somerset and also of Warwick as an accomplice in the Protector's 'treasons'.

In a series of meetings at Greenwich and at Ely Place, the majority of the Council made their plans. There seems to have been little secrecy about their activities, as the King recorded: 'The lords sat in open places in London, calling for the gentlemen before them and declaring the causes of accusation of the Lord Protector, and caused the same to be proclaimed.'[18] The court, meanwhile, had moved to Hampton Court. It maintained its usual routine and there was no attempt by the Dudley-Wriothesley grouping to gain possession of the King's person. The plotters, however, liaised closely with the royal household via their friends and relatives, including Robert and his brothers. Those about the King who knew what was afoot were at pains not to raise the boy's fears. Not until after the Protector returned to court on 1 October did the atmosphere become tense. Somerset only gradually became aware of the strength and unity of the opposition. By 4 October it was being whispered around the court that the Earl of Warwick had turned traitor, and Seymour began sending urgent summonses to all who might repair to him with loyal troops. After dark the next day the Duchess was brought with all haste to Hampton. There was no sign of any soldiers coming to Somerset's aid. The story going around the court now was that London was up in arms against the Protector. Long before dawn on Sunday, 6 October the alarm was sounded. Every member of the household was roused. All able-bodied men were ordered to arm themselves. The gentlemen and members of the guard had conventional weapons. The rest equipped themselves with clubs and iron bars. Doors and windows were barricaded. 'The stones in the court was digged up and carried up unto the leads over the gate'.[19] In the early morning light the Protector stood before the embattled household, the frightened King at his side, and made a rallying speech in which he stated that the rebellious lords of the Council intended to make away with their young sovereign as Richard III had disposed of the princes in the Tower. Messengers were sent into the surrounding countryside and by noon 'there was great resort of people, dwelling in the towns by, with such weapons as they had and armour'.[20] The young Dudleys must have passed several tense hours. Only recently they had seen the atrocities ordinary Englishmen were capable of when roused. But in Norfolk Ambrose and Robert had been on the winning side; now they were prisoners in the middle of an ill-disciplined mob.

But no opposing force came from London and Somerset decided to make a rush for the Tower. Taking the King, the bulk of the household and the royal guard, he made for the bridge at Kingston. There he was met by the news that the Tower was in the hands of his enemies. He turned westwards and rode hard through daylight and darkness for Windsor. It was a nightmare, headlong flight for all concerned and at the end of it the weary court arrived at the castle about midnight to find unmade beds, unfurnished chambers and an empty larder.

For two days the members of the household were kept on short rations and in uncomfortable quarters while letters passed to and fro between Seymour and the 'London lords'. They were a divided assembly and the Protector did not improve the situation by placing his own servants in the Privy Chamber and refusing Edward's usual attendants access to him. He harangued the King's companions on the subject of the disloyalty of the Council. But the opposition did not go unheard: pamphlets were smuggled into the castle setting out Somerset's crimes and making it clear that his removal from power was the sole object of the London lords' campaign. Disunited, demoralized and hungry, the household was in no mood to resist indefinitely. Nor was Edward.

The King's majesty is much troubled with a great rheum, taken partly with riding hither in the night, and partly increased by the subtlety of this air, as the gentlemen of his chamber say, and much desireth to be hence, saying that 'Methinks I am in prison; here be no galleries nor no gardens to walk in'.[21]

Seymour knew that all was up. On the morning of 10 October, having received assurances of his safety, he surrendered himself to his fellow Councillors. On 14 October the King and his household left Windsor for Hampton Court. On the same day the ex-Lord Protector and his guards left Windsor for the Tower of London. New provisions now had to be made for the guardianship of Edward VI. Thus, on the 15th, it was decided 'to have some noblemen appointed to be ordinarily attendant about his Majesty's person in his Privy Chamber, to give order for the good government of his royal person, and for the honourable education of his highness in these tender years in learning and virtue.'[22] Of the six noblemen appointed one was the Earl of Warwick. Four principal gentlemen of the Privy Chamber were also named. One of them was Sir Andrew Dudley, the earl's brother. That same day John Dudley resumed the office of Lord High Admiral.

On 17 October Edward was able to return to his capital. He came, decked in cloth of gold and silver, attended by his entire retinue and an augmented bodyguard. The household dined at Suffolk Place, Southwark, then rode across the bridge and through the City among crowds of cheering and relieved subjects. One of the King's first official acts at Westminster was to confirm the patent reappointing the Earl of Warwick as Lord High Admiral. On 17 November, an investiture was held to honour the visiting Duke of Luneberg. Among those chosen to receive the dignity of knighthood was Ambrose Dudley.

This might suggest that events were proceeding entirely in favour of Robert's family. It was not so: as Wriothesley and Arundel moved into the second phase of their plan they were helped by the fact that Warwick was suffering from one of his periodic illnesses. Council meetings had to be held at Ely Place – sometimes, in the Earl's bedchamber. The Catholic peers advanced friends and co- religionists to the Council. It was widely believed that the Reformation would soon be halted and persecution of Protestants would recommence. Somerset was rigorously examined in the Tower and sufficient evidence gathered to enable Southampton to demand his attainder. Archbishop Cranmer and the radicals were alarmed, and so, too, were a number of prominent men who were inclined to the old religion but were appalled at the prospect of an impending ruthless political purge.

The crisis was very real and none the less so for being obscured by secrecy and the non-survival of vital evidence. A lurch towards reaction could have halted the English Reformation in its tracks. As regent, with men like Gardiner and Wriothesley at her side, Mary might well have made a restored Catholicism and, in time, a restored papal allegiance unassailable. What saved England from this fate was the fact that Dudley was a better tactician than his rivals. While Wriothesley was using him, he was using Wriothesley. He made several minor concessions to the Catholic faction and hoisted apparently significant signals, such as ordering his own household to observe fast-days. At the same time he used friends about the King to obtain the royal consent for the appointment of new councillors to balance the Wriothesley-Arundel party.

The confrontation when it came took the form of one of those dramatic gestures at which Warwick excelled. The Council members were gathered about his bed and Wriothesley was holding forth about the 'treasons' for which Somerset deserved to die. Dudley silenced him with a scowl. A curved sword (falchion) lay beside him on the coverlet and now he placed his hand upon it. 'My Lord,' he observed, 'you seek [the Protector's] blood. He that seeketh his would have mine also.'[23] The meeting broke up in embarrassed confusion. The evangelicals were now strong enough to make their triumph public. At the end of October a royal proclamation was issued ordering, on pain of imprisonment, an end to all rumours that Somerset's imprisonment betokened a return to 'the old Romish service, mass and ceremonies'. The move for Seymour's attainder was quashed and the Catholic tide turned as suddenly as it had come in, leaving Warwick in a position of complete power. Waverers hastened to Ely Place to assure Dudley of their loyalty. Wriothesley's health broke under the shock of the complete failure of his plans (he died the following July after a long illness). In January the Earl of Arundel was sent to the Tower 'for certain crimes of suspicion against him'. Warwick did not seek the trappings of absolute power; he made no attempt to replace Seymour as Protector, contenting himself with the presidency of the Council. He did not acquire a dukedom (that of Northumberland) until two years after the 1549 coup. But he had, in fact, become uncrowned king of England, a position far in advance of anything his forbears had achieved and beyond the reach of later generations of Dudleys – although Robert would come very close to it. His objective was to restore conciliar government under his own firm leadership and in this he was successful. Under his regime the Council became once more the efficient administrative and executive body that Thomas

Cromwell had established in the 1530s and, thanks to Dudley having packed it with supporters and sympathisers, one, for the time being, not vitiated by factions.[24] Somerset's attempt to create divisions was the only serious threat to unity and it was firmly dealt with (see below).

According to the Imperial ambassador, the King's attitude towards his new mentor was one of love and fear.[25] There is no corroboration of this singularly unilluminating assessment and certainly Edward's journal throws no light on the relationship, but such evidence as we have suggests that there was more mutual respect between them than had existed between Edward the his uncle. The King had been brought up as a thoroughgoing evangelical and Warwick supported his sovereign's convictions, though how far this stemmed from a personal attachment to radical religion is dubious. The evidence is scanty and conflicting. From his first emergence as a political figure Dudley had been recognised as a supporter of the evangelical cause. Though he was no theologian, when the Council considered allowing Princess Mary to continue with her private mass Warwick made a virulent attack on papistical error.[26] It was under his leadership that the pace of Protestant revolution was furiously accelerated. It was Warwick's surviving sons, Ambrose and Robert, who were to be the main pillars of Elizabeth's Protestant state. Yet, when confronting his own death, he confessed a reconversion to the old religion. If it is possible to tease out a thread of consistency it is probably to be found in that almost mystical attachment to the anointed sovereign which, in our egalitarian and democratic age we find difficult to comprehend. His own political upbringing had been in the court and government of a charismatic despot. Though Edward was only a lad he was Henry VIII's son and he was the lawful ruler of England. As such, Dudley rendered him that loyalty he had given his father. In all his efforts to train Edward for the assumption of royal power, Warwick never treated him as a cypher, never used him to bolster his own authority. We should not underestimate the deep hold which reverence for the anointed king had on his mind. In the end it would contribute to his downfall, as it had contributed to his father's. In religious matters he did not dissent from the convention that a ruler had the right and duty to determine the belief of his subjects. He, therefore, threw his weight behind the Protestant revolution.

The long-accepted verdict on John Dudley, that he was 'exceedingly ambitious of power and very greedy'[27] has to be challenged. He allotted genuine authority to the Council. In fact, his own declining health meant that he was often absent from its deliberations.

Frequently he expressed his longing for the day when the young Tudor would assume full kingship and allow Warwick to take his sick and aged body into weary retirement.

That this was no disarming false humility is borne out by his tutelage of the King. Warwick made considerable changes in Edward's daily routine. His two major concerns were to lead the King into a more rapid assumption of sovereignty and to relieve the studious solemnity of his life. Increasingly, the Earl involved his charge in government discussions and decisions. Edward attended Council meetings and spent long periods closeted with Dudley learning about the day-to-day concerns of his ministers. To counterbalance the burdens of state Warwick organised court entertainments and encouraged Edward's interest in martial arts. Within months Warwick assumed the office of Lord Great Master of the Household and with it the supreme control of the court. Now his family came into full prominence in the King's inner circle. Sir Andrew was the keeper of the Wardrobe, keeper of the Palace of Westminster, was appointed Chief Gentleman of the Privy Chamber in 1552 and was nominated to the Order of the Garter the following spring. John Dudley, Viscount Lisle, was Master of the Buckhounds, and in April 1552 became Master of the Horse. With his brothers, Ambrose and Robert, John was frequently to the fore in court 'triumphs' – chivalric exercises such as jousts, tilts and barriers, accompanied by spectacular masques, pageants and interludes.[28] In May 1550 the King recorded in his diary the entertainment provided for some French ambassadors: 'After dinner [they] saw a pastime of ten against ten at the ring, whereof on the one side were the Duke of Suffolk, the Vidame [of Chartres], the Lord Lisle and seven other gentlemen apparelled in yellow; on the other Lord Strange, Mons. Hunaudaye and eight others in blue'.[29] In December 1551 Lisle and three companions issued a challenge to all comers at tilt. Ambrose and Robert were among the gentlemen who took up the gage, each running six courses as a part of the Christmas festivities. They all appeared on Twelfth Night to bring the celebrations to a rousing conclusion of plays and fast combat. Eleven days later 'there was a match run between six gentlemen of a side at tilt'. The victorious team, which won by '4 taints [broken lances]' was led by John and Ambrose. The other was captained by Robert.

Robert Dudley was fast growing into manhood. In 1550 he was married. His love for Amy Robsart had, apparently, not lessened in the months following the Norfolk rebellion and his father eventually agreed to their union. It was certainly a love match, but other considerations were also involved. Territorial, financial and political issues weighed with John Dudley, as they did with all sixteenth-century men of property. During the last years of the previous reign he had formed alliances with two prominent members of the government. Ambrose had been betrothed to Anne, daughter of William Whorwood, the Attorney General, and Henry had been promised to Margaret, Lord Chancellor Audley's daughter. By the summer of 1550 Ambrose was already married, and would become, briefly, a father during 1551; his son, named John in honour of his grandfather, died soon after birth. Arrangements had probably already been made for Mary, the eldest Dudley girl. She was destined to be the wife of Henry Sidney, Gentleman of the Privy Chamber, and one of the King's closest associates. Warwick's heir was married to one of the Duke of Somerset's daughters. Alone of all the great Earl's children, Robert was allowed to espouse the child of an insignificant country squire.

The reason lies in the general political situation of 1550. Order had been restored throughout the country and a more united government had been established. The appearance of tranquillity, however, was only on the surface. Popular grievances had not been dispelled and the ex-Protector still had many supporters. Economic problems were worsening: grain prices had doubled since 1548, and as the year wore on it became obvious that the harvest would again be poor.[30] Warwick's government had many basic policy issues to contend with – the maintenance of peace with France; the restoration of the currency; the promulgation and enforcement of new religious legislation. But before success could be hoped for there had to be real stability, first of all within the governing class and then, through this class, in the rural areas. It was with this very much in mind that Warwick arranged a *rapprochement* with Seymour in the spring. Somerset was released from the Tower and, after a decent interval, he resumed his seat at the Council board.

Then it was decided that the restored friendship of the two great men should be cemented by a marriage alliance. Viscount Lisle was thus betrothed to Anne Seymour, and plans were laid for the wedding to be held at Somerset's great house of Sheen, beside the Thames on 3 June. The celebration was to be a lavish affair, attended by the King and his court. It was also arranged that Robert Dudley should marry Amy the following day, in the same place and before the same august assembly.

Warwick could obviously have made a better match for his fifth son. He did not do so because he was unwilling to force his will upon the young people and because the Robsart alliance did have certain advantages. Even in those days of arranged marriages

sensitive parents did not ride roughshod over the wishes of their
children. The attraction of Robert's marriage was that it would
make him a prominent Norfolk landowner. Amy was heiress to the
manors of Syderstone, Newton and Great Bircham in the north-
west corner of the county. Warwick settled on the couple the
reversion of the neighbouring lands of Coxford Priory. The estates
of the old Augustinian house were extensive.[31] They were all
itemised in the marriage settlement down to such parcels as 'all that
warren of coneys called Brockling, and of the courses of foldage of
sheep with the appurtenances called "the Gouge" in West Rudham'.
By the terms of the settlement Warwick paid the couple £50 a year
out of the rents of Burton Lisle, Leicestershire, and Sir John
Robsart provided them with another £20 per annum. At one stroke
Robert became the wealthiest landowner in north-west Norfolk.[32] In
November 1552 John Dudley made an exchange of lands with the
crown which brought him the manor of Hemsby, near Yarmouth.
This he also settled on Robert and Amy.[33] A few days before Edward
VI's death Robert received a grant of Saxlingham, near Holt.[34]
Together these estates made up a very considerable holding, but
their **significance** did not end there. They were the nucleus of a
widespread system of clientage extending among Robsart's relatives, friends and neighbours. These included such families as the
Appleyards, the Flowerdews and the Walpoles of Houghton, whose
lands and influence were considerable. Warwick knew how important it was to build on the goodwill of the Norfolk gentlemen which
had been established the previous summer. A county that had
blazed into revolt once might do so again, especially as the traditional authority of the Howards had been curtailed, at least for the
time being.

Warwick was not present at Sheen to see the double wedding:
illness had once again incapacitated him and detained him in
London. The wedding of Amy and Robert must have been an anti-
climax after the event of the previous day on which all eyes were
fixed. For John and Anne there was a 'fair dinner made and dancing' and their nuptials were graced by the King's presence. After the
meal Edward and his attendants retired to a shaded bower of
plaited branches to watch a joust between two teams of six gentlemen. No such lavish spectacle was provided for Robert. His friends
had to be content with a bizarre and less chivalric sport: a live goose
was tied to a post and the young men rode at it with drawn swords
to see who could be the first to cut off its head. There were,
however, more manly pastimes on the following (and final) day of
the celebrations: 'There was a tilt and tourney on foot with as great

staves as they [could] run withal on horseback.[35] On 6 June the royal party returned to Greenwich. One member was probably an ambitious 29-year-old lawyer, shortly to become Secretary to the Council. Years later he would sourly describe the relationship of Robert and Army as 'a carnal marriage, begun for pleasure and ended in lamentation'. His name was William Cecil.

The seventeen-year-old newly weds may have spent some part of the ensuing months in Norfolk. Certainly Robert had new responsibilities to attend to as landowner and royal agent in the shire. In 1550 he and his father-in-law were charged with the commission to collect the subsidy granted to the King by parliament. The following year he was on the commission for gaol delivery. In 1552 he was appointed Lieutenant of Norfolk, and in the same year he was elected MP. Twelve months later, when new legislation of an ultra-protestant kind had been introduced, it was Lord Robert Dudley* and Sir John Robsart who were in charge of removing objects of superstition from the churches in their area. Syderstone, we are informed, yielded up three sets of vestments, one cope and two candlesticks.

Yet Robert must have performed some of his shire duties by proxy for his responsibilities at court steadily increased. In August 1551 two of the King's former companions were sworn as gentlemen of the Privy Chamber. One was Edward's close friend and favourite, Barnaby Fitzpatrick. The other was Robert Dudley. In the following spring, on Viscount Lisle's appointment as Master of the Horse, Robert assumed the vacant post of the Master of the Buckhounds. This brought responsibility for arranging royal hunting parties, ensuring a supply of animals for His Majesty to pursue and keeping up the breeding standard of the King's hounds. For these tasks he was allowed £33. 6s. 8d. per annum. Robert's elder brothers were now increasingly involved in political and diplomatic activities. John, for instance, went on an important mission to France in 1552. But Robert's duties were purely concerned with ceremonial and court functions. In October 1551 we read of him being part of an impressive retinue of lords and gentlemen sent to welcome the dowager Queen of Scotland and to bring her to Hampton Court. The last appointment he received from Edward VI was to yet another household post – that of Chief Carver on 25 February 1553.[36] He was then nearly twenty years of age, had spent almost all his life at the royal court and, apart from the brief skirmish at Norwich, had not been stretched in any more demanding role. Had

* Robert received this courtesy title in 1551 when his father became Duke of Northumberland. At the same time his eldest brother became Earl of Warwick.

he been entrusted with more important tasks he might not have
failed his first major test.

For three years the Dudleys rode high, rich and powerful in the
realm. The family profited hugely from Warwick's pre-eminence.
The Earl awarded himself and his friends lucrative positions and
large grants of lands confiscated from ecclesiastical bodies and
enemies of the regime. There was nothing novel about this establishment of a secure power base and the buying of support but it was
destined to continue and to reach abnormal levels as the political
situation changed and Warwick found events slipping out of his
control. Warwick Castle, obtained in 1547,[37] now became the focal
point of Dudley power in the Midlands. The Earl's property and
influence extended throughout an area bounded by Birmingham,
Dudley, Worcester, Stratford-upon-Avon, Southam, Rugby and
Coventry. No man had held such unchallenged sway in the area
since the days of the great Beauchamp and Neville earls. On his
marriage, Viscount Lisle was established with lands at Balsall so that
he could familiarize himself with the estates and tenants which
would one day be his. Some of the land in the south-east – the
Guildford estates centred on Halden – went to Mary and her
husband, Sir Henry Sidney, on their marriage. The following year
Penshurst Place was granted to Henry's father on the attainder of
Sir Ralph Fane for plotting against Dudley. It became the centre of
the considerable Sidney landholding in the Kentish Weald and was
inherited by Henry in 1554. Together with Warwick's other lands
and iron foundries (he was a pioneer in the English iron and steel
industry) in Kent this was a considerable nucleus of Dudley territorial power.[38] Henry Dudley controlled the inherited Dudley lands in
London and Middlesex. Ambrose's lands were also in the home
counties, but when his first wife, Anne Whorwood, died of the
sweating sickness in 1552 he remarried within a few months. His
new bride was Elizabeth, Baroness Talboys, who owned in her own
right great estates in Lincolnshire and Yorkshire. In 1551, to
support John Dudley's new dignity of Duke of Northumberland, he
received enormous grants of land in the north, including parcels of
the old Percy estates and of the bishopric of Durham. One such gift
from the crown was bestowed in order to encourage Dudley's children to 'follow in his steps and exhibit a like example of the virtues
of true nobility'.[39]

As well as land, power brought other perquisites. The fees from
his various court posts provided Robert with over £100 a year. In
1553 he was granted the wardship of Sir Thomas Philpott, an
elderly Kentish knight of substance who had fallen beside his wits.

About the same time Robert also obtained property formerly belonging to Anne of Cleves. Henry VIII's only surviving wife was forced by the Council to part with certain manors granted to her for life. For £400 Robert obtained the reversion of some of these manors. By the spring of 1553, then, Lord Robert Dudley was comfortably provided for. He had every opportunity, through his court and county connections, to extend his possessions and, though Robert could look forward to a substantial inheritance on the death of his father, Northumberland may well have felt that he had given his fifth son a very adequate start in life. He was in favour with the King and, as Edward grew to manhood, there seemed every possibility that he would attain a position of considerable prominence in the state.

Before high summer his life and prospects lay in ruins.

CHAPTER FOUR

PRISONER

'If I should have [relied] more upon the speech of the people than upon the service of my master, or gone about to seek favour of them without respect to his highness' surety, I needed not to have had so much obloquy of some kind of men'.[1] Therein lay the dilemma of John Dudley. Most historians now agree that the reformed Council under his presidency, though it had its shortcomings, made a serious start on the solution of England's gravest problems. Law and order were restored at home, and peace (albeit at the cost of some national pride) was secured abroad. The currency began to regain some of its former value. The religious settlement favoured by the government involved a further lurch towards radicalism, which may have offended Catholics and moderate reformers but did have the support of the most vigorous and convinced, though perhaps not the largest, section of the church (not to mention landowners great and small who benefited from the new flow of ecclesiastical property onto the market).[2] Support for the religious radicals had the approval of the one person who, in the last analysis, mattered most – King Edward. The progress of the Reformation was dearer than anything to the boy's heart, and though Northumberland did not share Edward's bigotry he had always supported the evangelical cause. The Lord President saw, with the clarity of the military strategist, those things which required urgent and firm attention if national recovery were to be achieved. He replaced Somerset's hope-inspiring promises and impracticable policies with clear-cut plans and efficient action. This involved the ruthless suppression of civil disorder and reform of revenue collection methods. Such policies might have made for good government: they certainly did not make for popularity. Thus Northumberland came to be widely hated.

   He felt it keenly. Though he chose to present himself to colleagues and officials as a man of iron, impelled by a rigid sense of duty, he confided to intimates that every night he went to bed 'with a careful heart and a weary body, and yet . . . no man hath scarcely any good opinion of me.'[3] Depression and self-doubt were now his constant companions. His bouts of illness were frequent. He longed to hand over full executive power to the King and, at the end of 1552, obtained conciliar approval to advance Edward's majority from his eighteenth to his sixteenth birthday. He attempted, by showing leniency to individual members, to offset the harsher aspects of his policy. He urged his Council colleagues to assume a more credible stance: 'Let us show ourselves . . . ready not only to spend our goods but our lands and lives for our master and our country and to despise this flattering of ourselves with heaping riches upon riches, house upon house, buildings upon buildings . . . let us . . . fly from it as the greatest pestilence in the commonwealth'.[4] All this made little impression on the country at large. The people saw Northumberland as the man who had created a standing army to suppress their liberties. They believed that he and his cronies were milking the state; that they had the King in their power; that the Lord President was issuing coins bearing his own image: in short, that the Duke of Northumberland was a ruthless oppressor.

Somerset's tragic end only confirmed the popular verdict. There were faults on both sides but Seymour's pride was the main cause of his second – and final – downfall. He could not accept a position of equality with his colleagues. He became the leader of opposition to Warwick in the Council and within a few months government unity was in danger of disintegrating in faction struggles. The 'good duke' was still popular throughout the country – more so since his imprisonment – and some of his friends were planning, or at least discussing, his return to power. It was an intolerable situation but one which Dudley permitted to continue for more than a year while he sought, through intermediaries, to persuade Seymour to more reasonable courses. Not until 16 October was Somerset arrested on a charge of treason. Then the regime proceeded against him by the accepted Tudor method for dealing with political undesirables – the state trial. He was executed for felony on 22 January 1552.

The populace, the disgruntled Catholics and Northumberland's personal enemies now had a martyr. Somerset's death united opposition. From all over England came reports of justices examining men and women who spoke against Dudley and spread wild rumours about him. Northumberland's family had to share the obloquy heaped upon the head of the house. Yet as long as Northumberland had the support of and acted in the name of the sovereign he had little to fear whatever men might say about him. The lesson was not lost on Robert. Northumberland continued to enjoy the confidence of his prince. Edward had little love for his uncle and did not mourn his passing. Dudley gave much of his attention in this crucial period to keeping Edward diverted. The Christmas entertainments of 1551 were the most elaborate of the

reign. They were supervised by a lord of misrule and, on Northumberland's express instructions, there was no stinting on
costumes, props and ingenious devices. All the King's attendants
were impressed with the importance of keeping Edward's mind off
more sombre subjects The Dudley brothers played a prominent
part in the masques, mock tourneys and spectacular buffoonery
which lasted throughout the twelve days. But these jollifications
were not only laid on for the King's benefit: the citizenry of London
also needed humouring. On 4 January the court took its entertainment to the people. Ambrose and Robert were among the great
retinue of 'young knights and gentlemen' who boarded the royal
barges at Greenwich, dressed in gaudy silks as attendants of the lord
of misrule, and disembarked at Tower Wharf to caper merrily
through the streets, dispensing free wine and largesse.[5]

There were many other entertainments at court, though not as
lavish as those of Christmastide 1551, and Lord Robert was involved
in most of them. He and his wife now had quarters close to the royal
apartments in every house where the court lodged. He was
constantly in attendance upon his young master, keeping watch on
pages, grooms, sewers, cooks, tutors, huntsmen, and ensuring the
smooth day-to-day running of the household. He was present at
most of Edward's private and public engagements – ambassadorial
audiences, revels, receptions, and even those occasional meetings
between Edward and one or other of his very different sisters.

Though Elizabeth's visits were infrequent they were sufficient for
Robert to maintain his friendship with her. Northumberland made
a deliberate show of cordiality towards the King's half-sisters, and
since the Dudleys, their relatives and friends dominated the court it
was scarcely possible for the princesses to avoid close contact with
them. Elizabeth had good cause to be grateful to the Duke who was
largely instrumental in setting her up in sumptuous independence.
Life had been very difficult for her during Somerset's protectorate.
The £3,000 settlement made on her by her father had not been
carried into effect and she had been lodged for a time with
Seymour's brother, Thomas. The latter began to make amorous
advances to her which were not only offensive but politically
dangerous. When John Dudley came to power he immediately
concluded the arrangements for the Princess's household. He made
over to her his own palace and park at Hatfield and even provided
her with a surveyor to keep her affairs in order – Secretary William
Cecil. Elizabeth was to maintain a lifelong affection for both. On her
visits to the court she was accorded every dignity due to her estate.
On 21 January 1551 the seventeen-year-old Princess 'was most

honourably received by the Council . . . to show the people how much glory belongs to her who has embraced the new religion and is become a very great lady',[6] and on her entry to London she was met by a hundred of the King's horse. The years 1550-1553 were undoubtedly the most tranquil that Anne Boleyn's daughter had yet known. Robert was very busy with his court duties, his gay, luxury-loving wife, and with estate and local affairs in distant Norfolk, yet there was no reason to doubt that he could always find time to enjoy the company of the royal girl he knew so well.

Life was very full but very amiable – until the winter of 1552-3 Then it began to appear to those close to the centre that Northumberland's grasp on events was not as firm as it had once been. Illness had severely drained his energies. At times he seemed to lack the will to continue carrying the burdens of state. The great magnates, once firmly behind him, were now divided: some of them had been driven from office; others disliked his policies; still more were simply jealous of his power and wealth. The Duke had even been recently rebuffed when he sought the hand of the Earl of Cumberland's daughter for young Guildford. Yet all was well as long as the King continued to trust and rely on him. In February the King fell dangerously ill. A severe cold became a chill and, thus weakened, the boy fell a prey to pulmonary tuberculosis.* He grew very weak. Even in the worst moments he refused to accept the possibility of death but Robert and the others who watched over the slight, weak form in the great bed at Westminster saw the spectre draw near often. The King's high fever and his agonising struggles for breath forced them to face a future in which Mary Tudor would occupy the throne. For the Dudleys such a future would be bleak.

With the spring Edward recovered. He was able to move with the court to Greenwich. But by the third week of May he was confined to bed again and could not watch Northumberland's last triumph – the departure of Willoughby and Chancellor's expedition in search of a north-east passage to Cathay. As the three ships were towed down the Thames Robert must have been among the excited crowds waving and cheering along the Greenwich waterfront. His father had put a great deal of money and careful planning into this venture, had talked of it often, and, at last, despite the worrying situation at home, his brave captains and mariners were setting out to win for England a greater share in the orient trade.

It was a brief shaft of sunlight through the gathering clouds. Edward's condition worsened. Faced with the possible crisis of the

*This is the consensus of historical opinion; no sixteenth-century physician could diagnose such a disease.

King's death and the inevitable destruction of all he had worked for, Northumberland was unable to pursue a consistent policy. His tired mind could not cope with all the details that would require attention if he were to force his will ruthlessly upon the nation. In all probability he had no real desire to do so, and when Edward VI did die he could only make a muddled and half-hearted attempt to ensure the Protestant succession.[7]

It was that objective which underlay the events of June and July 1553. The legislative framework of the Reformation was largely in place. Churches had been stripped of Catholic icons. The mass had been abolished. Public worship was in the vernacular. The Bible was available to all who could read. Most ecclesiastical wealth had found its way into lay hands. It would be difficult, probably impossible, for two decades of change to be reversed. But the nation's new identity had yet to be accepted by all the people. There was widespread discontent, especially at the accelerated pace of innovation associated with Northumberland's rule. Time would be needed to win hearts and minds and time was a commodity the regime did not have. If Mary succeeded to the throne she would undo as much as possible of her father's and brother's religious policies – of that there could be no doubt. For those at the centre of government this posed the threat of England slipping back into papistical error or, at least, political instability as the queen became a prey to all the ambitious royal houses of Europe. It was the attempt to prevent that which led to the tragi-farce of the nine days' queen.

No-one was more passionate than the King to divert the succession away from his half-sister. The zealous royal evangelical was genuinely horrified at the prospect of his country being forced to turn its back on all he believed in. How far the details of the plot to debar Mary originated with him and how far they proceeded from Northumberland will always remain a matter for conjecture. What is beyond dispute is that Edward was determined, that Northumberland, in pursuance of his public policies and private interests, was bent on carrying out his master's wishes. Granted that premise there is an uncomplicated logic in the steps taken to place Northumberland's daughter-in-law on the throne of England.

The facts of the plot are well known: the King drew up a 'devise for the succession' in which he attempted, illegally, to leave the crown to a candidate of his own choice; at about the same time all the females who stood close in line of succession were married or betrothed to men Northumberland could trust. It was a great misfortune for Edward and Northumberland that there were no eligible male candidates. In his first draft of the 'devise', probably

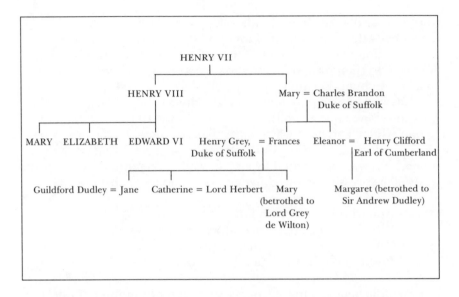

written before he knew he was fatally ill, the King excluded Mary and Elizabeth on the grounds of their bastardy and left the crown to Jane Grey's heirs male. Later he altered this to 'the L. Jane and her heirs male'. By that time the poor girl had a husband – the youngest Dudley boy, Guildford.

The arrangements for the wedding were made in April and were not welcomed by either of the principals. Jane, a pious, serious-minded fifteen-year-old, felt no attraction for Guildford, who seems to have had very little depth of character. Young Dudley, for his part, may well have resented being obliged to marry at his father's pleasure when brother Robert, only a year or two his senior, had been allowed to choose his own bride. The protests of the young couple were ignored; too much was at stake. On 21 May, the day after the departure of Willoughby's ships, the London crowds gathered outside Durham Place, Northumberland's town house, to watch all the great men and women assemble for the leading social event of the year. The whole Dudley family was there to witness the splendid nuptials of John and Jane's last two unmarried children. As well as Guildford marrying Suffolk's eldest daughter, little Catherine Dudley was united with Henry Hastings, Lord Huntingdon's heir and a great friend of the King. The third wedding celebrated that day was that of Catherine Grey to Lord Herbert, the Earl of Pembroke's son. The festivities were deliberately lavish – 'exceedingly splendid and royal', according to one Italian observer[8] – the object undoubtedly being to impress the populace and take their minds off present sufferings and future fears. The effect was achieved for at least one guest who, dazzled by the splendour and power of Northumberland and Suffolk, wrote, 'Who could then have imagined that Fortune was about to turn her coat and expend her fury upon those two great lords'.[9]

It was not blind fate which brought down Northumberland and his allies; it was public opinion (or the opinion of that section of the public which had political clout). The Dudleys were unpopular. Mary Tudor had always enjoyed widespread sympathy. Northumberland was confronted by a stout wall of common sentiment. It was well expressed by the courtier, Sir Nicholas Throckmorton.

> And, though I liked not the religion
> Which all her life Queen Mary had professed,
> Yet in my mind that wicked notion
> Right heirs for to displace I did detest.[10]

Most people believed that Princess Mary and her mother, Catherine of Aragon, had been appallingly treated by King Henry. Even convinced Protestants like Throckmorton were horrified at the thought that she should be deprived of her rights by the ambitious Dudleys.

No one could fail to notice the significant absence of one guest at the wedding celebrations. King Edward had promised to attend but his physicians would not permit him to leave his bed. In London the story rapidly spread that the boy was already dead. Hurrying back to Greenwich, Northumberland asked the King to stand at a window and show himself to the local people. Held by two gentlemen of the Privy Chamber, who carried more than supported him, Edward made a supreme effort to comply. Then he was laid back upon his bed never to leave it again. The ensuing days were tense and melancholy for Robert and the other close attendants of the dying King. Edward's long bouts of continuous, convulsive coughing now brought up a sputum which was 'livid, black, foetid and full of carbon; it smells beyond measure'.[11] His body was hot, dry and ulcerated. Speech was an effort. The swallowing of food was almost impossible. He longed for oblivion but doctors, goaded by ministers unwilling to let the King slip into an unconsciousness from which he might not wake, plied him with stimulants. Northumberland and other members of the Council came every day hoping to detect some improvement. Sometimes there were signs of a spurious recovery. Then Edward insisted on receiving ambassadors and other dignitaries to demonstrate to them that he was on the mend. But at all other times visitors were kept to an absolute minimum and those attending the King were sworn to complete secrecy about his condition.

The days and nights passed slowly in the close-guarded, stuffy, odorous death room. Robert and the other members of the Privy Chamber took turns at sitting with the feeble boy. In the absence of his favourite, Barnaby Fitzpatrick, who was in Ireland on family business, it was Sir Henry Sidney, Robert's brother-in-law, for whom Edward most often called. Sidney and Sir John Cheke were almost constantly at the bedside. The suffering and piety of the young king were alike affecting and, according to Sidney, 'had almost caused death to penetrate his dart into my own soul'.[12]

Robert shared the grief of all present but there was another strain upon him. He knew how critical the King's survival was for the nation and for the Dudleys. Probably he knew that Northumber-land was torn about what action to take in the event of the King's death. The arrangements made for the changed succession were made. Contingency plans existed to secure the Tower, station troops in strategic places and ensure the loyalty of the navy. But, at the same time, the Duke was keeping Mary informed about her half- brother's condition and had made no attempt to restrict her movements. In desperation Northumberland had dismissed the royal physicians and installed his personal doctor and two other practitioners. But Edward VI's condition was beyond sixteenth-century medical knowledge.

On 12 June Robert helped to prepare the King for an important audience. Terrified at the prospect of facing divine judgement without securing his country's religious revival, the devout adolescent summoned Lord Chief Justice Montague and the leading law officers and instructed them to draw up a new will. It was a tense meeting. Northumberland and a small group of councillors stood beside the bed. The judges knelt. The King spoke with a fervour enhanced by shortness of breath of his concern for the maintenance of true religion. Everyone waited for Montague's reaction. He knew that what the King was demanding was contrary to the law but could he say so to this dying boy? Falteringly he tried. The King grew angry. 'I will hear no objections,' he gasped. The judges withdrew in confusion. It took an angry demonstration by Northumberland and a further demand by Edward before they submitted to the royal will.

The King's physical and spiritual agony came to an end on the evening of 6 July. He died quietly in Henry Sidney's arms. Now was the time for resolute action. Northumberland and his friends began well. Two days previously the princesses had been summoned to their brother's bedside. Elizabeth pleaded illness but Mary set out cautiously from Hunsdon (near Hertford); so cautiously that by the evening of 6 July she had reached Hoddesdon, a mere five miles distant. When the King died the news was kept secret. But Northumberland's security system was faulty. Speculation and rumour had been rife for weeks. Observers watched the comings and goings at Greenwich with more than usual interest. Some of those necessarily privy to the plot were unhappy about it. The truth was out in a very short time. The imperial ambassador reported that the King's death and the plan to divert the succession were common knowledge in the capital within twenty-four hours. Certainly some-one went to Hoddesdon to warn Mary. In the small hours of 7 July the Princess's suite left hurriedly, travelling northwards with the objective of reaching Kenninghall, Mary's manor on the Norfolk-Suffolk border. By dusk the party had reached Sawston, south of Cambridge, where John Huddleston, a kinsman of one of the Princess's attendants, had a moated hall.

Meanwhile Northumberland had despatched his sons John and Robert towards Hunsdon with a force of three to four hundred mounted guards. There was nothing overtly sinister about this: it was the custom to escort the princesses into the capital. What more natural than that the Master of the Horse should personally attend the late King's sister? It has always been assumed that Northumber-land intended to lure Mary to London in order to place her under lock and key and force her to renounce the crown formally. The difficulty with this view is that it fails to explain why the Duke did not act quickly, decisively and forcefully. If he suspected on 4 July that Edward's end was near, he could have sent troops to Hunsdon, then. Even if he had waited until the King was dead he could have had horsemen at Hoddesdon before the Princess's informant arrived.

There is another interpretation of the known facts which avoids this difficulty and seems more in keeping with Northumberland's hesitancy and opportunism. His attitude to Mary was, to the very end of her brother's reign, a very proper one. Indeed, he seems to have gone out of his way to make himself pleasant to her. At the end of 1552 he sent his brother to offer to convey a message from her to the Emperor Charles V which, said ambassador Scheyfve, 'she must needs take in most comfortable part'.[13] In February Mary was received into London by the Duke and Duchess in person with a great display of affection. She was kept fully informed of the King's condition, as we have seen. And in May and June, when the Council certainly had many other problems to occupy it, it devoted consid-erable time to discussing the theft of some of the Princess's hawks.

The imperial ambassador felt sure he knew what lay behind this ostentatious wooing of Princess Mary: it was done 'in case other designs which he may peradventure be nourishing do not come to fruition, and so clear himself of the suspicion of aspiring to the crown'.[14] Scheyfve was wrong about many things but here he was probably close to the truth. It was in Dudley's nature to keep his options open as long as possible.

He had in his possession the King's will, endorsed by all the leading men of the realm. It had not yet been published and Jane Grey had not been proclaimed queen. He had control of London and had no reason for concern about the military situation. Very properly he sent an urgent summons to Mary so that she could be at her dying brother's bedside. If she had come, he would have been in a position to control the future: he would have been the queenmaker. He could have supported Mary on certain conditions and torn up Edward's will. If she proved uncooperative, he could have decided for Queen Jane. Whichever way the decision went he would have preserved his own position and the major government policies. In the event, Mary seized the initiative and forced Northumberland's hand. If this interpretation of events is accepted, Robert Dudley's role assumes greater significance.

He and John arrived at Hunsdon to find that the Princess had gone. The young men faced a real dilemma. Everything hinged upon Mary being brought safely to London but if they pursued her now their mission would drastically change its character: it would cease to be an honourable escort and become a police force. The brothers did not know what support Mary might have gathered. They did know that there was considerable public sympathy for her even among their own men. A decision had to be made quickly. John, Lord Warwick, ordered his brother to ride on after the Princess with the bulk of the men. If Mary was headed, as was suspected, for the coast, Robert would be able to raise loyal men from his own Norfolk estates to stop her. Warwick would make all haste to report back to the Council (he could trust no one else with the message) and return to Robert's aid with fresh troops if necessary.

Robert rode through the night, probably taking the highway (the present A10) to Cambridge. He thus lost track of Mary who had travelled by side roads to reach Sawston. Arriving at the university city well before dawn, he eventually gathered news of the Princess's whereabouts. Stopping only to augment his force with local supporters, he rode the seven miles to Sawston as the sun rose over the level East Anglian fields. Once again he was too late. Scarcely an hour before her pursuers arrived at Huddleston's house Mary had set out towards Newmarket. Robert must have been tired, worried and angry. He had already had trouble from some of his own men who had deserted during the night. Now he was faced with Huddleston's unhelpful servants. Under these strains his patience disintegrated and he did something foolish. He ordered his men to set fire to Sawston Hall. According to local legend, the Princess, looking back from rising ground to the north-east and seeing the smoke, promised to build Huddleston a new house. Within a few years the existing hall sprang up; Mary had been true to her word.

It was a time for resolute action, but that did not include petulant arson. If Robert had pressed on in pursuit, he just might have successfully accomplished his mission. But with every hour that passed his credibility waned. All that the country people knew (or guessed) was that their King was dead and that the Dudleys were in armed revolt against the lady who was now their sovereign. With reports reaching him of East Anglian gentry resorting to Mary along her route, Robert deemed it wiser to withdraw to Cambridge where he had some support and await Warwick's arrival. John met him there later that day and they set off together along the Newmarket road. They were like men riding into an enemy country. People in the villages along the route were sullen and uncooperative. Hours before those same people had cheered Mary. Her flight had become a triumph. In Bury St. Edmunds she had been given a civic reception. Long before the Dudleys could catch a glimpse of their quarry their force had diminished so much that further pursuit into hostile territory was impossible. The brothers decided to split up in order to raise more troops and Robert headed northwards into his own country.

In London, Northumberland could sit on the fence no longer. On this same day (8 July) he officially informed the Lord Mayor and aldermen of Edward's death and Queen Jane's accession. He sent out messengers to all the great landowners near the capital ordering them to gather forces and be ready to defend the realm. Mary, he reported, had fled towards the coast in the hope of escaping abroad and returning with a foreign army. But within hours the Princess was safely at Kenninghall, deep within friendly Howard country. Men of all estates flocked to offer their allegiance and Mary was ready to move on to the offensive. She proclaimed herself Queen, and wrote to the Council demanding immediate submission. England now had two sovereigns. The supporters of one of them would soon be traitors.

Robert laboured hard for the cause he had espoused. His first loyalty was to his family and, in the critical days when everyone else deserted Northumberland, Dudley unity held firm. The young lord of Syderstone worked strenuously to assemble tenants, neighbours and friends. He had some success in the area where he and the Robsarts had power and influence. He established control as far as Wisbech, and on 18 July he proclaimed his sister-in-law's accession in King's Lynn, being supported by the Mayor, George Rively, and 300 of the citizenry.[15]

Robert's achievement was the only ray of hope in a situation which had become very black for Northumberland. Mary had moved to the Howard castle at Framlingham and established her court there. The gentlemen and nobles of England either ignored the Council's order to levy powers or actually marched their men towards the Suffolk stronghold. Queen Jane and her government were secure in the Tower, but their fortress was rapidly becoming their prison. On 14 July the Duke reluctantly left at the head of an army and marched into East Anglia. He knew his cause was lost before he set out and his colleagues were relieved to be disembarrassed of his presence. He had 3,000 men. The camp at Framlingham had grown to some 20,000. In town after town Mary's accession was proclaimed. Royal ships in Yarmouth harbour defected to Mary. Northumberland's own officers grumbled and argued. Some left him. He reached Cambridge and there he stayed. His force was too depleted for him to continue the offensive. On 18 July he was deserted by his colleagues who surrendered the Tower to Mary, stripped the nine days' queen of her title, and even set a price on the Duke's head. It was all up. When he heard the news Northumberland personally proclaimed Mary in Cambridge. He was still there on 24 July when his old enemy, Arundel, came to arrest him. He was immediately sent under guard to London where crowds jeered and shouted at him all the way from the City gate to the Tower. With him went two of his sons, his brother and six of his principal supporters.

Robert's apprehension at King's Lynn soon followed. He was taken to Framlingham where he threw himself on the Queen's mercy.[16] Four days after his father arrived at the Tower Robert was also brought thither in the company of Bishop Ridley and the Marquess of Northampton.[17] At no time in its history were the prison quarters of the Tower so full as they were in Mary Tudor's reign. Northumberland's lodging in the Garden Tower (later popularly called the Bloody Tower, though no one quite knows why) had to be cleared of lumber in order to accommodate him. The five boys were first separated, Robert and Guildford being in the Bell Tower, John in the Beauchamp Tower, Ambrose and Henry in Coldharbour.

As more and more prisoners were crammed in, however, it was found necessary to put all the boys together in the Beauchamp Tower. Jane was lodged first in the Lieutenant's house and later in the Gentleman Gaoler's house, next to the Beauchamp Tower. Conspirators who had been unsuccessful in their attempts to cast all the blame on Northumberland soon occupied all the remaining prison accommodation. Within months political prisoners were joined by men detained for their religious convictions: Mary arrested many leading Protestants and preachers inimical to her regime.

Robert now passed the most unpleasant period of his life. He was in prison for eighteen months – most of them spent under threat of execution. He lost everything, and with a suddenness that was catastrophic. Gone was the luxurious, intimate life of the court and the airy freedom of great parks and chases. Yet it would be easy to exaggerate the unpleasant conditions of Robert's confinement. Prominent prisoners in the Tower were customarily permitted such indulgences as their rank demanded and their purses could command. They could buy whatever food they wished, have furniture, books and even pets sent in, and they were always attended by servants. Robert obtained permission for Amy to visit him at 'any convenient time' and we know that Jane and Guildford Dudley were sometimes together. He was allowed exercise every day on the leads joining the Beauchamp and Bell Towers. At such times, and when he was a guest at the Lieutenant's dinner-table, he was able to talk with other prisoners.

It was in their common room on the first floor of the Beauchamp Tower that John, Lord Warwick, said goodbye to Ambrose, Henry, Robert and Guildford on the morning of 18 August before going, with Northumberland and the Marquess of Northampton, to Westminster to be tried on charges of high treason. They were heard before their peers in a court presided over by the Duke of Norfolk, himself recently released from the Tower. The result was a foregone conclusion and the accused did not trouble their judges with a plea of 'not guilty'. They confessed their crimes though, as Northumberland pointed out, some of those who sat in the solemn and begowned ranks of the nobility were equally guilty. The court took no account of the fact that the Duke had acted in consort with the royal Council. They also chose not to be swayed by the Earl's tender years. All three were sentenced to be hung, drawn and quartered. They were then returned to the Tower.

In the event, it was only the chief conspirator who went to the scaffold. He was a sick and broken man but he was not left in peace to prepare for his end. The new regime (or, more particularly, his old enemies Gardiner, Howard and Arundel) wanted more than his head: they wanted his humiliation, degradation and recantation. In his draughty chambers Dudley was plagued with visits from councillors and priests urging him to confess publicly that all he had stood for had been wrong and, above all, that the Protestant faith was damnable heresy. To this end he was offered a pardon and other inducements that his enemies had no intention of honouring. He succumbed. The self-doubt to which he had always been prey now took over. Unable to resist any more he gave his enemies all they wanted.

On 21 August Robert and his brothers expected their father to be led out to execution. Instead they were summoned to St Peter's Chapel. When they had taken their places inside, along with a crowd of official guests, Northumberland, his brother Sir Andrew Dudley, the Marquess of Northampton, Sir Henry Gates and Sir Thomas Palmer (all now condemned men) were ushered into prominent seats at the front of the church. Then Bishop Gardiner entered, attended by priests all clad in the mass vestments which had been forbidden in England for four years. They performed the full Roman rite and everyone watched as the Duke and his companions went forward to receive the sacrament. At the end of the service John Dudley turned to the congregation and said: 'Truly, I profess here before you all that I have received the sacrament according to the true Catholic faith; and the plagues that is upon the realm and upon us now is that we have erred from the faith these sixteen years. And this I protest unto you all from the bottom of my heart.'[18]

It was the ultimate humiliation not only for Northumberland but also for his family who had supported him so loyally. Mary and her vengeful advisers were determined to rub salt into the wound and to break utterly the magnificent, impressive man who had built up the Dudley fortunes and held together a divided country for four years. We can only guess at the effect this had upon the captive brothers, but one fact is clear: it left Robert with a bitterness and loathing for the religion espoused by Mary and Gardiner.

At the nadir of the Dudley fortunes one is struck again by the strong bonds which held the family together. There was no destructive, *sauve qui peut* panic with everyone trying to extricate himself from the consequences of the Duke's failure. In a little devotional manual, which Lady Jane Grey gave to the Lieutenant of the Tower before her death, there is a touching little prayer written in a margin. It beseeches God to bestow long life on Northumberland. It is signed 'Guildford Dudley' and was obviously written in the early days of his imprisonment.[19] Forced, for political reasons, to marry a girl he did not love, obliged to play second fiddle to her when she was proclaimed queen and then, within days, thrown into prison, Guildford certainly had cause to reproach his father. From Jane, Duchess of Northumberland, there came no word of blame as, with nothing left of her great fortune but a house in Chelsea and some treasured keepsakes, she devoted all her energies to securing the release of her sons. But perhaps the most touching testimonial to family affection is the one which can still be seen by any visitor to the Tower. Beside the fireplace in the room which the boys shared the elder Dudley carved their heraldic devices – the bear and ragged staff, and the double-tailed lion – and his name on a scroll beneath – 'IOHN DVDLI'. With patient and elaborate care he encircled the legend with a border of leaves and flowers, whose significance was explained in an unfinished verse carved below:

> Yow that these beasts do wel behold and se
> May deme with ease wherefore here made they be
> Withe borders eke wherein*
> 4 Brothers names who list to serche the grounde

The names appear in the plants displayed: roses for Ambrose, gilley-flowers for Guildford, oak leaves for Robert (Latin *robur*=oak) and honeysuckle for Henry. It is a charming conceit, and one can imagine the obviously talented young man whiling away hundreds of tedious hours at it. Robert, too, left his mark in the room – a small carved oak branch and the initials R.D. And, if legend is correct, the simple word IANE, also engraved in the Beauchamp Tower, is the work of Guildford Dudley and suggests that he quickly developed a genuine affection for his unwanted bride.

On the morning of 22 August the Duke of Northumberland was led out to Tower Hill for his execution. His sentence had been commuted to simple beheading. It was soon over. The boys would not have been able to see their father's departure from their lodgings but they undoubtedly witnessed his return – a wooden box clattering about in an open horsedrawn cart which came through the Garden Tower gate, circled the green and came to a halt before the chapel of St Peter ad Vincula. Within, John Dudley was laid to rest under the altar. Besides him were the remains of his old friend and enemy, Edward Seymour. He was spared the final indignity of having his head displayed on a pole in some prominent place. One man was not ashamed to show loyalty and friendship:

*Words missing – perhaps 'there may be found'.

John Cork, Lancaster Herald, sometime servant to this Duke, begged of Queen Mary to bury the head of his old master in the Tower of London, which was granted him with the whole body and performed accordingly. In remembrance whereof the said Lancaster did ever after bear for his crest *a bear's head silver, crowned gold*.[20]

Queen Mary had no desire to start her reign with a bloodbath and, for the moment, only Northumberland, and two associates, Palmer and Gates, went to the scaffold. No date was set for Warwick's execution. No judicial process was begun against his brothers. But the Dudleys were extremely vulnerable. At any moment when the government decided that a show of firmness was desirable they would be the first to be sacrificed. Robert and his brothers had a vested interest in the peaceful transfer of effective rule to Catholic Mary.

It was not to be. The honeymoon period lasted weeks rather than months. The seemingly universal joy with which Mary had been welcomed soon gave way to mistrust, hatred and contempt. It began with protests against her attempt to dismantle the religious structures of the last twenty years. As early as 13 August the Queen's chaplain narrowly escaped death from a hostile crowd when he preached at St Paul's Cross. Parliament, when it met in October, proved uncooperative about repealing old statutes. Mary's Council was fast splitting into factions, a process accelerated by her inclination to rely on others – mostly priests and foreigners – for advice. Then towards the end of the year, the news was published that the Queen was negotiating a marriage with Philip, heir to the throne of Spain. National pride and hatred of papists now merged in a general outcry against the proposals. Country priests were manhandled. Scurrilous pamphlets were distributed. A dead dog with a 'tonsured crown' was thrown in through one of the palace windows. Mary was obliged to double her personal guard and Bishop Gardiner (now Lord Chancellor) received so many assassination threats that he was forced to take up residence in the royal household. Mary Tudor and England were moving onto a collision course.

Measures taken to ensure law and order rapidly filled the prisons. Hundreds of men and women did not stay to face arrest on suspicion of heresy or treason. They fled to Germany and Switzerland and took up their abode in the more congenial and more extreme centres of Protestant reform. It was England's first religious exodus. All this was bad news for the prisoners in the Tower. The Queen was constantly advised to take firmer measures against possible claimants to the throne in whose interests rebellions might be launched. Pre-eminent among these were Princess Elizabeth and Jane Dudley. Mary kept her half-sister at court most of the time and grew increasingly aggravated by her half-hearted outward conformity to the restored religion. Jane was now brought to trial. On 13 November she was taken with her husband, Archbishop Cranmer, and Henry and Ambrose Dudley to Guildhall. Jane and her relatives all pleaded guilty to the charge of high treason and all heard the inevitable sentence pronounced upon them. Then they were returned to their prison quarters. Probably Mary hoped that they could eventually be released, as Suffolk, Northampton and others had been already. Certainly, during the next few weeks, the conditions of their captivity were eased.

Robert was now the only member of the family not to have been formally charged. The reason appears to have been the comparative difficulty of gathering evidence against him. The others had all proclaimed Jane in London and levied their powers close to the capital. Robert's treasons, however, had been committed mostly in Norfolk and it was there that the justices had to gather witnesses to his activities the previous July. It was not until 9 January 1554 that a commission of oyer and terminer was held in the Shirehouse at Norwich to enquire 'of good and loyal men of the said county of Norfolk and neighbouring areas concerning all treasons, misprisions of treasons, insurrections, rebellions, etc, within the county of Norfolk by whomsoever perpetrated'.[21] The commission decided that 'Robert Dudley formerly of London, Knight' had 'possessed and in warlike manner fortified [King's Lynn] and there traitorously published and proclaimed to be Queen of this realm of England one Jane Dudley . . . and that . . . with the aforesaid Duke and the said other traitors he continued to levy very cruel war against the said Queen Mary his sovereign and . . . falsely and treacherously worked for, abetted and encompassed the utter destruction of the said Queen contrary to his allegiance and against the crown and dignity of the said Queen . . .'[22] On receipt of the Norfolk commissioners' report letters patent were sent to Thomas White, Lord Mayor of London, to assemble a court at Guildhall to hear Robert Dudley's plea to the charge, to consider the evidence, pass judgement and pronounce sentence.

On 22 January Robert was conveyed on foot through London, preceded by the Gentleman Gaoler of the Tower bearing the axe. The weather was bitter and the mood of the City grim. White had already arranged for a distribution of cheap sea coal to ease the situation, but the cold, the unchecked spreading of libellous pamphlets, the hatred of the Spaniards who were frequent visitors to the capital, and the growing rumour of a widespread rebellion in the country made the people discontented and tense. At the beginning of the month Spaniards had been pelted with snowballs as they rode through the streets of the capital. Few citizens gathered now to jeer at the last of the Dudleys going to receive his just deserts. At his trial Robert followed the example of those convicted before him: he pleaded guilty to all the charges. Thereupon judgement was given and he was sentenced to be hung, drawn and quartered.

There was still some room for hope that the sentence might not be carried out, though optimism dwindled rapidly in the next few days. The rumoured rebellion did break out. Though it collapsed in the west and Midlands, Sir Thomas Wyatt succeeded in raising Kent and advancing towards London at the head of 3,000 men. The veteran Duke of Norfolk turned out to confront the insurgents and suffered his last military humiliation: some of his men deserted and the remnant trailed back into the capital, 'their coats torn, all ruined, without arrows or string in their bows'.[23]

The Dudleys were witnesses of the bustle and alarm within the Tower as shipping was cleared from the wharf and cannon trained on the south bank of the Thames. Wyatt's men overran Southwark on 3 February but failed to take London Bridge. They were forced to continue up river and cross over at Kingston, advancing through the capital's western suburbs on the 7th. Hunger and faint-heartedness had diminished Wyatt's host and he gained little support from the citizens (nor, it must be said, did the Queen). For hours the outcome hung in the balance but, at last, the leader surrendered at Temple Bar. The Dudleys must have heard the shouts and jeers of the garrison as Wyatt and hundreds of his bedraggled supporters were marched into the Tower to be distributed among the overcrowded prison quarters.

There now followed a series of events which were both traumatic and creative in the life of Robert Dudley. First of all Mary, urged on by some of her Council, carried out savage reprisals against the rebels. Then Jane and Guildford were executed. Finally Princess Elizabeth was brought to the Tower. Ultimate responsibility for the death of Lady Jane and her husband must lie with the Queen, though she would probably have preferred to take the path of leniency. It was Gardiner and the advocates of the Spanish match who impressed upon her the need for removing all possible rivals to the throne. When she realised that the plans for her marriage to Philip were in jeopardy she agreed to the executions of Jane and Guildford and to the close examination of Elizabeth. On the morning of 12 February (execution had been arranged for the 9th but was unaccountably delayed) Robert, Ambrose, John and Henry embraced their younger brother for the last time. Then he was led out of the Tower to the spot where his father had perished. Probably the other members of the family did not witness Guildford's death. It is only recorded that the Marquess of Northampton was permitted to watch from the roof of the Devereux Tower.[24] The same author relates that the youngest Dudley made a good end, resolute in his faith to the end and refusing the ministrations of a Catholic priest. Jane was spared the humiliation of a public execution and she died with quiet fortitude. From the Beauchamp Tower the four remaining Dudley prisoners* had a clear view of the last earthly movements of their brave, tragic sister-in-law as she walked across the Green below to a specially erected scaffold, prayed, spoke briefly to a small group of bystanders, knelt and submitted her neck to the axe. One of her last acts was to give the Lieutenant, Sir John Bridges, a prayer book in which she had written a brief message. It is interesting to note that she did not despise or reject the name that had brought her to the scaffold but signed herself 'Jane Dudley'.

Suffolk, who had been re-arrested on 10 February, was taken out to the nearby execution site for his beheading on the 23rd. Wyatt, the leader of the rebellion, did not suffer a traitor's death until April. The bulk of the captured rebels were, at length, ostentatiously set at liberty, being led through London in bonds to the tilt-yard at Westminster where they knelt before the Queen, received pardon from her own lips and departed free men. But the large-scale hangings had by then left a bitter taste in the mouths of many – a taste which would shortly be revived when Mary's religious persecution began. Gallows were set up at every London gate – one at the end of London Bridge, four in Southwark, one at Leadenhall, two in Cheapside, six or eight in Fleet Street and Charing Cross, and in many other places. The prisons were so full that some offenders had to be locked in churches, forty or more at a time.[25]

Ironically, when Mary executed Jane and Guildford she removed the only obstacles to a revival of Dudley fortunes. Had the nine days' queen and her husband lived into Elizabeth's reign they would have been possible rivals and a constant embarrassment to the new Queen. The government would have been constrained to restrict their movements. It would scarcely have been possible for Robert and Ambrose to have won Elizabeth's confidence and affection.

On Palm Sunday the Queen's half-sister was brought by barge to the Privy Stairs (not Traitor's Gate, as spurious legend would have

*Sir Andrew's prison is unknown.

it) where, according to a contemporary chronicler, she made a brief speech to the Lieutenant and his officers: 'Oh Lord! I never thought to have come in here as a prisoner; and I pray you all good fellows, bear me witness that I come in no traitor but as true a woman to the Queen's majesty as any now living: and thereon will I take my death.'[26] The Princess was terrified of this place where her mother had been executed and now lay buried. She had pleaded not to be sent here but Gardiner had persuaded the Queen and bullied the Council. He was convinced that Elizabeth had been implicated in Wyatt's rebellion despite her repeated protestations to the contrary. Like his victim he thought of the Tower as one step from the grave. With Elizabeth out of the way the Protestant cause in England would be finished, the unfortunate sequence of events begun in 1529, with the summoning of the Reformation Parliament, totally reversed.

Elizabeth was lodged in the upper chamber of the Bell Tower, only a few yards from Robert's prison. They were even closer when one or other of them was taking exercise on the ramparts between the Bell and Beauchamp Towers (now known as Elizabeth's Walk). They were, of course, not permitted to be there together: the strictest security surrounded the Princess and she was not supposed to set foot outside her gaol without being guarded by five attendants. This does not mean that there was no contact between the two prisoners. They may have met as guests at the Lieutenant's table. Robert may well have smuggled messages conveying loyalty and encouragement to Elizabeth. It is not beyond the bounds of possibility that the two young people may have been able to snatch a few moments' conversation together. Despite the sternest injunctions, guards were always open to bribes. Only nine years later the Earl and Countess of Hertford found themselves in the Tower under royal displeasure. They were in separate lodgings and forbidden to meet. Yet during their captivity they managed to produce a baby. As public sympathy for Elizabeth became more manifest and conditions of her imprisonment were eased (she was, for example, permitted to walk in the Privy Garden). It is inconceivable that the Dudleys would not have attempted to make contact with her; almost inconceivable that they did not succeed in some way or other.

Put at its very lowest level, the shared experience of imprisonment in the Tower of London under threat of death must have created a strong bond between two people who had been companions on and off all their lives in much happier circumstances. There was no one else now for whom Robert could have felt a natural loyalty. The only other people who had ever filled that place in his life were dead –

his father, King Edward, Lady Jane. Certainly there was nothing to draw him towards the Queen who, after Easter, came with a fanfare of sackbuts and drums to St John's Chapel to be married by proxy to the Hapsburg king.

Natural loyalty was one thing; survival was another, as both Elizabeth and Robert knew. Throughout several examinations the Princess stoutly denied all prior knowledge of Wyatt's uprising (a lie), affirmed her loving allegiance to Mary (a lie), and declared her complete satisfaction with the Roman faith (a lie). Her duplicity won her release from the Tower on 19 May. She was permitted to retire to Woodstock. Later she was brought again to court. But wherever she was she remained the hope of Protestants and the fear of Catholics. It took all her ingenuity to survive the malice of her enemies and the embarrassing attentions of her friends, but survive she did. The Dudleys, too, worked hard for their restoration, and none strove more energetically than the late Duke's widow. She devoted the remaining months of her life to securing the pardon of her surviving children.

Jane was forty-five when her husband was executed. She mourned the passing of a much loved husband. A few months later she grieved over the death of a favourite son. To the heartache of a bereaved widow and mother were added the difficulties and stigma of greatly reduced circumstances. All Northumberland's property reverted to the crown on his attainder and an army of royal officials marched into his houses and estates to make an inventory of everything down to the last lamb, gown and joint-stool. All Jane had left was a manor and lands at Halesowen which had been part of her marriage portion and which John had subsequently settled on her. She was allowed to continue using her husband's house in Chelsea and the Queen gave her sufficient of the Duke's confiscated goods to enable her to furnish it in a style suitable to her rank.[27] For one who had lived in the utmost luxury and splendour for twenty years or more the shock of her sudden fall must have been considerable, though by the time Jane came to compose her will (in the winter of 1554-5) she was able to be philosophical about it: '. . . I had (rather) a thousand fold (that) my debts . . . be paid and the poor . . . be given unto than (that) any pomp (should) be showed upon my wretched carcase, that hath had at times too much in this world, full of all vanities, deceits and guiles; and whoever doth trust to this transitory world, as I did, may happen to have an overthrow, as I had.'[28] In her darkest hours Jane showed great strength of spirit. It was obvious to her that no members of the Queen's suite or Council would be prepared to defile themselves by befriending the tainted

Dudley family: all the English notables were far too busy playing down their involvement in Northumberland's regime. The same, however, was not true of the Spaniards, and Jane pinned her faith on the members of Philip's retinue who were coming to England in increasing numbers during the spring of 1554. In her endeavours she was aided by Sir Henry Sidney who, throughout the crisis years of Mary's reign, showed himself a good friend to his wife's family. Sidney had survived the political changes of July 1553 and was still at court though 'neither liking nor liked as he had been'.[29] In March 1554 he was chosen as one of a diplomatic mission sent to Spain in connection with the marriage negotiations. Jane must have discussed in great detail with her son-in-law how to make the most of this opportunity, for Henry worked hard on behalf of Jane's sons and to considerable effect.

The time was opportune for such an approach. Philip was anxious to make a good impression on the leaders of English society. Mary, who believed herself passionately in love with her new husband, could refuse him nothing. Henry seems to have made a good impression on the prince. The Spaniard stood godfather to Sidney's son, born later in the year, and gave the boy his name.* As a result, Jane Dudley found herself accepted at court in the summer and with many new friends among the lords of the King's Privy Chamber and their ladies. There was the Duchess of Alva, wife of the great general and Philip's leading adviser. There were the Duke of Medinaceli, Principal Gentleman of the Bedchamber, and the splendid Don Diego de Mendoza. These and others were remembered in Jane's will as those who 'did my sons good, beseeching them for God's sake to continue . . . good lords to my sons in their needs, and my trust is that God will requite it to them'.[30]

However, the favours Jane sought were not won easily. For months she demeaned herself by petitioning all who would receive her. Even with influential friends at court it was not easy to persuade Mary and her Council to set at liberty the hated Dudleys. A grudging mercy was shown towards the Earl of Warwick. At the end of the summer he fell ill and permission was at length granted for him to go to his sister's house at Penshurst. There he died on 21 October, three days after his release. He had not reached his twenty-fourth birthday. This further tragedy may well have proved more than the Duchess could bear. She took to her bed at Chelsea and died three months later on 22 January 1555, having devoted her little remaining energy to writing her will in her own hand. By her death Jane

*Ironically, when Sir Philip Sidney died thirty-two years later it was while fighting against Spain.

Dudley achieved what she had failed to accomplish by her constant pleading – the order for the release of Henry, Ambrose, Robert and their uncle was made out the same day.[31]

Robert now had his freedom and little else. His attainder was not lifted (and would not be for another two years) so he could not come into the modest inheritance left to him by his mother (fifty marks worth of land at Halesowen). Nor could he enjoy the property at Syderstone which had come to him in right of his wife on the death of Sir John Robsart on 8 June 1554. For some months Robert and Amy must have been in dire straits. Even meeting his late mother's debts presented problems. On 30 December 1556 Robert had to enter a bond of £20 with Thomas Borrowe, a London gentleman, to pay an outstanding apothecary's bill of £5.[32] There was little to do but to live off relatives and friends and haunt the antechambers of the mighty, hoping to be noticed. One task, of course, commanded urgent attention. The Duchess of Northumberland's funeral took place on 1 February. Despite her instructions that she be interred with the minimum of ceremonial – 'let me be wound up in a sheet and put into a coffin of wood and so laid into the ground with such funeral as pertaineth to the burial of a corpse'[33] – her obsequies were such as befitted a noble lady. Two heralds led the large company of mourners, all of whom were equipped with black coats.

There were seventy-two torch bearers and the coffin was preceded by two servants carrying branched candlesticks. On the short journey to Chelsea church the velvet-draped bier was borne on an open hearse, a sombre canopy held over the waxen effigy of the deceased. Years later her tomb was marked by a modest monument bearing a brass plate carved with images of herself and her thirteen children. In death she fared better than her husband.

Three discontented and under-employed young men may have found it rather difficult to stay out of trouble. There were many unquiet spirits thronging the taverns and meeting-places of London, people who hated papists or Spaniards or both. Some were loud-mouthed and too readily drew attention to themselves. Some conceived futile demonstration against the King and Queen. Some were involved in intrigues of an altogether more serious nature. The most far-reaching conspiracy hatched during the reign of Philip and Mary was conceived in the brain of a Dudley. Sir Henry Dudley was a younger son of 'Lord Quondam'. He had been employed on sundry diplomatic missions by Northumberland to whom he had been devoted. His brother Edward was restored to all the dignities and lands of the barony (including Dudley Castle) in 1553, soon after their pathetic father had been accorded a lavish state funeral (presumably to point the distinction between the loyal buffoon and the rebellious soldier). The new Baron Dudley soon found employment with the Marian regime and was Lieutenant of Hampnes from 1556 to 1558. Henry was apprehended after Northumberland's downfall and had a short spell in the Tower, but he satisfied his interrogators and was taken into the Queen's service. By the summer of 1554 Dudley was at the French court and, together with the enemies of England, constructing a plot which was as widespread as it was potentially dangerous. It involved French leaders, English exiles and several agents at home. In return for handing over Calais to France, Sir Henry was to have every assistance in conveying a thousand men to Portsmouth or the Isle of Wight. The scheme was very detailed and, considering the number of people involved, it was kept secret for a surprisingly long time. £50,000 was to be taken from the Exchequer to pay for the invasion. The conspirators who were to carry out this audacious robbery included an ex-Lord Mayor, the Keeper of the Star Chamber, the wife of an Exchequer teller, the customs officer at Gravesend, Henry Peckham, courtier and son of Sir Edmund Peckham, councillor and Master of the Tower Mint. The plan was betrayed. Peckham and his accomplices perished on Tower Hill in July 1555. Royal officials probed further into the Dudley conspiracy and, to their alarm, discovered more and more notable people involved. It was disturbing to realise that so many gentlemen close to the throne were seriously contemplating the murder of the Queen, the succession of Elizabeth and her marriage to the exiled Edward Courtenay, Earl of Devon.[34]

It would be unrealistic to expect to discover direct involvement in these plots by Robert and his brothers. Any contact they had with the activists would have to have been clandestine. What is clear is that from very early in the next reign Robert numbered some of the prominent anti-Marians among his friends and protégés. In 1565 Cecil made a list of men he considered to be Dudley's cronies. Among the names were James Croft, Henry Dudley, Henry Killigrew, Edward Horsey, Anthony Forster and Thomas Leighton. All these men were involved in conspiracies against Mary Tudor. In 1559-60 Robert obtained permission for some of them who were still in exile to return, and their subsequent careers were largely dependent on his. Robert may well have been cautiously in touch with these hot-heads on his release from the Tower. One contemporary report states that he and his brothers had attracted the attention of the authorities by resorting to St Paul's and there talking with known malcontents. For this indiscretion they had been warned to retire to the country and stay there.[35]

Robert did not stay out of town long. Friends at court at last succeeded in commending him to the King. In September 1555 Philip returned to the Continent to take possession of the vast territories now his by virtue of his father's recent abdication. Robert went as a junior member of his entourage. The King's greatly increased responsibilities obliged him to travel with a considerable suite composed of Spaniards, Flemings, Neapolitans, Dutchmen, Savoyards, Englishmen and Germans – men through whom he could maintain contact with the component states of his empire and with his allies. Robert Dudley, it seems, fulfilled the role of messenger, conveying reports from Philip to English ambassadors on the Continent and sometimes crossing the Channel in person. He travelled with the court through the Low Countries as, one by one, the seventeen provinces acknowledged the abdication of Charles V and the accession of his son.

It is not clear whether or not Robert's brother accompanied him. Perhaps Ambrose stayed to continue as a petitioner at court. Whatever advances were being made on the Dudleys' behalf they were quite unproductive until January 1557. On the 30th of that month letters patent were issued under the Great Seal raising the attainder on Ambrose, Robert and Henry.[36] It is no coincidence that in the same month the conflict between France and Spain, briefly halted by the Truce of Vaucelles (1556), broke out again. Philip had for a long time been demanding that an English army be sent to help him. Mary had done her best to carry out his orders, only to be thwarted by Council and Parliament. Robert now seized his opportunity: he pledged the King that if he and his brothers were restored to their lands they would raise troops to fight against the French. Other courtiers seeking favour made the same promises. Philip could not afford to ignore any of them. A few weeks later the King decided to visit England to commandeer the necessary supplies in person. It was Robert Dudley who was despatched to carry to Mary Tudor the glad tidings of her husband's approach. He reached Greenwich on 17 March.[37]

Robert immediately set about raising the cash necessary for his forthcoming military exploits. On 30 May he sold some Suffolk lands, which had formed part of Amy's marriage settlement, to Robert Armiger of Hollesley. The parcel comprised:

The manor of Bulcamp with the appurtenances and 16 messuages, 16 tofts, 16 cottages, 400 acres of land, 100 acres of meadow, 100 acres of pasture, 40 acres of wood, 400 acres of broom and heath, 40 acres of alder grove, 100 acres of marsh, and 40s. yearly rent with appurtenances in Bulcamp, Henham, Blytheburgh, Wenhaston, Blytheford, Westhall, Wangford, Roydon and Frostenden, and also some warren and fishing in Blythburgh and Bulcamp.[38]

The deal brought Robert £500. At the same time Robert raised money on the Halesowen estates. He borrowed sufficient sums to enable him to buy out his brother's interests and thus acquire the entire property himself. He had to pay Ambrose £800 and Henry £300 and guarantee his sister Catherine the charge of 50 marks a year, bequeathed to her in their mother's will. He then pledged the estate to Anthony Forster as security for loans totalling £1,928. 6s. 8d.* Forster was a gentleman of culture and learning who had lands in Worcestershire, Warwickshire and Shropshire. He had acted as steward on some of Northumberland's Midlands estates and was briefly involved in plots against Mary Tudor. He soon forsook the excitements of political life and had recently rented Cumnor Place, Berkshire, from Dr. George Owen, the royal physician. Forster was a well-respected member of Berkshire and Oxfordshire society and was married to a niece of Lord Williams of Thame. He served as sheriff and on various commissions. According to his epitaph he was a noted musician, builder and gardener. Certainly he made considerable improvements to the house and grounds at Cumnor after his purchase of the estate from William Owen (George Owen's son and heir) in 1561. Such was the friend and associate who was to be closely connected with one of the most tragic episodes of his patron's life.

It is very significant that it was Robert who took the initiative in these matters. Ambrose was the eldest brother. Sir Andrew was now the senior member of the late Duke's family. But Northumberland's brother was ill; he made his will in July when he described himself as 'sick of body',[40] and though he survived for another three years it was as an invalid living in retirement. It was Ambrose who might have been expected to shoulder the burden of responsibility. He did not lack courage or boldness. He would, in fact, prove himself a better soldier than Robert. Yet it was Robert who was recognised as the leader, the one to whom the others looked to effect a reversal of the Dudley fortunes. Robert was the strongest character – talented and extrovert. He was soon styling himself 'Lord Dudley of Halesowen'.[41] By persistence, flattery and graciousness Robert had brought his family out of the storm and back into the sunshine of royal favour. Following up the contacts made by his brother-in-law

*This was the sum repaid to Forster in 1558 and may have included interest.[39]

he had ingratiated himself with several of the prominent members
of Philip II's suite and, with the King himself. The pleasantries, the
gifts, the favours, the bribing of servants that went into achieving
this we can only guess at, but it is certain that he was heavily in debt.
In the years 1555 to 1557 Robert Dudley cast a great deal of bread
upon the waters. He made many friends among the Spaniards and
was still corresponding with them years later. Among the pictures
which would one day decorate Kenilworth Castle were portraits of
King Philip, the Duke of Alva, the Duke of Feria, Charles V and the
Duchess of Parma.[42] It was Robert, with the gifts of the perfect
courtier, who led the way back to fame and fortune. As in the past,
the rest of the family fell in behind its natural leader.

Another reason for Robert to assume control of the family
fortunes was his friendship with Elizabeth. Again, we are starved of
substantial evidence of their continued relationship during the dark
days of Mary's reign. On 16 June 1561 the scholar and diplomat,
Hubert Languet, wrote to Augustus, Duke of Saxony:

> The English leaders had made it plain to her [Queen Elizabeth]
> that her too great familiarity with my Lord Robert Dudley
> displeased them and that they would by no means allow him to
> wed her . . . The Queen replied . . . that she had never thought of
> contracting a marriage with my Lord Robert; but she was more
> attached to him than to any of the others because when she was
> deserted by everybody in the reign of her sister not only did he
> never lessen in any degree his kindness and humble attention to
> her, but he even sold his possessions that he might assist her with
> money, and therefore she thought it just that she should make
> some return for his good faith and constancy.[43]

A seventeenth-century author, Gregorio Leti, adds flesh to the bare
bones of this story of Robert's financial help. He writes of a gift of
£200 sent by the hand of a lady, together with an exaggerated
assurance of devotion from one who 'would willingly lose his life it
that would be of any service to her or procure her liberty'.[44]
Unfortunately Leti was a notorious romancer, and anything from
his pen must be read with the greatest of caution. Yet the story bears
some relation to known facts. Not until Robert's return from the
Low Countries in the summer of 1557 would he have been in a position to render the Princess any assistance. At that time he was
certainly selling large parcels of land with the support of his brothers. Genuine affection and an eye to the main chance might both
have prompted Robert to give the Princess tangible proof of his

loyalty. Other gentlemen were certainly sending secret messages of support to Elizabeth. One, for example, offered to come to her aid with troops if ever she needed him.[45] Support for the Princess grew stronger from the end of 1556 when the Queen's health began to fail. Elizabeth was the hope of all men disillusioned with Catholic Mary. Such was the measure of sympathy for her that she had to be very careful whom she met and spoke to as she progressed around her manors close to the capital.

Although we have no direct evidence of contact between Robert and Elizabeth in this difficult period, we do know that Dudley had friends and contacts in the Princess's household. William Cecil was still her surveyor and a man in whose skill and discretion she reposed considerable trust. And Cecil was someone Robert counted among his friends at this time; they had been closely acquainted ever since Northumberland took the ambitious young lawyer under his wing. John Dee, Robert's teacher and later protégé was another contact, as was Giambattista Castiglione, Elizabeth's Italian tutor.[46] Both of these men were apprehended by Mary's officials on suspicion of plotting an Elizabethan coup. The necessary secrecy which guarded all Elizabeth's dealings at this time has prevented historians from unravelling the relationships which undoubtedly existed between the Princess and her many friends at home and abroad. That Robert held an important place among Elizabeth's supporters can scarcely be doubted. His situation was almost unique: he had friends in the Princess's household, among the leading members of society who supported her, among the adventurous partisans, most of whom were in exile, and also in King Philip's entourage.

It was the latter who were the most important. Elizabeth's survival during her half-sister's reign owed more to Spanish influence than to her English supporters. As long as Mary had not named her as her successor, had not despaired of having a child, and was under pressure to dispose of her half-sister, Elizabeth was in real danger. Her survival was largely due to Philip. The King was not attached to his wife but he was very much attached to the Anglo-Spanish alliance. If anything happened to Mary, he wanted to be sure of remaining on good terms with the next ruler. He urged the Queen to show kindness to Elizabeth. As a member of Philip's suite Robert was able to speak to influential people on the Princess's behalf and to convey messages to the royal captive about the prevailing Hapsburg attitude towards her.

Robert commended himself to Philip as a potential military commander, and when the King returned to the Netherlands in July 1556 with a force of 6,000 Englishmen led by the Earl of

Pembroke, he, Ambrose and Henry went with him. The brothers had managed to raise small contingents to take part in the expedition. Robert was designated Master of the Ordnance. Little time was lost in preparation; at the beginning of August Philip's main army was despatched across the French frontier led by the Duke of Savoy. It struck deep into enemy territory and began the investment of St Quentin, an important wool-producing centre on the Somme, not eighty miles from Paris. On 10 August the Constable of France, de Montmorency, brought a relief column up from the south. It was annihilated. The Spaniards took many prisoners, including the French commander. The town fell almost immediately. If the Earl of Bedford is to be believed, the action begat horrors far worse than those Robert had witnessed during the Norfolk campaign:

> . . . for my part, I have not seen the like in all my life. The *sault* was soon won and with the loss of no great number, but the slaughter was in the town about the spoil. The Swartzrotters, being masters of the King's whole army, used such force as well to the Spaniards, Italians and all other nations as unto us, that there was none could enjoy nothing but themselves. They have now showed such cruelty, as the like hath not been seen for greediness. The town by them was set afire and a great piece of it burned.[47]

Philip's mercenaries may have grabbed the lion's share of the loot but some was left for the other officers and Robert seems to have more than covered his expenses on the campaign. But once again the Dudleys paid a high price for success. Young Henry, not yet twenty years old, was killed beneath the walls. According to Holinshed, he paused to adjust his hose and was killed by a cannon shot.[48]

Philip did not press home his advantage. He disbanded most of his army and sent the rest into winter quarters. St Quentin was reoccupied by the French, and during the next few months the army of Henry II was able to capture Calais and enter Luxemburg. Long before then the Duke of Northumberland's two surviving sons were back in England. It may have seemed to them that there was a curse on their house. Their father had married but once and his wife had borne him thirteen children – eight sons and five daughters. There seemed every prospect of the line flourishing for generations. Now there were only four Dudleys left and neither Ambrose nor Robert yet had any children.

The England to which the triumphant soldiers returned was a realm in the grip of intense religious persecution. Between 1555 and 1558 three hundred Protestant men and women passed through the flames of martyrdom. Thousands more were examined by Mary's bishops and suffered great distress of spirit when they were forced to recant publicly. About eight hundred people who could afford to do so escaped the dilemma by going into voluntary exile on the Continent. Persecution, of course, strengthened and deepened the English Reformation rather than eradicating it. Even those who were not disciples of the new faith admired the fortitude of those prepared to die for their convictions and were revolted by an oppressive regime which hounded their fellow countrymen to death. Mary Tudor and her government were fast losing all credibility except with a minority of Catholic fanatics. The involvement in foreign war, the loss of Calais, the frequent clashes between Spaniards and Englishmen, the failure to deal with the realm's economic problems – all these were bitterly resented.

They were resented by Robert. His Protestant upbringing had never been rooted out, despite his outward conformity. The scanty records suggest that St Quentin was a turning point in his life. Before the battle all his energies had been directed towards restoring the family fortunes in the only way open to him – service to King and Queen. His reward had been the sight of his young brother's shattered, bloody corpse. Once back in England Robert made no attempt to capitalise on his faithful service. For the only time in his life the court did not draw him. He did not seek some household post for which his experience and his proven loyalty would have equipped him. On the contrary, he now retired to his Norfolk estates to live the life of a country gentleman – at least as long as Mary Tudor remained Queen.

He settled his debt with Anthony Forster straight away, presumably out of his share of the St Quentin loot. Then he placed the Halesowen property in the hands of two agents, Thomas Blount and George Tuckey, to be sold. In October 1557 a deal was concluded with John Littleton, a distant kinsman whose lands at Frankley bordered the Halesowen estate. Negotiations did not go smoothly: for months there was haggling over various parcels of land, and Robert did not receive full payment until Ash Wednesday 1561.[49] The sale of these lands left him with a total profit of over £3,000. In addition, he had the income from his Norfolk estates and whatever booty was left over from the St Quentin raid. It was sufficient for him to settle his debts and establish himself and Amy in reasonable style in East Anglia.

They went to Syderstone. It was the first time that they had been able to contemplate living together in their own home. But the house at Syderstone, as Robert soon realised, had considerable disadvantages. He set his agent, John Flowerdew, to search for a more suitable residence. As he explained, 'I must, if to dwell in that country, take some house other than mine own, for it wanteth all such chief commodities as a house requireth, which is pasture, wood, water, etc.'[50] Mr Flowerdew learned that the hall at Flitcham, some eight miles to the south-west of Syderstone was vacant. He visited it, together with Amy's brother-in-law, James Bigot, and reported to his master that it seemed ideal. It stood on the Babingley river, had plenty of pasture around it and a protective screen of woodland. Robert wrote back in the summer of 1558 approving what his agent had so far done and asking him to discover what stock the estate would carry and whether the furniture in the house was worth buying. If the answers to these questions were satisfactory, Dudley would come himself to view the property.[51] But he never did, or if he did the bargain was not struck. By the summer of 1558 the political situation was once more in the balance: Queen Mary was dying. Her half-sister was her only possible successor, and with Elizabeth on the throne Robert's fortunes would be distinctly brighter.

On 8 November the Queen accepted the inevitable and nominated the Princess as her successor. But it was not until the early hours of 17 November that Mary Tudor breathed her last. The lords of the Council immediately set off into Hertfordshire. In the park at Hatfield they found Elizabeth walking beneath the bare trees. They knelt to offer their allegiance. The new Queen's first reaction was to render thanks to God. Afterwards she sat in conference with Cecil and some of the others to discuss immediate arrangements.

There were certain people who had to be informed urgently of Elizabeth's accession. A secretary made the first memorandum of the reign:* 'To send messengers to the Emperor, Sir William Pickering, Sir . . . Wooton; to the King of Spain, Sir Peter Carew, Lord Robert Dudley; to the King of Denmark, Sir Thomas Ch . . .'[52]

*The document was damaged by fire.

CHAPTER FIVE

MASTER OF THE HORSE

On the first day of Elizabeth's reign Robert Dudley was appointed Master of the Horse, a household post of importance and one which entailed close and frequent contact with the Queen. All the potential for their future intimacy lay in that initial appointment, and many historians have been at a loss to understand why Elizabeth should have become deliberately involved with such a man as Lord Robert. It has generally been assumed that she was infatuated with his good looks and accomplished courtly manners. In fact, there was more to it than that. The young Queen was already a shrewd judge of men, and bitter experience had taught her to be wary about whom she admitted to her confidence. She certainly did not judge by externals alone.

It is true that, at twenty-five, Dudley was a magnificent figure of a man. Tall, by the standard of the age (a little under six feet), and slender, he wore fashionable clothes with a casual grace, his cap invariably tilted at a jaunty angle. When astride a horse his athleticism and pride were seen to their full advantage, for few Englishmen rode better than he. The stylised early portraits of him which have survived reveal a thin face accentuated by a wispy beard. The nose is long; the set of the mouth haughty. The eyes beneath their arching brows are watchful but there is about them a suggestion of sardonic humour. It was the eyes that captivated Elizabeth and she soon gave him the playful nickname 'Two-eyes'. Often he would write to her, signing himself simply ō ō. Others about the court, less enamoured of his dark good looks, called Dudley 'the Gypsy'. He was full of life and had an outrageous sense of fun. The many anecdotes and also the vivid language of his letters testify to this. This was one of the qualities that must have attracted Elizabeth. Surrounded as she was by solemn councillors pressing her for decisions on matters of state, she needed someone constantly at hand to divert her and provide light relief. Lord Robert was a master both of organised and spontaneous entertainment. Over the years he would be responsible for arranging hundreds of tourneys, banquets, masques and plays. He could also delight Elizabeth with a piece of unrehearsed coquetry, such as solemnly suggesting to a Spanish bishop that he marry the Queen and her favourite on the royal barge in the middle of the Thames.

A characteristic which commended Robert to Elizabeth more

emphatically, however, was his utter devotion. In selecting her councillors and household officials the Queen had many people to choose
from – representatives of the ancient nobility, sage councillors who
had served under one Tudor monarch or more, experienced court
officials, young hotheads who had engaged in rebellion against Mary
for her sake. Elizabeth was surrounded by thousands of potential
servants but few friends. She could dip into a treasure chest of
wisdom, talent and experience, but she could find there few real
companions, men and women she could trust with her fears, doubts
and secret thoughts. But there were some people she knew well, with
whom she had grown up, people who had taken what opportunities
they could during the last five years to assure her of their continued
devotion. Lord Robert was among them. Furthermore, he had not
been one of the hotheads whose well-meaning activities had only
heightened the Princess's danger. Elizabeth appreciated that: she had
no time for rebels or for men whose thoughtless zeal bordered on
fanaticism. Robert Dudley was a man she knew she could trust – and
she was right. As well as the personal affection he felt for Elizabeth,
Robert had inherited from his father and grandfather that utter
respect for the crown which Elizabethans referred to as 'dread'. Never
over the next thirty years did his devotion falter. Every letter Robert
wrote to his sovereign bore extravagant protestations of loyalty:

> It is easier for me to confess how much I am tied to you by innu-
> merable benefits than to attain to my desire to be worthy of so
> great favour. I may not begin, lest I should not make an end, to
> tell of that I have received, but am ashamed that I have deserved
> so little; only I offer you a most faithful and loyal heart. God grant
> me no longer breath than it be most unspotted to you.[1]

Such sentiments may be partly explained away by convention – but
only partly. In Dudley's case they are amply borne out by his
actions. Other ministers and courtiers used their favoured position
to accumulate landed wealth for themselves and their posterity.
Robert's person and property were always at the disposal of his
Queen. He spent lavishly on costly gifts for her, and the performance of his official duties frequently left him out of pocket.

The man who was to hold the centre of the social and political
stage for three decades was proud and more than a little vain. He
was a showman capable of exploiting to the full his not inconsiderable talents. Rivals frequently complained of his arrogance and even
close members of his family feared that *hubris* might prove his undo-
ing. The reign was no more than a few months old when Robert's
sister, Catherine, Countess of Huntingdon, wrote:

My good brother, after my heartiest congratulations and thanks for your gentle letter, I assure you I was as sorry that I could not see you at my departing as you were but I trust that we shall both meet full merrily when our quartans* be gone, whereof I would be glad to hear you were delivered though mine remain still in me, good brother. I hear God hath increased you with honour since my departure. I pray let me desire you to be thankful unto him that showeth himself so gratious unto you. I am bold to write this because I know honour doth rather blind the eye than clear it . . .[2]

He had a natural panache but he was very careful to cultivate it by dressing well and in the height of fashion. Certainly he did not stint when ordering material from European markets:

Touching the silks I wrote you about, I wish you to take up and stay for me 4,000 crowns worth of crimson and black velvet and satins and silks of other colours. And if there be any good cloth of tissue or of gold or such other pretty stuff, stay for me to the value of £300 or £400, whatever the charge shall be . . .

P.S. Make stay of as much stuff as I have written for and the money shall be sent you immediately . . . Let it be of the best sort of every kind I have written for . . .[3]

No wonder is it that he could comment ruefully in his will, 'I . . . have lived always above any living I had'. When, in later life, he had inventories made of all his possessions they ran to thousands of items, many of them costly and of exquisite workmanship.

The portraitures of the Queen's majesty and my lord, cut in alabaster.

A ring of gold enamelled black with a fair table diamond in it, cut lozenge wise with these letters in it 'E.R.'

A salt, ship fashion, of the mother-of-pearl, garnished with silver and divers works of warlike ensigns and ornaments, with sixteen pieces or ordnance, whereof two on wheels, two anchors on the fore part, and on the stern the image of Dame Fortune, standing on a globe, with a flag in her hand.

A fair, rich, new, standing bedstead of walnut tree, all painted over with crimson and silvered with roses, four bears and ragged staves, all silvered, standing upon the corners, the tester, ceil, double valance and bases of crimson velvet, richly embroidered with cinqfoils of cloth of silver, with my lord's arms very richly embroidered in the midst of the ceil and tester, supported with the white lion and the bear, silver, lined through with red buckram.

*Quartan fever – one which was marked by major paroxysms every third or fourth day.

A chess board of ebony, with chequers of crystal and other stones layed with silver, garnished with bears and ragged staves and cinqfoils of silver, the thirty-two men likewise of crystal and other stones set, the one sort in silver white, the other gilt, in a case of leather, gilded and lined with green cotton.[4]

His wardrobe was immense, running to several hundred items listed under a profusion of headings: 'Night gowns, short gowns, cape cloaks, short cloaks, long cloaks, riding cloaks, riding slops, cassocks, hose paned and slops, doublets jerkins, buttons, brooches, tags and points of gold, caps and hats, boothose and stockings, rapiers and daggers with their girdles and hangers, fawchions, woodknives, buskins, shoes, pumps, pantophels, slippers and boots'.[5]

One type of pride that Lord Robert certainly possessed was family pride. He remained for many years in his father's shadow and longed to emulate Northumberland's political and military exploits. Like Northumberland, Robert also wanted to make himself acknowledged head of the Dudley family. He had an elder brother, but Ambrose acquiesced in allowing the mantle of Northumberland to fall upon the late Duke's younger surviving son. Sir Andrew, the last senior member of the family, died in 1559 and Robert was a major beneficiary under his will. Almost immediately he attempted to give tangible expression to his headship of the family. He approached Baron Edward Dudley with an offer to buy Dudley Castle. He had a list made of all the baronial lands, together with the outstanding mortgages and calls upon them.[6] Cousin Edward, although affirming that 'if God does not send us issue there is no one I would rather see inherit than your Lordship', was not prepared to sell,[7] and by the end of 1560 Robert had been obliged to give up his plans to acquire the ancestral home. But he retained his interest in the areas of traditional Dudley influence. His estates were largely concentrated in the Midlands and when he was offered an earldom he chose the title that had been considered for his father – Earl of Leicester (Ambrose had already been made Earl of Warwick).

Other aspects of Dudley's character will emerge subsequently. He was a man of hearty appetites – his liking for good food was a standing joke in the Queen's circle of intimates. He enjoyed gambling and seldom drew a bow or took up a tennis racket without having a wager on the outcome. He was a warm friend. He was generous and forgiving to enemies. He was heedless of the many rumours and insults which circulated about him. The only person whose opinion he valued was the Queen's and he was extremely jealous of his standing with her. When he felt that he was being supplanted by a rival or that enemies were misrepresenting him to Elizabeth he was capable of sudden rage or prolonged sulking. He adhered firmly to the Protestantism in which he had been reared (which is not to say that he always lived up to its moral precepts). He was a patron of scholars, clergy, actors and artists. He encouraged scientific and philosophical enquiry and through this sought to make up for his own lack of intellectual attainment. His was not a brilliant or incisive mind but it was one that was capable of application. He lacked appreciation of political subtleties and tended to see issues in black and white. In this, and in many other ways, he was a complete contrast to Elizabeth. It was partly the attraction of opposites that brought the two together.

But we must be careful not to antedate the intimacy which sprang up between Robert and Elizabeth. When Dudley rode to Hatfield (traditionally on a milk-white steed) on that November day in 1558 it was to receive a household appointment and not to be accepted as a lover. The new Queen was too conscious of the enormous weight of her responsibilities to give thought to affairs of the heart. The treasury was empty. The nation was facing the threat of diplomatic isolation. Calais was lost to France and French influence was paramount north of the border. Her brother and sister had failed catastrophically as rulers of England. None of her subjects relished the accession of another woman to the throne. Everyone expected her soon to marry, and thus enter for the good of the country on a different form of bondage to the one she had just escaped. These and other problems had to be faced with the aid of wise and loyal councillors and, at the same time, Elizabeth had to achieve and maintain the independence befitting a sovereign. Such considerations were uppermost in her mind as she selected those who were to be the members of her Council and her household. The people the Queen chose were not, for the most part, newcomers but those who either had themselves served Henry VIII or Edward, or belonged to traditional court families. Public opinion and her own inclination urged her to surround herself with safe, anti-Catholic men and women, to create a court which was strongly reminiscent of the royal household of twelve years and more earlier.

It was under these circumstances that the Dudley family achieved the unique distinction in the Tudor age of recovering twice from total disgrace. Just as John overcame the disaster of 1510 and emerged with a prestige and power even greater than his father's, so Robert, in 1558, began to revive a political influence which had seemed extinct five years earlier. In addition to Robert's appointment as Master of the Horse, Ambrose became chief pantler at the coronation and received the manor of Kibworth Beauchamp which went with the office. He was also granted the important post of Master of the Ordnance,* vacated by the Catholic Richard Southwell.[8] Mary Sidney was welcomed at court and became one of the Queen's principal and best loved ladies-in-waiting. Robert's importance was obvious to interested observers from the start. Writing to his master on 14 December, the Spanish ambassador advised him to revise the list of English courtiers to whom he paid retainers: 'I think a different course must be adopted with the pensioners. It will be best to pay them to the end of the year and afterwards to pay those who may be needful, such as Cecil, who, I think, should receive 1,000 crowns, the Comptroller, Lord Robert and the Earl of Bedford, who should reach receive a similar amount as they are necessary now'.[9]

There is, however, no indication that Robert's appointment was greeted with surprise or disapproval. No one who knew Dudley could doubt that he was in every way the obvious choice for the post he now occupied. His eldest brother had held it, and, in that Robert had followed John as Master of the Buckhounds, it may well be that the Mastership of the Horse had also been destined for Robert in due course had Edward VI lived. He was a good judge of horse flesh, an expert in the hunting field and the tilt-yard and an experienced courtier well acquainted with ceremonial occasions and royal progresses. The position was no sinecure: the Master of the Horse headed one of the busiest departments of the household. He was responsible for the transport of the Queen and the court on all occasions, ceremonial and otherwise; for the supervision of the royal studs, together with the purchase, training and equipping of horses for all purposes; for the provision of mounts for household officials and royal messengers; for the organisation of the Queen's annual progresses; and for the planning of ceremonial journeys. He had to provide war-horses, 'great horses' for the joust and for pulling the unsprung carriages just coming into fashion, coursers for the Queen's gentlemen, palfreys and amblers for the maids of honour, cobs and rouncies for lesser attendants, mules and pack-horses for baggage, and a supply of hacks and hunters for the Queen's sport. The stable employed a large staff of aveners†, grooms, clerks, farriers, purveyors and baggage-men. In 1554 the wages of all these employees was £1,132. 10s. $2^1/2d.$, in addition to which some of them received bouge‡ of court and other perquisites.

---

*This was, in effect, the same post Ambrose's father had earlier held and which was then called 'Master of the Tower Armouries'.
†Officers in charge of obtaining provender for horses.
‡Board and lodging at court.

The sum had almost certainly increased by 1558. Fodder and other running costs of this large household department accounted for at least another £1,000 per annum. A great deal of the routine work was done by subordinates but Robert maintained close personal control and much of his time was spent considering reports on horses at stud; instructing foreign agents to buy new bloodstock; planning the stages of the royal progresses; organising tourneys and accompanying the Queen in the hunting field. It was work he enjoyed. He had a flair for it and he continued as Master of the Horse until the last year of his life.

Robert's salary was 100 marks at the beginning of the reign, and as Master he enjoyed his own suite of rooms in the household where he dined with senior stable officials and was attended to by his own servants. He was usually allowed four horses for his own use, and a surviving document headed 'The Master of the Horse's allowance in the great warrant for two years' itemises minutely the livery (in royal green and white) and equipment he was permitted:

First 4 bits with slots, 4 pair of silk laces to the same bits, 4 head-stalls and reins of leather, 4 double collars double paired, 8 pair of pasterns, 8 trammels, 4 leading reins, 12 [cloth] circingles, 8 double circingles of white twine, 4 horse harnesses of white and green cloth lined with canvas borders with white and green cloth . . . 4 rugs with buckles, 4 travel saddles of buff leather, 4 double harnesses of black leather with caps varnished black, 8 pair of white girths of double fustian, 8 pair of stirrups, the new varnish-ing of 8 pair of stirrups, 8 pair of double stirrup leathers, 8 ells of canvas for bags and dusting cloths.[10]

Another warrant tells us that Dudley was allowed £400 a year for new horses and harness.[11] In addition, the Master was allowed a cart to carry all his personal and stable equipment whenever the court was on progress. On all such occasions the Master himself rode immediately behind the sovereign.[12]

His work began immediately. The first few days at Hatfield were spent largely in Council meetings, but Elizabeth found time to ride with her Master of the Horse in the park. Robert continually urged her to take plenty of exercise as an antidote to work and it was his advice she followed to the end of her days. Then the Queen began the journey to her capital. It was not just a journey, it was a triumph. From the villages of Hertfordshire and Middlesex and further afield, men, women, and children rushed for a glimpse of the new Queen and her glittering court. Through cheering crowds Elizabeth made her way to Lord North's home, the Charterhouse, not far from the City wall and Aldersgate. On 28 November the cavalcade set out again. Deliberately avoiding the main thorough-fares (they would welcome the Queen during the coronation procession) the entourage rode over freshly-gravelled streets close by the wall and came, via Fenchurch and Gracechurch Streets, to the Tower.

The next few weeks were hectic for the Queen and all her officials. Cecil and the Council had to establish the machinery of a new government within the land and the credit of that government abroad. Household officers had to master the workings of their departments. But, in addition, everyone was involved in the plan-ning and celebration of Elizabeth's first Christmas, which was to be followed (nine days after Twelfth Night) by the coronation. The arrangements for the ceremonial and festive events were, in part, Dudley's responsibility and must have taken up almost all his time throughout December and the first half of January. After five days in the Tower the court travelled by water to Somerset House, whence, after a brief stay, they continued to Whitehall. There the Queen gave careful consideration to the most propitious date for her crowning. Robert was involved in these discussions and it was he who brought to court the man who eventually decided the matter. At the age of thirty-one John Dee was already a much travelled scholar, widely known and respected among the international community as England's foremost exponent of Euclidian geometry and its terrestrial and celestial application. Robert now commis-sioned Dee to cast the Queen's horoscope. Dee made his observations and calculations and concluded that 15 January was the appropriate day for the coronation.

Robert had overall charge of arrangements for the coronation procession and the London pageant series. Although the Lord Mayor and aldermen were principally responsible for the City's ceremonial welcome everything they planned had to be vetted by court officials. Robert, a born impresario, attended personally to all this as well as to the equipping of the royal cavalcade, arranging it in the correct order, ensuring sufficient troops to keep the route clear, and making provision for the smooth transit of the thousands of dignitaries, guards and servants from the Tower to Westminster. At the same time he was engaged as planner and performer in the Christmas court revels. There can be no doubt that he made every effort to excel in his performance of these duties. Having received his great opportunity he must have been determined to grasp it by impressing Elizabeth both with his efficiency and his personal bear-ing towards her.

The Christmas and coronation festivities had a great deal in common. They were marked by exuberant enthusiasm and relief, and they were vigorously anti-Catholic in tone. We know very little about the masques, banquets and entertainments at court but we do have a disapproving summary of them by the Mantuan agent – a Catholic:

> . . . your Lordship will have heard of the farce performed in the presence of her majesty on the day of the Epiphany, and I not having sufficient intellect to interpret it, nor yet the mummery performed after supper on the same day, of crows in the habits of cardinals, of asses habited as bishops, and of wolves representing abbots, I will consign it to silence . . . Nor will I record the levities and unusual licentiousness practised at the court in dances and banquets . . .[13]

Elizabeth brought a new splendour and gaiety to court. Most visitors commented on the new Queen's love of beautiful clothes, trinkets, dancing, hunting, riding, masques and mimes. When diversions were arranged for her she abandoned herself to their enjoyment. Her capacity for pleasure was enormous. She could outdance many of her courtiers, enjoy cards or music till far into the night, and her love of riding fiery horses alarmed even Robert; when he wrote to order some 'good gallopers' from Ireland he commented that whenever the Queen had new mounts 'she spareth not to try as fast as they can go. And I fear them much, but she will prove them.'[14] It was in arranging this aspect of her life with skill and panache that Robert Dudley was invaluable to Elizabeth.

On 12 January the court returned to the Tower. On the following day Elizabeth created several Knights of the Bath and complied with other traditional pre-coronation formalities. Saturday, 14 January, was London's day. Under Robert's direction the court rode forth – ladies, nobles, gentlemen, servants and horses, all decked out in costly new finery. Citizens and countrymen from far and near came to gaze upon their betters and to see the 'pageants, fine paintings, and the rich cloths of arras, silver and gold'[15] which decked the streets. At the centre of the procession rode the Queen in a horse-litter decorated with cloth of gold and white satin. Elizabeth herself wore cloth of gold and silver with ermine trimmings. In close attendance upon her as she acknowledged the 'prayers, wishes, welcomings, cries, tender words and all other signs' of her 'most obedient subjects'[16] were the Dudley brothers. Ambrose came on foot leading one of the litter horses. Robert rode immediately behind leading the fully caparisoned palfrey of honour. The Queen paid close attention to the pageants and orations presented to her at various stages along the way. Here, from elaborately decorated platforms, the citizens acquainted the monarch with their aspirations and gave her advice under cover of flattering addresses. They presented a Bible, urging her to uphold Protestant truth and tread down superstitious error. They desired her to choose wise councillors, banish rebellion, encourage and reward virtue, and maintain peace. She should, they suggested, consider herself another Deborah who was sent by God and governed Israel with courage and piety for forty years.[17] The next day Elizabeth came to the Abbey for her crowning. The banquet that followed marked the end of the long series of celebrations. The serious work of the reign now began in earnest.

For Robert this basically meant his duties as Master of the Horse. The most important task, and the one which was to occupy him throughout his tenure of office, was the improvement of the native strain of horses. This meant reforming the management of the royal studs[18] and importing new bloodstock. Henry VIII had begun the systematic improvement of English horsebreeding but subsequently 'the officers, waxing weary, procured a mixed breed of bastard races, whereby his good purpose came to little effect'.[19] Elizabeth and Robert set about redeeming the situation. The Queen enforced existing statutes requiring landowners to keep a specific number of mounts commensurate with their station. Robert started a stud exclusively for rearing Barbary horses at Greenwich. He brought in Italian experts to advise on the improvement of the royal establishment and he was always despatching agents to the Continent to buy mares and stallions.

The latter, in itself, was no easy task. As with every other aspect of her household and government administration, Elizabeth expected the best results to be achieved with shoestring budgets. Moreover, the buying of horses abroad sometimes involved diplomatic entanglements, and passport arrangements were not mere formalities. The point is illustrated clearly by Bernardine de Granada's mission to the Low Countries in the summer and autumn of 1559. Bernardine was one of Robert's stable officers and he was sent over in July to acquire horses, probably the Hungarian greys introduced there by the Hapsburgs, which made such magnificent mounts for ceremonial purposes. The trip began well: Bernardine could report by 23 August that he had delivered a gift of English hounds to the Duchess of Lorraine and had already bought two horses in the Netherlands.[20] The Spaniard made good progress with the colonial grandees of the Netherlands, and by the beginning of October he had obtained another four horses. He stabled them at Mechlin (conveniently near the port of Antwerp), bought fodder for them and sent to his master for transport instructions. Robert wrote on 15 October, but his letter went astray and did not reach Bernardine until 9 November by which time the agent had run out of money and into trouble. Apparently he had no documentation to show the authorities and they declined to believe that the horses were for the Queen. Bernardine, therefore, could not obtain passports. He appealed to the ambassador, Thomas Challoner, who tried his persuasive powers with the customs officials – to little avail.[21] As soon as Dudley's letter arrived, Bernardine hurried to Brussels to see the top officials. At the same time Elizabeth, petulantly expressing to Challoner her surprise that so much difficulty was made over the transport of a few horses, asked the Spanish ambassador in London to intervene on her behalf.[22] Despite this top-level activity, Bernardine had to do some hard talking. Very strict regulations governed the export of quality horses (they were, after all, vital in warfare), and relations between England and Spain were not at their most cordial. A week of argument, cajolery and, perhaps, bribery resulted in a compromise: Bernardine could have passports for four horses, not six.

By this time Challoner had the animals on his hands, since Bernardine's funds had run out, and he did not want to take the responsibility of selling off two of the Queen's steeds and thereby acquiescing in the diplomatic snub Elizabeth had received. He solved the problem by smuggling the horses out of Spanish territory. He persuaded the Count de Helvestein, who already had a passport, to substitute the two remaining horses for two of his own and he told the Count that they were his (Challoner's) own. On 23 November he reported to Dudley, with some relief, that the Queen's cargo was ready for shipment. Her majesty, he said, would have to be content with these six horses for the time being. The fault was not with Bernardine, for, though the agent had not achieved all that Dudley had required of him, it had not been for want of trying.[23] To the Queen Challoner wrote more circumspectly the next day but did not fail to let her know the pains he had been to on her behalf. Could she ensure, he pleaded, that no such business was set in hand again without licences being obtained beforehand. He concluded with the reminder that 'the charges sustained about the keeping of these horses are not small'.[24]

Alas for Challoner, his troubles were not over. On 20 December another string of horses was led up to the door of his Antwerp lodgings. They were 'a Spanish horse, another good stepper, an ambling

Turkish horse' and a poor creature 'blind in one eye from a pistol shot'. They came as a result of an agreement made two months before between Bernardine de Granada and one of the German Lutheran princes. They had been delayed because one animal had gone lame through a nail in the hock and they now arrived at a time when Anglo-Spanish relations were becoming even more sensitive. Poor Challoner had no alternative but to stable the horses at an inn and write for instructions. Should he accept delivery or send them back? Then, on 7 January, he learned that the Regent of the Netherlands had issued an order prohibiting entirely the export of 'man, armour or victuals' to England and France. This time it took a personal letter from Elizabeth to the Regent to obtain the necessary passport.[25]

As well as importing fresh breeding stock whenever he could Robert was always on the look-out for skilled riding masters and horse breeders. In 1572 he authorised Walsingham (then in Paris) to secure the services of a top French trainer-breeder at a salary of £30 plus food, drink and stabling. The daunting reply came back that £50 plus perquisites was the going rate.[26] He was, however, more successful in securing the services of two Neapolitan experts (the Neapolitans were widely recognised as the finest horsemen of Europe). Claudio Corte was the author of a book on equitation, entitled *Il Cavallerizzo**, which he dedicated to Dudley. He had obviously been in England some years for in 1565 Thomas Blundeville had commended Dudley's employment of Corte in his *Four Chiefest Offices Belonging to Horsemanship*. But even more accomplished was Prospero d'Osma, an Italian master, who for many years ran a highly successful *école de manège* at Mile End. In 1575 Dudley commissioned him to make a survey of the royal studs and to suggest improvements in the breeding and training of the Queen's horses. The resulting report, delivered the following year, detailed all the mares and stallions currently at stud and contained some excellent advice on improvement of pasture, covering mares, rearing foals, breaking colts and counteracting diseases.[27] Dudley seems to have valued Osma's work and relied on it considerably in the future management of studs, which improved steadily throughout the reign. The expertise gained by horse owners in these years was an important foundation upon which the next generation would begin the breeding techniques which produced the English thoroughbred.

Long-term plans had to take second place to the pressing day-to-day work of the Master of the Horse. There were, for example, the

*1572, translated into English by Thomas Bedingfield, 1584.

itineraries of the royal progresses to be organised; no small task
when there were hundreds of men and women of all ranks, plus
their horses, to be fed, housed and transported from point to point.
Times and distances had to be calculated and all details of accommodation fixed in advance. A note relating to court movements in
August and September 1572 gives some indication of what was
involved:

	Days	*Miles*
Saturday 23 August from Kenilworth to Sir Thomas Lucy's to dine and to Compton to supper and [rest].	3	14
Tuesday the 26th from thence to Mr Laysford to dine and to Woodstock to supper and rest.	11	12
Saturday 6 September from thence to Sir Christopher Brown's house and [rest].	3	
Tuesday the 9th from thence to Wallingford and rest.	2	
Thursday the 11th from thence to Yattenden to dine and to Newbury to supper and rest.	4	
Monday the 15th from thence to Ingleford or Aldermaston and rest.	2	
Wednesday the 17th from thence to Reading and rest.	7	
Wednesday the 24th from thence to Windsor and there during the Queen's majesty's pleasure.[28]	13	

Robert obviously delegated details to underlings but he was never
the sort of departmental head who left his subordinates unsuper-
vised or scorned to do a job himself if occasion demanded. This was
particularly true when he felt that the personal touch was called for
(perhaps it was an art he learned from his royal mistress). It was, for
example, this sensitivity to the feelings of others that brought him in
person on a wet night in the atrocious summer of 1582 to the gates
of Rycote Park, Oxfordshire. It had been the Queen's intention to
call there on her progress and spend time with her old friend
Henry Norreys and his wife Marjory (known affectionately by
Elizabeth as her 'old crow'). At the last moment the plans had been
changed and, rather than send a messenger, Robert decided to

break the news himself. He could not have expected a warm reception from the loyal couple who had spent weeks preparing for the royal visit. His expectations were fully realised, as he reported to Hatton:

> I found a very hard journey yesterday, after I departed from you. It was ten of the clock at night ere I came here and a more foul and ragged way I never travelled in my life. The best was, at my arrival I met with a piece of cold entertainment at the lady's hands of the house here . . . for she was well informed ere I came that I and you were the chief hinderers of her majesty's coming hither, which they took more unkindly than there was cause indeed. But I was fain to stand to it that I was one of the dissuaders, and would not for anything, for the little proof I had of this day's journey, that her majesty had been in it . . . Well, I did, I trust satisfy my lady, albeit she saith she cannot be quiet till you have part of her little stomach [i.e. till you have also felt the sharp edge of her tongue] too. Trust me, if it had not been so late, I think I should have sought me another lodging, my welcome awhile was so ill, and almost no reason could persuade but that it was some device to keep her highness from her own gracious disposition to come hither. But I dealt plainly with her, that I knew she would have been sorry afterwards to have had her majesty come at this time of year to this place. I assure you, you should find it winter already. Thus much I thought good to tell you, that, when my lady comes hither, you may satisfy her, as I hope I have done. But her majesty must especially help somewhat or else have we more than half lost this lady . . . I rest here this sabbath day to make peace for us both. What remains you shall do at their next charge upon you . . .[29]

Elizabeth's passion for riding and hunting never abated. In August 1565 the Spanish ambassador recorded a chase at Windsor at which, 'The Queen went so hard that she tired everybody out, and as the ladies and courtiers were with her they were all put to shame. There was more work than pleasure in it for them'.[30] Accompanying Elizabeth on such outings was highly enjoyable for Robert: it was at these times that their two spirits were closest, indulging the sport they loved free from cares of state and the claustrophobia of the court. Other duties were more onerous. There were lists of requisitions to be checked:

> A rich litter covered with velvet laid upon
> with gold lace.

A litter for the ladies.
Saddles for my lord swathed and guarded with
velvet and spare furnishings.
Saddles of calves leather for the gentlemen.
Three pairs of gilt stirrups, etc.[31]

Horses were sometimes given as presents to visiting dignitaries
and representatives of foreign princes. Thus the Emperor's ambassador had a gift of 'Dun Sidney with a velvet saddle' and the
representative of the Regent of the Netherlands was presented with
'Layard Amightly with a velvet saddle'.[32] Such were the activities
which formed the constant background of Robert Dudley's life, and
it is against them that his political and diplomatic activities and his
relations with Queen and councillors must be seen.

Robert also had a domestic life to maintain. He had a wife, estates
and an army of servants to support. In eight and a half years of
marriage he and Amy had had very little life together. Political
upheaval, imprisonment and service abroad had kept them apart
most of that time. With the reversal of their fortunes in November
1558 this situation might have been expected to change. It did not.

Robert's court duties allowed him little freedom and he could not
afford a house in or near the capital where he might establish his
wife with a *ménage* suitable to his position. By the same token he
shunned the enormous expense of keeping his wife and her
servants at court. Amy, perhaps, had little desire for the stuffy life
of royal palaces (many ladies preferred the independence and
fresh air of the country and chose to forsake their husband's
company) though equally she had no wish to be completely isolated
in north Norfolk. She, therefore, spent her time in long visits to
friends, most of whom lived near London where Robert could also
come for short stays. At Christmas 1558 she was in Lincolnshire.
On her way south she visited relatives near Bury St Edmunds.
There was little point in her being near the court at a time when
the seasonal activities and the preparations for the coronation were
keeping Robert fully occupied. Spring saw her once more within
visiting distance of her husband, and during the ensuing months
she stayed twice with her mother's people: the Scotts of
Camberwell. Her principal residence, however, was Mr William
Hyde's house at Denchworth, near Abingdon, Berkshire.[33] Hither
Robert came as often as he could, and when he could not messengers and gifts atoned for his absence. His account books provide
some details of these to-ings and fro-ings:

To Thos. Jones to buy a hood for my lady	35s.		
To Gilbert the goldsmith for 6 doz. gold buttons of ye Spanish pattern, and for a little chain delivered to Mr. Forrest for my lady's use	£30		
Delivered for my lady's charge riding into Suffolk with 40 pistoles [Spanish coins] delivered to Huggins to put into her ladyship's purse	£26.	13s.	4d.
For spices bought by the cook when your Lordship rode to my lady's	22s.		
For bringing venison to Mr. Hyde's	5s.		
Delivered to your Lordship at Mr. Hyde's at sundry times; by my hands 20s.; by Huggins 11s.; and by Mr. Aldersey 28s. Total	67s.[sic]		
To Mr. Hyde which he lent your Lordship at play at his own house[34]	40s.		

These entries speak to us of a busy husband, yet one attentive to his wife's needs, sending messages and remembrances, obtaining for her in the smart London shops 'sewing silk', '2 pair of hose, a looking glass', '2 ell of fine Holland cloth'[35] for ruffs, etc. We see Robert thoughtfully augmenting Hyde's larder with meat and spices before descending on Denchworth with his attendants, and we can envisage the Dudleys and their friends relaxing over the card table late into the candlelit evenings.

Nor was it always Robert who visited Amy. Lady Dudley did occasionally come to court and when she did so it was in some style.

To hire of 12 horses when my lady came from Mr. Hyde's to London	60s.

Sometimes she came to stay in the neighbourhood when the court was away from the capital.

To Langham for two days board wages attending upon my lady at Christchurch your Lordship being at Windsor	3s. 4d.[36]

There is, thus, no hint of estrangement between husband and wife. On the contrary, their marriage seems to have stood up remarkably well to the strains placed upon it almost from the beginning. They had no children but that is not to say that Amy had no pregnancies or that the couple did not enjoy a normal sexual relationship. As the months passed, however, and the ties between Robert and Elizabeth grew stronger Amy's absence from court must have been convenient. The Queen was always jealous of other women in the lives of her male companions and would have found it difficult to tolerate Robert's wife. For this reason it was politic for Robert to leave Amy in the country. It is hard to see what else he could have done if he wished to please Elizabeth and encourage her affection for him. He may also have wished to spare Amy the unpleasant gossip that was very soon circulating around the court and the capital – gossip which made obscene references to the Queen and her Master of the Horse. We may be sure the stories spread and that, sooner or later, Amy heard them – heard that she was a sick woman and that her husband was only waiting for her to die to become King of England. It was not a fantastic notion: her father-in-law had been uncrowned king; her brother-in-law had been consort to a Queen for nine days. The rumours must have been distressing for her. Perhaps they hastened the illness and depression she appeared to be suffering from a year later. If she really was a sick woman in the spring of 1559 and if there was any substance to the court gossip about her, the affliction must, as yet, have been slight. Her frequent travels and her obvious delight in the latest fashions[37] do not square with a picture of Amy as a semi-invalid, distracted by pain or discomfort from the vanities of the world.

Like any good wife, Lady Dudley was also able to deputise for her husband in matters of estate management, and was fully trusted by her lord to do so. One of the two surviving letters in her hand deals with just such an issue and gives us a further indication of her feelings for Robert. It was written to John Flowerdew, their Norfolk agent, in August 1559.

Mr Flowerdew, I understand by Gryse that you put him in remembrance of that you spoke to me of, concerning the going of certain sheep at Syderstone; and although I forgot to move my lord thereof before his departing, he being sore troubled with weighty affairs and I not being altogether in quiet for his sudden departing, yet, notwithstanding, knowing your accustomed friendship towards my lord and me, I neither may nor can deny you that request, in my lord's absence, of mine own authority. Yea, and [if] it were a greater matter, as if any good occasion may serve you to try me; desiring you further that you will make sale of the wool so soon as is possible, although you sell it for 6s. the stone, or as you would sell for yourself, for my lord so justly required me, at his departing, to see those poor men satisfied, as though it had

been a matter depending on life. Wherefore I [hesitate] not to
sustain a little loss thereby to satisfy my lord's desire, and so to
send that money to Gryse's house to London, by Bridewell, to
whom my lord hath given order for the payment thereof. And
thus I end, always troubling you, wishing that occasion may serve
me to requite you. Until that time I must pay you with thanks.
And so to God I leave you.

   From Mr. Hyde's this 7 August
      Your assured during life,
         Amy Dudley.[38]

It is, surely, the letter of a wife who enjoys an excellent understanding with her husband and can confidently speak for him. It is also
the letter of a wife still in love with her husband. She is not ashamed
to acknowledge her distress at the brevity of Robert's recent visit
and his appearance of being 'sore troubled with weighty affairs'.

By the spring of 1559 the relationship between Robert and the
Queen certainly provided good reason for Amy to be anxious. On
18 April Feria, the Spanish ambassador, reported:

During the last few days Lord Robert has come so much into
favour that he does whatever he likes with affairs and it is even
said that her majesty visits him in his chamber day and night.
People talk of this so freely that they go so far as to say that his wife
has a malady in one of her breasts and the Queen is only waiting
for her to die to marry Lord Robert. I can assure your Majesty
that matters have reached such a pass that I have been brought to
consider whether it would not be well to approach Lord Robert on
your Majesty's behalf promising your help and favour and coming
to terms with him.[39]

Nor was this a fantasy or exaggeration on the part of the Spaniard:
other, Italian observers eagerly related this latest piece of court
scandal:

Robert Dudley . . . [is] a very handsome young man towards
whom in various ways the Queen evinces such affection and inclination that many persons believe that if his wife, who has been
ailing for some time, were perchance to die, the Queen might
easily take him for her husband.[40]

My Lord Robert Dudley is in very great favour and very intimate
with her majesty. On this subject I ought to report the opinion of
many but I doubt whether my letters may not miscarry or be read,
wherefore it is better to keep silence than to speak ill.[41]

On 23 April Elizabeth bestowed her first public honour on Lord Robert. He was one of three men nominated as Knights of the Garter. The names of the others now admitted to this ancient order, which existed to enable the sovereign to reward personal service, cannot have evoked any surprise: the Duke of Norfolk was the premier peer of England and Earl Marshal; the Earl of Rutland already had a long and distinguished career as soldier and diplomat behind him. But Lord Robert, the traitor's son, with nothing to commend him but his dark good looks and his ability to sit a horse? No wonder, as the Venetian ambassador hinted, there were malicious tongues wagging at court. The chronicler, William Camden, commented that Lord Robert's new award aroused 'the admiration [i.e. wonder] of all men'.

It is thus clear that at some time during the tense, problem-filled winter of 1559 the Queen realised that she was in love with her Master of the Horse. Those historians who disapprove of Dudley (and they are in a large majority) prefer to speak of Elizabeth's 'infatuation', as though there was something disreputable or, at least, odd about her feelings for Robert. It is assumed that Dudley must have deliberately 'cast a spell' over her so that, despite her better judgement, she surrendered to his importunate wooing. Such arguments surely reveal as little understanding of human nature as of the atmosphere of Elizabeth's court. The young Queen was under considerable strain and had not yet fully learned how to master men and events. She was surrounded by flattering courtiers, councillors and ambassadors, all of whom, as she knew, were motivated by self-interest as much as loyalty. Often she worked alone late into the night, sifting in her mind the conflicting advice she had received during the day. There were few men in whose company she could relax. One of them was her handsome, extrovert Master of the Horse, whom she had known and liked all her life.

Wooing and talk of marriage were in the air during those early months of the reign. It was the courtier's role to make ostentatious display of loyalty and devotion to the sovereign. When that sovereign was an unmarried woman such behaviour inevitably took on the character of flirtation and even courtship. It was a game that Elizabeth loved and all her close attendants had to play. But sometimes reality became confused with the roles in the comedy. For some months the Earl of Arundel, one of Elizabeth's most senior councillors and household officials, considered himself a serious contender for the Queen's hand. He was one of the few Catholic holders of high office to survive into the new reign. At forty-seven he was an urbane, cultured and proud representative of the old

nobility. He owned the finest house in the land – Henry VIII's extrav-
aganza, Nonsuch – and entertained the court lavishly in the summer
of 1559. In February, within days of assembling, Elizabeth's first
parliament had fallen to discussing her marriage. Some members
voiced the hope that she would choose within the realm[42] and they
may have had Arundel in mind. The Earl was the Dudleys' implacable enemy. It was he who had been imprisoned without trial by
Northumberland, had promised to hold London for Queen Jane and
subsequently hastened to Cambridge to arrest the Duke and convey
him to the Tower. Robert's emergence to favour may have originated
in some fresh manifestation of the rivalry between the two families.

The Queen did not lack for advisers in matrimonial affairs. The
most exalted was Philip II who, from distant Madrid, tried to play
the puppet-master and had sent de Feria to England largely for the
purpose of arranging the marriage which all men supposed must
shortly follow the coronation. At first he was prepared, magnani-
mously, to offer himself, but even his religious zeal flinched at the
prospect of a second Tudor wife. He contented himself instead with
patronising a succession of 'safe' Catholic suitors. Elizabeth kept the
ambassador at a polite distance and obliged the baffled grandee to
hover about the court, picking up whatever snippets of information
he could. When necessary she kept him happy with vague promises.
Only after several months, and when the diplomatic situation had
changed in her favour, did she inform Philip that she had decided
not to marry for the present.

It was the same answer she had returned to parliament. On 10
February she graciously thanked them for their concern, assuring
them that they need have no fear of her choosing an unsuitable
husband: 'Whensoever it may please God to incline my heart to
another kind of life, ye may well assure yourselves my meaning is
not to do or determine anything wherewith the realm may or shall
have just cause to be discontented'. For herself, however, she had no
desire for the wedded state: 'In the end, this shall be for me sufficient, that a marble stone shall declare that a Queen, having reigned
such a time, lived and died a virgin'.[43]

Such were Elizabeth's public sentiments (her speech was printed
for general circulation) and we may not doubt that they were
genuine as far as they went. Personal and political considerations
gave her a predilection for the maiden state. Yet she was a healthy
young woman with normal susceptibilities and in February or
March 1559 she fell victim to the romance-scented air of the court,
to the unremitting pressure to seek a consort, and to the charm of
Robert Dudley. Furthermore, by allowing herself to fall for her

Master of the Horse she could indulge both sides of her nature: she could be in love and remain a virgin. Unlike all the other wooers, within the realm and without, Robert was not a contender for her hand; he was safely married.

The knowledge that he had won the Queen's heart, with all that implied, probably dawned slowly on Robert. Its effect must have been staggering. However genuine Robert's feelings were for his wife, he must have been flattered by the Queen's affection for him and was certainly committed to doing everything possible to foster it. It was not a matter in which he had any choice. If he wanted to continue enjoying prosperity, prestige and a large clientage, he had to indulge Elizabeth. Perhaps that did mean telling her she was the only woman he really loved and perhaps he did promise to prove that to her if his wife died. But Amy was very much alive, so the Queen and her Master of the Horse could indulge in the most outrageous love play without having to face the responsibility of mutual commitment.

Gratifying as his position now was within the court it carried with it as many problems as privileges. It was extremely precarious: Robert was totally dependent on the Queen's bounty, having as yet no major grants of land to support his dignity. It made him a focus of attention for all who had suits to press upon the sovereign. The work of his secretaries rapidly increased as nobles, ladies, gentlemen, merchants and courtiers inundated Dudley with requests, gifts and information in the hope of ingratiating themselves with the new favourite.

> Seeing the great affairs whereat your honour is continually travailed I have been afraid to trouble you with my humble suit but now am of pure necessity constrained most humbly to beseech your honour to stand my good lord to further this my suit whereof I have here enclosed a brief note unto the Queen's Majesty . . . if I may by your Lordship's good means obtain it it will something release my present necessity which is such [that] if I be [rejected] by your Lordship I shall be utterly unable to pass the rest of the short time which I have yet to come in this world in quietness of body or mind which I most humbly beseech your honour forthwith to consider for whose prospering and state I do and shall daily pray.
> Your Lordship's most bounden
> George Gilpin[44]

Such letters came to Dudley in their scores week in and week out. George Gilpin was a poor gentleman seeking speedy execution of an overdue land grant. He became a protégé of both Dudley and the Earl of Bedford. Sir James Croft, Governor of Berwick, appealed on behalf of a widowed gentlewoman, trusting to Dudley's kind nature 'which I have known always to be favourable to women'.[45] Lady Elizabeth Darcy sought a post at court for her son.[46] The Earl of Ormonde sent a servant to claim a position as groom of the stable, 'according to your promise'.[47] The Bishop of Worcester begged Dudley to maintain his 'honest and righteous causes'.[48] Thomas Benger, a disgraced courtier, entreated Dudley to intercede with the Queen and assure her 'although I live from her Highness, as I take it, like a banished man, yet would no worm fainer creep to his food than I on the knees of my heart's desire to serve and follow her'.[49] A merchant called John Stow, desiring to leave trade and follow the scholar's calling, presented Lord Robert with a manuscript copy of his grandfather's treatise, *The Tree of Commonwealth*.[50] Artists, writers and craftsmen in profusion sought Dudley's patronage. Few, it seems, sought in vain.

One who had himself tasted the lees in fortune's cup readily sympathized with those who had fallen on hard times. On many occasions his generosity and friendship were extended to those he had little cause to love. Sir Thomas Cornwallis was one such. Cornwallis was an ardent papist. He had resorted to Mary Tudor at Framlingham in July 1553 and was there when Robert Dudley was brought in. As a member of Mary's Council he had been a trusted adviser throughout the reign and became Comptroller of the Household in 1557. He showed himself hostile towards the Queen's opponents and behaved with scant courtesy towards Princess Elizabeth. Naturally he fell from favour in November 1558, was stripped of his offices and placed under house arrest. The following summer he appealed to Dudley with some confidence that the favourite's goodwill would not fail him:

My good Lord, understanding by my wife and my brother your Lordship's great courtesy in suffering them to have recourse unto you in the time of their suits . . . and what great cause I have to owe you my poor service during my life, and although it is not in me to deserve any part of this your goodness, yet hath your own good nature in this point emboldened me to use your friendship further: that, forasmuch as I am constrained (by my wife's sickness and the absence of other of my friends) to send my servant Waterhouse to be a suitor to my Lord for my further liberty, it may please your Lordship to further him in the same, and to give him leave sometime to resort unto you for his better furtherance, with hope whereof and promise of my good will and service for ever, I humbly take my leave. From London, 29 July, 1559.

Your Lordship's most assured to command,
Thomas Cornwallis[51]

The ex-councillor was shortly afterwards given leave to retire to his Suffolk estates, where, in quietness, he passed the remainder of a long life, outliving both his Queen and his benefactor.

Yet, human nature being what it is, for every may or woman who had cause to be grateful to Lord Robert there was another who was jealous and resentful of his privileged, influential position. Feria's statement, 'he does whatever he likes with affairs', need not be taken at face value. The disgruntled Spanish ambassador, deliberately excluded from the influential position he regarded as his due, was not an objective reporter. Yet there were others who murmured against Robert in private. By the end of 1559 the Duke of Norfolk was acknowledged leader of an anti-Dudley faction at court who 'cannot put up with his being king'.[52] There was even talk of a plot on the favourite's life, in connection with which the soldier, Sir William Drury, and his brother, Dru, Gentleman of the Privy Chamber, found themselves in the Tower for several months.[53] Abroad, Dudley's position roused comment in diplomatic circles. In December Thomas Challoner, writing to Cecil from the Netherlands, dismissed current rumour about Lord Robert as 'most foul slander' but suggested that 'a princess cannot be too wary what countenance of familiar demonstration she maketh more to one than another . . . No man's service in the realm is worth the price of enduring such malicious tales'.[54]

The fungus of bitter envy grew naturally and luxuriantly on the tree of Elizabethan court life. When all courtiers were competing for the favours of the young virgin Queen and using the language of love it could scarcely be otherwise. Elizabeth encouraged this rivalry. She was not so much under Robert's spell that she could resist the temptation to tease him. She encouraged the Earl of Arundel and spent five days at his house in August 1559.

In the autumn she was flirting with a more obscure, but no less comely, bachelor, Sir William Pickering, a 43-year-old courtier-diplomat. The Queen entertained him in private and allowed him rooms in the palace, where he set himself up in pretentious style. His intimacy with the Queen encouraged him to great extravagance and to give himself airs. He upset Bedford, Arundel and probably others. When Arundel tried to stop him sauntering through to the Queen's private chapel and told him to wait in the Presence Chamber as befitted his rank, Pickering haughtily upbraided the Earl as an impudent, discourteous knave. In October, the piqued Arundel was heard to mutter that if Pickering won the Queen's hand he would sell his estates and go abroad.

The romances with Pickering and Arundel passed like summer showers; that with Dudley did not. By mid-November, as we have seen, there was a sizeable opposition to him at court. De Quadra, the new Spanish ambassador, could report:

> The Duke of Norfolk is the chief of Lord Robert's enemies, who are all the principal people in the kingdom . . . he said that if Lord Robert did not abandon his present pretentions and presumptions, he would not die in his bed . . . I think his hatred of Lord Robert will continue, as the Duke and the rest of them cannot put up with his being king.[55]

There was every reason why Thomas Howard, fourth Duke of Norfolk, should emerge as Dudley's principal opponent. He was grandson and heir of that other Thomas who had been Northumberland's most implacable enemy. When Robert had been learning courtcraft in Edward VI's household, Thomas had sojourned in the country overshadowed by his family's disgrace. Later, Howard had enjoyed royal favour while Dudley had been in the Tower. Norfolk was by upbringing inclined to the old religion. As England's only duke and representative of an ancient family, Howard believed that he merited, as of right, a place among the Queen's closest companions and advisers. Yet, both in his shire and in the court, he found himself checked by Dudley. In Norfolk Dudley was soon able to take up the threads of clientage he had manipulated in his early years as a landowner there. Thomas was an athletic young man (some five years Robert's junior) yet could not match Robert's prowess in the tilt-yard and the tennis court. An incident that particularly rankled in 1559 arose from the payment of the parliamentary subsidy. Howard's first instalment of £160 was one of the highest in the country. As if that were not bad enough, Dudley was specifically excused payment by royal warrant. It was impossible that the two men could be friends: their lives touched and clashed at too many points. Norfolk could not acquiesce in Lord Robert's position of special favour without denying all that he stood for. From the beginning of the reign he was impelled along the path that led to self-destruction.[56] In December he confronted Dudley face to face about his interference in state affairs, and angry words passed between them. A few days later Howard received a new appointment, which can scarcely have been unrelated to the quarrel: he was sent to the border country as Lieutenant General in the north.

Elizabeth had been on the throne barely a year but already the main characteristics of her attitude to Dudley were manifested – deep affection and a determination to protect him from his enemies. Her favour had already begun to take a tangible form. During 1559 Robert received various parcels of land in different counties: Knole in Kent, Burton Lazar manor and hospitals, Leicestershire, Beverley manor, park and borough, Skidby and the site of Meaux Abbey, all in Yorkshire, and a house on the river at Kew, convenient for London and Windsor.[57] On 24 November letters patent were issued appointing Dudley Lord Lieutenant of Windsor Castle and Park, a post vacant by the decease of William Fitzwilliam. At the same time Sir Francis Englefield was obliged to surrender to Robert his life constableship of Windsor Castle.[58] Dudley still did not establish his own household, however, and it was about the turn of the year that Lady Dudley took up residence with Robert's friend and steward, Anthony Forster, in his newly rented house, Cumnor Place.

CHAPTER SIX

'CAREFUL FOR THE QUIET OF THE STATE'

It was not only Robert's intimacy with the Queen which some English courtiers and statesmen found difficult to forgive, they also mistrusted him for his political ambition. The son of Northumberland believed he had a duty and a right to be at the centre of national and international affairs. From the outset of the reign he indicated that he was not content with a purely ceremonial role. The writs for Elizabeth's first parliament were dated 5 December, and Lord Robert indicated to the electors of Norfolk that he was available for their consideration. Probably we should see this as one of many moves he was making to regain his former influence. He had been returned as knight of the shire in 1552 and in 1553. Norfolk had turned upon him most decisively on his father's downfall and some of its prominent landowners had given evidence against him in the Shirehouse at Norwich. Robert now pointed out to these leaders of local society that the whirligig of fortune had taken another turn. They hastened to respond, anxious to win the approval of this local landowner whose star was evidently rising, and Lord Robert Dudley was duly elected.

Dudley was never to show himself an original political thinker, nor did he possess the diligence and acumen of a man like Cecil to sift the intricacies of the ever-changing international situation. But involved he always was, and industrious. He kept himself well informed about all major events at home and abroad, and to all problems he applied those general principles he had absorbed from his upbringing and from his father's tutelage.[1]

At the beginning of the reign the European scene was dominated as much by religion as politics. Indeed, all but the most incisive sixteenth-century minds found it difficult to distinguish between the two. Philip II had placed himself at the spearhead of the counter-reformation, determined to extirpate heresy throughout his dominions and beyond. He was supported by the papacy, the Inquisition and the Jesuits. France was involved in spasmodic internal warfare between the supporters of the Catholic Guises and the Protestant Chatillons. Calvin's Geneva had shown that a Protestant theocracy was technically viable. Other city-states had set up similar polities and these attracted religious extremists from other lands;

extremists who eventually went home burning with zeal to establish godly commonwealths in their own domains. Spain and France were the dominant powers, but a useful counterbalance on the Protestant side which English statesmen sometimes found helpful was the league of German Lutheran princes.

The religious issues which had rent the ancient fabric of Christendom divided English life also. The Marian regime had filled many rectories and episcopal palaces with convinced Catholics. It had also persecuted the Protestant church into a position of unprecedented strength. That strength was now in the process of being redoubled as religious radicals returned home from exile in Geneva, Zurich, Frankfurt and other continental havens.

The two urgent matters facing the framers of English policy in the early months of 1559 were the conclusion of a foreign peace and the elaboration of a formula which would ensure a measure of religious peace at home. England's involvement in the Franco-Spanish war on the side of Philip II had gained her nothing and lost her Calais. The major contenders were now tired of conflict and were negotiating a Treaty at Cateau-Cambrésis. England had elbowed her way to the negotiating table but looked like having to accept whatever terms her more powerful neighbours agreed – and they would not include the return of Calais. Cecil and the leading diplomats involved were resigned to the permanent loss of England's last continental foothold. The Secretary, indeed, was in favour of peace at almost any price. But there were those who were appalled at the thought and at the suggestion of the new reign starting on such a negative note. They also feared the prospect of a united France and Spain, seeing in it the beginnings of a Catholic union which would launch a crusade for the reconversion of Europe.

These radicals did not yet constitute a party or faction but we can distinguish certain groups who, for reasons of religion or national pride, advocated broadly similar policies. The most vociferous protagonists of an unyielding politico-religious stance were the returning exiles. Then there were the enthusiastic young gentlemen who had intrigued for the overthrow of the Marian regime and wanted Elizabeth's England to take a leading place among the reformed nations of Europe. Lastly there were the traditionalists among the nobility and gentry, men who had fought at St Quentin, men who regarded France as the old enemy, men who felt the loss of Calais almost as a personal humiliation. Where were such bold spirits to look for leadership? The answer for some of them at least was to Lord Robert Dudley and Francis Russell, Lord Bedford.

Writing in the winter of 1558-9, John Aylmer, the Protestant scholar and pamphleteer, singled out these two courtiers as men 'careful for the quiet of the state, the safety of our sovereign, and the wealth of the whole realm'.[2] Bedford had spent part of Mary's reign among the continental exiles before being reconciled and serving under Philip II at St Quentin. He became one of the leaders of the Puritan party and a close friend and colleague of the Dudleys.

Many men who had found favour with Northumberland in the old days looked to his son now. There were Protestant ministers, scholars and political agents who expected Robert to use his influence on their behalf. They had good reason to hope for his aid and, in many cases, they did not hope in vain. For Robert was committed to the cause of international Protestantism. Like his father he stood firmly against Spain: an attitude which often led him to take a pro-French stance. His was a highly nationalistic attitude. Like many men of the younger generation he looked to the government to defy England's enemies, both potential and real; to lead Protestant Europe in opposition to the monolithic Hapsburg alliance. These principles inspired most of his official actions.

Dudley's patronage of Thomas Wilson well illustrates the point. Wilson was a considerable scholar who had enjoyed the support of Robert's father and eldest brother and who had married the daughter of his grandfather's colleague, Sir Richard Empson. After Northumberland's fall he had fled to the continent only to be pursued by Mary Tudor's vengeance. It was probably at her instigation that Wilson was imprisoned and tortured by the Inquisition. After many adventures he returned to London in 1560. The Dudleys were not slow to reward his loyalty and to make use of his considerable talents. Wilson was an MP in the parliament summoned in 1563 and received important judicial appointments. Later he served on embassies to Portugal and, as well as his official duties, he was invaluable to Robert as an agent in secret discussions with Spanish and Portuguese officials. In 1571 it was Thomas Wilson who conducted interrogations in the Tower of Dudley's rival, the Duke of Norfolk, when the latter was under investigation for treason. He was returned to parliament again in 1572 and reached the summit of his career five years later as principal secretary to the Council. The presence of such men in his entourage tells us much about how Dudley maintained his position and also the causes he used his influence to support.

Years later Robert could justifiably claim a consistency of public behaviour:

I am no hypocrite nor Pharisee. My doings are plain, and chiefly in the causes of religion. I take Almighty God to my record, I never altered my mind or thought from my youth touching my religion, and you know I was ever from my cradle brought up in it . . . I thank God I never rejoiced in no worldly thing so much as in this good establishment of it which we ought to be thankful for . . . look for all the bishops that it can be supposed that I have commended to that dignity since my credit any way served . . . Look of all the deans that also in that time have been commended by me . . . Besides this, who in England hath had or hath more learned chaplains belonging to him than I, or hath preferred more to the furtherance of the church of learned preachers? Or what bishop . . . doth give so large stipends out of his purse to them as I do? And where have I refused any one preacher or good minister to do for him the best I could at all times, when they have need of me either to speak or write for them . . .[3]

This claim is born out by an anonymous note which was addressed to him very early in Elizabeth's reign and which commended to him for immediate employment in the church twenty-eight 'godly preachers which have utterly forsaken antichrist and all his Romish rags'.[4] In 1561 and 1562 two Calvinist works appeared, dedicated to Lord Robert: Robert Fills' *Laws and Statutes of Geneva* and Jean Veron's *Treatise of Free Will*. They were but early fruits from an abundant harvest of Protestant piety addressed to Dudley. As the years passed Dudley clearly emerged as the most influential leader of the reformed party, but this alliance was no sudden change of face decided on for political or personal motives. His convictions had been fashioned during his formative years at the courts of Henry VIII and Edward VI and, from the very beginning of Elizabeth's reign he was recognised as a Protestant activist, a member of a group of influential men (including Bedford, Huntingdon, Pembroke and Ambrose Dudley) more unequivocal in their support of reform than Cecil and his circle.

From the beginning, also, this religious bias was associated with political action. As early as 23 November 1558 the Spanish ambassador, realising Dudley's importance, could mistakenly report, 'Lord Robert, the Master of the Horse, is in the Council'[5] Within weeks he was complaining about the 'heretics' close to the Queen. Some of them were urging her to take a tough line in the Cateau-Cambrésis negotiations, 'persuading her that she has power to resist the French'. He believed he could detect two rival groups bringing pressure to bear upon the Queen: 'Pembroke, the Treasurer

[William Paulet, Marquess of Winchester] and Robert' and 'Cecil, the Admiral [Edward Clinton, Earl of Lincoln] and Mason' [Sir John Mason, an old and experienced diplomat]. Winchester was a trimmer but the 'oldest and most respected member of the Council'. Pembroke, though he had served Mary, was a thoroughgoing Protestant, a soldier who had fought against the French and who had been for a time Governor of Calais. According to de Feria, Pembroke was 'always about the palace and does not leave her [Elizabeth's] side'.[6] Together with the rising star, Robert Dudley, these men formed a heavy counterweight to the cautious Cecil and his friends. The sympathies of leading courtiers were well known further afield. When, in January 1561, members of the foreign Protestant community in London were petitioning for an extension of their privileges it was Sir Francis Knollys and Sir Robert Dudley whom they lobbied.

The policy they were advocating was an insistence on the return of Calais, backed, if possible, by an alliance with the German Protestant princes. Robert received frequent reports from friends and protégés abroad. These were Protestant exiles, diplomats and young men who had been involved in plots against Mary. George Gilpin, acting as his agent in the Netherlands, kept him informed of the situation there and could report on 6 March 1559 that 'some of the wisest [statesmen here] be of opinion that, if a peace be made and Calais left in the Frenchman's hands, it will never be kept two years.[7] More important, however, was Henry Killigrew. From December to February he was involved in secret negotiations in Germany with the celebrated Paulo Vergerio, agent of the Duke of Wurttemberg.[8] Letters passed back and forth between Killigrew and the radical group at the English court concerning the details of a possible alliance. One of these letters, written in Latin and dated 6 February 1559, made quite clear the attitude of at least one member of the Dudley's group. It was sent from the court to Vergerio: 'Nothing is more gratifying to me than to take part in this cleansing of the church and her restitution to her primitive beauty. Although I am far inferior in learning to others, I would not yield place in labour and diligence to the best workman in the Lord's vineyard. The Church of Christ in England is once more reviving after enduring great and miserable afflictions. I commend [her] to your prayers and whatever aid you can render . . . We must make our enemies understand that the princes of the Evangelical Alliance regard English affairs with as great interest as their own. We must be as vigorous in our defence as they are in attack'.[9] The letter bears no signature but clearly came from one of the leading court evangelicals. The most likely contenders are Pembroke, Bedford and Dudley himself.

These plans at length foundered on the Germans' insistence that Elizabeth subscribe to the Augsburg Confession. The Queen was never prepared to yield to such pressures, but in the winter of 1558-9 the domestic religious situation obliged her to keep as many options open as possible. The terms of the Treaty of Cateau-Cambrésis were agreed on 19 March. Mason, definitely committed to accepting any face-saving formula which would ensure peace, was sent over for the final stages of the negotiations. Calais remained in French hands but was scheduled to be restored to England at the end of eight years. Everyone knew that it would not be. Scapegoats had to be found to assuage public indignation and these were the unfortunate captains who had been in charge of the fortifications at Calais at the time of its capture. Thomas, Lord Wentworth, Sir Ralph Chamberlain and John Harleston were committed to the Tower and all subsequently stood trial on charges of high treason. Wentworth was acquitted. The others were found guilty and sentenced to death but their sentences were commuted and, when public interest in them had waned, they were quietly released, ruined men but alive.

Despite the Spanish ambassador's assessment of Lord Robert's importance, there was, as yet, no place for him on the Council. Nor would there be for three years. The only political arena he could enjoy was the Commons chamber of parliament, which assembled on 25 January 1559. Unfortunately there are no detailed records of debates so we cannot assess his performance there. Court business may have kept him away on some occasions. But on the major items of business he was certainly no neutral and it is unlikely that he was a passive member of the assembly. Few members were: the lines of religious and political division were too sharply drawn. The most urgent issue was the achievement of a religious settlement. After the upheavals, burnings, doctrinal changes and spoliations stretching back over a generation, the Queen's subjects were now looking for peace and religious stability. At every level of political influence Catholics and Protestants were urging their own solutions to the nation's ills and seeking aid in their cause from powerful friends at home and abroad. In the Lords and Commons, where liturgical and doctrinal guidelines for the Elizabethan church were laid down, powerful factions argued long and earnestly and ministers had no easy task in guiding the assembly to desired conclusions. The Queen herself gave no unequivocal lead. She was not a fanatic and no clear statement of her faith has ever been possible. At Christmas 1558 she

refused to remain at mass for the elevation of the host and she
ostentatiously rejected excessive religious ceremonial at her coronation. Yet in the following November she celebrated the feast of All
Saints at Westminster Abbey, where the French ambassador noted
that the high altar was restored, embellished with silver crosses, and
that the Queen lit two tapers upon it – at which behaviour 'the
Protestants in this city are wonderfully surprised and cry out'.[10] At
the Garter ceremony in April no crosses were carried and the
Queen absented herself from the mass for the dead. Yet within days
she was telling the Spanish ambassador that in matters of religion
'she differed very little from us'.[11]

Throughout February and the first half of March parliamentary
debated centred round two main issues: the nature of royal
supremacy and the form of worship to be sanctioned. In Parliament,
in Council and in the court individuals and groups argued their
own points of view. Catholics were stiffened by Spanish and French
ambassadors, radicals by the growing number of returning exiles.
The Queen, as was her wont, permitted freedom of debate, listened
to all who proffered advice and returned gracious words which
permitted 'papist' and 'heretic' alike to hope. By 22 March a
cautious Supremacy Bill was ready for the royal assent and it
seemed that parliament would be dissolved before Good Friday (24
March). Then Elizabeth changed her tactics drastically: parliament
was simply adjourned until 3 April and in the new session the
government introduced firmer anti-Catholic measures, including a
new Act of Supremacy to which all clergy were obliged to swear.

Many reasons have been suggested for this sudden plotting of a
more aggressively Protestant course. The treaty with France and
Spain was all but signed. The strength and vociferousness of the
returning exiles were increasing and Elizabeth reluctantly
concluded that she needed their support. The Commons had shown
an unexpected solidarity and had to be wooed. Radicals at court
were gaining in boldness. All these pressures undoubtedly played
their part in influencing the Queen's decision. However, it was
precisely at this time that the Queen fell under Dudley's spell and
there can be no doubt about the advice he gave her on the religious
issue. His closeness to Elizabeth allowed him to exercise considerable boldness in urging religious policy. He may even have taken
considerable liberties from time to time. If the Spanish ambassador
is to be believed, various items offensive to evangelical eyes were on
occasions during the 1560s removed from the Queen's private
chapel without her permission and at Dudley's instigation.[12]

In the second half of 1559 most of the Marian bishops were

deprived and during the next year no less than twenty-one new appointments were made. All of them were Protestants, some of them were radicals, most them acknowledged the debt they owed to the favourite. Recently a historian has identified fourteen bishops, six deans and seven other higher clergy advanced wholly or partly by Dudley in the early years of the reign.[13] Among them were Thomas Young, Archbishop of York (1561), Edmund Grindal, Bishop of London, Robert Horne, Dean of Durham (and Bishop of Winchester, 1561), Edwin Sandys, Bishop of Worcester, and Edmund Scambler, Bishop of Peterborough (1561).

It was not only in the ecclesiastical sphere that Lord Robert exercised patronage. He advanced friends and clients to positions at court. His aid was sought, and given, in connection with the government of the shires. For example, he insinuated his relative, John Appleyard, into the position of sheriff of Norfolk in the autumn of 1559 against the Duke's appointee. Through Killigrew he was in touch with some of the young activists still lingering in exile and it was largely thanks to his intervention that Henry Dudley, Leighton, Horsey and others were allowed to return.[14] Within a few years Cecil was able to identify, in one of his many private memoranda, the leading members of a Dudley faction active within and without the court: 'Sir H. Sidney, Earl of Warwick [Ambrose Dudley], Sir James Croft, Henry Dudley, Sir Francis Jobson, Appleyard, Horley [Horsey?], Leighton, Mollyneux, Middlemore, Colshall, Wykeman, Killigrew, John Dudley, ii Christmas, Forster, Ellis, Middleton'.[15] The patronage system made it impossible for a favourite not to be a political figure. In deciding whom he would help the favourite inevitably chose men he approved of, men who could be useful to him, men whose policies, opinions and beliefs matched his own. He became associated with specific causes and was able to advance these causes. It was a short step to attempting to influence directly the thoughts and actions of the monarch. Even if Dudley had had no political ambition he would have found it impossible to avoid playing a political role.

This very soon brought him into conflict with the 'professional' politicians, foremost among whom was Sir William Cecil. Mr Secretary brought his cool, analytical mind to bear upon the relationship between Elizabeth and Robert and, therefore, he was never able to understand it. He found it profoundly regrettable that such a cultured, intelligent woman should throw herself away on a mere court exotic. He found it frustrating when the favourite countered his own policies and urged the Queen towards courses he considered disastrous. His bewilderment and annoyance are best summed up in the words of his protégé, William Camden, 'the inclination of princes to some men and their disfavour towards others may seem fatal'.[16]

It is well known that Elizabeth held Cecil in high regard and valued his advice until the end of his life, but in the early years of the reign his position became increasingly insecure in direct proportion to Lord Robert's rise to favour. The personal rivalry of Lord Robert and Sir William was at its peak in the 1560s and, on at least one occasion, Cecil seriously contemplated resignation and complete withdrawal from public life. That he did not do so was because of his underlying philosophy rather than any weakening of Dudley's influence. Self-interest dominated his attitude to royal service, just as it did for all the Queen's men. It was for this reason that, during Mary's reign, he had publicly disavowed his earlier religious 'errors', attended mass regularly and ostentatiously sported a large rosary.[17] And it was for this reason that he was careful to make no open demonstration of hostility towards Lord Robert. He understood too well the necessity of preserving a right attitude towards his social superiors. In rank he was only a knight and was tolerated by the great lords of the household and Council because he enjoyed the Queen's favour and because he was suitably deferential towards them. Dudley's special relationship with the Queen drew from Cecil no demonstrations of resentment. On the contrary, he did all in his power to show friendship towards the favourite. It was a policy he was later to advocate to his son:

> Be sure to keep some great man thy friend, but trouble him not for trifles. Compliment him often with many and small gifts and if thou hast cause to bestow any great gratuity let it be something which may be daily in sight. Otherwise, in this ambitious age, thou shalt remain like a hop without a pole, live in obscurity, and be made a football for every insulting companion to spurn at.[18]

At the same time Cecil was careful to cultivate Dudley's rival, the Duke of Norfolk, for whom he seems to have had a real affection and whose character he completely misread.

Neither Cecil, nor Howard, nor indeed, any other critic could or did accuse Lord Robert of a lack of conscientiousness. His days were filled with a wide variety of duties and cares. For example, the six months from May 1559 began with the arrival of the French mission which had come to ratify the Treaty of Cateau-Cambrésis. On 23 May Robert was one of the dignitaries who met the visitors at Tower Wharf and escorted them to their lodgings. There followed five days of banquets, processions and entertainments, all of which demanded his presence. On 6 June Robert was at Windsor for the lavish ceremonial of his Garter installation. A few days later the court moved from Westminster to Greenwich. Thither, on 2 July, came the City musters to demonstrate their skills in manoeuvres and mock battle before the court. Dudley helped to organise a tournament, followed by banqueting and masques, on 11 July. The feasting took place in pavilions of 'fir poles . . . decked with birch and all manner of flowers of the field and garden [such] as roses, gilliflowers, lavender, marigolds and all manner of strewing herbs'.[19] On the 17th the summer progress began and Dudley was responsible for seeing that the royal cavalcade safely reached Eltham, Dartford, then Cobham, Nonsuch, Hampton Court, on to 'my Lord Admiral's house' and thence to Windsor in late August. The Queen spent much of her time at the castle riding and hunting in the Great Park. After a month the court was back at Westminster to receive the latest foreign suitor for Elizabeth's hand. This was Prince John of Sweden, who came representing his oft-repulsed but persistent brother, Eric. At the beginning of October Robert set out with the Earl of Oxford towards the east coast. They met the Prince's party at Colchester and brought him, by stages, to the capital. On the 5th they rode through Aldgate, to be met by a large escort of honour led by Northampton and Ambrose Dudley. And so they conducted him in pomp to his lodging at the Bishop of Winchester's house. Another round of festivities followed during which, on the 19th, Lord Robert was host at a court banquet. On 27 October he and the Prince of Sweden stood godfather when Sir Thomas Chamberlain's son was christened at St Bennet's, Paul's Wharf. On 5 November a tournament was arranged for the Prince's benefit at which Dudley and Lord Hunsdon were the defenders against eighteen contenders. An observer noted with satisfaction that many lances were broken and the Queen showed great favour to Hunsdon and Dudley.[20]

Amid all this activity Robert kept a close watch on the political situation. As the summer of 1559 shaded into autumn this was increasingly dominated by affairs in Scotland and France. Henry II died in July after a jousting accident, and Mary Stuart, the wife of the dauphin, suddenly found herself the new French queen. She and her supporters had always claimed not only the crown of Scotland but also that of England, and now, it seemed, she was in a powerful position to press that claim. She was supported by the ambitious Guise faction who filled the Edinburgh government with Frenchmen and planned to send more troops across the North Sea. Elizabeth saw the neighbouring kingdom being turned into a base for the invasion of England but was hampered in her response by her desire to preserve peace and also by the Treaty of Cateau-Cambrésis. The situation was complicated by the beliefs and activities of the Scottish Calvinists and their mouthpiece, John Knox. In the name of religion and patriotism they opposed Catholic Mary and her friends and appealed to England for help. Politically such an alliance was welcomed by Elizabeth's government, but philosophically Knox's party, which told the Scots that they had a divine commission to depose their queen, was abhorrent to her. However, by the end of 1559 she had been obliged to strengthen her border garrisons. Through the winter the Earl of Norfolk and Lord Grey de Wilton waited at Berwick for clear instructions while Elizabeth havered between commitment to military intervention and diplomacy. Cecil and the majority of the Council urged her to confront the French in the field but the Queen shrank from a course which would be both sanguinary and expensive. Not until the end of March did she allow herself to be persuaded to sanction Grey and Howard to lead their men against Leith. The siege was a disaster from beginning to end. The climax came on 7 May when Norfolk's assault on the town was repulsed with heavy losses. The effect on Elizabeth was such as to cause her advisers great embarrassment, as Cecil reported to Nicholas Throckmorton the ambassador in France.

The Queen's majesty never liketh this matter of Scotland. You know what hangeth thereupon; weak hearted men and flatterers will follow that way. And now, when we looked for best fortune, the worst came. Upon Tuesday the seventh of this month our men offered an assault at Leith, and being not saltable they were repulsed with loss of a thousand men . . . I have had such a torment herein with the Queen's majesty as an ague hath not in five fits so much abated.[21]

That Dudley was among the 'flatterers' who supported Elizabeth in her reticence we need not doubt. He rejoiced at Norfolk's discomfiture, and every mishap in Scotland which embarrassed Cecil strengthened his position.

Robert's attitude towards the Scottish situation seems to have been that, as long as the English succession was undecided, it would be best to arrive at a negotiated understanding with the Stuarts. This would weaken their links with France. That country was so distracted by internal politico-religious divisions as to pose no serious threat to England. The real potential enemy was, and always would be, Spain. Such considerations he urged on the Queen, whose mind was always attracted by the prospects of peace and economy.

Even while the military conflict in Scotland continued, Elizabeth's mind was already turning to thoughts of negotiation. In May the French and English courts appointed commissioners to discuss terms. The Queen chose Cecil to head her delegation, and before the end of the month he and his fellow representatives were travelling northwards for the conference, which eventually convened in Edinburgh. The Secretary and his friends had grave misgivings about his absence from the centre of activities. Cecil suspected that Dudley was behind the decision to send him away from the court. He was far too cautious to mention names in his correspondence but he confided in Throckmorton:

> My journey is to me very strange and diversely judged of. My friends in Council think it very necessary for the matter and convenient for me. My friends abroad think I am herein betrayed to be sent from the Queen's majesty. Whatsoever it is, I content myself with service and being wearied at home shall feel no difference of trouble abroad . . . The most comfort is that by this means shall be tried what we shall trust unto. You shall do well to write now circumspectly; for how you shall be judged of in my absence I know not . . .[22]

Sir William had reached a crisis point in his career. 'Wearied' with the situation at court he was in one sense glad to be away, and the peace negotiations did provide an opportunity for him to gain credit with his mistress. At the same time he knew that the power vacuum would be completely filled by Lord Robert and that, on his return, he might find himself permanently ousted from his position of principal political adviser. His absence might, indeed, try 'what we shall trust unto'.

One immediate result of Cecil's departure was a sudden change in religious policy. Dudley and his radical friends were able to act without restraint. Several deprived bishops and Marian officials who had been allowed to live in semi-retirement or had their movements only slightly restricted were now thrust into prison. On 10 June Nicholas Heath, late Archbishop of York, was sent to the Tower. He was swiftly followed by John Boxall, Mary's secretary, the erstwhile bishops of Exeter, and Bath and Wells, and others.[23]

At the end of July the court left Greenwich for the summer progress. Lord Robert was, of course, in daily attendance as the household travelled by easy stages south of the river to Windsor. It was reported that Elizabeth and he spent most of their time hunting and riding together. The Queen's affection for and reliance upon her Master of the Horse was now common knowledge. A Spanish diplomat in Antwerp treated Challoner to a disquisition on the state of England as he saw it: '. . . disunion, disfurniture, miscontentment of the old sort for change, of the new for want of liberty, the grudge of our nobles and gentlemen to see someone in such special favour, the little regard the Queen hath to marriage'.[24] And in Essex a gossip was examined by the magistrates for spreading the story that the Queen was pregnant by Lord Robert.[25] It was the kind of slander that crops up often in the records over the years and which was doubtless circulating almost continuously at all levels of society. In January 1563 Edmund Baxter of Suffolk was in trouble for saying that the Queen was a 'naughty woman' kept by Lord Robert; Lady Willoughby declared that when the Queen came to Ipswich she looked 'like one lately come out of childbed'. In December 1574 the Spanish ambassador confidently reported that there was a daughter born to Elizabeth and Robert. She was 'kept hidden although there are bishops to witness'.[26] Some people went beyond gossip and showed their disapproval of the favourite in petty ways. On 4 June 1560 Henry Manners, Earl of Rutland, sent Robert a present: '. . . one of the best dogs that ever hath been in this country. Yet notwithstanding, for the enmity that some beareth your Lordship, but specially towards me, they found means to steal the same dog, so as in ten days he could not be heard of, and besides that they did dye him of sundry colours . . .'[27]

Meanwhile, Cecil and his colleagues brought off a considerable diplomatic coup. The terms of the Treaty of Edinburgh were very favourable to England. The Secretary sent long despatches itemising the details of the agreement and the means by which they had been reached. He might reasonably have expected some commendation from his mistress. Instead he received letters full of bitter complaint. He had failed to obtain the restitution of Calais. He had not obliged the French to pay an indemnity to cover her war expenses. These were sensitive issues with Elizabeth but Cecil suspected that it was his rival who had nerved the Queen to stand on such an extreme position. When he returned south his suspicions were confirmed. He was received very coolly at court and Elizabeth refused to reimburse him for the bulk of his expenses. Norfolk, also, received nothing for his pains. Sir William was plunged into melancholy. Within days he wrote to the Earl of Bedford:

> The court is as I left it and therefore do I mind to leave it, as I have too much cause, if I durst write all. As soon as I can get Sir Nicholas Throckmorton placed [i.e. as Secretary] so soon I purpose to withdraw myself, which if I cannot do with ease I will

rather adventure some small displeasure for so have I cause rather to do than to continue with a perpetual displeasure to myself and my foolish convenience.[28]

To Throckmorton in Paris he wrote:

You must needs return . . . I dare not write that I might speak. God send her majesty understanding what shall be her surety. And so full of melancholy, I wish you were free from it . . . God send me hence with words to pray and sue for her majesty with all the power of mind and body . . .[29]

What he dared to say to the Queen in private we do not know but there is no mystery about what troubled him. He spoke confidentially to the Spanish ambassador and itemised his concerns.

I met the Secretary Cecil [de Quadra wrote to his master] whom I know to be in disgrace. Lord Robert, I was aware, was endeavouring to deprive him of his place. With little difficulty I led him to the subject, and after my many protestations and entreaties that I would keep secret what he was about to tell me, he said that the Queen was going on so strangely that he was about to withdraw from her service. It was a bad sailor, he said, who did not make for port when he saw a storm coming, and for himself he perceived the most manifest ruin impending over the Queen through her intimacy with Lord Robert. The Lord Robert had made himself master of the business of the state and of the person of the Queen, to the extreme injury of the realm, with the intention of marrying her, and she herself was shutting herself up in the palace to the peril of her health and life. That the realm would tolerate the marriage, he said he did not believe. He was, therefore, determined to retire into the country although he supposed they would send him to the Tower before they would let him go. He implored me for the love of God to remonstrate with the Queen, to persuade her not utterly to throw herself away as she was doing, and to remember what she owed to herself and to her subjects. Of Lord Robert he said twice that he would be better in paradise than here . . . He told me the Queen cared nothing for foreign princes. She did not believe she stood in any need of their support. She was deeply in debt, taking no thought how to clear herself and she had ruined her credit in the City.

Last of all, he said that they were thinking of destroying Lord Robert's wife. They had given out that she was ill, but she was not ill at all; she was very well and taking care not to be poisoned.

God, he trusted, would never permit such a crime to be accomplished or so wretched a conspiracy to prosper.[30]

This piece of unscrupulous, deliberate, gossip-mongering reveals just how desperate Cecil was. He was fighting for his political life and using every weapon that came to hand. He knew full well that telling de Quadra something in confidence was the best way of ensuring its rapid dissemination. It would reach the ears of the Queen, her friends and her enemies at home and abroad. The long term consequences of these poisonous calumnies were of little concern to Cecil as long as they achieved the short term objective of cooling Elizabeth's ardour for Lord Robert. The Queen was supposed to be alarmed at the wild stories which came to her ears and dismayed at the prospect of her Secretary's resignation. The large degree of exaggeration and half-truth contained in Cecil's complaint make it difficult to distinguish the realities around which it was woven. What is evident is that the Queen and her Master of the Horse were indulging in intimate behaviour of the type usually associated with lovers. Lord Robert exercised a strong influence over the sovereign and thereby had become a political figure of consequence. The talk of the couple getting married and of removing Amy from their path by poison was malicious gossip based only upon the most sinister kind of conjecture. Had Robert and Elizabeth planned a murder they would not have been so stupid as to advertise the fact. In her more abandoned moments of passion the Queen certainly wanted to marry Robert. He would have been less than human if he had not encouraged such a desire which would have brought him a prize far beyond the outstretched grasp of his ambition. But such a consummation could only be in a hazy future in which Amy had died from natural causes and political circles had been persuaded to accept Elizabeth's union with a subject. The sudden death of Robert's wife in suspicious circumstances would have been disastrous for any romantic plans the couple may have had. The only person in England who might have gained from such a tragedy was William Cecil. Within days of his telling de Quadra that Lady Dudley was doomed she was found with a broken neck at the foot of a staircase at Cumnor Place.

CHAPTER SEVEN

'SO PITIFULLY SLAIN'?

The sequence of events which led up to one of the most celebrated mysteries of the sixteenth century began in the autumn of 1559. William Owen, from whom Anthony Forster leased Cumnor Place, was married to Ursula Fettiplace, whose family were neighbours of the Hydes of Denchworth. Amy was among friends who belonged to a fairly close group of the leaders of Oxfordshire and Buckinghamshire society. Probably the new arrangement was designed to provide her with a more permanent base, somewhere that she could regard as her own home. She had for a companion Elizabeth Odingsells, a widowed sister of Mr Hyde. The ladies had their own quarters over the great hall in the west wing of the build-ing. The Forsters had their own apartments, as also did the elderly widow, Mrs Owen, William's mother. Cumnor Place was a grey stone, fourteenth-century, quadrangular building which had been built as the summer residence of the abbots of Abingdon. Although modern features, such as a long gallery, had been added it retained its essentially medieval character. Under Forster's cultured eye the house and, especially, the gardens began to take on a pleasing and comfortable appearance. He liked Cumnor, eventually bought it and was finally laid to rest beneath an impressive monument in the parish church. Forster was an accomplished singer and performer at the virginals, a travelled and interesting person who was well thought of in the area and well connected. Doubtless Amy and her companions exchanged visits with other leading local families, such as the Norreys of Rycote and the Williams of Thame. Life in the household of such a congenial man must have passed very pleasantly.

On Sunday, 8 September, however, the atmosphere at Cumnor Place was highly charged. It was the first day of Abingdon fair and Amy gave permission for all her attendants to go. She urged Mrs Odingsells to attend, but that lady refused, saying that it was not seemly for her to be in Abingdon when the town was full of servants and ill-bred people. At this Amy became unaccountably angry. Her companion tried to reason with her: if she went to the fair, who would dine with Lady Dudley? Amy replied that she would eat alone with Mrs Owen. This, apparently, is what she did, every other

member of the household having gone to Abingdon except the
determined Elizabeth Odingsells. It was the returning servants who
found Amy's body. She was lying at the foot of the shallow staircase
which led from her rooms to the hall

One of the men, by the name of Bowes, was sent off immediately
to Windsor to inform Lord Robert. On the road the next morning
he met someone he knew. It was Sir Thomas Blount, the principal
officer of Dudley's household, who was frequently employed carrying messages between and wife and who had just been despatched
to Cumnor on routine business.[1] Bowes hurried on to Windsor and
blurted out his story. Robert obtained little more than the bare facts
from the man, but the implications of those facts were not slow in
occurring to him. That evening a mounted messenger was pound-
ing along the road in pursuit of Blount.

> The greatness and the suddenness of the misfortune doth so
> perplex me, until I do hear from you how the matter standeth,
> or how this evil should light upon me, considering what the
> malicious world will bruit, as I can take no rest. And, because I
> have no way to purge myself of the malicious talk that I know the
> wicked world will use, but one which is the very plain truth to be
> known, I do pray you, as you have loved me, and do tender me
> and my quietness, and as now my special trust is in you, that
> [you] will use all the devises and means you can possible for the
> learning of the truth; wherein have no respect to any living
> person.[2]

Dudley ordered Blount to ensure that an impartial coroner's jury
was sworn and that no efforts were spared to ascertain all the facts.
At the same time he despatched a messenger to Norfolk to acquaint
Amy's next of kin, John Appleyard, of the tragedy. Blount knew
perfectly well that the important issue at stake was his master's
good name. He did not await Lord Robert's instructions. Instead of
riding directly to Cumnor he put up for the night at an inn in
Abingdon in order to sound out local opinion. Posing as a traveller
en route for Gloucestershire, he questioned the landlord about the
news that had set the entire district buzzing. How did people
account for Lady Dudley's death? Well, some said one thing, some
another. But what did the landlord think? 'By my troth,' the man
replied, 'I judge it a very misfortune [i.e. accident], because it
chanced at that honest gentleman's house, his great honesty doth
much curb the evil thoughts of the people.'[3]

When Blount arrived at Cumnor Place the next day (10 September)
and came into possession of Dudley's letter he found the coroner

already with his jury. He conveyed to them his master's wishes that they should do their work thoroughly and without respect of persons. He was able to report to Lord Robert that the jury were 'as wise and as able men to be chosen upon such a matter as any men, being but countrymen, as ever I saw.'[4] He thought that there was no chance of their being overawed by their social superiors since some of them were 'very enemies to Anthony Forster'.[5] It is interesting to note that locally the important issue was not only Dudley's involvement in any possible foul play but also Forster's. Common rumour probably asserted that the two men were in collusion to dispose of Robert's wife. Blount went on to make his own enquiries among the servants, and especially with Amy's maid, Pinto (or Pirto). What did she make of her mistress's strange death – was it chance or villainy?

> She said by her faith she doth judge very chance, and neither done by man nor by herself. For herself, she said, she was a good virtuous gentlewoman, and daily would pray upon her knees; and divers times she saith that she hath heard her pray to God to deliver her from desperation. Then, said I, she might have an evil toy in her mind. No, good Mr Blount, said Pinto, do not judge so of my words; if you should so gather, I am sorry I said so much.[6]

The gentleman was not wholly convinced. Amy's unusual behaviour on the morning of the death, the odd circumstances of her fall and other inexplicable things she had said and done in recent weeks disturbed him: 'My Lord, it is most strange that this chance should fall upon you. It passeth the judgment of any man to say how it is; but truly the tales I do hear of her maketh me to think she had a strange mind in her.'[7] In concluding his report Blount urged Lord Robert to turn from sorrow to joy in his innocence, which fearless enquiry would soon reveal and then 'malicious reports shall turn upon their backs'.[8]

Meanwhile the news had exploded like a bombshell in the court. Robert and his friends were in a state of considerable agitation. Enemies, and all who enjoyed tittle-tattle, were enjoying the situation hugely. Elizabeth was deeply distressed. Her first reaction was to distance herself as far as possible from the tragedy. She sent Dudley away from her. He was ordered to remain in his house at Kew until the coroner's verdict was announced. There he stayed for several days, his anxiety made worse by idleness. If he had been allowed to remain at Windsor or to go to Cumnor, he could have kept close watch on the situation, could have taken some action to safeguard his position. At Kew he could only fret, send messages and interrogate such visitors who deigned to come to him.

One such was William Cecil. The see-saw which had plunged Robert into disfavour had raised him instantly into the Queen's confidence. With her dearest companion banished and under a cloud Elizabeth needed someone else to turn to for advice and support. Mr Secretary was at hand. Events had fallen out remarkably well for him. But he was far too clever to be openly exultant. Elizabeth would not have tolerated such an attitude towards a man who was, in addition to his other problems, mourning a dead wife. Cecil, therefore, visited his despondent rival at Kew, bringing words of conventional consolation and, probably, personal messages from the Queen. Within days Robert wrote to thank him.

> Sir, I thank you very much for your being here, and the great friendship you have shown towards me I shall not forget. I am very loath to wish you here again but I would be very glad to be with you there. I pray you let me hear from you, what you think best for me to do. If you doubt, I pray you ask the question [i.e. if you do not know what to advise me ask the Queen if she will permit me to return], for the sooner you can advise me [to come] thither, the more I shall thank you. I am sorry so sudden a chance should breed me so great a change, for methinks I am here all the while as it were in a dream, and too far, too far from the place I am bound to be, where, methinks also, this long, idle time cannot excuse me for the duty I have to discharge elsewhere. I pray you help him that sues to be at liberty out of so great a bondage. Forget me not, though you see me not and I will remember you and fail you not, and so wish you well to do. In haste this morning.
>
> I beseech you, Sir, forget me not to offer up the humble sacrifice you promised me.
>   Your very assured,
>   R. Dudley[9]

The fortunes of the two men had changed drastically. Yet a close reading of the letter suggests that their positions were by no means completely reversed. Dudley begs for Cecil's aid but he still is able to offer a bargaining counter, 'I will remember you and fail you not'. Robert, it seems, still believed himself to have considerable influence with the Queen.

Everything now depended on the result of the inquest. Elizabeth waited for it as anxiously as Robert, eager for the decision that would make it possible to reinstate her favourite. She was reported to be pale, listless and irritable, seldom venturing from her private apartments. Dudley wrote more letters urging Blount to ensure a full, unbiased investigation. The servant wrote back assuring his lordship that all was being done thoroughly and correctly. It was about 13 or 14 September that Robert received an unofficial letter from the foreman of the Cumnor jury, a man named Smith. Probably the fellow, realising how concerned Dudley was, thought to earn some reward for setting his mind at rest. Robert certainly was very relieved to hear that the jury had so far found nothing to indicate that Amy's death was due to anything other than accident. But he was also anxious lest this irregular correspondence should suggest that he had been tampering with the course of justice. He was passionately concerned that justice should be done and be seen to be done. He had to clear his name of every vestige of suspicion. Everything depended on it – his position in the court, his wealth, his political influence and certainly any prospect of marriage with the Queen. For though technically that now became a possibility, morally it was more impossible than it had ever been. In his eagerness Robert toyed with the idea of a second investigation and with calling in impartial referees.

> Assuredly I do wish that another substantial company of honest men might try again for the more knowledge of truth. I have also requested to Sir Richard Blount, who is a perfect honest gentleman, to help to the furtherance thereof. I trust he be with you, or before long, and Mr. Norreys likewise. Appleyard, I hear, hath been there, as I appointed, and Arthur Robsart her brother. If any more of her friends had been to be had, I would also have caused them to have seen and been privy to all the dealing there.[10]

Inconclusive though the news from Cumnor was, it was sufficient for Elizabeth to send for her ō ō and to welcome him back to her court and her love. Her relief was as intense as her previous depression had been. She grasped eagerly at the indication of Robert's innocence and when, some days later, the coroner's jury formally brought in a verdict of death by misadventure she announced the matter closed and Lord Robert restored to full favour. The court was ordered into mourning for Lady Dudley and remained so until mid-October.[11]

The funeral itself took place on Sunday, 22 September in St Mary's Church, Oxford. It was a lavish affair, as befitted a lady of her station: the church was draped in black, with coats of arms prominently displayed; a large, raised hearse to receive the coffin and round it a rail and velvet-covered stools for the principal mourners. The service was attended by representatives of the court, the university and the corporation of Oxford. The Queen's proxy as chief mourner was her old friend, Margery Norreys. Presiding over the ceremony were the great kings of arms, Garter, Lancaster and Clarenceux with Rouge Croix pursuivant, all resplendent in their heraldic gowns. Forty poor men and women in black gowns, provided for the occasion, led the procession from Gloucester College outside the city. They were followed by the choir and clergy, immediately before the pall bearers. After the coffin came Mrs Norreys and a large group of gentlewomen, yeomen and representatives of town and gown, followed by 'all that would'. The preacher at the service was Francis Babington, Master of Balliol and a protégé of Dudley. He was a celebrated trimmer, having achieved steady ecclesiastical preferment under Henry VIII, Edward VI, Mary and Elizabeth. Years later it was affirmed that this career-conscious cleric had tripped up in his sermon and referred to 'this lady so pitifully slain'. The story first appeared a quarter of a century after the event in *Leicester's Commonwealth* and it is very unlikely that there is any truth in it. After the ceremony there was 'great dinner and dole of monies [for] as many as came'.[12] It was very solemn and splendid and it cost Dudley 2,000 marks. Robert's absence from his wife's funeral has been commented on unfavourably by some historians. In fact, it has no significance at all: it was by no means the custom in the upper ranks of society for widows and widowers to follow their spouses' coffins. Principal mourners were usually, as in this case, of the same sex as the deceased.

Amy was buried but she was not forgotten. For the rest of his life Robert was held responsible in the public imagination for his wife's tragic death. Days after the affair at Cumnor, Thomas Lever, a Puritan minister in Coventry, wrote to inform the Council 'in these parts seemeth unto me to be a grievous and dangerous suspicion and muttering of the death of her which was the wife of my Lord Robert Dudley'.[13] It was the same all over the country, and the decision of twelve good men and true had little impact on popular opinion. Nor were the English alone in enjoying evil gossip. At the end of October Throckmorton wrote to his fellow diplomat, Sir Thomas Chamberlain:

My friends advertise me from home that my Lord Robert's wife is dead and hath by mischance broken her own neck, and here it openly bruited by the French that her neck was broken, with such other appendances I am withal brought to be weary of my life. I

Pray God hold his holy hand over us, and so evil be the reports as I am ashamed to write them. But as you are a wise man and can consider how much it importeth the Queen's majesty's honour and her realm to have them same ceased, so I trust you will by your letters thence, as I do from hence, help to do some good for the appeasing of the same . . . I write unto you because . . . we be both in one ship and . . . the tempest must touch us both alike.[14]

The rumour was never stopped, and the 'murder' of Amy remained until the end of his days the blackest stain on Dudley's reputation. The story entered popular folklore, was from time to time deliberately revived by enemies and libellers, and achieved its final, highly embellished form in Walter Scott's *Kenilworth*.

Modern historians, even those inimical towards Dudley, now accept the verdict of the coroner's jury. Medical knowledge unavailable to those sixteenth-century yeomen has been called upon to provide likely interpretations of Amy's behaviour and the circumstances of her death, and it is now possible to piece together the story of Lady Dudley's last months in such a way that even the most suspicious incidents can be explained.

A few days after the event Robert received a note of condolence from his brother-in-law, Huntingdon. It came as a postscript to an inconsequential letter accompanying a gift of venison pies:

As I ended my letter I understood by letters the death of my lady your wife. I doubt not but long before this time you have considered what a happy hour it is which bringeth man from sorrow to joy, from mortality to immortality, from care and trouble to rest and quietness, and that the Lord above worketh all for the best to them that love him. Well, I will leave my babbling, and bid the buzzard cease to teach the falcon to fly, and so end my rude postscript.[15]

It seems that members of the intimate family circle knew that, for Amy, death was a happy release. This hints at some affliction of body or mind from which she was known to be suffering. The first positive suggestion we have of any such condition occurs in the report, already mentioned, written by de Feria on 18 April 1559. Referring to the relationship between Robert and Elizabeth he said 'people talk of this so freely that they go so far as to say that his wife has a malady in one of her breasts, and the Queen is only waiting her death to marry Lord Robert'.[16] De Feria's successor seems to have known nothing about Amy's alleged ailment but, in March 1560, he reported having heard Dudley say 'if he lives a year he will be in another position from that which he at present holds'.[17] Four days before the Cumnor accident de Quadra had a much less ambiguous statement from the lips of the Queen herself. She told him 'that the Lord Robert's wife was dead or nearly so, and begged me to say nothing about it'.[18] This squares with Cecil's claim that Elizabeth and her favourite were putting it about that Lady Dudley was ill. Cecil denied that Amy was anything of the sort; he chose, instead, to circulate the poison rumour. It suited his book to do so. The thought that Robert's wife should die, thus freeing him to marry the Queen, was anathema to Cecil. However, if die she must, it were better that foul play be suspected than that she succumb to an illness. It is hardly surprising, therefore, to discover that the Secretary's statement is the only one which goes against the general run of the evidence. Blount, it will be recalled, unearthed evidence of Amy's disturbed state of mind, and Pinto had spoken of her mistress praying to be delivered from desperation.

Irritability, depression, afflictions of the breast, death from a broken neck – all these suggest two possibilities. One is breast cancer. It is a painful and emotionally disturbing disease and there was no means of combatting its inexorable encroachment. A woman suffering from such a malady might well become 'desperate' and be prone to bouts of irrational anger. Amy's husband would have known that she was dying and thus no sinister interpretation need be placed upon Robert and Elizabeth's prophecies. Furthermore, as the disease develops, cancerous deposits are built up in the bones. If the cervical spine is affected in this way, the slightest jolt (such as would arise from simply walking down stairs) is enough to cause a fracture (in other words a broken neck).[19] A slightly less convincing theory, but one which adequately takes account of the available medical evidence, is that Amy was suffering from an *aortic aneurism*, a morbid enlargement of the great artery of the left ventricle of the heart. The symptoms of this condition are pains in the chest, sometimes accompanied by a swelling on the chest wall, and a secondary complaint known as *ischaemia*. This is mental instability caused by insufficient blood reaching the brain. The patient would certainly be given to fits of rage and depression. Again any slight sudden pressure can burst the aneurism, whereupon death is instantaneous. If such a death had overtaken Amy, even near the foot of the staircase, she might well have pitched forward awkwardly and struck the floor with sufficient force to break her neck.[20] Natural causes can thus be made to account for all the circumstances surrounding Amy Dudley's death. Robert's behaviour is also entirely consonant with that of a man expecting his spouse to die but not in the way she did. His urging of the fullest and frankest enquiry is not the action of a guilty wife-murderer.

Throughout the whole sorry affair we find no statement of affection by Robert for Amy, no evidence of grief, no sense of loss, only a frantic concern with his own predicament. This has sometimes been taken, quite unfairly, as evidence that all love had gone out of his marriage, that 'as a husband he had . . . been a failure'.[21] We know nothing of what Robert felt or said in private. The only letters extant concern the coroner's examination and the reaction of the Queen. But even if these few documents did accurately reflect all the emotions he felt after his wife's death they would provide inadequate evidence to charge him with heartlessness. Let any man put himself in Robert's situation – his wife dead and himself suspected of her murder. Even the deepest personal sorrow would take second place to the instinct for self-preservation. As well as being concerned to clear his own name, Robert had the responsibility – to Amy herself, her kinsmen, to Anthony Forster and all the people at Cumnor – of ensuring that the circumstances of the tragedy were fully investigated and the truth discovered. The responsibility he clearly discharged diligently. That the first youthful passion had gone out of his relationship with Amy there is no reason to doubt. Their long periods of enforced separation and Robert's involvement with the Queen must have taken their toll. If we are right about Amy's illness, that, too, will have played its part: the 'malady in one of her breasts' must have inhibited their moments of intimacy. Yet, as we have seen, within the limitations imposed by his office, Robert remained a dutiful and attentive husband to the end. The evidence will not support the traditional view of Dudley as a man who callously cast aside his wife and waited impatiently for her to die so that he could marry the Queen.

But as the dust of the Cumnor affair settled that was precisely the issue that dominated English politics. At court and in diplomatic circles men were speculating on what would happen now that the obstacle to Elizabeth's marriage with Lord Dudley was removed. Everyone closely involved seems to have over-reacted to the situation. The couple were watched and any sign that their relationship was cooling or intensifying was noted. Cecil and his supporters continued to do all they could to keep the recent scandal alive, and to raise at home and abroad the gruesome spectacle of 'King Robert', another infamous Dudley ruling the country. Robert's supporters vigorously declared his proven innocence. It is no exaggeration to say that the court was in a turmoil. Old friendships became strained. Traditional enemies were united in support of, or opposition to, the favourite. Many who should have been giving the Queen disinterested advice were afraid to declare their opinions, and with some cause; even the beloved Kate Ashley, who had been Elizabeth's principal attendant since her childhood, fell from favour over the issue. Her husband was heard to utter words against Lord Robert and this was enough to send the Queen into a frenzy of rage. Kate and John were dismissed from the court and a distraught Mistress Ashley had to seek Dudley's aid to gain reinstatement.[22] In November there was a 'great affray' between some of Dudley's men and Pembroke's retainers. No details are recorded but it is not difficult to see what it was that caused a temporary rift between the two friends.[23] Nor is it surprising to find letters to and from courtiers at this time carrying contradictory information. Sir Henry Killigrew was convinced that 'Lord Robert shall run away with the hare and have the Queen'. But one of Throckmorton's correspondents reported to him, 'The Queen's majesty looketh not so hearty and well as she did by a great deal. And surely the matter of my lord Robert doth much perplex her. And if [the marriage] is never likely to take place, and the talk thereof is somewhat slack, or generally misliked . . .'[24]

In Paris Mary Stuart scoffed 'The Queen of England is about to marry her horsemaster'.[25] Yet by mid-December Cecil was confident: 'I know surely that my Lord Robert hath more fear than hope, and so doth the Queen give him cause'.[26] Throckmorton was not so sanguine. He wrote to Cecil a letter which was designed to give the Secretary additional ammunition for his battle against Dudley:

> . . . if her majesty do so foully forget herself in her marriage as the bruit runneth here, never think to bring anything to pass, either here or elsewhere. I would you did hear the lamentation, the declamation, and sundry affections which hath course here for that matter. Sir, do not so forget yourself as to think you do enough because you do not further the matter. Remember your mistress is young and subject to affections. You are her sworn counsellor and in great credit with her. You know there be some of your colleagues which have promoted the matter. There is nobody reputed of judgement and authority that doth to her Majesty disallow it, for such as be so wise as to mislike it be too timorous to show it, so as her majesty's affection doth find rather wind and sail to set it forward than any advice to quench it. My duty to her, my good will to you doth move me to speak plainly.[27]

But such letters were counter-productive. A few days later Cecil had to write warning Throckmorton not to make any more comments upon the situation at the English court, and Killigrew told him bluntly that criticisms of Dudley only made the Queen angry.[28]

The two people at the centre of this controversy were, obviously, under an enormous emotional strain. Elizabeth, like Dudley, railed against fate which had so cruelly intervened to complicate her life. Amy's death was a double disaster for the Queen: it obliged her to make good her private protestations of love for Robert; at the same time it made it virtually impossible for her to do so. She was vigorous in defence of her ō ō and became more so as suspicion against him mounted. When, in November, a messenger from Throckmorton cautiously voiced the version of Lady Dudley's death which was common currency in France, Elizabeth retorted angrily 'that the matter had been tried in the country and found to be contrary to that which was reported, saying that [Lord Robert] was then in the court and none of his [people] at the attempt at his wife's house, and that it fell out as should neither touch his honesty nor her honour.[29]

In October the Queen decided to grant Robert Dudley an earldom. This was to be a further public acknowledgement of her regard and, perhaps, a move to make him more acceptable as a potential husband. It was not well-advised. If the Dudleys were to have some of their father's honour restored to them, Ambrose should have been the first to be ennobled. It was an act which could only exacerbate jealously and ill-feeling. Some of her advisers may have been bold enough to protest. Nevertheless, all preparations went ahead for the investiture. The patent was drawn up. Then, at the last moment, in a fit of rage, Elizabeth took a penknife and cut the document to shreds. Again we are left to conjecture about the feelings of this complex woman. What prompted this sudden reversal? Was it, perhaps, a resentment that Robert could not share her sacrifice? She could go on giving to him. She could make him richer and more powerful. And he would go on taking all she gave. Yet she was denied the one thing that she wanted from him. Whatever the Queen's motives were, they temporarily dashed Dudley's hopes, and his enemies were exultant.

Throckmorton, at Cecil's prompting, gave highly coloured reports about the French reaction to a possible royal alliance with Lord Robert, but there were other important foreign powers and the Queen avidly enquired about opinion in these lands. The most important was Spain. De Quadra's predecessor, it will be recalled,

had marked Dudley's potential importance very early in the reign
and urged his master to renew the friendship with Robert which
had begun in the previous reign. King Philip had acknowledged
that Elizabeth might choose a husband from within her own realm
and, if this happened, he wished to be on good terms with the
fortunate man. This was important for international peace and also
for Philip's dream of reuniting England and the papacy. Robert
and Elizabeth now played upon the Spanish King's pious hopes. In
January Henry Sidney went to de Quadra as their representative
with a startling question: should Philip support Elizabeth's
marriage with Dudley if it were to be the means of restoring
Catholicism in England? The ambassador was suspicious and non-
committal but he wrote home for advice and sought interviews on
the subject with the Queen and with Lord Robert. Elizabeth was
coy but she did not deny the scheme Sidney had suggested. As for
Dudley, he urged de Quadra to commend the plan heartily to both
sovereigns.[30]

If we were to take these clandestine negotiations at face value, we
should have to conclude, with Dudley's detractors, that he was a
man who totally subordinated religious conviction to personal
ambition. In fact, few historians have accepted that the Queen or
any of her advisers contemplated overthrowing the recent church
settlement and turning back the clock to the days of Queen Mary.
It is not possible to say with certainty what lay behind these
manoeuvrings or even whether the Queen and Dudley were pursuing the same objectives. They have to be seen against the
background of European affairs. In November the Council of Trent
was reconvened and England was invited to send representatives. A
direct refusal would have been undiplomatic and the government
always had to consider the threat of a Catholic alliance against
heretic states. In December Francis II of France died and the position of his widow, Mary Stuart, once again became uncertain.
Relations with both Scotland and France thus had to be reassessed
and there was the possibility that the Pope might support Mary's
claim to the English throne. Lines had to be kept open to all potential allies. Holding out tantalizing promises to other governments
was to be a feature of Elizabethan diplomacy and it may well be that
that was all the Queen intended when she sanctioned the overtures
to de Quadra. Robert may well have hoped for another outcome:
that Elizabeth would conclude that there was sufficient rapport
abroad for her to follow the urging of her heart. As for promises
about religion, they were only promises and more easily broken
than kept.

Within the court Elizabeth kept everyone guessing, Cecil remained in her confidence. He disapproved of the backstairs diplomacy but seems to have been powerless to put a stop to it. Robert's intimacy with the Queen was encouraged but he received no firm answer from her on the subject of marriage. By April he was lodged in apartments next to the Queen's at Greenwich and he and Elizabeth were almost inseparable. It was a frustrating situation for him. According to one report, Robert at one stage demanded that the Queen either marry him or give him leave to go abroad and serve as a captain in one of the Spanish armies. Elizabeth declined both alternatives and Robert remained dutifully at court.[31] The negotiations with de Quadra dawdled along, each side demanding impossible conditions and guarantees. They would have slowed to a gradual standstill within a few months. But in April Cecil reasserted his authority and put a sudden check upon them. He discovered compromising correspondence carried by a chaplain of Sir Edward Waldegrave, a Marian councillor. Upon this slender foundation he constructed a Catholic 'plot'. Waldegrave and other prominent papists were arrested, English Catholics were given a serious shock, and the Spanish ambassador's negotiations came to an abrupt end. The whole incident illustrates very clearly the different ways in which the two men closest to Elizabeth approached their problems. Robert always worked directly with, or upon, the Queen. He sought to enforce her wishes. He tried to persuade her to see matters his way. He worked through others to influence her. And because of the hold he had on her affections he was often successful. Where Dudley was open Cecil was devious. Subtlety and unscrupulousness came naturally to him. He always contended for what he thought was best for Elizabeth and England, not for what Elizabeth wanted or could be persuaded to want. If circumstances were against him, he went about by intrigue to change circumstances.

The crises passed and gave way to a summer of relaxed gaiety in the royal court. The relations between Elizabeth and Robert had settled down. There was less talk of marriage but Sweet Robin was clearly established as 'most favoured person'. He still had not achieved a position of formal political authority but he was content, for the time being, with the very real informal influence he wielded. During the progress there were lavish entertainments at which the Queen and Lord Robert presided, presenting to all observers the vision of a happy and devoted couple. On one occasion Elizabeth and her ladies went, disguised, into Windsor Park to watch Robert shooting a wager with other courtiers. It was all light-hearted and less intense than the preceding months. The situation had stabilised and people could now adjust themselves to it.

One group of such people were the benchers of the Inner Temple. These worthy men of the law were, during the summer of 1561, anxiously seeking a patron. A dispute had arisen over the ownership of Lyon's Inn, an inn of chancery. The Middle Temple, who also claimed it, had powerful allies in Sir Nicholas Bacon, the Lord Keeper, and the two Chief Justices, and seemed certain to win the day. The Inner Temple did not lack for influential members – the Duke of Norfolk, Lord Hunsdon, Howard of Effinghamn, to mention but a few – but seemingly they could do little for the Inn. The Parliament of the Inner Temple, therefore, appealed to the one man who was closer to the Queen than all others. And Lord Robert did not disappoint them. He persuaded Elizabeth to stay all proceedings in the case by sending her ring to the Lord Keeper. The benchers were extremely grateful. In November they passed a resolution that:

> no person or persons whatsoever now being or which at any time hereafter shall be of the fellowship or company of this our House of the Inner Temple, shall, in any wise or by any manner of means, be retained of counsel or otherwise give any counsel, help, or aid in any matter or cause against the said right honourable Lord Robert Dudley or against any of his heirs, but that we and every of us and our successors shall at all times hereafter be of counsel with the said Lord Robert Dudley and his heirs upon his and their pleasure therein signified to us or them in that behalf; and that the arms of the said right honourable Lord Robert Dudley shall be set up and placed in some seemly and convenient place in the hall of this our House of the Inner Temple as a continual monument of his lordship's said goodness and great good will towards this House.[32]

This event began a long association between Dudley and the Inner Temple. The very next Christmas Robert (who was admitted to membership of the Inner Temple on 22 December) held court there. It was the custom of the inns to stage elaborate festivities throughout the holiday. The revels of 1561, however, were celebrated with a richness of display and an extravagance in feasting probably never before equalled. Events began with a procession through the City:

> The 27th day of December came riding through London a lord of misrule, in clean complete harness, gilt, with a hundred great horse and gentlemen riding gorgeously with chains of gold and their

horses goodly trapped, unto the Temple, for there was great cheer all Christmas . . . and great revels as ever was for the gentlemen of the Temple every day, for many of the Council was there.[33]

And not only of the Council: noblemen, officers of the royal household, the Lieutenant of the Tower, aldermen and members of the livery companies all made up the complement of the benchers' guests. Over them all presided Lord Robert, in the revels guise of Prince Palaphilos, sitting on a raised dais, his arms (a winged horse argent on a field azure) blazoned above. Here he received the homage of his court, dubbed Knights of the imaginary Order of Pegasus, and was

> served with tender meats, sweet fruits and dainty delicates, confectioned with curious cookery, as it seemed wonder a world to observe the provision. And at every course the trumpets blew the courageous blast of deadly war, with noise of drum and fife, with the sweet harmony of violins, sackbuts, recorders and cornets, with other instruments of music as it seemed Apollo's harp had tuned their stroke.[34]

Robert had good cause to celebrate. The previous day the reinstatement of the Dudley family had been completed: Ambrose had been created Earl of Warwick and had received a grant of a large portion of his father's confiscated lands.

The entertainments included a tilt, a tourney, a masque and a play. Both dramatic presentations, as was customary, were full of topical, political allusions. The masque was a classical allegory based on the story of Pallas, Perseus and Medusa. The hero, Perseus, was a representation of Lord Robert, who was figured as a champion ridding England of the Gorgon whose many heads – false religion, foreign enemies, rival claimants to the throne, etc. – threatened its peace and security. The play was the early tragedy *Gorboduc*, written for the occasion by Templars Thomas Norton and Thomas Sackville. It told the sanguinary tale of a British king who plunged the realm into war and unleashed all kinds of evil and misery upon his family by setting aside primogeniture and choosing his own heir. The moral was that sovereigns should marry and put an end to the hopes and ambitions of rival claimants to the throne. Taken together, the two productions conveyed clear, if oblique advice to Queen Elizabeth to take as her husband Prince Palaphilos.

Marry him she did not, but she did continue to bestow favours. At the time of Ambrose's ennoblement, grants of old Dudley lands also came to Robert.[35] In the following summer he received licences to export 80,000 undressed white cloths, an enormously lucrative

concession which enabled him to raise money at any time by sub-
letting all, or part, of his rights. In October he was given a pension
of £1,000 a year, chargeable on the London customs.

These were all signs of the complete confidence Elizabeth now
reposed in the man who was still only, officially, her Master of the
Horse, but the year 1562 was to bring forth much more dramatic
evidence.

'WORTHY TO MARRY THE GREATEST QUEEN'

It was Robert's advocacy of the Huguenot cause which persuaded the Queen, uncharacteristically, to become embroiled in the 'Newhaven adventure'. The unstable position in France had, by April 1562, degenerated into civil war. The rival groupings were decided largely by religious allegiance; the Catholics led by the Guises and the Huguenots by the Prince of Condé and Admiral de Coligny. The plight of French Protestants seemed grave and they cast about for allies. Throckmorton urged Elizabeth to come to the aid of her co-religionists and his appeal was echoed in English Protestant circles. The man who made himself the leader of an interventionist policy was Robert Dudley. Most of the Council were sympathetic to his point of view but it was Dudley, who was not a member of the Council, who led them. Cecil was forced into a subordinate role. He tried, and failed, to commend a policy of conciliating the rival parties in France. Having failed, there was little he could do but implement the policy of his colleagues. The Secretary wrote the letters, sent the messengers, passed on conciliar instructions, but it was Lord Robert who initiated those instructions. His increasing political activity was based upon his widespread contacts throughout the Protestant world and his English friends and agents. During the winter he had been in correspondence with Huguenot leaders and in May he sent Henry Sidney to France as his representative. It was Sidney who effected a reconciliation with Throckmorton. No longer urged on by Cecil, the diplomat did not find it difficult to revise his opinion of Lord Robert, a man who shared his own forthright Protestantism. That summer Dudley stood godfather to Throckmorton's youngest child. It was the cementing of a relationship that was to prove strong, creative and long-lasting. After Throckmorton's permanent recall to London in 1564 John Aylmer wrote to him expressing sentiments that many English Protestants shared: 'God be thanked that hath joined that noble and good-natured gentleman's heart and yours, for both shall in the end have cause to rejoice in one another's amity, seeing that likeness of minds, especially in the chiefest point of faith and religion, have knit you thus fast together'.[1] Other agents soon followed Sidney across the Channel.

They were men who had identified themselves with the Dudley interest and would continue to serve him for years to come – Henry Killigrew, Thomas Leighton and Edward Horsey.

Negotiations continued throughout June and July. Condé was asking for men and money. In return he proffered a prize Elizabeth could scarcely resist – Calais. Unfortunately Calais was not in Huguenot hands. Newhaven (Le Havre), however, was and it was eventually agreed that this harbour would be ceded to England until the more northerly one had been captured. Meanwhile, the Catholics were everywhere triumphant in France and even Cecil had come to realise that positive, military support was the only practicable policy for Elizabeth's government. But the actual terms of the English aid were not decided till early October. Then the order went out for 6,000 soldiers to be despatched to Newhaven and Dieppe. Probably Robert begged the Queen to allow him to take command of this force. Elizabeth would not permit him to leave her side but she did the next best thing – she gave the generalship to Ambrose Dudley, Earl of Warwick.

All was ready for Ambrose's departure when a new crisis at home halted him. The Queen was dying. 1562 had been a bad year for smallpox. Hundreds of people of high and low degree had succumbed. Soon after arriving at Hampton Court Elizabeth developed a fever and became delirious. Her physicians gathered round but could do little except encourage the disease to reach – and pass – its crisis. But the crisis did not come; the pustules were slow to develop and the Queen grew weaker. She would only allow her favourite maids to attend her. The lady who was most constantly at her bedside was Robert's sister, Mary Sidney. Her devotion proved costly. Sir Henry, years later, described what had happened: 'When I left my wife at court to go to Newhaven she was a full, fair lady; in my eyes the fairest. On my return I found her as foul a lady as the smallpox could make her . . . Now she lives solitary, *sicut Niclicorax in domicilio suo*'.[2] At the time, of course, all attention was focused not on Lady Sidney but on the Queen and the succession. Elizabeth hovered on the brink of death, too ill to make her wishes known. In the Council support was divided between the claims of Catherine Grey, currently in the Tower for marrying without royal permission, and the Earl of Huntingdon. There is no reliable evidence of Robert's preference. Presumably he would have supported his ultra-Protestant brother-in-law. Fortunately he never had to declare himself. The smallpox eruptions broke out, dried, formed scabs and began to fall away. The crisis had passed.

Those few anxious days were crucial for Dudley. He was at the height of his influence and had begun to establish himself as a real political power in the land. Suddenly his only support seemed to be removed. Whatever fracas might ensue on the Queen's death it seemed unlikely that he would survive. It was, therefore, all the more gratifying when, in one of her moments of clarity, Elizabeth made a staggering demand of the assembled councillors. In the event of her death they were to appoint her beloved Lord Robert Dudley as Protector of the Realm with a salary of £20,000. She went on to tell them of her trust and love for Robert – love, she assured them, which had never involved them in any impropriety. She gave another, very significant, order: Robert's body-servant who slept in his bedchamber (a man named Tamworth) was to receive £500 a year. This highly-trusted servant was probably the only third party who could confirm her statement about her degree of intimacy with Dudley. He had witnessed the comings and goings between their chambers late at night; had stood guard at the door while Robert and Elizabeth enjoyed their moments of intimate friendship. His continued loyalty was important if her reputation was to remain unsullied. It was worth a £500 annuity.[3]

Even those who knew of Elizabeth's deep feelings for her favourite must have been taken aback at the realisation of just how complete her trust in him was. The Council, of course, were never called upon to carry out her request. They were, however, obliged to receive Lord Robert into their midst. The Queen appointed him and Norfolk to the Council on 20 October. It was perhaps the most gratifying of all the marks of favour that had so far come his way. Elizabeth kept her Council fairly small and only nominated men whose judgement she valued and respected. Robert had worked hard to merit a place in her government. He had interested himself in every aspect of national and international affairs. He had given advice when called for. He had provided the Queen with snippets of information gleaned from his own sources. He had negotiated on her behalf with councillors, diplomats and local officials. When given the chance he had initiated policies of his own and shown himself skilful in carrying them into effect. He deserved his place at the Council table, he valued it, and to the end of his days that place was seldom empty.

The Newhaven affair was a failure. This was not Warwick's fault. Like most of Elizabeth's few military enterprises it suffered from divided counsels at home and unreliable allies abroad. For a start Elizabeth would not allow many English troops to be sent to the main areas of conflict. As a result Rouen and Dieppe fell to the Catholic besiegers and Warwick's army was penned down in

Newhaven. Then the rival French parties began to draw together against the 'intruder'. National pride was outraged at the prospect of losing Calais, and the English were now everyone's enemies. For Warwick and his Puritan suite* the Protestant crusade had now degenerated into a grab for Calais. Elizabeth was determined to force her allies into meeting their obligations to exchange Newhaven for the old English port. Warwick was therefore ordered to stay and defend his position, come what may. For weeks he and his troops held on bravely, even when contrary winds prevented supplies being brought in. Warwick urged the government to sanction a larger military commitment. If he could move on to the offensive while French affairs were still in some disorder, he argued, he might be able to make important gains which would give England a good bargaining position. He was strongly supported by his brother, but the Queen would have none of it. She would not even provide sufficient funds for repairing the defences of Newhaven. She could, and did, demonstrate her confidence in Warwick by admitting him to the Order of the Garter in April but that was the extent of her commitment.

Meanwhile plague struck the besieged garrison. In July, with his men dying in large numbers every day, Ambrose was forced to seek Elizabeth's permission to surrender.

The Queen agreed and Warwick offered to discuss peace terms with the attackers. It was while standing on the wall and parleying with his opposite number that he was shot in the leg by a French musketeer. The wound never healed properly and for the rest of his life Ambrose was lame and had to use a stick. Though feverish and in pain, he remained at Newhaven until he had concluded arrangements for the honourable withdrawal of his army.

Ambrose arrived back at Portsmouth on 31 July, was conveyed to the house of a Mr White at nearby Southwick and was there put to bed. Thomas Wood, one of Warwick's Puritan companions, wrote immediately to Robert to tell him of his brother's condition. The Earl's preservation, he said, was miraculous. Fortunately he had been so distressed by sea-sickness during the crossing that he had been able to forget the pain in his leg, but now he was suffering considerably.[4] As soon as he received the letter Robert set out to visit Ambrose, a compassionate move which earned him the Queen's displeasure. She sent a message after him complaining that Robert was putting himself in contact with the plague and warning him to stay his return for fear of introducing it at court.

*He had with him as chaplain William Whittingham, the Calvinist leader of the Frankfurt exiles, and many other prominent Puritans.

Elizabeth did not blame the Dudleys for the failure of the Newhaven venture. They were too firmly lodged in her affection and she was too angry with her fickle French allies. Indeed, it was in the summer of 1563, while Ambrose was struggling with a discontented garrison and an angry citizenry, that Robert received more striking proof of royal favour. Ever since the beginning of the reign he had been seeking to rebuild the Dudley interests in the Midlands. He had failed to acquire Dudley Castle but his brother had received Warwick Castle and between them they now controlled much of their father's former territory in the area. Yet Robert still lacked an impressive Midlands seat of his own. There were few suitable buildings available under royal ownership. But there was Kenilworth, which belonged to the Duchy of Lancaster. In 1553 it had been granted to Robert's father but his ownership had only lasted a few months. Much needed doing to the buildings to make them into a residence sufficiently splendid and comfortable for Robert to live in and to entertain the Queen in, but they had many advantages. Kenilworth was only five miles from Warwick. It had been, however briefly, a Dudley possession. It was at the heart of traditional Dudley country. Some time after Ambrose's elevation to the earldom of Warwick Robert asked Elizabeth for Kenilworth. At first she would only give him smaller lands and less important offices – the constableship of Warwick Castle, the stewardship of Warwick (together with Steward's Place), the stewardship of Barford – but at last she relented and, by letters patent under the Great Seal dated 9 June 1563, he became the owner of Kenilworth.[5] He took possession at the end of the same month. Now the Dudley's had regained their position as substantial territorial magnates. Whatever their enemies might say about them, they could not dismiss them as mere court exotics. Almost at once Robert set in hand costly renovation and rebuilding work at Kenilworth. Whenever he could take a few days' leave from the court he travelled thither. Within a decade the castle had been transformed into one of the great Elizabethan houses.

After the signing of the Treaty of Troyes with France in the following April (1564) a period of real peace ensued for England. The Queen and her people had more time and energy to devote to internal problems. The issue which dominated conversation from alehouse to Council chamber was the succession. Bishop Jewel spoke for many when he said, 'O how wretched are we, who cannot tell under what sovereign we are to live! God will, I trust, long preserve Elizabeth to us in life and safety.'[6] This urgent problem had been debated by the gentlemen and burgesses summoned to parliament in January 1563. Elizabeth's recent illness had brought home to them just how frail was the life which stood between them and the abyss of anarchy, chaos and civil war. The Commons asked the Queen to receive a delegation, and she graciously heard their representatives on 28 January. The spokesman made only a brief mention of Elizabeth's marriage. It was too delicate a subject now for open debate. The Queen's preference for Dudley was all too obvious. The parliamentarians thought it safer to concentrate on urging their sovereign to declare herself with regard to the other claimants to the crown. Elizabeth returned them an answer which was tactful, firm and evasive. She promised them that she was very conscious of her duty to her people but that she would not declare herself yet on the succession issue 'because I will not in so deep a matter wade with so shallow a wit'.[7] She would take further advice before reaching a decision. Robert was almost certainly present at this exchange and he had copies made of the petition and the reply.[8]

He was certainly more than an intersted bystander in a matter which touched the interests of the nation and, more particularly, his own destiny. The initiative in this matter undoubtedly came from the Council. Parliament would not have dared to pursue so delicate a question so determinedly without the backing of some of the great men of the realm. Robert was admitted to the Council sometime in 1562 and it is significant that the Queen's marriage reached the top of the legislature's agenda within months of his inclusion in government. In January 1562 he had sponsored a performance of *Gorboduc* at court. This tragedy waxed eloquent about the evils that befall a state when the hereditary succession fails. A year later it was a Dudley protégé, Alexander Nowell, Dean of St Paul's, who preached the sermon at the opening of parliament and who, in the course of it, directly urged the Queen and her advisers to take thought for the provision of a legitimate heir. In the ensuing debate members of Dudley's clientage fervently pressed the Queen to take a husband.[9]

If Elizabeth thought her soft answer had put an end to parliamentary importunity she was mistaken; a few days later it was the turn of the House of Lords to make representations. The nobility also wanted the succession dispute settled as a matter of urgency and particularly to put paid to the aspirations of Mary Stuart. Perhaps it was in the hope of persuading the Queen to act on this issue that they showed unprecedented magnanimity over her marriage. The asked 'that it would please your Majesty to dispose yourself to marry, where it shall please you, to whom it shall please you, and as soon as it shall please you.'[10] The majority of their lordships had apparently decided that even Robert Dudley was better than no king at all. We might have expected Elizabeth to be greatly encouraged by this but there is no evidence that she responded at all positively to it. In her speech at the closing of parliament in March she assured her listeners that if they thought she was opposed to marriage they should 'put out that heresy'. But yet she declined to say whether or not she was contemplating taking a husband in the near future. When it came to the settlement of the succession she hinted that 'other means than ye mentioned have been thought of, perchance for your good as much, and for my surety no less'.[11]

The 'other means' included a plan to marry Robert Dudley to Mary, Queen of Scots, a scheme which staggered contemporaries and has puzzled some historians. Since her return from France, Mary had not lacked for suitors anxious to share her Scottish throne and her pretensions to the English one. It was an issue which profoundly affected Elizabeth. A husband who brought close ties with one of the major continental powers would obviously be undesirable. So would a husband who strengthened Mary's claim to the English crown. It was in January 1563 that Elizabeth came up with an idea which she hinted at to parliament, and in March that she mentioned the possibility to William Maitland, the Scottish Secretary. He did not take the suggestion seriously, intimating that if anyone was to marry Lord Robert it would surely be Elizabeth herself. When the proposition became widely known many contemporaries shared Maitland's incredulity.[12] Some observers assumed that Elizabeth would never agree to be parted from her lover and that her scheme was merely a delaying tactic designed to keep Mary from contracting an unsuitable match. However, Elizabeth prosecuted the plan for over two years and seemed genuinely annoyed when it eventually failed.

What lay behind the proposed royal solution? Had the relationship between Elizabeth and her õ õ developed to the point where she could seriously contemplate his virtually permanent exile? Elizabeth was in love with Robert in 1559 and prepared to dream about marriage with him as long as Amy's existence made it impossible for her to commit herself. During these tense months following Lady Dudley's sudden death the possibility of matrimony became distinctly more real. She was concerned, above all else, to stand by her Robin, to support him and believe his innocence, though all the world was against him. The winter of 1560-1 was a time of cruel torment for her. Love pulled her one way, duty another. She and Robert explored every stratagem that might enable them to wed with the support of at least some of her people. At this juncture

Robert became importunate. In the early days of their relationship it was the Queen who made the running. Now Robert took the initiative. Having such a glittering prize set before him he was reluctant to relinquish it without a struggle. Elizabeth, however, was descending from the summit of passion. Reason was asserting itself. She began to realise that England's well-being, her own safety, and probably Robert's, would be more secure if she remained unmarried. There were individuals and groups who would never accept a Dudley on the throne. Rebellion and assassination would become real possibilities if she set Robert beside her. She remained as devoted to him as ever. She gave ample proof of this by her lavish gifts and by widening the scope of his political activity. But Robert wanted more. He pressed the Queen for a decision on the marriage issue. She wanted to oblige him but knew that she could not.

Was her severing of the Gordian knot an inspired piece of statecraft? Although it would be hard for her to be parted from him, Robert would have a crown; he would remain faithful to Elizabeth and would use his position for her advantage; the two nations would be brought closer together than ever before; the corrosive influence of Catholicism in Scotland would be stopped; and there would be a check to the influence of foreign powers in the British islands.

The scheme commended itself to the hard-headed Cecil. He, of course, had personal reasons for wanting Dudley removed permanently from the English political scene, but the vigour with which he prosecuted the Queen's policy suggests that he, too, appreciated its diplomatic advantages. The enthusiastic terms in which he described the suitor to Maitland contrast remarkably with an analysis he made of Dudley's character two years later when his marriage with Elizabeth again seemed possible. Lord Robert, he wrote,

> is a nobleman of birth – yea, noble also in all qualities requisite, one void of all evil conditions that sometimes are heritable to princes and in goodness of nature and richness of good gifts comparable to any prince born, and, so it may be said with due reverence and without offence to princes, much better than a great sort now living. He is also an Englishman and so a meet man to carry with him a consent of this nation to accord with yours, which amongst all other aspects hath not the least interest. He is also dearly and singularly beloved [sic] esteemed of the Queen's majesty, so as she can think no good turn nor fortune greater than may be well bestowed upon him.[13]

The two people who were least in favour of the scheme were the

prospective bride and groom. For months Mary kept the negotiations alive, though she had no desire to be palmed off with the man
she regarded as Elizabeth's discarded lover. She instructed her
diplomats to insist, as a condition, that the English Queen should
name her as her successor and that this be ratified by Parliament.
She must have known that this would be quite unacceptable.
However, Elizabeth was prepared to make some concession on the
succession issue and there was room for negotiation if Mary had
genuinely wanted a settlement. As for Robert, he had no desire at all
to spend the rest of his days in Edinburgh. He opposed the scheme
as openly as he dared and, if Mary is to be believed, he actually
wrote to her to say that the marriage proposal was no more than a
diplomatic ploy to keep her from offering her hand elsewhere.[14] He
certainly would not have gone behind Elizabeth's back in this way if
he had not been genuinely alarmed that the negotiations might
prove successful. He later complained that the entire scheme had
been dreamed up by Cecil in order to get him out of the way.[15]
Indeed, the Secretary had to induce Thomas Randolph, the English
ambassador in Scotland, to write directly to Dudley and remonstrate
with him: 'if in so good a cause so much to her majesty's contentation, so profitable to your country, so comfortable to your friends
and honourable to your Lordship's self there be found a stay in you,
as all men hitherto have judged your Lordship worthy to marry the
greatest queen, so will they alter their opinion of you, worse than I
can speak or would be glad to think.'[16]

As far as Robert was concerned the only key which would unlock
his diplomatic prison was Henry Stuart, Lord Darnley. This young
man was descended, in the female line, from Henry VIII's sister
Margaret, Queen of Scotland, and thus had a place in both the
Tudor and Stuart successions. It was believed in some circles that, as
a follower of the Old Religion, he would be the natural choice of
English Catholics to succeed Elizabeth. His inordinately ambitious
mother, Lady Margaret Lennox, had long aimed to marry Henry to
Mary Stuart. All this was well known at the English court and, in
1561, Darnley and his parents were summoned to London and kept
under close observation. They appealed for permission to return to
Scotland and Darnley's father was given leave to travel north in
August 1564. Once across the border he began earnestly working
for his son's cause, particularly among the Catholic nobility.

Meanwhile Elizabeth showed no sign of wavering. In the summer
of 1564 she decided to grant Robert the earldom she had denied
him in 1560. Her main (perhaps her only) intention was to render
her Robin more acceptable to the Scottish Queen. Cecil hinted, in

the letter to Maitland referred to above, that Elizabeth would be prepared to advance him still further in order to bring the marriage plans to a successful conclusion. Perhaps there was another purpose behind her decision: it may have been a further bribe to induce Robert to accept his destiny. He was becoming increasingly restless as the months passed. He frequently interceded on behalf of Lady Lennox and her son, urging the Queen to permit their travel to Scotland. He quickly made friends with the new Spanish ambassador, Guzman de Silva, and promised his support in return for de Silva's influence against the Scottish marriage.

The ceremonies of ennoblement were fixed for the end of September and took place at Westminster. On the 28th Robert was created Baron Denbigh. The next day he received the title that had been suggested for his father seventeen years before – the earldom of Leicester. The court was thronged with spectators, including the French and Spanish ambassadors and Sir James Melville, Mary Stuart's representative. When Elizabeth entered the Presence Chamber she was preceded by a sword-bearer, specially chosen for the occasion. It was Henry Darnley. Robert knelt to receive his new honour and the Queen fastened the ermine-lined mantle around his shoulders. As she did so she could not restrain herself from tickling his neck. Elizabeth turned to Melville. 'How like you my new creation?' she asked. The ambassador made a polite reply. The Queen pointed suddenly to Darnley. 'And yet you like better of yonder long lad,' she said, apparently with humour rather than malice.

It is Elizabeth's sense of humour that suggests a possible alternative interpretation of this bizarre episode in her relationship with her favourite. She was very annoyed at parliament's presumption in pressing her on the marriage issue and she knew full well the origin of the propaganda. What better way to silence the clamour for a royal bedfellow than to cut it off at source? Robert wanted a crown? Very well, she would arrange for him to have one. It was a brilliant counter stroke. It silenced Dudley. It gave Cecil temporary hope that he was about to see the back of the royal favourite. And Elizabeth could secretly enjoy the joke of turning the tables on her troublesome councillors and parliamentarians.[17]

Whatever the truth of the matter, Elizabeth eventually abandoned the Dudley-Mary match. A few days after the investiture Melville was in the Queen's bedchamber with Leicester and Cecil. Elizabeth offered to show him some of her treasures. Opening a cabinet she took forth a miniature wrapped in paper and labelled simply, 'My Lord's Picture'. It was a portrait of Robert. Immediately Melville begged that he might have it for his mistress. Elizabeth replied that she could not part with it as she had no copy. 'But,' pointed out the ambassador, 'your Majesty has the original.' One cannot help wondering whether there was not a greater depth to these words than at first appears. For another six months the marriage negotiations continued but the Queen's enthusiasm seemed to fade. The following February she yielded to the blandishments of Leicester, Lady Lennox and others, and permitted Darnley to travel to Scotland. Though the pretence of negotiations was kept up for a few weeks longer Elizabeth had already abandoned the scheme. According to de Silva, she changed her mind because Leicester would not consent to marry the Scottish Queen. Certainly the decision to release Darnley was a fateful one for whose consequences she partly blamed Leicester. The tall young Stuart set out for a brief, turbulent and bloody career in Scotland. Before he was blown to pieces at Kirk o'Fields he had sired the next ruler of England.

CHAPTER NINE

'I HAVE LIVED ALWAYS ABOVE ANY LIVING I HAD'

On 17 December 1576 four of Robert Dudley's closest friends and relatives, Henry Hastings, Ambrose Dudley, Henry Herbert and Sir Henry Sidney, entered into a bond to pay off, on his behalf, a debt of £10,000 (the residue of a £15,000 debt) to the Queen. In return Robert assigned to them the profits of his manor of Denbigh. The legal documents were all drawn up but they were never executed,[1] and Robert subsequently mortgaged his Denbigh lands for £16,000 to a consortium of London merchants.

When Robert confessed in his will, 'Touching my bequests, they cannot be great, by reason my ability and power is little, for I . . . have lived always above any living I had (for which I am heartily sorry)', he was speaking the unvarnished truth, for his estate was heavily encumbered with debt. In this he was not unique. All men of substance had their wealth in property and suffered a greater or lesser shortage of ready cash. Mortgages, bonds, leases and assignments were their means of achieving liquidity and keeping pace with inflation. Yet the problem was more acute for men prominent in the political and ceremonial life of the state. Though they stood to profit hugely from royal favour, they also had to spend large sums out of their own pockets both on the work of government and on the maintenance of that lifestyle which convention demanded of them.

When all that has been said, however, it is clear that many of Robert's colleagues in court and Council were able to leave their heirs better provided for than he did. For this his natural extravagance and generosity are partly to blame. He loved beautiful things and he loved display for its own sake. Doubtless he indulged himself more than he could afford. His account books show frequent expenditure on pleasure and luxury. In the first year of Elizabeth's reign, for example, he paid 'for apparel and goldsmith's work', £824. 17s. 5d.[2] and during the same period he had 'for playing money' £109. 7s. 10d.[3] These two items alone account for a sizeable proportion of his total personal expenditure during 1558 and 1559 which amounted to £2,589. 2s. 1½d.[4] But it was not only on himself that Leicester spent money. He made frequent lavish

1a   The only authenticated picture showing Robert's father dates from Edward VI's reign. John Dudley is the second man on the boy king's left

1b   the memorial to Robert's mother, Jane Dudley, in Chelsea Parish Church

1c   Carving by Robert Dudley in the Beauchamp Tower at the Tower of London. It shows an oak sprig and his initials

The quenes maieſtie In her litter vnder the canapie borne by

The lord Robert Dudley mr of the horſes leading the palfrey of honor

The lorde ambroſe dudley leading the ſeconde litter horſe

The lord gilef paulet leading the firſt litter horſe

2a Elizabeth's coronation procession, detail from a contemporary drawing. Ambrose and Robert are seen close to the Queen, Ambrose leading the second litter horse and Robert leading the royal charger

2b This coronation picture of Elizabeth was perhaps given to the Dudleys by the Queen or commissioned by them. It hung for many years in Warwick Castle

3a   Robert Dudley at about
the time of Elizabeth's
accession. Artist unknown

3b   Robert's third (or second)
wife Lettice Knollys, Countess
of Essex, a celebrated beauty
of the day

4a   Robert's sister, Mary, who married Sir Henry Sidney

4b   Robert's elder brother, Ambrose. The picture is wrongly titled 'Robert Dudley, Earl of Leicester' in a later hand

5   Kenilworth Castle as it might have appeared when Elizabeth visited it in 1575

6a A portrait of the Queen at Wanstead. Two of the figures in the courtyard may be Robert and Lettice

6b   An 18th century engraving of Wanstead House. In Robert's day the courtyard was enclosed, a range of buildings and a gatehouse lying between the two front towers

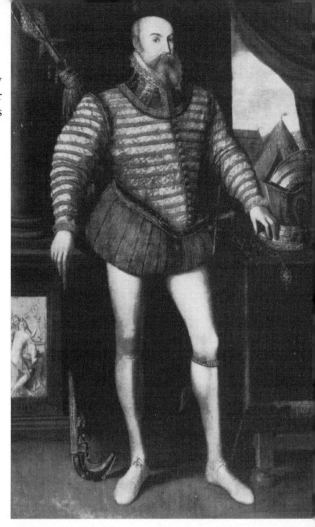

7a   A portrait commissioned by Leicester during his time as Governor General of the United Provinces

7b   This bitter satirical cartoon shows the Dutch cow and its would-be owners. Philip of Spain hangs onto the tail; the French lead it by a rope that breaks; Leicester tries to milk it, with little success

8a *and* b   Medal struck by Leicester on his departure from the Netherlands. The inscription on the reverse states 'Reluctantly, I desert not the flock; only the ungrateful ones'

8c   On the cover of a note Robert wrote to her from Rycote the Queen wrote simply 'his last letter'. She kept it with her most treasured possessions

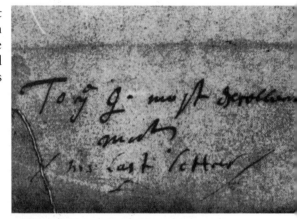

8d   The splendid tomb erected by his widow over Robert's grave in the Beauchamp Chapel of Warwick Church

gifts to the Queen. Regularly on New Year's Day, and sporadically as occasion and fancy served, Robert amused his royal mistress with costly and ingenious baubles. At the New Year in 1572, for example, he presented a gold bracelet, set with emeralds, diamonds and pearls, which opened to disclose a tiny timepiece – one of the first recorded wrist-watches. Lesser mortals also had a call upon his bounty:

> Mr Peacock, I pray you deliver to this bearer four ells of black taffeta for a short gown and three yards of black velvet to guard the same, which gown my Lord doth give to Mr Smith, the Queen's man. And also three yards [and a] quarter of crimson satin for a doublet which my Lord giveth to the Mayor of Abingdon and seven yards of black satin for two doublets which my Lord giveth to two of the mayor's brethren of the town of Abingdon. Thus heartily fare you well. This 16 May, 1566.
>
> Anthony Forster[5]

There were also gifts of a charitable nature which Dudley was obliged to make. The rich were always enjoined to help the needy. As the Queen's first subject and the patron general of Puritans, he had to give a lead. Evidence of his generosity abounds. Scores of protégés and admirers applauded his 'compassion on the distressed',[6] his succour of 'poor, friendless suitors',[7] his 'setting forth of God's glory and help of such as were the unfeigned professors thereof',[8] and his 'charitable alms unto the poor'.[9] In addition to such casual disbursements of largesse, he made two provisions of a more permanent nature. He paid for the education of two scholars at University College, Oxford, and in his will bequeathed some of his Welsh lands for the maintenance of this charity in perpetuity. The other was the establishment of a foundation which still survives and bears his name: the Hospital of Robert, Earl of Leicester in Warwick (now officially called 'Lord Leycester Hospital, Warwick'). Poverty and vagrancy were grave problems in Elizabeth's England and ones which regularly exercised the government. The poor laws enacted by parliament sought to control poor relief in three ways: to differentiate between the genuinely needy and 'sturdy beggars'; to restrict the movements of jobless people; and to encourage or force each parish to care for its own destitute inhabitants. It was fully in line with this official thinking that, in 1571, Robert obtained an Act of Parliament permitting him 'to establish one hospital within the town of Warwick or within the town of Kenilworth . . . for the finding, sustentation and relief of poor, needy and impotent people'. Probably Robert already had in mind the location of his foundation for, in the same year, he persuaded the burgesses of Warwick to grant him the fourteenth-century Guildhall and other buildings adjacent to the West Gate. The hospital provided food and shelter for twelve poor brethren who were in the charge of a master. The recipients of this charity were drawn from the town or, failing that, from the counties of Warwickshire and Gloucestershire. Preference was given to men 'maimed or hurt in the wars, in service of the Queen's majesty'. Dudley endowed it with lands producing an annual income of £200 and provided in his will for the continuance of this income.

Leicester also accumulated considerable business expenses. He was the foremost patron of enterprising commercial ventures and industrial pioneers. When, in 1565, William Humphrey, a mining expert, needed capital and influential support to back initial surveys in various parts of the country, it was to Dudley, Pembroke and Cecil that he turned. Leicester declined to help Humphrey and his colleagues in a plan to mine calamine in Somerset, but the extraction of copper in Ireland and iron in the Forest of Dean seemed more promising. Humphrey assured his hoped-for patrons that if they would help him to acquire a patent, he would soon be in a position to reward them to the tune of several thousand pounds. Notwithstanding this tempting offer[10] the progress of a rival concern, led by Thomas Therland, a royal chaplain, and a German technician, Daniel Houghsetter, seemed much more interesting. When first approached in 1565 Leicester had been very cautious,[11] but the success of exploratory diggings in Cumberland was such that he was soon joining with Cecil and Pembroke to combat the activities of the Earl of Northumberland who was proceeding against the miners for trespass. By September 1567 Therland and Houghsetter could report the discovery of first-grade copper ore in Cumbria and Borrowdale.[12]

The result of all this activity was an event of considerable significance in the economic history of these islands: the formation of the first industrial joint stock companies. These were the Mines Royal and the Mineral and Battery, both incorporated in 1568. Leicester was a member of these companies, which were licensed to 'work for all manner of mines or ores of gold, silver, copper and quicksilver' in specified areas on both royal and private ground. The Mines Royal Charter linked Leicester, Pembroke, Cecil, Lord Mountjoy and eighteen other shareholders in a venture,

> whereby great benefit is likely to come to us and this our realm of
> England, which also will the rather come to pass if the persons

now and hereafter having interest in the privileges aforesaid might by our grant be incorporated and made a perpetual body politic, thereby to avoid divers and sundry great inconveniences which by the several deaths of the persons above said or their assigns should else from time to time ensue.[13]

All the shareholders were, of course, looking for profit, but they were prepared to take considerable risks and, in fact, all those involved in the new mining projects lost money. Nor, presumably, did Robert ever see a return on his investment in an esoteric group calling itself the 'Governor and Society of the New Art'. This body, incorporated in 1571, had as its objective 'the making of copper out of iron and quicksilver out of antimony and lead'.[14]

Another venture which ended in failure was the Barbary Company. It was floated in 1585 and Dudley was its principal shareholder with an investment of £3,000. The objective was to organise and control the export of metals to Morocco and the import from there of saltpetre. Leicester already had considerable mercantile interests in the Mediterranean. His ships had been trading to the North African coast since at least 1581. But the activities of Barbary and Malta-based corsairs, the rivalry of English and foreign freelances, as well as the occupational hazard of 'the dreadful touch of merchant-marrying rocks', rendered the Moroccan trade particularly difficult. After two seasons the company folded.

Yet, whatever the balance of success and failure and however mixed the motives of those who underwrote brave new ventures, we must not underestimate the importance of Leicester and his forward-looking colleagues in the story of Elizabethan expansion. Pioneers with bold schemes and little money traditionally looked to the merchant community of London or Bristol for backing. But the cautious men of trade were more interested in 'safe' investments than speculative ventures. They could not afford to let imagination, or even national pride, overrule commercial common sense. It was here that Leicester, Pembroke, Hatton and the others gave a vital lead. When the leaders of society proclaimed in favour of an enterprise they quickened the spirits and loosened the purse-strings of other men. The startling successes of some ventures (notably, of course, Francis Drake's circumnavigation) and the growing rivalry with Spain were spurs to enterprise, but the steady support of courtiers for pioneering activities at home and abroad over many years was of greater consequence. Leicester was the very active figurehead of this movement. The Queen was not, could not be. Although she invested in a number of commercial undertakings, she often did so secretly. She could not be seen to support captains whose activities were, at least in part, piratical, and she did not choose to be publicly associated with enterprises which appeared to many observers foolhardy. Sometimes her financial gambles were concealed even from Lord Treasurer Cecil. But such speculations were entirely suited, in the public mind, to the larger-than-life, luxuriant figure of the Queen's favourite. They fitted the glamorous, extravagant image he created; an image which was the envy of young courtiers, the inspiration of would-be-adventurers and the despair of wise greybeards.

The principal setting for Leicester's gorgeous display was Gloriana's court, but he did build for himself another stage, grand and sumptuous, where he could live and entertain on a lavish scale. This was Kenilworth. The building that Robert was granted in 1563 was one of the great twelfth-century castles of England. Its massive keep and curtain-wall, defensively surrounded by lake and moat, had served the Angevins well. John of Gaunt had added a great hall and a range of chambers to transform it from a purely military building into a princely residence. Thereafter it remained little changed until Robert set to work upon it in about 1570. Basically what he did was to improve upon the plan laid down by 'time-honoured Lancaster'. At a time when other courtiers were providing themselves with new Renaissance palaces (Cecil built no less than three). Leicester contented himself with a medieval house. So untypical is he of the great men of his time in this regard that his attitude seems to call for some explanation. We know him to have been a man of culture, closely in touch with the fashion centres of France and Italy, yet he did not choose to compete with Burghley, Hatton, Walsingham and the great merchants and country gentlemen who were all building in the latest style to express their own personalities and leave something fine and impressive to posterity. The same is true of Ambrose, who left no mark at all on Warwick Castle. Perhaps residence in these large medieval fortresses emphasized their noble ancestry, their links with the past – factors which were more important than elaborate *nouveau riche* statements of wealth and taste. He spent £60,000 on enlargements and improvements, an impressive sum but not excessive in an age of great house building. The splendours of Burleigh House, Longleat and Hardwick Hall swallowed up greater fortunes and, a generation later, Thomas Howard would spend £200,000 on Audley End.

Robert's expenditure was all directed to one end: the creation of a magnificent pleasure house where Elizabeth and her court could be brought to take their ease and to be diverted with a great variety of entertainments. He made the most of the impressive natural surroundings:

> It hath, hard on the west, still nourished with many lively springs, a goodly pool of rare beauty, breadth, length, depth, and store of all kinds of fresh water fish, delicate, great and fat, and also of wild fowl beside . . . [there is] a fair park on the one side . . . And on the other side, north and west, a goodly chase, vast, wide, large, and full of red deer and other stately game for hunting, beautified with many delectable, fresh and shaded bowers, arbours, seats and walks, that with great art, cost and diligence were very pleasantly appointed.[15]

Within the curtain-wall Dudley laid out a formal garden. He connected the castle to the west chase with a 600 foot wooden bridge, converted the old south causeway into a tilt-yard overlooked by viewing galleries, constructed a large stable range, and raised on the north side a three-storey gatehouse to command the approach from the town. Within the main buildings he made extensive alterations to the keep and further embellished the already beautiful hall. But his main contribution was a new rectangular tower (known as 'Leicester's Building') opposite the keep, providing spacious apartments for visitors. The rough horseshoe-shaped plan of the finished castle lacked symmetry and balance, a fact which William Spicer, the Earl's master mason, was at pains to point out:

> The new tower will make a very good show at the height that is appointed already but the same cannot be so agreeable as the height of Caesar's Tower [i.e. the keep] . . . being both in sight at one time coming into the castle. This is a very heavy piece of work already both in workmanship and all other profession, and yet I beseech your lordship to think of the best way to the satisfying of your lordship's pleasure, that your lordship repent not hereafter what is left undone . . .[16]

Spicer's plea seems to have gone unheeded. Leicester's Building was certainly appreciably lower than the keep, yet its width, graceful dimensions and large oriel windows prevented it being dwarfed by the older structure.

Robert was no careful businessman like Cecil but his extravagant building and decoration at Kenilworth did not proceed totally regardless of expense. The following letter, written to Anthony Forster shortly before the Queen's visit in 1572, probably displays as clearly as anything can his determination to have everything done properly, his concern for economy and his cheerful delegation of financial detail to trusted servants:

I willed Ellis to speak with you and Mr Spinola again for that I perceive that he hath word from Flanders that I cannot have such hangings thence as I looked for for my dining chamber at Kenilworth. Yet he thought there would very good be had at this present in London and as good cheap as in Flanders. Palmer's wife told me at Hatfield that she was offered very good [hangings] for 11s or 12s an ell. In any wise deal with Mr Spinola hereabout for [he] is able to get such stuff better cheap than any man and I am sure he will do his best for me. And, though I cannot have them so deep as I would, yet if they be large of wideness and twelve or thirteen foot high it shall suffice . . . I hope you have made the provision of spice for me and have had the officers of the Queen's household to help, who promised me all at the [Queen's] majesty's price . . . I pray you send down with speed some such spice as is needful for all other matters against my chiefest day.

I have no mistrust of your care of such things as is to be sent thither. I have given this bearer £12 to buy trifles withal for fireworks and such like. When he hath provided his stuff, cause it to be safely sent hereafter, for that I have appointed him after four or five days to go to Kenilworth for a banqueting house that must be made. I have no leisure as you may see by my haste. If I forget [anything] you may judge meet to be thought of for this present, I refer it to further order. So fare you well Anthony, in much haste, this 16 July.

Your loving master.

Leicester[17]

The effects Dudley could create at Kenilworth were magical. But they were not solely expressions of Robert's vanity nor even of his desire to captivate the Queen. The building of the stately pleasure dome reflected both the public and the private man. It was necessary. Necessary because Leicester had to enthral, entrance, enchant, amuse, entertain his royal mistress. Necessary also because he had to impress the Queen's subjects and foreign visitors. He personified Elizabeth's court. Therefore, whether he was giving a banquet to the burgesses of Warwick, or entertaining the French ambassador in his apartments at Westminster, or dining some London merchants at Leicester House, he had to do it in the grand style. Kenilworth was only the pinnacle of the iceberg. Daily, Leicester incurred expenditure which was inescapable if he were to perform the role Elizabeth had devised for him:

The choirs your Lordship [employed when] . . . the Frenchman (Alençon) dined with your Lordship . . .   £9. 18s.

For the banqueting stuff at the
  Queen's highness being at your Lordship's . .   £6. 14s.
For banqueting stuff bought when
  the Scottish ambassador dined with
  your Lordship at Whitehall . . .   14s. 6d.[18]

It was the same with Dudley's career as patron. The breadth and variety of his interests were demonstrated by the large number of artists, writers, scholars, preachers, philosophers, adventurers, actors, dramatists and scientists he supported and encouraged. Leicester's princely household was the resort of some of the greatest talent in the land and of foreign genius, as Edmund Spenser later recalled:

For well I wot, sith I myself was there,
To wait on Lobbin [i.e. Robin] (Lobbin well thou knewest)
Full many worthy ones then waiting were,
As ever else in prince's court thou viewest . . .[19]

In the *Prothalamion* of 1596 the poet again recalled the concourse of great thinkers and artists who habitually assembled at Leicester House. Spenser was for a time a member of an 'inner core' of Dudley protégés and supporters, a society which included, among others, Sir Philip Sidney and Dr John Dee. It was this group *par excellence* which originated and sustained the doctrine of Elizabethan imperialism and reform. Dee was the high priest of this cult, whose beliefs were set out most clearly in his *General and Rare Memorials Pertaining to the Perfect Art of Navigation* (1577). He saw the Queen as having an inescapable destiny, arising from her supposed descent from King Arthur and the great heroes of imperial Rome. This destiny was a politico-religious destiny: Elizabeth would carry the standard of reformed religion into Europe and, through the development of the navy and mercantile enterprise, into lands beyond the seas.[20] Dee was the prime originator of this creed; Spenser and other writers expounded it in a variety of books and tracts (Puritanism must be regarded as a vital part of this programme); and Dudley was its foremost exponent in the political arena. The causes and policies Robert urged in the Council chamber were, for the most part, under-girded by the semi-mystical teachings of the Dee circle. The appeal to nationalism and religious fervour was the main plank in the Dudley party's propaganda.

In leading this group of adventurous spirits, Leicester, almost inadvertently, became a prime mover (perhaps *the* prime mover) of the Elizabethan Renaissance. He was certainly the leading patron of the pre-Shakespearian drama. He had grown up with court entertainments – masques, mimes, plays and pageants. He enjoyed participating in them and presenting them. He found theatrical performances a useful vehicle for expressing his own policies to the Queen. It was only natural that he should encourage playwrights and actors. Leicester died just as the golden age of Elizabethan drama was dawning. Marlowe, Greene, Nashe and Peele were already entertaining Londoners in the Curtain and the Theatre out at Finsbury Fields, but Shakespeare's first production was not staged till 1591. Yet it can reasonably be claimed that without Robert Dudley's activities in the immediately preceding decades that great explosion of literary and dramatic talent would have been somewhat dampened.

In 1559 Robert engaged his own company of players, who in later years were called the Earl of Leicester's Men. There was nothing remarkable about that event in itself; noblemen and other prominent citizens had for generations employed entertainers on a more or less permanent basis. When the patron did not need them they gave public or private performances elsewhere. Dudley's troupe was no exception for, in 1559, he wrote to ask the Earl of Shrewsbury to grant his players a licence valid in the Earl's 'country'. What did distinguish this group of men from rival companies was the eminence and discernment of their patron. Robert could attract the best available talent. It was vital to him that he did so for his actors often performed before the Queen, to whom he dared offer only the best. Having gathered an excellent company, Robert was able to ensure them profitable engagements. At Leicester House, Kenilworth, Wanstead and the royal court they played before all the leaders of English society as well as distinguished foreign visitors, most of whom showed their appreciation in money. In 1585-6 their patron took them to the Netherlands[21] where, no doubt, the wealthy burghers rewarded the Governor General's men for their entertainment. When they went on tour in the English provinces, players who came in the name of the great Lord Leicester could be sure of a good reception.

However, life for the Earl of Leicester's Men was not entirely *couleur de rose*. Puritan objections against these 'lewd fellows' grew in volume. Church leaders and pious laymen demanded greater control over players. City corporations carried out their own censorship of plays offered for performance. There was some reason for all this concern. Many bands of wandering players were little more than gangs of thieves, pickpockets and card-sharpers. Performances attracted prostitutes and confidence-tricksters. Plays, not infrequently, made transparently clear references to contemporary personalities and religious and political issues. Elizabeth's poor laws, which made some attempt to deal with vagrancy and unemployment, clearly included 'common players in interludes, and minstrels, not belonging to any baron of this realm or . . . any other honourable personage' among the undesirables who were to be 'deemed rogues, vagabonds and beggars' and punished accordingly.[22] This did not affect Leicester's Men, but a royal proclamation of the same year did. Its object was to restrict the numbers of retainers kept in noble households. To avoid dismissal, Dudley's actors wrote to ask him to keep them on the payroll as 'household servants and daily waiters'.[23] This subterfuge saved them until their patron was able to take a more positive step to ensure their future. In 1574 he obtained from the Queen a royal patent, the first ever issued to a company of players. It authorised them to perform throughout the realm, without hindrance from local authorities, any play which had been approved by Elizabeth's Master of the Revels. The importance of this development for the history of the English theatre can scarcely be exaggerated. As well as giving a company of actors permission to ply their craft anywhere they could obtain an audience, it bestowed a new dignity on their profession. It was, furthermore, a step away from reliance on noble patronage towards complete independence. Within a decade it was followed by two more significant events – the forming of the Queen's own company and the building of the first permanent English theatre.

The latter was the inspiration of James Burbage, a joiner until the lure of the stage proved too strong. He was an early member of Dudley's company, and by 1574 he seems to have been its leader. When Leicester's Men claimed the immunity given by the royal patent and organised performances in London, they found that the Lord Mayor and aldermen refused to recognise royal jurisdiction within the City. Acrimonious exchanges ensued between the Puritan burghers on the one hand, and Leicester and his actors on the other. At length, Burbage thought of a scheme to thwart the enemy. With the Earl's approval, if not with his backing, he obtained a twenty-one year lease on some land in the parish of Shoreditch, scarcely half a mile beyond Bishopsgate. There he built the Theatre and thither, by the middle of 1577, the citizens were flocking to see Leicester's actors and to enjoy the novelty of their very own playhouse. It was a great financial success and, within months, a second theatre (perhaps also built by Burbage), the Curtain, appeared nearby. All the leading companies performed in these buildings and, when no plays were on, competitions and exhibitions of fencing, quarterstaff and athletics took place. The Queen's company came into being in 1583 and

Robert was obliged to release some of his better performers for it. They were accounted as grooms of the Chamber and received wages and liveries as such. However, Leicester's Men remained the most prestigious troupe. It continued for some years after the Earl's death but eventually its leading members joined the Lord Chamberlain's company, for which Shakespeare wrote most of his masterpieces.

Some writers have linked Shakespeare's early career with Leicester and, though the connection is problematical, it is by no means fanciful. It is generally accepted that the future playwright travelled to London in 1586 or 1587 and almost immediately found employment as an actor at the Curtain or the Theatre. By 1594 he was a member of the Lord Chamberlain's company. The inference that he became one of Leicester's Men soon after his arrival in the capital is a reasonable one. An ambitious young man determined to make his career on the stage would certainly hope to gain admittance to the best professional troupe in the land. In all probability Leicester's Men was the professional company he knew best. It would have appeared often in and around Stratford-upon-Avon, for Shakespeare's home town was in the heart of Dudley country. Indeed, we know that Burbage and his colleagues performed in Stratford on their 1586-7 tour, about the time that Shakespeare left for London. What more natural than that, through friends in the company, he should have sought the patronage of the great Earl himself?

With other men prominent on the Elizabethan stage we can be more definite. Richard Burbage, James Burbage's more famous son, was a member of his father's company from a very early age, probably appearing first as a boy actor in juvenile and female roles. Richard became the most celebrated actor of his day and a great favourite of the Queen. He inherited his father's theatrical properties in 1597, and two years later built the most famous of all Elizabethan playhouses, the Globe, home of the Lord Chamberlain's company and the scene of Shakespeare's greatest triumphs. The two most celebrated comedians of the age certainly began their careers in Dudley's employ. According to a seventeenth-century account, Richard Tarlton was a Shropshire swineherd until one of Robert's servants found him and, impressed by Tarlton's native wit, introduced him to his master.[24] He became a jester and, probably, one of Leicester's Men. Soon he made himself the reputation of being one of the funniest men on the London stage, famous for his playing of clown parts, his dancing and his extemporising of jokes and rhymes. He was one of the actors taken over into the Queen's company on its formation in 1583. His death five years later was a great loss, for, as Stow said, 'for a wondrous, plentiful, pleasant, extemporal wit he was the wonder of his time'.[25] The gap was largely filled by Will

Kemp, colleague of Shakespeare, and later to attain a bizarre fame for his nine days' dance from London to Norwich. Kemp was a member of Dudley's company by 1585. Perhaps he was employed when Tarlton left to join the Queen's players. He accompanied Leicester into the Netherlands in that year and received payments for such antics as 'leaping into a ditch before your Excellency and the Prince Elector as you went a walking at Amersfoort'.[26] As a juggler, tumbler and dancer he performed at banquets, as well as in plays put on by the Governor General for his guests. Kemp, too, is later found in the Lord Chamberlain's company, where he 'jested and jigged' for many years. Several of Shakespeare's clown roles were written for Kemp who enjoyed an excellent reputation at home and abroad.

Professional actors were not the only ones who attracted Dudley's patronage. There was a venerable tradition at the universities and Inns of Court which demanded the performance of plays and masques by students and their superiors at Christmas, other festivals and on the occasion of royal visits. Themes and characters were drawn from mythology and British and classical history, but these pieces were not merely displays of erudite allegory, they were comments on the prevailing issues of the day. Using this device, writers and patrons could, without giving offence, proffer to Queen and Council their advice on matters of policy which they would not otherwise have dared to do. Dudley was an enthusiastic supporter of and participator in many of these performances, particularly those staged by the Inns of Court. Year after year the players continued to serve Dudley's interests. In March 1565, for example, he brought some players from Gray's Inn to Whitehall to entertain Elizabeth.

> On the 5th instant the party of the Earl of Leicester gave a supper to the Queen in the palace . . . There was a joust and a tourney on horseback afterwards. The challengers were the Earl of Essex, the Earl of Sussex and Hunsdon . . . When this was ended we went to the Queen's rooms and descended to where all was prepared for the representation of a comedy in English . . . The plot was founded on the question of marriage, discussed between Juno and Diana, Juno advocating marriage and Diana chastity. Jupiter gave the verdict in favour of matrimony, after many things had passed on both sides in defence of the respective arguments. The Queen turned to me and said, 'This is all against me.' After the comedy there was a masquerade of satyrs, or wild gods, who danced with the ladies, and when this was finished there entered ten parties of twelve gentlemen each, the same who had fought in the foot tourney, and these, all armed as they were, danced with the ladies . . .[27]

De Silva, the Spanish ambassador who wrote that report, thought the event 'very novel'. In his native country people did not make oblique criticisms of the monarch to the monarch's face. Dudley, however, made full use of this very English custom and, throughout the reign, those able to help him enjoyed his patronage.

To the impoverishment of our literature, very few of these court and college entertainments have survived. Fortunately there are exceptions, such as the work of George Gascoigne, poet, dramatist, moralist, 'novelist', reporter, literary critic; described by C.S. Lewis as 'the first streak of dawn' heralding the Elizabethan Renaissance.[28] Gascoigne was a troubled and troublesome spirit who failed to find a niche for himself before Leicester took a hand in his career. He studied at Cambridge but received no degree. His subsequent course at the Inns of Court was similarly interrupted. He concluded an unsuccessful marriage. He fought in the Low Countries with more fury than distinction. He was a confirmed gambler, and many of his adventures were spurred on by his desire to escape angry creditors. Intermittently he wrote poems and dramatic works but lacked the confidence or stability of character to offer anything for publication. In the 1560s his obvious talents commended him to the patronage of Lord Grey and the Earl of Bedford, but they were able to do little for him in the way of preferment.

However, through these men, Gascoigne came to the attention of Dudley. The writer-adventurer must have made a considerable impression on Leicester for he included Gascoigne in the committee which arranged the Kenilworth entertainments of July 1575. He wrote and took part in a dramatic dialogue between Echo and A Savage Man, in which Elizabeth and Robert were praised with effusive flattery. Gascoigne was chosen to deliver the parting oration to the Queen, which he did, somewhat breathlessly, running beside her horse as she rode away from Kenilworth. This was not the end of his activities that summer. Thanks to Dudley's support, Gascoigne was allowed to join the royal entourage and at Woodstock he had a further opportunity to commend himself to the Queen. His *Tale of Hermetes the Hermit* was well received by Elizabeth who asked for a manuscript version. Gascoigne did not waste this golden opportunity: he presented the Queen with a most elaborate copy of the play in English, French, Latin and Italian. In his dedication he begged for employment, expressed repentance for his former dissolute life and promised to give diligent service. He was remarkably true to his word. Within the next twelve months he published: *The Princely Pleasures at the Court of Kenilworth*; *The Steel Glass* (a verse satire – the first in English); *A Discourse of a New Passage to Cathay* (a treatise supporting the work of Gilbert and Frobisher); *The Drum of Domesday* and *A Delicate Diet for Dainty-mouthed Drunkards* (two moral tracts); *The Spoil of Antwerp* (an eye-witness account of the situation in the Netherlands); and *The Grief of Joy* (a collection of poems in praise of the Queen). In November 1577 he died. Leicester's support had come too late to save him from the inevitable consequences of a wild and impoverished youth. But not too late to save his reputation and finest works for posterity. Within a few years all Gascoigne's extant writings, published and unpublished, were collected and printed. They included early plays, such as *The Glass of Government, Supposes* and *Jocasta*, and an important treatise on the poet's craft, *Certain Notes of Instruction Concerning the Making of Verse*. Were it not for Robert Dudley Gascoigne's life would have filled a far slimmer volume – and that volume would probably never have been published.[29]

In any survey of the poetic and dramatic forerunners of Shakespeare, Jonson and their fellows, the circle of playwrights, versifiers and translators from the universities and Inns of Court who looked to Robert Dudley as their chief patron must have a central place. They established popular themes which were taken up by later writers. They gave the stage a measure of respectability. They extended the range of the drama: buffoonery and bombast were contributed by the wandering players, subtlety and grace by the lawyers. They created a wider audience for serious plays.[30] And this they were able to do so effectively because their patron had a passion for the drama in all its aspects.

There was one other category of actors active in and around London, and its members also enjoyed Robert's support. They were the boys of St Paul's and of the Chapel Royal. These precocious lads, as well as singing services, appeared frequently before the court in masques, pageants and plays. They also gave public performances. Whether acting for the 'quality' or the 'commons' they enjoyed the popularity always commanded by juvenile entertainers. For many years William Hunnis was the master of the Children of the Chapel Royal and he was devoted to Dudley, as he had been to Northumberland who first preferred him to royal service. Hunnis was a fellow prisoner of Robert in the Tower for conspiring against Queen Mary. Elizabeth restored him to his office. He was employed in the 1575 Kenilworth festivities and three years later dedicated a devotional work, *A Hive Full of Honey*, to his patron. In return for faithful service and for schooling the boys to be the mouthpiece of his own policies, Robert extended protection and support to Hunnis. When, for example, the owner of a property in Blackfriars refused permission for the boys to give public performances there, Leicester wrote to assure him that such 'practice' was essential 'for the better training them to do her majesty's service'.[31] This was sufficient to remove the obstacle.

Sebastian Westcote, Hunnis's counterpart at St Paul's, is a more interesting example of a Dudley client. He was appointed to his post about 1550 and was a steadfast Catholic. He refused to compromise his principles by attending the Reformed rite of Holy Communion and, quite predictably, he at last faced disciplinary action from Bishop Grindal who suspended him from office; but the sentence was never carried out. Robert Dudley intervened and the Bishop was forced to withdraw. He allowed Westcote a few months' grace and, meanwhile, wrote to Dudley and Cecil explaining why, in his view, the man must either recant or lose his job. But Westcote did not lose his job. Apart from a spell in prison for heresy in 1577-8 he continued to teach the boys of St Paul's and to present them occasionally at court until his death in 1582.

Two factors emerge from this story. One is the power Dudley could wield on behalf of a protégé. Grindal was a man of principle; later in his career he resisted Elizabeth herself rather than compromise on a matter he thought important. Yet Lord Robert's displeasure obviously distressed and worried him. Moreover, Grindal was supported by the largely Puritan City council. Seemingly, the combined weight of civic and ecclesiastical authority was not enough to move one man supported by the favourite. We have seen that in such contests Robert did not always have his own way, but clearly it was no light matter to oppose his will.

The other factor concerns Dudley's sincerity. He was a convinced Protestant yet he deliberately kept a Catholic in a position which gave him considerable influence over the tender minds of the young. There was certainly a degree of inconsistency in Robert's attitude, as Puritan friends were only too ready to point out:

> I humbly beseech your honour to take heed how you give your hand either in evil causes or in the behalf of evil men, as of late you did for players to the great grief of all the godly. But as you have showed your forwardness for the ministry of the Gospel, so follow that course still. Our city hath been well eased of the [pestilence] of those wickednesses and abuses that were wont to be nourished by those impure interludes and plays that were in use, surely the schools of as great wickedness as can be. I trust your honour will herein join with them that have long out of the [Bible] cried out against them, and I am persuaded that if your honour knew what sinks of sin they are you would never look once towards them . . .[32]

Dudley's support for actors and known Catholics, and also for their arch-enemies, the Puritans, cannot be wholly reconciled. Yet they do not stand in such stark contradistinction to each other as might at first appear. For Robert subscribed to the Protestant-humanist concept of the Christian commonwealth in which the rich and powerful were 'but ministers and servants under the Lord our God' who must in the last day 'render straight account of their administration'.[33] It followed that the extending of charity and succour was a solemn duty for all those to whom God had given great wealth and influence. If talent and diligence counted for anything, a man like Westcote was one deserving of support and he also enjoyed the Queen's favour. Therefore Robert helped him.

The most outstanding of the non-dramatic writers who enjoyed Dudley's patronage was Edmund Spenser. In 1576 Spenser left Cambridge, a scholarly and ambitious young man intent on entering the Queen's service, preferably in some post involving travel to the great centres of European culture. His first stepping-stone to this goal was employment as secretary to the Bishop of Rochester. Then, early in 1579, he gained an introduction to Leicester and was appointed to a similar post in the Earl's household. From letters Spenser wrote to his university friend, Gabriel Harvey, it is obvious that the poet was delighted with his good fortune. At Leicester House Spenser wrote his first major work, *The Shepherd's Calendar*, and dedicated it to Sir Philip Sidney. Its extolling of love, its flattering praise of the Queen, its Puritan sentiments and its overall charm brought the poem considerable acclaim.

But, when he turned his talents to political satire, he considerably overreached himself. *Mother Hubbard's Tale* was an allegorical fable written as ammunition for Dudley's party in its opposition to Elizabeth's marriage to the Duc d'Alençon (see below pp. 224 ff.). It chronicled the evil adventures of a monkey and a fox who attempted to overthrow king lion. Unfortunately, the identification of the principal characters was a little too obvious. The Queen was not amused to hear that Jean Simier, Alençon's representative, was being lampooned as a gibbering ape and Cecil represented as a half-crazed chicken-thief. The poem was an embarrassment to Leicester who had no option but to dismiss Spenser from his house. The rift was clearly not serious as far as the poet was concerned for he continued to support his ex-patron and revered Leicester's memory long after his death.[34]

Dudley, for his part, did not desert his protégé. He obtained for him the post of secretary to his friend, Lord Grey, newly appointed Lord Deputy of Ireland, and towards the end of 1580 Spenser crossed the Irish Sea to take up his new appointment. Although his long sojourn in the troublesome province ended in disaster, with the loss of everything during Tyrone's rebellion in 1598, it provided

him with opportunities to win fortune and promotion. He occupied
successively a number of posts in the administration and obtained
an estate of over 3,000 acres at Kilcolman. While in Ireland he
worked intermittently at his great work, *The Faerie Queene*, begun at
Leicester House. The involved allegory of this incomplete epic will
probably never be completely understood but one of the themes in
the poet's mind was the praise of his great patron and the policies
for which he stood. It seems difficult to deny that in some passages
Spenser intended the heroic figure of King Arthur to represent
Leicester. In Book I, Canto IX, for example, the King describes how
he first fell in love with Gloriana, the fairy queen, and was subsequently parted from her:

> From that day forth I loved that face divine;
> From that day forth I cast in careful mind,
> To seek her out with labour and long tyre [sorrow],
> And never vowed to rest till her I find:
> Nine months I seek in vain, yet ni'll [never will]
>   that vow unbind.

To this the Red Cross Knight responds:

> And you, my Lord, the patron of my life,
> Of that great Queen may well gain worthy grace,
> For only worthy you through prowess priefe [proved],
> If living man might worthy be to be her liefe [darling].

What is this but a return to the old theme sung by so many of
Dudley's protégés that if any man was suitable as a husband for
Elizabeth it was Lord Robert? But we do not need to rely on debat-
able interpretations of Spenserian allegory. In the (now lost)
Stemmata Dudleiana he praised his patron's ancestry. In *Colin Clouts
Come Home Again* he upbraided ungrateful colleagues who dispar-
aged Leicester's memory. In 1590 he wrote an elegy on his patron
in *The Ruins of Time* and, as late as 1596, he was still lamenting his
death in *The Prothalamion*.

   Another famous writer who acknowledged his debt to Dudley,
long after the latter's death when he could have had no ulterior
motive for flattery, was John Stow. In 1604 he recalled, 'It is now
nigh 45 years since I, seeing the confused order of our late English
chronicles, and the ignorant handling of ancient affairs, as also (by
occasion) being persuaded by the Earl of Leicester (leaving mine
own peculiar gains) consecrated myself to the search of our famous
antiquities'.[35] The Renaissance, as Agnes Heller suggests, was 'the
first era which *chose for itself a past*'.[36] Certainly rediscovery of antiquity

and the intense self-consciousness of the Protestant English state created for educated Elizabethans a new interest in history. Scholars turned to the past for elucidation of present problems and for justification of existing regimes. It was to this end that Robert Dudley, who bore, as Stow said, a 'great love . . . to the old records of deeds done by famous and noble worthies',[37] urged the chronicler to trace the ancient lineage of the house of Tudor and extol the Protestant imperial ideal. The results were the *Summary of the Chronicles of England* (1565) and the longer *Chronicles of England, from Brute unto this present year of Christ* (1580), both dedicated to Leicester.

Support for Stow did not prevent Dudley from also patronising his rival, Richard Grafton. Or perhaps one should put that the other way round for it was Grafton who had a prior claim on Robert's support. Printer as well as author, Grafton had enjoyed the patronage of Dudley's father in earlier years. He published the two Edwardian Prayer Books, the proclamation of Queen Jane in 1553 and other official documents. In 1563 he dedicated to Lord Robert his *Abridgement of the Chronicles of England*, acknowledging not only his patron's love of learning but also 'the special private causes of good will, whereby I am most bound to you'. In his account of the nation's history Grafton was careful to praise the exploits of Robert's ancestors and particularly to set the activities of his father and grandfather in the most favourable light.

Raphael Holinshed also drew the attention of readers to John Dudley's services in the dedicatory epistle of his History of Scotland:

> I offer this parcel of my travails . . . in regard of the honour due to your noble father, for his incomparable valour, well known and approved, as well within that realm as elsewhere, in service of two kings of most famous memory, Henry VIII and Edward VI, sounding so greatly to his renown, as the same cannot pass in silence, whilst any remembrance of those two most peerless princes shall remain in written histories.

This was a part of his massive *Chronicles of England, Scotland and Ireland* which brought him instant fame and, through the historical plays of Shakespeare, lasting fame.

It was in 1571 that Edmund Campion dedicated to Leicester his *History of Ireland*. Whereas most ambitious protégés hoped that Dudley would commend them to his mistress, in Campion's case the procedure seems to have worked in reverse: it was Elizabeth who recommended the historian to her favourite. Given this fact, Robert could scarcely fail to do all in his power to further Campion's career. And Campion was grateful.

... there is none that knoweth me familiarly, but he knoweth withal how many ways I have been beholding to your Lordship. The regard of your desserts and of my duty hath easily won at my hands this testimony of a thankful mind. I might be thought ambitious, if I should recount in particular the times and places of your several courtesies to me. How often at Oxford, how often at the court, how at Rycote, how at Windsor, how by letter, how by reports, you have not ceased to further with advice and to countenance with authority, the hope and expectation of me, a single student.[38]

It is necessary to be cautious about taking at face value the praise heaped upon patrons by clients eager for preferment but Edmund Campion is a man it would be hard to accuse of insincerity. At the time he wrote the above words he was a secret Catholic struggling with his conscience. Within months he had fled to Douai. Subsequently he joined the Society of Jesus and headed the mission for the reconversion of England. He had no cause to love the 'public' Dudley, the Puritan's champion, but, in all honesty, he had to acknowledge the debt he owed to the 'private' Dudley. Campion's subsequent history indicates the real bond that existed between the two men. In July 1581 the Jesuit was arrested and imprisoned in the Tower.

On the following day he was taken publicly to the house of Robert, Earl of Leicester and examined before him, the Earl of Bedford, and two secretaries of the realm, in the same clothes he wore when he went to the Tower . . . He answered them with such learning, prudence and gentleness as to draw praise from the earls . . . The earls greatly admired his virtue and learning and said it was a pity he was a papist . . . They ordered his heavy irons to be removed and that the keeper of the Tower should treat him more humanely, giving him a bed and other necessaries.[39]

There was little more that Dudley could do for his old protégé in the prevailing climate of political fear and Puritan fury. Campion was tortured to extract information, offered every opportunity to recant, and, failing to do so, was tried and executed. It is remarkable that Robert did so much (according to one source Campion was offered life, liberty and land in return for a recantation at the Leicester House conference)[40] at a time when the Puritan party was vigorously urging upon him the role of avenging Protestant crusader. The story offers further proof that personal client-patron relationships were often more important than matters of policy or dogma.

There were hundreds of other talented men whom Dudley befriended and who bound themselves to him: artists such as Zuccaro,

William Segar and Gheeraerts; writers of treatises of chess, military strategy, the rearing of horses, politics and philosophy; translators of original work in Latin, Greek, French and Italian; and musicians. He was a supporter of progressive techniques in the field of medicine and an encourager of scientific studies. Throughout the second half of the century university-trained surgeons and physicians were striving to establish themselves and their new methods of treatment against, on the one hand, quacks and charlatans, and on the other, superstitious conservatives who put their trust in astrology and ancient books rather than in empirical science. The men who looked to Dudley for aid needed powerful patrons who could defend them and ensure the circulation of their ideas. Such were Thomas Gale, William Clowes, John Jones and Richard Forster. Gale was one of the first surgeons to make a close study of gunshot wounds and made his knowledge available to Lord Ambrose's camp doctors at Le Havre. His first major treatise, *Certain Works of Chirurgery*, was dedicated to Robert in 1563. William Clowes, physician, was one of those who went on campaign with Warwick and later accompanied Leicester to the Netherlands. In *A Proved Practice for all Young Chirurgians* he acknowledges the help the Dudleys have given to the dissemination of practical medical knowledge. Jones enlisted Leicester's aid in spreading information of basic medical terms and techniques, information which some doctors wanted to keep within the profession. Jones was a great believer in the properties of natural springs, and it may have been as a result of his encouragement that Dudley resorted frequently to Buxton to bathe in the waters. Forster was one of the leading medical teachers of the day and his lectures at the College of Physicians were very popular. He too was fulsome in praise of his patron (Dudley was probably instrumental in gaining him his lectureship) who had advanced his own career and that of many of his colleagues.[41]

Leicester used his position as chancellor of Oxford University to advance the careers of protégés. He often nominated heads of colleges. In 1576, when the Vice-Chancellor demurred about admitting Antonio de Corro to a doctorate of divinity at Dudley's request, he was removed from office. The Spaniard was certainly a hot-tempered and troublesome man but he was also an independent and creatively-minded theologian and one well deserving of support. De Corro was a member of the community of foreign Protestants in England. This community counted Leicester its especial patron and not without cause, for the Earl, ever anxious to promote the cause of international Protestantism, did all in his power to help individual exiles.

Dudley's interest in maritime matters grew steadily. The only major work on these subjects dedicated to him was William Cunningham's *The Cosmographical Glass, Containing the Pleasant Principles of Cosmography, Geography, Hydrography and Navigation* (1559), and from the author's dedicatory epistle we learn not only that Lord Robert had given science 'within your breast a resting place' but that he had already encouraged Cunningham 'both in words and most liberal rewards'. In 1570 John Montgomery addressed to Leicester his treatise, *On the Maintenance of the Navy*,[42] in which he set forth several ideas – navigational aids, the building of larger ships, restrictions on mercantile vessels, etc. – designed to increase the size and efficiency of the royal navy. Montgomery could speak from long experience; he had begun his career under Northumberland's protégé, Sebastian Cabot, and had since spent nineteen years at sea. Dudley was one of the foremost supporters of commercial, exploratory and privateering ventures. In this sphere he was able to combine financial interest with doctrinaire expansionism and anti-Spanish policy.

In 1562 John Hawkins made his first voyage to the West Indies, an area theoretically closed to all except Spanish ships. He was backed by a syndicate of London merchants and, officially, the government knew nothing about his expedition. When, after a highly profitable venture – shipping African slaves to Hispaniola in exchange for hides, pearls, ginger and sugar – he planned a more ambitious voyage in 1564 he had little difficulty in interesting more exalted backers. Herbert and Dudley headed the list of subscribers. They chartered a royal vessel, the *Jesus of Lubeck*, at a charge of £500,[43] and this became Hawkins' flagship when he sailed from Plymouth on 18 October 1564. The arrangement probably enabled Elizabeth secretly to have a share in a venture which had all the appearance of being a private mercantile enterprise. This time things did not go so smoothly. Regulations against 'foreign' interlopers had been tightened, and at several points on the Main the English had to force the colonists to trade at gunpoint. The trip, however, which ended in September 1565, was highly profitable, and on 2 January 1566 Leicester received his share of the profit – £301. 16s. 6d. – which probably represented a return of at least three hundred per cent on his capital.[44]

Robert and Ambrose were the principal backers of Frobisher's first search for the North West Passage in 1576, though their stake (£50 each) was modest. The following year saw Leicester more enthusiastically pledged to Francis Drake's expedition which went on to circumnavigate the globe and become one of the most famous voyages of all time (see below, p. 237). His connection with the greatest mariner of the age probably began in 1566 when Drake and John Lovell led one of Hawkins' ventures to the New World. The names of the backers were kept secret for political reasons but it would be surprising if Dudley; who had profited handsomely from Hawkins' earlier enterprises, was not among them. By the end of the 1570s the Spanish ambassador was reporting 'Leicester and his party are those who are behind Drake', and also complaining that the favourite was an enthusiastic patron of privateers.[45] Robert followed Drake's career closely, entertained him in his London house and their names were linked in many ventures. He possessed at least two maps of the circumnavigation voyage and an inventory of his goods also included 'a fine Turkey bow' given to Leicester by 'the Turk that came with Sir F. Drake'.[46]

In 1581 Robert bought a fine 40-gun armed merchantman which had been built by Matthew Baker, the leading shipwright of the day, and renamed it the *Galleon Leicester*. He planned to send it on a journey to the Spice Islands to take up the concessions gained by Drake from the Sultan of Ternate. Drake, himself contributed £663.13s.4d and the Bark Francis. Other backers included the Earl of Shrewsbury, the Muscovy Company and the Levant Company but, with £2,200 at stake, Dudley was by far the largest shareholder. Unfortunately, the expedition, led by Edward Fenton, collapsed within weeks of its departure because of disputes among the captains. *The Galleon Leicester* sailed later on a number of privateering trips, at least once (1585) under Drake's command.

Dudley frequently shared in expeditions under the auspices of the Muscovy Company and the Merchant Adventurers. Despite the risks and the substantial losses he sometimes sustained, his enthusiasm never faltered: 'I am fully persuaded it will fall out the best voyage that ever was made out of this realm . . . I assure you that if I had £10,000 in my purse I would have adventured it every penny myself'.[47] So he wrote about a Muscovy Company venture of 1574. He was the driving force behind the foundation of the Barbary Company set up in 1585 after years of fruitless negotiation with the rulers of Morocco, aimed at obtaining saltpetre. The commercial, military and diplomatic importance of established friendly relations with the North African state account for Leicester's large investment of money and effort in the undertaking which, despite his endeavours, failed to show a profit because Moroccan saltpetre proved too expensive for English merchants to buy.[48] He also backed smaller voyages. In 1575, Andrew Baker, merchant of Bristol, lost everything when his ship was seized by Spaniards at Tenerife. Baker was determined to be revenged. He planned a privateering voyage to the Spanish Main and set about finding backers. With their help he 'furnished two barques'. The records give no details of Baker's supporters but we can reasonably infer the name of one when we read that the two barques were named (or renamed) the *Bear* and the *Ragged Staff*.

If the benefits Dudley's protégés obtained from their exalted patron were considerable, those that he gained from them were both extensive and varied. They extolled him in pulpit oratory, printed word or paint. They advanced his interests in distant corners of the realm. They acted as his spies and agents, gathering information both at home and abroad. In a variety of ways they enhanced his prestige.

It was vitally important for Leicester to know the mood of the country. Every county harboured personal foes, potential enemies of the state, and agents working for court rivals. Writing in 1571, William Overton, canon of Chichester, was at pains to point out the importance of friends in distant places:

> . . . for be you out of doubt right honourable that when the enemy strikes at me and such as I am, who are used to stand in your defence and have our care abroad to guard you that cannot guard yourself and have our mouths oftentimes employed in answering for you when you . . . cannot answer in your own behalf; be you out of doubt, I say, that the enemy is striking the blow towards your own self, and you shall feel the blow . . . except [using] your authority now, when you may, you defend these your poor friends, as I defend you at all times.[49]

As we have seen, Robert received privately foreign intelligence from both ambassadors and personal agents. George Gilpin, Henry Killigrew, Thomas Gresham were, from very early in the reign, among the established diplomats who corresponded frequently with the favourite. But there were humbler men like the Puritan scholar, William Rowe, who kept Dudley supplied with snippets of information. Writing in March 1573 the young zealot suggests that he can probably tell his patron nothing that he does not already know:

> . . . yet may I not but of duty testify my ready will and purest service at all times. May it please your honour, therefore, to understand that God hath guided me to Middleburg, where I have for the most part remained and mind by the grace of God to stay this summer within Dr Emmanuel, the Hebrew professor, his house attending [to] whatsoever service you lordship shall command me. The Prince Palatine* will not league with the French

---

*Frederick III, 'the Pious', who was the Champion of Calvinism in Germany.

murderer.† The Prince himself in person daily laboureth refor-mation of religion, as also in civil government. He personally attendeth to what his council decideth in all matters, even such as are of little importance. [Yet] truly doth he first seek the glory of God and then the wealth public.[50]

There were many such men – scholars, merchants, lawyers and younger sons of the nobility anxious to serve the favourite on their travels abroad or to receive more permanent employment. William Malim, for example, was a Cambridge graduate, a student of law and languages, who was already well travelled before Elizabeth came to the throne. In 1561 he became headmaster of Eton, but, after only a short incumbency, he decided that the court held out better prospects for advancement. About 1564 he was sent by Dudley to the Levant, where his knowledge of Italian and Turkish enabled him to render invaluable service to his patron. For three years he served as a kind of semi-official ambassador at Constantinople, providing both informa-tion for the Council and intelligence for Dudley's eyes only. He also acted as a commercial agent for his master who had important connections in Italy.* On his return, he entered Leicester's household where his knowledge and skills proved of considerable value and did not go unrewarded. In 1569 Dudley obtained a prebend for him at Lincoln Cathedral (this did not involve Malim's residence) and four years later Malim was appointed headmaster of St Paul's School. In a busy life Malim found some time for authorship and translation. In 1572 he inscribed to Leicester a tract upon the Turkish siege of Famagusta. It is remarkable only for the fact that of its forty-eight pages, seven are devoted to the author's dedication. He had good reason for gratitude.

How was all Robert's generosity and extravagance financed? Leicester had several official appointments, grants and licences which brought in a steady revenue. Apart from his household posts, among the offices of profit under the crown which he held were those of Constable of Windsor Castle and Keeper of the Park; Constable and Steward of Warwick; Chancellor of Oxford University; High Steward of Cambridge University; Chamberlain of the County Palatine of Chester; Warden of the New Forest; Steward of Snowdon Forest; and Ranger of Wichwood Forest. The royal

†Charles IX of France had sanctioned the Massacre of St. Bartholomew the previous August, an appalling evernt which horrified all Protestant Europe, though in fact it was the King's mother, Catherine de Medici, who had been its principal instigator.
*In 1575 he entered a partnership with the Venetian merchant, Acerbo Velutelli, for whom he obtained a monopoly on imports from the Republic. Cecil and other councillors tried in vain to annul this lucrative transaction.[51]

bounty was also poured on him in the form of trade concessions and monopolies and the farm of import duties. In 1564 Dudley sold to a consortium of Merchant Adventurers his licence for transporting finished cloths for the sum of £6,266. 13s. 4d. He farmed the duties on sweet wines, oils, currants, silks and velvets. All of these concessions were subcontracted. For example, he received £2,500 annually from Thomas Smith, Customer of the Port of London, for his farm of sweet wines. His household offices brought him far more than the formal fees attached to them; the sale of minor offices and 'considerations' for the placement of contracts constituted a valuable source of income.

Since suitors seldom came empty-handed, patronage also could be lucrative. It might be no more than a jar of conserve or a chicken for his larder, but there were those who could offer much more. Sir Philip Chowte of Cambre sent Dudley a fine sapphire, 'wishing it to be an orient diamond and so it were worth [to express my thanks] but, as it is, King Henry VIII wore it in a ring'.[52] Dudley enjoyed several stewardships, mainly from ecclesiastical bodies. These involved the receipt of an annual fee (virtually a retainer) in return for which Robert was expected to lend his support in any suits or disputes which might arise. For example, he was paid yearly £10 by the Dean and Chapter of Norwich, £100 by the Bishop of Winchester, £4 by the Corporation of Yarmouth and £40 by the Archbishop of York.[53] Eleven town corporations, nine bishops, two cathedral chapters and both universities offered Dudley stewardships.[54] The administrative work involved in these posts was farmed out to sub-stewards.

Other kinds of payment might be less tangible though nonetheless welcome. The Inner Temple, as we have seen, had cause to be grateful to Leicester and expressed that gratitude by admitting him to membership and pledging all their members to give him legal support whenever necessary. But Robert's contact with the lawyers and their house was much closer than that and remained so throughout his life. He frequently nominated followers and friends to membership of the Inner Temple. By the 1580s the benchers were becoming concerned at the numbers of courtiers and gentlemen gaining admittance because of the favour of mighty patrons, but they never, as far as the records show, refused a Dudley nominee. In 1576 they permitted Dudley to 'have certain buildings, erected by him, for term of his life, and he, and his heirs, and executors for sundry years might dispose of them'. The following year Robert extended these buildings. The Earl was thus provided with chambers where he could entertain his friends and business associates. These buildings adjoined a private garden, and to make it more private it was ordered in 1585, 'that all doors which open upon the Earl of Leicester's garden near his office in the Temple Garden shall be walled up before Michaelmas next, by the owners of the chambers whereunto the same doors belong'. Clearly Robert Dudley was regarded as the most honoured member of this sixteenth-century gentleman's club and enjoyed unique facilities there.[55]

The bulk of his income, however, came from estates and commercial grants lavished on him by the Queen. These were many and generous. For example, between 1560 and 1562 he received Watton Priory, Yorkshire (leased for £306 p.a.), the reversion and rent of pasture rights at Beverley Park, an annuity of £1,000 and the licence to export cloths, among many other gifts. His landed holdings changed continually as a result of fresh grants, sales and exchanges. However, a jointure on his wife made in 1584 and his will written three years later reveal that he had consolidated most of his estates in four areas: the Midlands (more specifically, in the modern counties of Warwickshire, West Midlands, east Hereford and Worcester and north Gloucestershire), North Wales, Essex and Kent. His principal residences were Kenilworth, Wanstead and Leicester House in London's Strand. Some of his Norfolk lands had reverted to members of the Robsart family on his wife's death. The remainder he dispersed in the 1570s.[56]

Like all the great figures of the court and government, Leicester was an absentee landlord who delegated most of the responsibility for estate management to stewards. These were usually men well-established and respected in the areas where they lived. Like all magnates struggling to maintain their living standards in an age of inflation, Leicester had to exploit his lands to the full. Most income came from rents and fines (sums paid at the commencement of a new lease or tenancy). Many rents were fixed or could, according to custom, only be increased by small amounts. Fines were much more controllable but, being of a sporadic nature, they did not provide a regular income. Faced with the problem of rising prices and static revenues, most landowners manipulated their tenancy arrangements in various ways. For example, they might bribe a yeoman or gentleman tenant into accepting a higher rent or shorter lease by keeping his entry fine to a minimum. Where possible they also sought to reclaim and enclose land. So relentless were the inflationary pressures that the efficient landlord or agent had to resort to every device to increase income.[57] Such exploitation and tampering with ancient custom was, of course, not popular, particularly when carried out in the name of an absentee owner. Robert Dudley certainly did not escape the odium poured out upon landlords in general by the tenantry in general:

>Proud Dudley held awhile this noble fort,
>With cruel arts he fleeced its fair domain;
>And Salisbury's sons, who dared to make retort,
>Were falsely charged and then as basely slain.[58]

So one local bard assessed Leicester's behaviour as a major landowner in North wales. It was not an altogether fair judgement.

In June 1563 Robert received the lordships of Denbigh and Chirk and the office of Chief Forester of the Forest of Snowdon. This made him the greatest landholder in the area. By virtue of his close friendship with Henry Sidney, President of the Council of Wales, he was also the most powerful politically. Soon after his appointment Dudley visited his new estates and discovered that they were suffering from years of neglect. He appointed a commission to report and advise on the more efficient management of the lands. As well as his own representatives the commission was staffed by the leading tenants: Sir John Salisbury, the Bishop of St. Asaph, Dr Ellis Price and Robert Wyn ap Cadwalader.[59] The committee examined and deliberated for almost a year and came up with a detailed package of recommendations. Rents were raised, vague boundaries properly defined and waste lands enclosed. The major tenants and leaders of local society were anxious to ingratiate themselves with the new lord who was so admirably placed to reward faithful service. The recommendations of the commission were thus much to Dudley's liking, as was the present of £2,000 given by his freeholders on his induction.

There were, however, wilder spirits whose national pride, social conscience and sense of tradition were outraged by the activities of one who lived in London and, as they thought, milked his Welsh domains simply to pay for his own pleasures. Bands of young men went about pulling down Leicester's hedges and fences. The ringleaders were Sir John Salisbury's two sons, who were eventually apprehended, tried and hanged at Shrewsbury.

But the brutal efficiency of Dudley's agents also roused the ire of several men of substance. When Robert sold to London speculators a thousand acres of 'dimesne' at Y Maes Gwyn for £1,508. 5s. local landowners protested that it was not his to sell. They found Dudley, backed by Henry Sidney and the Council of the Marches, a powerful opponent but they finally obtained a compromise or 'composition' on this and other disputed territorial matters.[60] A similar situation arose in 1575 when Leicester obtained the Forest of Snowdon by letters patent. His representatives enquired closely into crown land which had been encroached on by tenants and freeholders in Caernarfon, Merioneth and even Anglesea. Again there were local riots, while official protest was carried to the Queen herself. The opposition was led by Sir Richard Bulkeley, Constable of Beaumaris, sometime sheriff and M.P. for Anglesea. He was a member of the royal household and was thus able to make repeated petition to Elizabeth over many years. In this manner concessions were obtained, although Dudley largely gained his own way by prosecuting recalcitrants through the Council of the Marches and by exploiting long-standing local feuds and rivalries. By astute business methods, not untinged with ruthlessness, Leicester was able to increase his revenues from North Wales to £1,500 p.a., considerably more than they had paid his predecessors.*[62]

A superficial reading of all this evidence might suggest that Dudley was indeed a prime example of the bad absentee landlord. There is, however, another side to the coin. Robert fully shared the prejudices and convictions of his class: that the divisions of society were immutable and that peasants and tenants were to be kept in their duty to the crown and their superiors. Any other policy would lead to anarchy and the bloodshed Robert had witnessed at first hand in 1549. But he also accepted fully the obligations of his position. He extended his patronage to local people and their families. After Sir John Salisbury's sons had been executed it was Dudley who took Salisbury's grandsons, Thomas and John, under his wing. He placed the boys at Trinity College, Oxford, then welcomed them into his service at court. The elder eventually went to the bad, becoming involved with his friend, Edward Jones (another of Dudley's young Welsh protégés) in the Babington plot, but John prospered, became a Squire of the Body to Queen Elizabeth, and restored the family fortunes.[63]

Leicester was determined to leave his mark on North Wales. He intended to make Denbigh the centre of the region, furnished with buildings appropriate to its importance. The town was not very impressive in the mid-sixteenth century. The 300-year-old castle was in a semi-ruinous state. Only since the end of the Wars of the Roses had the citizenry emerged from its protective walls to build straggling streets of houses down the hill-side. There was no civic centre. The only church was the small garrison chapel of St Hilary. All this Leicester resolved to change and to give the townspeople a Denbigh of which they could be justly proud. He immediately set in hand

*It should not be supposed that Leicester was the only royal officer seeking to exploit his position to the full. In 1570, for example, the Queen had to intervene in a dispute betwen Robert Colshill, one of her Gentlemen Pensioners, and certain Somerset farmers. Colshill held the Forest of Exmoor under patent from the crown and had increased the rates payable for pasturage. Elizabeth, in this case, urged the parties to 'have some end by quiet manner without further charges'.[61]

important repairs to the castle. He gave land for the building of a shire hall and instructed that work should begin urgently because 'the officers and inhabitants of the said town are greatly desirous to proceed with some expedition, in respect it is a thing so needful unto them, as also so expedient and necessary for all the inhabitants of that whole country'.[64] But this was not to be the crowning glory of Robert's building work. He decided to establish nothing less than a cathedral in Denbigh. On 1 September 1578 the foundation stone of a new church was laid and Leicester was soon appealing to the English bishops to gather funds for the completion of this holy work. The building was not large, but it was the first church in post-Reformation England and Wales designed to reflect Protestant doctrines and to be the setting of simple, non-ritualistic liturgy. Dudley intended that it would be a symbol of the reformed faith in this corner of the realm and that Denbigh would replace St. Asaph as the seat of the bishopric. He was probably prompted, in part, by the need to combat a Catholic revival in North Wales. Under the lax episcopate of William Hughes recusancy had increased, and only the previous year the bishop had had to defend himself against the charge of not enforcing Anglican orthodoxy. The Lord of Denbigh's pious plans, however, came to nothing. Sufficient funds were not forthcoming and the work went forward very slowly. The church was unfinished at Dudley's death and, though fresh monies were raised for the project later, the building was never completed.

Of the men who faithfully served Dudley's interests in North Wales the name that stands out is that of Dr Ellis Price. Price was already advanced in years* when Robert received his Welsh estates. He was a man of distinct Protestant conviction and in the 1530s had been one of Thomas Cromwell's monastic visitors. This had not prevented him holding important office under Mary Tudor, and by 1563 Price had already served more than once as MP for Merionethshire, and as sheriff of Merionethshire, Caernarvonshire and Denbighshire. He was a member of the Council of Wales and a considerable landowner in his own right. After 1563 he adhered firmly to Dudley and, as a result, his local standing was considerably enhanced. He served even more frequently as sheriff and MP between 1563 and 1585 and added considerably to his estates. His son, Thomas, became 'a gentleman of plentiful fortune', partly out of wealth inherited from his father and partly as a result of the benefits of Leicester's patronage. He accompanied Dudley to the Netherlands in 1585 and served as a garrison commander at Tilbury in the Armada year. He was one of the eager young men about the court who supported Leicester's adventurous

*DNB suggests 1505 as the year of his birth.

foreign policy, who joined expeditions led by Drake and Raleigh and who later organised his own privateering voyages.

The Prices were not mere 'creatures' of Dudley. They were men whose roots ran deep into Welsh culture. Thomas was a poet who wrote much of his verse in his native tongue. Ellis was not untalented and was a close friend of the great bard, William Cynwal. Of the same circle of Protestant Anglophile Welshmen was the pamphleteer and linguist, William Salisbury (a cousin of Sir John) who gained Leicester's support for the translation of the Bible and Prayer Book into Welsh and himself laboured for many years on these projects.[65] Yet another was Humphrey Lhuyd, physician, historian and geographer who, thanks to his patron's influence, was MP for Denbigh from 1562-8.[66]

Not all Robert's agents and supporters in North Wales were local men. John Hubaud was his constable at Kenilworth. John Nuttal was a friend and fellow Inner Templar. So was John Yerwerth, MP for Chester. Richard Cavendish, Member for Denbigh, was used by Robert on diplomatic missions. But whether they were new men or members of established families, they were bound to Dudley by bonds of self-interest. He was by far the most powerful man in the area, especially after his appointment as Chamberlain of the County Palatine of Chester (1565) and his brother's grant of the lordship of Ruthin (1564). That does not mean that they did not genuinely share his attitudes and support his basic policies. Indeed, when Leicester led the expedition to the Netherlands in 1585, most North Wales MPs went with him.[67] In their reliance on the Earl, Welsh communities did not lose their independence. In 1572, for example, Denbigh rejected their lord's nominee for the Commons even though he wrote them a hurt and angry letter.[68]

It was the same all over the country. If we consider parliamentary seats alone it is clear that Dudley had influence in elections at Southampton, Wallingford, Windsor, Lichfield, Abingdon and Coventry, among many others. These MPs were important to him. Indeed, one of the most serious breaches between Leicester and Sussex was over the right to nominate the member for Maldon, Essex. They gave support in the commons to the policies he and his circle were urging in court and Council and which his preachers were declaiming from pulpits throughout the land. In return, Leicester's patronage provided ambitious men with a stairway to wealth and influence. It also worked for the benefit of communities such as the town of Chester which, in 1571 looked to the favourite to 'work an honourable and charitable deed to help to reform our decay'.[69]

CHAPTER TEN

'HER MAJESTY MISLIKES'

By 1565 Robert Dudley stood at the centre of English political life. He shared this position with three rivals: William Cecil, Thomas Howard and Thomas Radcliffe. At court and in the localities these political princes influenced elections and nominations to most important offices, for where they did not possess estates their political associates among the nobility did. They were courted by ambassadors. Groups of friends and allies formed around them. The movement of national affairs during the next decade was dominated not only by policy makers in Europe's capital cities but also by the interaction of Leicester, Cecil, Norfolk and Sussex with the Queen.[1]

International affairs were certainly troubled. In Scotland the conflicts of Mary Stuart and her nobles frequently threatened to spill civil and religious strife across the border. In France the continuing faction struggle prevented any consistent relationship with England. The Netherlands flared into open rebellion against Spain inevitably involving thousands of Elizabeth's subjects who had close commercial and religious ties with the Low Countries. In 1570 Pope Pius V excommunicated the Queen, thus absolving all wholehearted Catholics from their allegiance to their sovereign.

The political climate in the English court was similarly marked by frequent storms – personality clashes, divisions on policy, even rebellion – but at its centre there was a new stability. Some of Elizabeth's ministers had begun to accept the possibility that their Queen might indeed 'live and die a virgin'. The personnel of the Council and the household remained fairly static. Elizabeth had a knack of maintaining strong personal relationships with her servants. This held together the members of her faction-ridden court, obliged rivals to cover their real feelings with a veil of civility and prevented them from destroying each other. The prospect of marriage with Robert faded but it was not entirely defunct. There were occasions when Leicester fell from grace, but nothing that passed between them was ever able to destroy their deep friendship. The shrewd Cecil realised this. After a brief estrangement between Queen and favourite in 1566 he remarked, 'I think the Queen's majesty's favour to my Lord of Leicester be not so manifest as it was to move men to think she will marry with him and yet his lordship hath favour sufficient.'[2] This was why, for all their disagreements, Cecil never permitted himself to be drawn into prolonged, open hostility with the favourite. For it always remained true that Sweet Robin had 'favour sufficient'.

If Cecil was circumspect in his dealings with Leicester, others were not. Throughout 1565 and 1566 there were many clashes between Robert and the Norfolk faction. They took advantage of the fact that Elizabeth blamed Dudley for frustrating her plans for Mary Stuart. Her annoyance was prolonged as news arrived of Darnley's courtship of Mary and the couple's hurried wedding in July 1565. These developments gave Robert's personal and political enemies cause to hope that his star was declining, and hope lent them boldness.

The first public quarrel between Dudley and Norfolk occurred early in 1565. Howard and Dudley were playing real tennis before the Queen in one of the Whitehall courts built by Henry VIII. After a while Robert went across to Elizabeth and borrowed her napkin to mop his sweating brow. At this Norfolk lost control of himself. He raged at Dudley for his presumption and 'swore that he would lay his racket upon his face'. The Queen was naturally angry with the Duke, who now hated Dudley even more for giving rise to his public humiliation.[3]

Petulance was a characteristic of Thomas Howard. He was a man self-tortured by the conviction that his talents went perpetually unrecognized. Thwarted ambition warped his judgement and left him a prey to flatterers and plausible men. He easily fell under the sway of more forceful personalities and now he found such a one at his elbow, ready to help nurse his injured pride. It was Cecil who recorded the forging of this new alliance: 'My Lord of Norfolk loveth my Lord of Sussex earnestly, and so all that stock of the Howards seem to join in friendship together . . .'[4] Thomas Radcliffe, Earl of Sussex, was, at forty, a soldier of experience if not distinction. He had but recently returned from nine years as Lord Lieutenant of Ireland, where his government had been marked by vigour, ferocity and failure. He had done his best in an impossible situation and served until the toll on his health and nerves forced him to request a recall. The treachery of the Irish princelings and their stubborn determination not to be ruled by the English were hard enough to combat. When the home government failed to provide the necessary men and money, when Queen and Council were incapable of understanding the Irish situation, and when critics from the comfort of the court indulged in career assassination, the Lord Lieutenant's work became impossible.

Dudley had been one of Sussex's sternest critics. He had his own informants across the water, and in Henry Sidney, who had served under the Earl, he had a close friend, who knew the Irish situation intimately. What particularly rankled with Radcliffe was the fact that in 1563-4 his administration had been subjected to examination by a special commission. He detected Dudley's influence here and in all probability he was correct. The men who headed the mission, Sir Thomas Wroth and Sir Nicholas Arnold, were the favourite's supporters. The major fly in the Irish ointment was Shane O'Neill, rebel Earl of Tyrone. Sussex had used force and treachery to bring him to book, both without effect. The Earl returned in mid-1564 to find the story freely circulating that he had aided and abetted O'Neill's resistance. Sussex thus had ample cause to hate Dudley and he now provided the motive force necessary to weld a disparate group of disgruntled and jealous courtiers into a faction. Norfolk was its titular head but Radcliffe was effectively its leader. Dorset, Howard of Effingham and Hunsdon, were among the followers, while Cecil – cautiously, of course – gave encouragement. By midsummer 1565 the rival earls and their followers were carrying arms at court. Six months later the two factions were distinguished by the wearing of coloured favours: yellow for the Howard-Radcliffe alliance, purple for Leicester. There were occasional brawls between groups of supporters and Sussex complained directly to the Queen that his life was in danger.

Elizabeth knew that Robert's arrogance and his familiarity with herself were, in part, the cause of this tension. She must often have warned him about this in private, and she certainly did so on occasions in public, telling him in the Privy Chamber or Presence Chamber that her affection was not so locked up in him that she had none left for others. It may well have been to demonstrate this fact, and to take some of the heat out of the situation, that in the summer of 1565 she began a flirtation with Sir Thomas Heneage, one of the gentlemen of her Privy Chamber. Heneage was about the same age as Elizabeth and Robert but he was married, so that nothing more than harmless dalliance can ever have been intended by the Queen. Furthermore, he had been a member of the royal household since the beginning of the reign, so it seems unlikely that Elizabeth became suddenly aware of his charms for the first time. The initiative clearly came from the Queen, and the 'affair' lasted six months or more. It was like the Pickering incident all over again (interestingly, Sir William and Heneage were close friends) and it was certainly successful in goading Robert into foolish reprisals.

Concluding that what was sauce for the goose was sauce for the gander, Leicester declared his affection for one of the ladies-in-wait-ing. He followed this up with a request to be absent from court for a few days. According to one story, Throckmorton was the brains behind this scheme which had as much to do with politics as with romance. Elizabeth was again toying with the possibility of a Hapsburg match. The Leicester group wished to discover once and for all how serious she was and whether she would really let Robin go in the interests of a marriage alliance. Elizabeth's jealous anger when she heard of the affair was both gratifying and frightening. There was no volcanic outburst of royal wrath. Instead Elizabeth grew cold towards her favourite. For his benefit she 'wrote an obscure sentence in a book at Windsor'[5] (presumably a cryptic expression of displeasure). In conversation with others she lamented that she had wasted her time on Robert Dudley. She refused him favours, such as his request for a Council place for Throckmorton, and she continued her association with Heneage. Yet she knew that this only perpetuated an explosive situation, and in November she tried to patch up the quarrel between Dudley and his enemies. When Sidney, awaiting passage for Ireland, heard the news he was both hopeful and sceptical: 'I hear of a great reconcile-ment lately made with you. If so, I trust I am remembered in the contract. I care not in regard of any subject your enemy in England, but [I] would be accounted a feather in your wing, and a principal one, too. There may be fairer semblances between you and others, but trust not before trial, for in such trust is oft treason.'[6]

The 'reconcilement' was only skin-deep and matters came to a head once more at the close of the Christmas festivities. Heneage was presiding over the merry-making as player king and he commanded a game of questions and answers on the day of the Epiphany. He ordered Lord Robert to ask the Queen, 'which was the most difficult to erase from the mind, an evil opinion created by a wicked informer, or jealousy . . . Lord Robert, being unable to refuse, obeyed. The Queen replied courteously that both were diffi-cult to get rid of, but that, in her opinion, it was much more difficult to remove jealousy.' The point of the question, as Leicester fully realised, was whether Elizabeth's anger was a response to false rumour or to a genuine desertion on the part of the favourite:

The game being ended, Lord Robert, angry with that gentleman for having put this question to the Queen, and assigning, perhaps a sense to this proceeding other than jest, sent to threaten him through the medium of a friend, that he would castigate him with a stick. The gentleman replied that this was not punishment for equals and that if Lord Robert came to insult him, he would discover whether or not his sword cut and thrust and that, if Lord Robert had no quarrel with him, Lord Robert was to let him know where he was to be found because he would then go to Lord Robert quite alone . . . The only answer Lord Robert gave was that this gentleman was not his equal and that he would postpone chastising him till he thought it time to do so.

When Heneage reported all this to the Queen she was furious with Robert. She told him that 'if by her favour he had become insolent he should soon reform and that she would lower him just as she had, at first, raised him.' Robert responded with a fit of sulks for four days,

> placing himself in one of the rooms of the palace in deep melancholy . . . showing by his despair that he could no longer live . . . The Queen, moved to pity, restored him again to her favour. Yet, as the ambassador told me, his good fortune, if perhaps not impeded, will at least have been delayed a little, for it had been said that she would surely proclaim him duke and marry him.[7]

Distressed though Robert must have been by these events he had the comfort of knowing beyond doubt how deep Elizabeth's affection for him was. It was clear that if she could not marry him she would either not marry at all or, if she did choose a husband, she would ensure that Robert's position was secure. He now realised afresh how strong were the cords which bound Elizabeth to him.[8] Perhaps Robert realised that Heneage had inadvertently performed a real service for him. Perhaps he simply forgave the courtier out of the goodness of his heart. However we explain it, the fact is that the two men became close companions and 'Sir Thomas Heneage, my good old friend' was mentioned in Leicester's will.

Elizabeth had already decided upon a public truce between the two great rivals in her court. In return for the award of the Garter, Charles IX of France had expressed a desire to confer the Order of St Michael on two of the Queen's subjects. She selected Leicester and Norfolk and fixed the date for 24 January. Howard was with great difficulty prevailed upon to take part in the ceremony, and did so only to please his sovereign. At the time appointed the two peers met in the 'great closet' at Whitehall and embraced each other before proceeding to the investiture. Then, magnificently arrayed in white and russet velvet, tricked out with fur, lace, gold and silver, they proceeded to the chapel to receive their chains of office from Charles's deputies. The reconciliation was as hollow as the honour.[9]

Within days Norfolk demanded of the favourite that he abandon his pretensions of marriage with the Queen and support the current negotiations for a marriage alliance with Archduke Charles of Austria. Robert replied cautiously that he would do whatever he could as long as it did not involve forfeiting her majesty's affection. If Elizabeth's statement to the Spanish ambassador soon afterwards is to be believed, Leicester was as good as his word. He had, she said, urged her to marry for her own sake, for the benefit of the realm, and, indeed, to deliver him from the blame of preventing her espousal. Yet the situation was obviously tense and both rivals thought it wise to leave the court. Norfolk stayed away until September. Dudley was absent until late March and, as he told Cecil, would have liked to extend his self-imposed exile.[10]

The last few months had taken their toll and left him deeply depressed. He had come to realise that the role of royal favourite was synonymous with that of royal scapegoat. Whatever others might choose to believe, he no longer had great influence over the Queen's state policies. That period of their relationship was over. Elizabeth consulted him on most matters and valued his honest appraisal of men and events, but her decisions were always her own. If those decisions were popular, men praised the Queen. If they were unpopular, men damned Leicester. Robert knew, for example, that Elizabeth would never marry the Archduke Charles (or probably anyone else) however strongly he might urge her to do so. He knew also that he would always be blamed for her continued spinsterhood. He was not very concerned about the opinions of the world but there were times when he felt the loneliness of his privileged position. A letter he wrote in February from Sir Harry Lee's house at Quarrendon, Buckinghamshire, to the Secretary breathes gloom and despondency. He thanked Cecil for his 'gentle and friendly letter' and for keeping him informed of the Queen's deliberations about the Austrian match. Nothing, he wrote, would settle her good estate better than marriage. Yet he despaired of a happy outcome.[11] Throckmorton was also keeping him informed about the situation, and advised Dudley that he was wise to stay away from the court so that no one could blame him for the cumbersome and difficult process of the negotiations.[12]

Yet not all Robert's friends proffered the same advice. His agent, John Dudley, wrote at the end of March:

Touching your coming here, I hear divers opinions; some say tarry, others, come with speed. I say, if you come not hastily, no good will grow, as I find Her Majesty so mislikes your absence that

she is not disposed to hear of anything that may do you good. I
talked with Mrs Dorothy after her coming from [Sir Richard]
Sackville before she saw Her Majesty, by whom I perceive fully her
affection to your hasty repair, and Her Majesty's unkindness taken
with your long absence.[13]

The Queen had already shown her 'unkindness' by refusing to
accommodate Leicester over a land transaction, despite the inter-
cession of Cecil and other Council colleagues.[14]

Robert decided to return, but his stay at court was a short one. By
the end of April he had obtained leave of absence once more, this
time to visit his Norfolk estates. Even here palace feuds pursued
him. On 4 May, while staying at Norwich, he received a bundle of
letters. One was from Throckmorton. Another was from the Queen
– and it did not make pleasant reading. Obviously something had
happened to put fresh strains upon their relationship, so recently
patched up. Whatever it was, it plunged Robert back into deepest
melancholy:

I have received yours [he replied to Throckmorton] and another
from one whom it has always been my greatest comfort to hear
from, but in such sort that I know not what to impute the difference to. If there is any cause found in me to deserve it, I am
worthy of much worse, but as there is none living that can so
uprightly keep themselves from error, so this far can I, in
conscience, acquit myself: that I never wilfully offended, nor did
anything that both fear and duty went not withal toward . . . Time
has been when my doings should never have been worse taken
than they were meant, nor my meaning so scanned as [to] stretch
. . . an unwilling stepping aside to a wilful slipping away [i.e. to
interpret unwitting error as wilful disobedience] . . . Foul faults
have been pardoned in some; my hope was that one only might
have been forgiven – yea, forgotten – [in] me. If many days' service
and not a few years' proof have made trial of unremovable fidelity
enough, without notable offences, what shall I think of all that past
favour which [I still enjoy in large measure, when] my first oversight [results in] an utter casting off of all that was before? . . .
    P.S. I see I shall not need to make so great haste home, when so
good opinion is conceived of me. Either a cave in a corner of oblivion or a sepulchre for perpetual rest were the best homes I could
wish to return to.[15]

Well might Robert be despondent: the pattern of conflict, reconciliation and renewed conflict went on. Hardly had he returned to

court before his enemies were seeking other means to discredit him. In the summer they discovered a disgruntled follower of Leicester who might, it seemed, serve their purpose. This was none other than John Appleyard, Amy Robsart's half- brother. Kinship with the great Earl had brought its rewards: as well as the offices Robert had acquired for him in Norfolk, in 1559 he had sent Appleyard to Ireland with £100 and an introduction to Henry Sidney in his pocket plus an annuity of 100 marks. In 1564 Dudley obtained letters of marque for him as a privateer working off the east coast. As late as 1566 the favourite acquired for him (through his friend Bedford) the office of Gentleman Porter of Berwick and entered a bond for £400 of Appleyard's debts. But this poor relation was not satisfied with opportunities for self-advancement. He wanted fat handouts in the way of cash, lands and offices. Moreover, he felt that Leicester *owed* him more than he had already paid. For Appleyard claimed to know details about Amy's death that had never come out; details that, so he implied, reflected upon her widower.

The Duke of Norfolk heard something of the wild stories and resolved to sound Appleyard out. While the malcontent was at Hampton Court (visiting his brother-in-law, William Hogan) he received a summons to a secret assignation across the river with a man he subsequently described as a 'merchant'. This go-between offered, on behalf of his principals, an immediate payment of £1,000, with more to follow, if Appleyard would provide evidence of Dudley's implication in his wife's death and also of his determination to prevent the Queen's marriage. Unfortunately for the conspirators, William Hogan, one of Dudley's servants, became suspicious and reported to his master. Dudley sent Thomas Blount to examine Appleyard and the whole story was eventually dragged out of the wretched man, including the statement that he understood Norfolk, Sussex and Heneage to be the instigators of the plot. Blount took Appleyard to Greenwich to confront Leicester who gave him an angry dressing down and eventually dismissed him.

But Appleyard simply could not learn from his mistakes. Almost a year later (8 May 1567) the Council were investigating the activities of one Trendle, another Norfolk man of dubious reputation. He reported a conversation with Appleyard in which the latter had claimed that he 'covered the murder of his sister' for the Earl's sake. Appleyard was summoned, as were Blount and Hogan, and all the activities of the previous summer were disclosed. Appleyard was thrown into the Fleet with orders to produce any relevant evidence he had concerning Lady Dudley's death, and the Council provided the prisoner with a copy of the coroner's verdict. It took Appleyard very little time to change his tune. Having studied the relevant document 'he not only finds such proofs, testified under the oaths of fifteen persons, how his late sister by misfortune happened of death but also such manifest and plain demonstration thereof as hath fully and clearly satisfied him, and therefore commending her soul to God, he has not any further to say of that cause'.[16] The Council left Appleyard to cool his heels a little longer. On 9 June Sir Henry Neville wrote to a friend in the country informing him of the eventual outcome of the affair:

> On Friday in the Star Chamber was Appleyard brought forth, who showed himself a malicious beast. For he did confess he accused my Lord of Leicester only of malice and that he hath been about it these three years, and now because he could not go through with his business . . . he fell in this rage against my Lord and would have accused him of three things: 1. of killing his wife; 2. of sending the Lord Darnley into Scotland; 3. for letting the Queen from marriage.[17]

Of Appleyard's punishment we know nothing, though Neville surmised he would be set in the pillory. The poor man was incapable of self-reform. Within weeks of his release he was trying to sell his Berwick post. In 1570 Appleyard was arrested in his own shire for taking part in a rebellion in support of the Duke of Norfolk. He was sentenced to life imprisonment and spent the next four years in Norwich Castle. In the spring of 1574 he was in failing health and on 31 May an order was issued in the Queen's name for the prisoner's removal to the house of the Dean of Norwich.[18] It is no surprise to discover that George Gardiner, Dean of Norwich, was an old friend and protégé of Robert Dudley. Characteristically setting aside personal malice, Leicester did what he could to ease his troublesome kinsman's last months. Appleyard was still resident in the cathedral close at the time of his death, though when that occurred is not known.[19]

Even before this unsavoury affair came to light Leicester and Sussex were at loggerheads over another issue. Since Sidney's appointment in Ireland, Radcliffe had sued for the grant of Sir Henry's former post as Lord President of the Marches of Wales. Sidney wished to keep this office and had installed a deputy to perform the duties, which were not onerous. Dudley supported his brother-in-law but Sussex continued to petition the Queen, and in April 1567 she gave in to his importunity. But she put a price upon the honour: she would not let the Earl leave court until he had been reconciled to Leicester (through Pembroke's good offices) and only then 'on condition that he gives his word not to complain further on the matter, nor of Lord Robert; and so it was agreed'.[20] Despite this settlement Sussex never got the Welsh job; Sidney held the position and enjoyed its revenues to the end of his days.

It was almost certainly Appleyard's revelations (which followed rapidly upon the event just recorded) that tilted the scales against the Norfolk faction and obliged them to make their peace with the favourite. The Spanish ambassador, who did all he could to maintain the breach between Dudley and his enemies, could report on 7 April that Norfolk was still at Kenninghall and under the influence of his Catholic wife. This, 'together with the enmity of Leicester, will, I hope aid in bringing the duke round, since Lord Robert is returning to the Queen's favour, to the great displeasure of many'.[21] By 24 May, however, de Silva had been disconcerted to hear from Leicester that he and Howard were now completely reconciled, although he commented sourly, 'I do not believe such friendship will last long.'[22] He was right – only three weeks later Cecil was complaining, 'this court here is not free from many troubles, amongst others none worse than emulations, disdains, backbitings and such like, whereof I see small hope of diminution.'[23]

At the beginning of 1566 Sir Henry Sidney was appointed to the Irish post vacated by Radcliffe. Soon his reports were arriving reinforcing with fresh evidence the alleged ineptitude of Sussex's rule. Sidney pursued different policies and they began to be effective. Sussex could do nothing but oppose the activities of the new Lord Deputy. But as the rebels were forced farther and farther back into the mountains his objections began to look like tardy vindication of his own ineffectual tenure of office. In the summer of 1566 he and Dudley almost came to blows at the Council board. Leicester accused Sussex of responsibility for O'Neill's rebellion. Sussex angrily countered with the calumny that Leicester had written letters of encouragement to Tyrone. Had the Queen not intervened the rivals would probably have fought a duel. Meanwhile Sidney's success continued until O'Neill was driven to seek refuge with kinsmen who turned against him and murdered him. Sussex was at least saved the final humiliation of receiving this news at court. Days before it arrived he had been despatched on an embassy to Vienna.

These petty intrigues spilled over into the important sphere of international politics. So determined were Norfolk, Sussex and their conciliar supporters – and even sometimes Cecil – to destroy Dudley's influence that they espoused policies which, had they materialized, would have brought disastrous consequences.

Leicester's political judgement had now matured considerably but his vision was also clouded by his desire to please Elizabeth, his need to safeguard his own position and his determination to ward off the attacks of his enemies. Foreign affairs were sufficiently complex without these added distractions.

On 29 July 1565 Mary Stuart had married Darnley. Elizabeth's Council responded by appointing Bedford (who was already Governor of Berwick and Warden of the East Marches) as Lord Lieutenant of Northumberland, Cumberland, Westmorland and the Bishopric of Durham and providing him with extra men and money. But conciliar unity broke down when he and Thomas Randolph, the ambassador in Edinburgh, urged support for the Protestant rebel lords, led by the Earl of Moray. Leicester, Cecil and the majority of their colleagues were in favour of going to Moray's aid in order to restore the politico-religious balance and to persuade Mary to renounce her claim to the succession. But Elizabeth shrank from sanctioning the use of force against an anointed monarch, and in this she was supported by Norfolk and Sussex. It is difficult to escape the conclusion that Howard and Radcliffe opposed inter-vention because it might strengthen the hand of the favourite and his Puritan followers. The result was a policy of advance and retreat. At first Bedford was authorised to make 300 men and £1,000 avail-able to Moray. Then he was ordered to keep the troops at Berwick. As a result Mary drove her enemies from their stronghold and forced them to seek refuge over the border. Bedford hospitably received these victims of English policy at Carlisle, and for his pains was severely reprimanded by his Queen.

Now that Mary Stuart was clearly established on her throne and safely married, Elizabeth had come down firmly on the side of negotiation but the tumultuous course of events in Scotland made this difficult. The murder of Rizzio, and subsequently of Darnley, and the birth of Mary's son forced constant reappraisals of the diplomatic situation. As long as events in Scotland were unsettled Cecil and Dudley were able to pursue a common policy, for they were concerned only to turn the situation to England's advantage. It was partly this which enabled Leicester to effect a reconciliation between Throckmorton and the Secretary in May. Cecil complained about Sir Nicholas's extreme policies but, on the latter's promise of future good behaviour, he held out the hand of friendship. By the middle of 1567, however, Mary's cause had collapsed completely and this once more drove a wedge between Secretary and favourite. Mary's subjects, Catholic and Protestant alike, had had their fill of royal lust and bloodshed. In June the Queen of Scots and her new husband, Bothwell, were defeated. Bothwell fled, Mary found herself a prisoner in Loch Leven Castle and the triumphant Moray was proclaimed Regent.

Throckmorton was sent north to negotiate with the victors while his masters in London wrangled over the instructions he was to be given. Cecil believed that Throckmorton should confine his activities to reaching a settlement with the triumphant Moray. Leicester, knowing how deeply Elizabeth felt about the sanctity of Kingship, realised that she would insist on Mary's release as a precondition of negotiations. His policy was based upon this reality and, though it upset his Puritan friends to see him going to the aid of the papist murderers, it was more likely than Cecil's to achieve the desired effect. The two basic elements in Dudley's political thinking at this time were his extreme Protestant conviction and his determination to try to give coherent form to the Queen's thoughts and feelings. These elements could not always be successfully combined.

Elizabeth was furious at the way the Scottish Lords of the Congregation of Jesus Christ (as the Reformation leaders called themselves) had treated their queen. The Lords were scarcely less angry at the English sovereign's coolness towards them. Poor Throckmorton was in the middle, trying to dissuade the Lords from sterner measures against Mary Stuart, to explain to Elizabeth that the new regime could not release a queen who had proved totally untrustworthy, and to make some arrangement for the upbringing of Prince James. At the Council board Leicester was in much the same position, having to convey Elizabeth's policy to a body, the majority of which opposed it. At the same time, he knew from Sir Nicholas's private reports that events in Edinburgh had reached a complete stalemate. The Queen recognised this on 11 August when she ordered Throckmorton's withdrawal in the strongest possible terms. Cecil affected to believe that Elizabeth's rage, of which he bore the brunt, was a charade, 'that she be not thought to the world partial against the Queen' and that no encouragement be given to any of her own discontented subjects.[24] He was wrong: Elizabeth's belief in what a later generation would call 'the divine right of kings' was profound and total. In 1566 she told parliament, 'I am your anointed Queen. I will never be by violence constrained to do anything . . . it is monstrous that the feet should direct the head'.[25] It was the Secretary's refusal to appreciate the depth of his mistress' feelings on this issue that led to his partial eclipse during these crucial months, and it was Leicester's support which cemented his return to favour.

The wedge driven between the two ministers and their policies was not, as has been often suggested, Dudley's overweening ambition, but

Elizabeth's concept of her role. Leicester supported that concept; Cecil did not. The Secretary persisted in thinking of the Queen as a pawn in the game of international relations. Although he would never have used that word and would have been shocked at its disrespectful implications, nevertheless it accurately represents his concept of the sovereign and her responsibilities. Elizabeth had to be manoeuvred. In particular she had to be persuaded to marry. One of his neatly reasoned private memoranda, written in 1566, clearly reveals his attitude:

> To urge both marriage and establishing of succession is the utter-most that can be desired. To deny both is the uttermost that can be denied. To require marriage is the most natural, most easy, most plausible to the Queen's majesty. To require certainty of succession is the most plausible to the people. To require succession [i.e. agreement on who should succeed in the event of the Queen's fail-ure to produce an heir] is the hardest to be obtained both for the difficulty to discuss the right and for the loathsomeness in the Queen's majesty to consent thereto . . . Corollary: the mean betwixt these is to determine effectually to marry, and if it succeed not, then proceed to discussion of the right of the successor.[26]

Leicester approached the problems of Queen and country from quite a different angle. He was devoted to Elizabeth and sympa-thetic to her insistence on her prerogative rights. To say that this enabled Elizabeth to use her favourite as a political tool would be an exaggeration, but that he was useful to her in enabling her to with-stand Cecil's pressures is clearly true. The resulting rift between the two political camps was inevitable. Leicester supported Mary. That suggested an alliance with France to procure the peace and eventual union of the two British kingdoms through the accession of James. This policy might well place a strain upon relations with Spain. But clashes over religion, commerce and maritime activities were already pushing Spain and England farther apart. Catholic, world-striding Philip II was the real enemy, as Dudley and his radical supporters saw clearly. Cecil, on the other hand, put his faith in the Protestant Lords of the Congregation. This reinforced his belief that the succession must be secured by the Queen's marriage. That marriage must be with some foreign prince who would strengthen England against her traditional enemy, France, for it was only the French who could threaten a Scottish settlement and attempt to place Catholic Mary on the English throne. The right man would be a candidate approved by Spain, for a pro-Hapsburg policy was vital to England's security and commercial prosperity. Cecil, therefore,

worked hard to secure Elizabeth's marriage to the Archduke
Charles of Austria. He kept open his connections with the court in
Vienna and laboured to enlarge the pro-Spanish group in the
Council. Leicester's candidature for the hand of Mary Stuart had
given him fresh cause to hope, and the emergence of the Norfolk
faction had brought him allies whose support for the Austrian
match rested largely upon their determination to stop Leicester
marrying the Queen. Cecil shared this determination, of course, for
personal and political reasons. In 1566 he drew up memoranda
setting out the relative merits of the Earl and the Archduke as royal
suitors. Two versions have survived. One concentrates more on
personal attributes and was, perhaps, for use in discussion with the
Queen:

	Charles	Earl of Leicester
In birth	Nephew and brother of an emperor	Born son of a knight. His grandfather but a squire.
In degree	An archduke born	An earl made
In age	Of – and never married	Meet
In beauty of constitution	To be judged of	Meet
In wealth	By report 3000 ducats by the year	All of the Queen and in debt
In friendship	The Emperor, the King of Spain, the Dukes of Saxony, Bavaria, Cleves, Florence, Ferrara and Mantua	None but such as shall have of the Queen
In education	Amongst princes always	In England
In knowledge	All qualities belonging to a prince – languages, wars, hunting and riding	Meet for a courtier
In likelihood to have children.	His father, Ferdinando, hath therein been blessed with multitudes of children. His brother Maximilian hath plenty. His sisters of Bavaria, Cleves, Mantua and Poland have already many children.	*Nuptiae steriles.* No brother had children, and yet their wives have . . . Himself married and no children.

In likeli-   His father, Ferdinando,   *Nuptiae carnales a laetitia*
hood   *ut supra*   *incipiunt et in luctu*
to love his   *terminantur*. Hated of
wife   many. His wife's death[27]

The other contained political arguments for use with Council colleagues.

Reasons to move the Queen to   Reasons against the E. of L.........
accept Charles..........................
Beside his Person, his Birth
his Alliance.

I. She shall not diminish the
Honor of a Prince, to match
with a Prince.

                          I. Nothing is increased by
                          marriage of him either in riches,
II. When she shall receive   estimation, power.
messengers from kings, her
husband shall have of himself
by birth a countenance to
receive them.

III. Whatsoever he shall bring   II. It will be thought, that
into the . . . realm, he shall   the slanderous speeches of
spend it here in the realm.   the Queen with the Earl have
                          been true.

IV. He shall have no regard to
any person, but to please the
Queen.

                          III. He shall study nothing but
V. He shall have no opportunity to enhance his own particular
nor occasion to tempt him to   friends to wealth, to offices
seek the crown after the   to lands, and to offend
Queen, because he is a stranger, others.

Sir H. Sidney	Middlemore
Earl of Warwick	Colshall
Sir James Croft	Wykeman
Henry Dudley	Killigrew
Sir Francis Jobson	John Dudley
Appleyard	ii Christmas
Horley(Horsey?)	Forster
Leighton	Ellis
Mollyneux	Middleton

and hath no friends in the
realm to assist him.

VI. By marriage with him, the
Queen shall have the friendship
of King Philip, which is
necessary, considering the
likelihood of falling out with
France.

VII. No prince of England ever remained without good amity with the house of Burgundy; and no prince ever had more cause to have friendship and power to assist her estate.

VIII. The French King will keep Calais against his pact.

IX. The Queen of Scots pretendeth title to the crown of England, and so did never foreign prince, since the Conquest.

X. The pope also, and all his parties are watching adversaries to the crown.[28]

IV. He is infamed by death of his wife.

V. He is far in debt.

VI. He is like to prove unkind, or jealous of the Queen's majesty.

p 326

   This is not a catalogue of objective observations nor does it simply represent Cecil's prejudices about Dudley. It is a list of arguments which the Secretary drew up for use in debate; a list deliberately exaggerating Charles's virtues and Leicester's defects. It omits such inconveniences as, for example, that Charles was a Catholic and, as such, unacceptable to the majority of Englishmen. Again it was certainly true that Dudley was 'hated of many' but he was also admired and followed by many others, especially the Protestant radicals. It is as well to remind ourselves of these facts, for documents such as this have sometimes been taken at face value by historians assessing Robert Dudley's career and character.
   For Elizabeth the one advantage of the marriage/succession issue, which was the bane of her life, was that for every avenue along which her advisers tried to propel her there were numerous intriguing side roads down which she could meander in order to waste time. One such cul-de-sac in 1565 was the possibility of a French alliance. Since the Treaty of Troyes, Catherine de Medici had been trying to interest the Queen of England in a marriage with Charles IX, a boy half her age. The Queen Dowager transmitted her enthusiasm through her ambassador, Paul de Foix, and de Foix received warm encouragement from Leicester. For several months the favourite kept up diplomatic relations with him and the French court through Throckmorton and Killigrew.[29] For Catherine, desperately seeking means to maintain the independence of the

crown, the proposed match was important. Young Charles was well schooled and vowed that he loved Elizabeth.[30] For the English Queen, however, it was nothing but a diversion. Dudley knew it; Cecil knew it; all the supporters of the Hapsburg match knew it and saw in it further proof of Leicester's desperate scheming to prevent Elizabeth marrying anyone but himself. In July the Queen politely informed de Foix that she had accepted her Council's advice to reject Charles IX's offer on the grounds of disparity of age.

From this point Cecil, Sussex and Norfolk worked strenuously to bring off the desired Austrian marriage. Involved as they were in their scheming on various levels, the protagonists simply could not see that they were fighting for a lost cause. De Silva, though he gave the Archduke's friends every assistance, was never sanguine about the outcome. In June he reminded his royal master, 'I have on many occasions written to your Majesty that the Queen has always brought up the subject of the Earl to me and has frankly told me that she would marry him if he were a king's son.'[31] It was a fact he reiterated often in his despatches, urging on Philip the necessity of maintaining good relations with Leicester while seeming to support his enemies. It is highly significant that the two men Elizabeth appointed, with Cecil, to negotiate with the Austrian envoy, Zwetkovich, were Leicester and Throckmorton.[32] For all her repeated avowals, Elizabeth probably never had any intention of marrying the Archduke.

In the aftermath of the abortive French bid Norfolk demanded Leicester's acquiescence in the Hapsburg negotiations, if the Emperor's envoys were to take the English marriage offer seriously. Dudley had to agree. The Queen was encouraging the matchmakers and he had no other diversion to commend. The French had fallen back on urging Elizabeth to marry her favourite but, apart from taking every opportunity to assert his devotion, there was little Robert could do to advance this old cause.[33] In December Cecil deliberately activated the absent Norfolk by hinting that Dudley had renewed his wooing,[34] and a month later Leicester himself was obliged to deny reports that he had opposed the Hapsburg alliance in Council. He protested to Sussex that he and others had been misrepresented by a courtier.[35]

Throughout the ensuing months the desultory negotiations continued, prosecuted by Cecil and Norfolk and resisted by de Foix (who even spread the rumour that Elizabeth and Robert were sleeping together in an effort to shatter the brittle marriage plans)[36] while most informed observers looked on sceptically. Diplomatic to-ings and fro-ings only established three facts: that Charles would not come to England before all arrangements had been made; that Elizabeth would not consent to marry a man she had not met; that the Archduke demanded the right to continue practising his own faith. Whatever accommodation the two principals might have reached, the religious issue was the one which loomed largest with the people, especially as the necessity of reconvening parliament became inescapable. Norfolk believed it was not insurmountable. Cecil, according to de Silva, 'seems to desire this business so greatly that he does not speak about the religious point'.[37] This wishful thinking cost them months of fruitless endeavour.

When Parliament of 1563 reconvened in October 1566 it was in a truculent mood over the marriage and succession issues. The Commons deliberately held up debate on the government's finances and demanded to know the Queen's intentions on the subject of an heir to the throne. For months a vigorous pamphlet war had been waged in favour of rival claimants, the two most earnestly favoured being Mary Stuart and Catherine Grey.[38] Leicester's brother-in-law, Henry Hastings, had comparatively few supporters at this time and certainly Dudley, still tending towards the Queen of Scots, was not one of them.[39] Various councillors were sent down to the parliament chambers to try to buy off Lords and Commons with promises. They failed. The poor men were trapped between the Queen's angry determination to keep these issues to herself and the representatives' equally firm commitment to have the succession publicly decided. Among them, no one was more hard pressed than Dudley. The issue of Crown versus Commons, whose first rumblings were now heard, would lead to bloodshed in the next century and would cost the lives of more than one royal favourite. But Robert Dudley was not a man of such mettle as Thomas Wentworth. He joined with his colleagues in urging the Queen to receive a joint delegation of Lords and Commons and to return them a fair answer.

Elizabeth was furious. She lashed the leading nobles with her tongue. Norfolk she called a traitor and conspirator. Pembroke, she said, had all the empty braggadocio of a swaggering soldier. Northampton's own domestic life was such a disgrace she wondered he had the gall to lecture her about marriage. She castigated each one individually but her sternest reproach was kept for Leicester. She had supposed, she said, that he would have stood by her though the whole world was against her. He replied that he would die at her feet if that would serve her cause. 'What has that to do with the matter?' she retorted. Before she dismissed them she forbade them her presence till further notice. The ban included Sweet Robin.[40] However violently she might vent her spleen on those closest to her, the Queen could not avoid a confrontation with her Parliament. She summoned representatives of both houses before her on 5 November and delivered one of her most celebrated speeches. Calculated wrath was mingled with graciousness in an oration designed to silence argument while leaving the points at issue unanswered. She had promised that she would marry, she said. Was the promise not enough?

> I say again, I will marry as soon as I can conveniently, if God take not him away with whom I mind to marry, or myself, or else some other great let happen. I can say no more, except the party were present. And I hope to have children, otherwise I would never marry.
>
> A strange order of petitioners, that will make a request and cannot be otherwise ascertained but by their Prince's word, and yet will not believe it when it is spoken! But they, I think, that moveth the same will be as ready to mislike him with whom I shall marry as they are now to move it . . .

She then passed to the matter of nominating successors outside the direct line.

> Your petition is to deal in the limitation of the succession. At this present it is not convenient; nor never shall be without some peril unto you and certain danger unto me. But were it not for your peril, at this time I would give place, notwithstanding my danger. Your perils are sundry ways; for some may be touched, who rest now in such terms with us as is not meet to be disclosed, either in the Commons House or in the Upper House. But as soon as there may be a convenient time, and that it may be done with least peril unto you – although never without great danger unto me – I will deal therein for your safety.

It did not silence the parliament men. Elizabeth was obliged to send a more conciliatory message to the Lower House a few days later. Even the Lords, apparently, considered a further approach on the subject of marriage. Among his papers Robert kept a draft petition dated 10 November 1566.[41] No other version appears to have survived and it seems probable that their lordships lacked the courage of their convictions. Yet, in the end, the Queen was right: no husband would have pleased all the people, and a delineation of the succession would have led to conflict rather than peace. The existing situation meant frustration for everyone, none more so than Robert Dudley, but it was the best the country could hope for. Yet still the charade of the Austrian match continued. The following spring a more exalted envoy, the Earl of Sussex, was sent to Vienna to conclude negotiations and to confer the Garter on the Archduke. And that was all Charles ever got from England. By the autumn, when the Austrians had made virtually every concession possible, Elizabeth realised that she could not keep this particular ball in the air any longer. She rejected her Hapsburg suitor on the grounds of religion.

The ringing down of the curtain on this latest matrimonial comedy coincided with a distinct turn for the worse in Anglo-Spanish relations. It was at about this time that John Man, Dean of Gloucester, was sent to Madrid as ambassador. It might almost have been a deliberate act of provocation, for Man was an outspoken, intemperate Protestant. He constantly ridiculed the religious practices of his host country, habitually referred to the Pope as a 'canting little monk', and lost no opportunity in urging his government to have nothing to do with the 'powers of darkness'.[42] In April 1568, Man was expelled from Philip's court and two months later Elizabeth recalled him. He was not replaced. The event coincided with de Silva's departure. The new Spanish ambassador, Don Guirau Despes, was scarcely less abrasive than Dr Man and did nothing to foster Anglo-Spanish amity.

Events in the Netherlands also gave rise to alarm and suggested the need for England's statesmen to reappraise the direction of national policy. Protestant and nationalist fervour had grown steadily over the years and by 1567 outrages against Spanish officials and Catholic churches were frequent. Faced with a breakdown of law and order, Philip resorted to Draconian measures. He despatched the Duke of Alva to Brussels with 10,000 men – a number soon increased to 50,000. With this, the largest standing army in Europe, Alva had no difficulty in stamping out incipient revolt. William of Orange, the principal leader of Netherlands resistance, fled to Germany. The English government was faced with an immense Spanish garrison just across the Narrow Seas and received frequent pathetic appeals for aid.

Most members of the Council sympathized with the persecuted Protestant Netherlanders but, recalling the Newhaven adventure, few were prepared to recommend any kind of English intervention. As early as April 1567 Leicester was marked as the most extreme of Elizabeth's advisers: 'Lord Robert is now a strong heretic, and I am told is very sorry that affairs in Flanders are prospering, speaking evil of the Prince of Orange and saying that he has deceived the sectaries by promising them help and then abandoning them.[43] De Silva lamented that there were no Catholics left on the Council and asserted that Dudley had converted Pembroke to a radical Protestant belief. This is an interesting observation, for Pembroke had for some years occupied the middle ground in domestic politics, sometimes playing the role of peace-maker between members of the rival factions. His adherence to Dudley now is one more sign that the politico-religious issues were becoming more clear-cut. A simple soldier – which is essentially what William Herbert was – could see that England's interests now were against Spain and with whatever allies she could find to support her against the Catholic monolith. This meant, among other things, that England had to be made strong at sea.

Since the beginning of the reign naval and mercantile affairs had featured prominently in Council business and parliamentary debates. The necessity to maintain a sound merchant navy which would form the basis of England's defence in time of war was widely recognised. One means of achieving that was to obtain for English captains a greater share in trans-oceanic commerce. Hawkins, to give him his due, had tried to obtain permission from Spain to trade with the New World colonies. But the Spaniards, and also the Portuguese, were determined to maintain their monopolies. Attempts to break them continued on two levels: Hawkins and other English captains followed the French in piratical forays to the Main, and they were very soon followed by Dutch mariners sailing under letters of marque from William of Orange; while on a political and diplomatic level Elizabeth's ministers sought to clear the seas for native enterprise and to equip the navy for a more aggressive role in world trade.

The letters, the memoranda, the draft bills went through Cecil's office and bear his stamp but this should not blind us to the contributions made by other members of the Council. Leicester was assiduous in his attendance at meetings. In 1565, for example, out of 103 meetings Dudley was present at 81. Only Cecil and Knollys were more regular and, since the average attendance was about seven or eight out of a total membership of twenty-two, it is obvious that Leicester was one of a handful of men shouldering the burden of day-to-day administration. He was certainly the most active of the peers on the Council.[44] Leicester's extant correspondence and the opinions of colleagues attest his conscientious attendance to government business. He wrote letters to and received news from all the principal capitals of Europe. He had regular bulletins from Ireland and Wales. He expressed his opinion on religion, foreign relations, enclosures, mining, trade, customs duties, appointments at Oxford, examinations of state prisoners and a host of other topics. Even Dudley's political opponents, who rejected his views and questioned his motives, never dismissed him as an ill-informed dilettante. Their complaint was rather that he immersed himself too deeply in all affairs of state.

CHAPTER ELEVEN

'I MAY FALL MANY WAYS'

By 1569 a party had emerged within the Church of England which was given the label 'Puritan', and Robert Dudley was its most exalted supporter. His patronage of preachers and radical clergy was of inestimable value to the movement. He opposed unsympathetic bishops, obtained preferment for 'sound' men, argued in Council for further reformation, and interceded with the Queen on behalf of 'persecuted' Puritans. This made him the focus of attack for Catholics and religious moderates. Unfortunately, his consistent support did not win him the unqualified approval of the sizeable radical minority. The difficulty was his private life. His relationships with the Queen and with other ladies of the court provided a constant source of gossip. The fact that most of it was slanderous was of little consequence: Dudley was the sort of charming, handsome extrovert of whom any scandal is readily believed. His enemies, therefore, could – and frequently did – claim that Leicester was a man lacking in moral and religious scruples whose support for the Puritans was merely a matter of political convenience. Some of his friends could not rid themselves of the suspicion that there might be an element of truth in this claim.

Within Elizabeth's church there were many shades of belief between those at the one extreme who hankered after Rome and those at the other who looked to Geneva. One observer reported 'the hotter sort of Protestants are called Puritans'.[1] More precisely, however, the Puritans were those Anglicans who objected to some aspects of official liturgical practice, such as the use of vestments and the 1559 Prayer Book, and who refused to conform in such matters. In the 1570s and 1580s there emerged from this party a smaller group, called the Presbyterians, who carried their protest still further. They wanted to do away with episcopal government and to introduce a system which gave greater autonomy to the local congregations.

By upbringing and by personal conviction Robert was, as we have seen, a religious radical, and one who used his influence in the cause of international Protestantism from the beginning of Elizabeth's reign. It has been suggested that he was much more circumspect in the early years of Elizabeth's reign until he could see which way the religious wind was blowing.[2] Certainly it is true that Robert Dudley did not belong to that rare breed of men who are prepared to sacrifice everything for the sake of their faith. But nor did any other politically prominent Elizabethan Protestant. Henry Hastings, Earl of Huntingdon, served faithfully at the court of Philip and Mary. Walter Mildmay began his career in government during the same reign. Francis Russell, Earl of Bedford, did, it is true, obtain leave to travel abroad in 1555 but he served under King Philip at the Battle of St Quentin alongside the Dudley brothers. Cecil and Walsingham had nothing to do with politics during the reign of Catholic Mary, yet of all Puritan patrons they were to prove the most circumspect. Robert had helped several returning exiles to important posts in the English Church and over the years was the dedicatee of many works of Protestant devotion and propaganda. It was clearly no sudden or even gradual conversion that the French ambassador reported in 1568, when he said that Leicester was 'totally of the Calvinist religion'.[3]

Dudley's service to the Puritan movement increased in direct proportion to his wealth and power. As his landed wealth grew so did the number of benefices in his gift and so did his influence over tenants and neighbours responsible for other parochial incumbencies. The religious influence of the great landowners can scarcely be exaggerated. Men like Russell, Hastings and Dudley could ensure Puritan dominance throughout large areas of England, just as Catholic patrons, such as the Howards and Talbots, could keep the conservative witness alive despite government policy. Robert Fills called them 'nurses of religion'.[4] Partisan lay patronage created great problems for the bishops, who were virtually powerless to control recalcitrant clergy who had the backing of great noblemen. Many clergy received their livings at Dudley's hands and were regarded as his chaplains. As well as the regular clergy there were itinerant preachers who were paid by individual benefactors or town corporations to give instruction in private houses, public buildings and churches. Such lectureships (Dudley instituted at least one – at Warwick – and the Earl of Huntingdon established another at Leicester) were entirely outside episcopal control. It was inevitable that certain individuals should attract considerable followings and that the bishops should become increasingly alarmed by the influence they were wielding and by the breakdown of traditional authority.

One such radical who was supported by Leicester and his friends was William Whittingham, one of the leaders of the exiled community in Geneva. On his return in 1561 Huntingdon supported him as an itinerant preacher in Leicestershire and tried, unsuccessfully, to have him appointed to the living of Loughborough. In 1563 he went as a chaplain to Newhaven with Ambrose Dudley. Subsequently, it was the influence of Robert and Ambrose that won for him the deanery of

Durham. In 1565 Thomas Sampson, Dean of Christ Church, Oxford, became one of the first Puritans to suffer for his convictions. The Queen deprived him of his Oxford appointment and not even Dudley, who had been Chancellor of the university since the previous December, was able to save him (as we have seen, he was not on the best of terms with Elizabeth for much of that year). But he certainly stood up for the man: he persuaded the Bishop of London to allow Sampson to air his views at Paul's Cross, and when the trouble blew over he and Huntingdon were instrumental in having the Puritan appointed to the mastership of Wigston's Hospital, Leicester.

The Dudley interest in the Midlands ensured a large Puritan stronghold in that area. In 1567 Robert took pains to provide 'the preachers of the Gospel in the county of Warwick' with a greater degree of security. He and other benefactors provided certain lands and funds, and Leicester obtained letters of incorporation for a body of trustees to administer them. The trustees were Huntingdon, Warwick, Sir Ambrose Cave, Sir Nicholas Throckmorton,[5] Sir Thomas Lucy, Sir Richard Knightly and Clement Throckmorton. This was a considerable step forward in establishing an independent church structure dominated and funded by laymen and quite separate from episcopal control. Town corporations had endowed lectureships in perpetuity. Wealthy men had left funds for the support of Puritan preachers in their wills. But Dudley's initiative in its scale and its potential challenge to the religious establishment was something new.

One of the returning exiles for whom Robert found a post in the Midlands was the fiery Thomas Lever. He had been a protégé of Northumberland in Edward's halcyon days and naturally looked to the Duke's son when he came back from the Continent in 1559. Robert succeeded in placing him as rector and archdeacon of Coventry. He faithfully supported his patron but did not consider that loyalty absolved him from the responsibility to offer godly criticism in the matter of Lady Amy's death. That crisis over, Robert was able to resume his benevolent oversight of Lever's career. In January 1563 the preacher became master of Sherburn Hospital, Durham, and a year later he gained a canonry at Durham. Then the trouble began. Lever refused to conform with 'popish' practices, such as wearing the surplice, and used his position to champion the cause of diocesan clergy who were being persecuted for their Puritan stand. He clashed with his bishop and appealed to Dudley for support. Even Leicester could not save him from being dismissed from his canonry. However, Lever held his other posts, filled his archdeaconry with non-conformist ministers, preached in London, Coventry, Durham, and elsewhere against his 'heretical' superiors, was cited before church courts for breaches of discipline and all the time relied heavily on his patron for support and protection. At length even his own bishop, the easy-going, Puritan sympathiser Thomas Bentham (another Marian exile who probably owed his promotion to Dudley), became exasperated with Lever and ordered him to control the unseemly conduct of clergy in his archdeaconry. He was still at the centre of controversy when he died in 1577. Not long before his death he reaffirmed his lifelong gratitude to his patron: 'I and many others have by your means had quietness, liberty and comfort to preach the gospel of Christ'.[6]

The most celebrated of the radical leaders who enjoyed Dudley's patronage was Thomas Cartwright, 'the head and most learned of that sect of dissenters then called Puritans'.[7] The foremost advocate of Presbyterian government, he was a lecturer and preacher at Cambridge where his challenge to the establishment, based on a clear, logical exposition of scripture, excited a generation of students. It led to widespread nonconformity at Cambridge and elsewhere, and precipitated the expropriation of his professorship and fellowship (1570-1). In 1573 a warrant for his arrest was issued because he had openly supported John Field (another Dudley protégé), imprisoned for making an attack on the Elizabethan settlement and for refusing to conform. He crossed the Channel and spent the next eleven and a half years abroad, mostly visiting Reformed churches and writing or translating religious works which could only be regarded as seditious by Elizabeth and her bishops. Among the many English friends and supporters with whom he maintained contact was the Earl of Leicester. In 1582 a group of Catholics in exile at Rheims produced an English version of the New Testament which was full of controversial doctrinal glosses and intended as a tool for the reconversion of England. Dudley and Walsingham pressed Cartwright to prepare a refutation of the work. He did so, but the book was so aggressive in tone that Archbishop Whitgift ardently and successfully opposed its publication. Two years later Dudley joined with Cecil in begging the Queen to permit Cartwright to return home. Elizabeth refused, and it was without permission that the exile came back early in 1585. He was immediately put in prison.

The Presbyterian firebrand was now fifty years of age. He needed powerful friends who could engineer his release and provide him with some security for his old age, more than ever before. His supporters at court quickly extricated him from prison and the threat of prosecution, but Leicester's attempts to obtain a preaching licence for him were firmly opposed by Whitgift. For some months Dudley employed him as a private chaplain, and in the autumn

Cartwright was in the Netherlands to herald Leicester's advent among the Protestant congregations. Before departing on this campaign Robert appointed Cartwright to the vacant mastership of Leicester Hospital in Warwick. The post carried a generous stipend out of the £200 yearly income allotted to the hospital and, in addition, Robert provided Cartwright with a £50 annuity. As well as meeting the preacher's material needs this arrangement gave him a pulpit, which he occupied regularly until his death eighteen years later. According to one commentator, Cartwright now 'grew rich and had great maintenance to live upon and was honoured as a patriarch by many of that profession'.[8] The new Master, however, did not confine his activities to Warwick: he toured the surrounding countryside and other Puritan havens throughout the Midlands and sometimes he returned to Cambridge. His sermons always drew crowds and were a source of continual irritation to the hierarchy. But Dudley protected him, and for a short while after Leicester's death Ambrose took up the mantle of patronage. It is significant that within months of the latter's demise (20 February 1590) Cartwright found himself on trial and his revenues at Warwick in danger of alienation.

The extent of Dudley's personal involvement in the careers of religious extremists and the trouble he went to for them was sometimes quite remarkable. In 1570, Percival Wiburn was invited by local gentry to establish a Presbyterian model of church government in Northampton. Wiburn was a minister who had already been deprived of his London benefice for refusing to wear the surplice and who had recently returned from Geneva and Zurich where he had presented the Reformed leaders with his *State of the Church of England*, a highly critical document. The experiment was soon successful and Northampton was the setting for the most complete example of Genevan polity that England ever saw. Clergy and magistrates jointly ruled a society of enforced morality where the citizens were compelled to attend worship, hear sermons and receive regular instruction in the scriptures. Ministers met regularly for 'prophesyings' and mutual criticism. Breaches of discipline were firmly punished. However, Wiburn and his colleagues were not without their opponents. Some were content to grumble among themselves or circulate scurrilous verses. Others complained to their diocesan, the Bishop of Peterborough.

When the Bishop, Edmund Scambler, intervened, Wiburn and his supporters appealed to Leicester. This led to a protracted correspondence between the Bishop and the Earl. Dudley laboured hard on behalf of his protégés and took a close personal interest in the situation at Northampton. One of Scambler's letters preserved among the Dudley Papers carries many underlinings and marginal notes in Robert's own hand. The Bishop was in a difficult position: he personally owed much to Leicester yet he hugely resented the Earl's interference in the affairs of his diocese, as he hinted in a letter to Cecil shortly afterwards.[9] To Dudley he pointed out that unless Wiburn was prepared to conform he would have to refuse him a licence to preach. There were, he pointed out, other zealous and godly ministers who submitted to episcopal direction. If he allowed Wiburn to continue unchecked, his diocese would soon be filled with all sorts of troublemakers.

> [Wiburn] is, as it seemeth to me, studious of innovation. For although your lordship doth like the substance of his doctrine, or the most part thereof, even as do I, yet know you not . . . as I do, the contention and discord that is in Northampton between Bourne's men and [Wiburn] which is about matters, ceremonies and things indifferent, about which he showeth as much zeal as about the principal grounds of religion.[10]

Dudley was not in a strong position when it came to defending the likes of Wiburn, which makes it all the more remarkable that he should so often have stuck his neck out on their behalf. For religion was the one matter above all others on which he and the Queen could not agree. Elizabeth had no love for zealots and a genuine fear of ecclesiastical indiscipline. Any breakdown of order in the church, she sensed, must be paralleled by a challenge of authority in the state. Robert's appreciation of the work of Puritan clergy, his sympathy with their doctrines (which matched his own radical approach to political affairs) and his fear of Catholic revival blinded him to the potentially disruptive nature of the movement. Indeed, his support of religious extremists became something of a trap for him. It goaded him into more and more independent policies which the Queen could not support, and it made him look for support to a sectarian group outside the mainstream of national life.

Gradually the dangers of Presbyterianism dawned upon him and he saw not only that by helping separatists he was isolating himself, but also that the movement itself was disruptive. He lost the battle over Wiburn, who was forced to leave Northampton in 1572 (though he continued his activities in neighbouring villages with the support of the local gentry). This seems to have helped to clarify Leicester's thoughts on the Presbyterian issue, for it was about the same time that he wrote to a Puritan friend:

> . . . as some of the higher sort have been over hard, perchance, to some of their inferior brethren, so are they of the inferior sort that

show more wilfulness in some cases than reason or charity will well allow. For undoubtedly I found no more hate or displeasure almost between papist and Protestant than is now in many places between many of our own religion . . . For my own part, none hath travailed more from the first than myself hath done to have the sincere conscience of faithful preachers and ministers to be preserved. Neither have I left [any] means undone that might make reconcilement between them and others.[11]

From this time onward Robert tried hard to prevent the disintegration of English Protestantism into rival camps. For example, in an effort to settle the vestments controversy he initiated, in 1573, through the Queen's Latin Secretary, Sir John Walley,* discussions with John Sturm, the Strasbourg leader, and the German Protestant princes.[12]

But he could not control the hotheads and blind zealots of the movement. Matters came to a head at Southam, Warwickshire, in 1576. One of the most important aspects of the Puritan movement was the 'exercises' or 'prophesyings': meetings of local ministers for mutual exhortation and Bible study, sometimes accompanied by public sermons. Large numbers were attracted to these orations and Dudley certainly attended on his occasional travels into the country. Some of them were harmless enough, but their potential as rallying points of dissent was obvious from the beginning. They were anathema to the Queen, who urged her bishops to be vigilant in suppressing the meetings. Some were disbanded but the diocesans hesitated to offend the leaders of local society who supported them. Among Puritans the exercise in Southam was considered 'undoubtedly without exception . . . the best exercise of this realm.' However, those who did not share this view complained to the Queen about the behaviour of the Presbyterian ministers and gentlemen (including Robert's friend, Sir Richard Knightly). Elizabeth referred the matter to Leicester – Warwickshire was, after all, 'his' county. Robert could not in all honesty, defend his protégés this time. The Southam men had gone too far. In so doing they had endangered the whole movement and seriously embarrassed their stoutest champion. In the event, Southam had to be sacrificed in the hope of preserving the other gatherings. Leicester passed on Elizabeth's protests to Archbishop Grindal and the Southam exercise was closed down. The faithful were dumbfounded. Some accused Dudley of deserting them.

The truth was otherwise, as an exchange of letters written within weeks of the Southam business demonstrates. Thomas Wood, a Leicestershire gentleman, an old servant of the Dudleys and a

*Walley had been one of Dudley's secretaries before being preferred to royal service.

leader of the Midlands Puritans, wrote to both Robert and Ambrose
on 4 August. He did not mince his words:

> It is commonly reported among the godly . . . that your Lordship
> hath been the chief instrument, or rather the only, of the overthrow
> of a most godly exercise at Southam, to the great hindrance of
> God's glory and the grief of all good men that have heard it or
> heard of it, which maketh them afraid lest the rest of such most
> profitable exercises both for the preachers and people . . . shall like-
> wise be overthrown, which God forbid. Ah, my Lord, I have known
> you and so you have been taken to be an earnest favourer and as it
> were a patron of these zealous and godly preachers who have been
> the setters forth and maintainers of these worthy exercises. They
> are the same men now they were then, and only seek God's glory as
> zealously as ever they did. And can you then become enemy to them
> now and not show yourself enemy to him whose faithful messengers
> they be and whose glory they only seek to advance?[13]

The replies were not long in coming. Ambrose's was dated 16
August. It was dignified and restrained yet throughout its tone was
one of scarcely suppressed indignation:

> . . . since there is no man knoweth his doings better than I myself,
> I must therefore declare my knowledge without any brotherly
> affection but even as the truth shall lead me. First, whereas he is
> charged to be the only overthrower of the godly exercise used at
> Southam, I can assure you there is nothing more untrue . . . he
> hath always had a special care in maintaining of it, so far forth as
> it might tend to the edifying of the Church of God. But when
> there began some abuses among them to be reformed, I think
> then that not only he but myself also, with divers others, did seek
> by all the good means we could to have them brought in that
> order indeed as that they might continue in their well doing and
> not to be cut off . . . I cannot a little marvel that either you or any
> other will so lightly condemn him upon every slight report who
> hath done so great good amongst you as he hath done.[14]

Robert's own answer was penned three days later. It is a long,
important letter. In no other extant writing of his do we find such a
vigorous and heartfelt religious testament. He was clearly stung by
accusations made by those who above all men had most cause to be
grateful to him. He catalogued all the services he had done for the
Puritan cause. He affirmed his lifelong, constant dedication to the
Protestant faith. He acknowledged himself a sinner and one, moreover, who stood 'on top of the hill, where . . . the smallest slip

seemeth a fall' but he categorically denied being a traitor to the godly exercise at Southam.

Once again he took the opportunity to state his opinion on current developments in the church:

> I am not, I thank God, fantastically persuaded in religion but, being resolved to my comfort of all the substance thereof, do find it soundly and godly set forth in this universal Church of England . . . And generally for the exercises which I have known and heard of in many places, there was never thing used in the Church that I have thought and do think more profitable both for people and ministers, or that I have more spoken for or more laboured in defence of, even from the beginning, especially where they are used with quietness to the conversation and unity of the doctrine established already and to the increase of the learned ministry . . . I fear the over busy dealing of some hath done so much hurt in striving to make better . . . that which is . . . good enough already that we shall neither have it in Southam nor any other where else . . . And this have I feared long ago would prove the fruit of our dissension for trifles first and since for other matters.[15]

Leicester's fears were soon realised. Within weeks Elizabeth summoned Edmund Grindal, Archbishop of Canterbury, to court and ordered him to see that all the Puritan exercises were suppressed. The poor man could not in conscience do so. He went away and, in the quiet of his study at Lambeth, he prepared a detailed, respectful defence of the exercises. In December he delivered it to Dudley and asked him to present it to the Queen. Whatever soft words Robert may have used in commending the Archbishop's letter evidently did not impress Elizabeth. Grindal was refused entry to the court and Leicester continued to act as his intercessor and intermediary. It was Leicester who suggested a compromise solution – that the exercises be allowed to continue but without lay participation – but the Archbishop would not yield ground. Nor would the Queen. Once more Dudley and virtually the whole Council found themselves united in opposition to their sovereign. They argued with her, spoke up for Grindal (now under virtual house arrest at Lambeth), and urged moderation. Elizabeth insisted that her orders be carried out and demanded the deprivation of the Archbishop. In the spring of 1577 Cecil sent out orders in the Queen's name to all bishops authorising the suppression of the exercises. But over Grindal she did not get her way. The old man's friends laboured hard on his behalf and, though he was never permitted to carry out all his functions, he retained his office till his death in 1582. That Leicester was still

among those interceding on Grindal's behalf over a year later is
proved by a letter from Sir Christopher Hatton to the Earl, in which
he says: The Bishop of Canterbury has oft sent to me to enquire of
your good Lordship's help in respect of his cause. I have now
answered that your Lordship hath effectually written in the same.
And I have dealt accordingly with her majesty, at whose hands, when
good may grow (which yet I find not) I will so deal . . .'[16] But Grindal's
opposition raised too important an issue: whether Queen or
Archbishop was the final authority in the Church of England. It was
a matter on which Elizabeth could not back down, even when
Leicester, Cecil and the majority of the Council stood against her.

Puritan leaders might have been less ready to accuse Dudley of
desertion if they had felt his private life was above reproach. When
Thomas Wood wrote his letter of 4 August 1576 he referred to
'other very common rumours very dishonourable and ungodly . . .
which I thought to have spoken with you about the last year
Kenilworth' (i.e. when Leicester was there for the royal progress in
July 1575).[17] In their replies both brothers made veiled references
to the subject of the gossip using almost identical words. Ambrose
declared that whatever the allegation was he hoped it would prove
to be unfounded, 'although I must needs confess we be all flesh and
blood and frail of nature, therefore to be reformed'.[18] Robert wrote:
'I will not justify myself for being a sinner and flesh and blood as
others be . . . But I will not excuse myself. I may fall many ways and
have more witnesses thereof than many others who perhaps be no
saints either'.[19] The sins of the flesh here virtually acknowledged
were his relations with certain ladies of the court.

How many such affairs Robert had had in earlier years we can
never know but it seems very unlikely that he was at all promiscu-
ous. He would not have wanted to do anything which would have
given Elizabeth the impression that she no longer held a monopoly
of his love. In 1565 he had deliberately flaunted his affection for
another woman and the results had been catastrophic. Whether or
not Robert had serious hope of marrying the Queen, as long as she
remained without a husband he had to maintain his courtship of
her. This meant forswearing marriage and probably intimate relations with any other. It was a high price to pay for Elizabeth's
continued favour. Not only did such abstinence involve sexual frustration, it also had serious dynastic consequences. It

> . . . forceth me . . . to be [the] cause almost of the ruin of my own
> house. For there is no likelihood that any of our bodies of men
> kind [are] like to have heirs. My brother you see long married and
> not like[ly] to have children. It resteth so now in myself, and yet, .

.. if I should marry I am sure never to have favour of them that I had rather yet never have wife than lose . . . yet is there nothing in the world next that favour that I would not give to be in hope of leaving some children behind me, being now the last of our house. But yet, the cause being as it is, I must content myself . . .[20]

Vague rumours there always were, persistent and insubstantial as coastal fog. The first firm linking of Leicester's name with any woman is found in a letter written by the twenty-year-old Gilbert Talbot to his father, the Earl of Shrewsbury, in May 1573.

My Lord Leicester is very much with her majesty and she shows the same great good affection to him that she was wont. Of late he has endeavoured to please her more than heretofore. There are two sisters now in the court that are very far in love with him, as they have been long; my Lady Sheffield and Frances Howard. They (of like striving who shall love him better) are at great wars together and the Queen thinketh not well of them, and not the better of him. By this means there are spies over him.[21]

If these amours had only just come to light the participants had been exceedingly discreet, for Robert and Lady Sheffield had been carrying on an affair for months – if not years.

Indeed, in that very same month – May 1573 – they were married.

Lady Douglas Howard, by repute a great beauty, was the daughter of William, first Baron Effingham, councillor and great-uncle of the Queen. She was married at an early age to Lord John Sheffield and widowed in 1568, when she was twenty. Shortly afterwards she came to court as a Lady of the Bedchamber. It was apparently not long before she fell under Leicester's spell. As their relationship deepened Douglas, inevitably, wanted the security and permanence of marriage. Robert explained to her – probably more than once – that this was out of the question.[22]

For a time, it seems, Leicester's mistress was content with her role, but then she began once more to clamour for him to do the honourable thing. This time Robert explained his position in writing. It was not a very gallant letter. He set down the reasons why it was impossible for him to offer her marriage. He assured her of his continuing affection. He told her that he realised how unsatisfactory her situation was and he offered her two alternatives, either of which would have his blessing: she could continue their relationship on the present basis or she could seek a suitable husband. This was the decision he had reached, he said, after having 'thoroughly weighed and considered both your own and mine estate' and with Douglas's best interests in mind: '. . . albeit I have been and yet am a man frail, yet am I not void of conscience toward God, nor honest meaning toward my friend, and, having made special choice of you to be one of the dearest to me, so much the more care must I have to discharge the office due unto you.'[23]

Douglas, it seems, did not accept the stark alternatives offered by her lover. Whenever she received the letter (and it is quite impossible to date from internal evidence) she had decided by the spring of 1573 to press Robert to marry her. Perhaps the letter itself gave her her opportunity. Nothing would have been easier for her than to let it fall in the Queen's Bedchamber. The mere threat of such action may well have prompted Leicester to be more accommodating. Or perhaps, intentionally or accidentally, Lady Sheffield let the mask of discretion slip, so that tongues in the court began to wag and Elizabeth's suspicions were aroused (as we know they were).

It seems that Robert lacked the ruthlessness to break with Douglas, or ever to stand by the firm decision he had made in his letter. He lacked also the courage and largeheartedness to acknowledge his love openly and face up to the consequences. Douglas or Elizabeth – whichever way, he decided he must hurt one of them. He could not do it. So he compromised. He agreed to a marriage, but one which must be kept secret. On a May evening, at a house in Esher, Robert Dudley was married for the second time. It was a clandestine ceremony attended only by close friends and servants of the couple. Douglas was given away by Edward Horsey, who, since his return to England, had been a close supporter of Dudley and had served his country as soldier, pirate and Captain of the Isle of Wight. Also present were Dr Giulio Borgarucci and Robert Sheffield, a kinsman of the bride. Robert espoused his new countess with a diamond ring given to him by the Earl of Pembroke.[24]

It seemed that Leicester really had found a way to have his cake and eat it. He continued to enjoy both Douglas and the Queen's favour. Even when news reached court that a son had been born to the couple (on 7 August 1574) there was, apparently, no outburst of royal anger, or if there was, no record of it has survived. The boy's existence (he was christened Robert – Ambrose and Sir Henry Lee standing godfathers), and therefore his parents' relationship, could scarcely be kept secret, although the marriage was. Leicester acknowledged the baby and referred to him as 'my base son' and 'the badge of my sin'. Elizabeth seems to have forgiven her favourite's 'lapse' (a far from unusual one in Tudor high society); the Countess of Leicester seemed content to enjoy her new station in the seclusion of Esher and Leicester House; and everything went on much as before. Or so it seemed.

But the appearance was a delusion, as Dudley soon realised. Once having practised to deceive he found himself having to spin an exceedingly tangled web. The comparative simplicity of his former situation had gone for ever. The opportunities for himself and his enemies were now more numerous and varied. His opponents were, at the least, supplied with a means of sullying Leicester's reputation, and we have already seen how his 'fornications' had upset his Puritan following. Of course, if any of them discovered the truth, they would have a way of scotching once and for all any hopes of a marriage with the Queen and perhaps of ruining the favourite entirely. Yet, paradoxically, the birth of a son brought potential advantages to Robert. He now had an heir, and one whose legitimacy he could reveal if it ever became desirable to do so.

Robert's indulgence in a private life had to be fitted into the brief hours spared him by his involvement in politics. In May 1568 Mary Stuart escaped, crossed the border and threw herself on her cousin's mercy. In the same year Catherine Grey died and the Queen of Scots thus became the only serious contender for the succession. Few men of consequence now seriously believed that the Queen of England would ever marry. On the face of it, therefore the internal situation had become greatly simplified. Mary was in Elizabeth's hands, and this meant that both a Scottish settlement and a decision on the English succession could be made in Westminster. This simplicity, however, was an illusion. Mary's arrival was a catalyst which produced among the unstable elements in public life a number of interlinked reactions – Catholic provincialism versus Protestant centralism, pro-Spanish versus anti-Spanish, conciliar nobility versus Secretary Cecil. The next three or four years were dangerous, uncertain years for Elizabeth, and scarcely less so for Robert Dudley.

Elizabeth's inclination was to restore the Queen of Scots to her throne on terms imposed by England. It was a policy strongly supported by Leicester and as strongly resisted by Cecil. The Secretary was in favour of detaining indefinitely the prisoner whom Providence had delivered into English hands, and of reaching agreement with the Scottish Regent. It was a point of view likely to commend itself to most Protestants. Yet Dudley's position was not an abandonment of his religious principles; he regarded a satisfactory ecclesiastical arrangement as a prerequisite of replacing Mary upon her throne. Both men, however, were agreed that Mary should be kept as securely as possible. They tried to persuade the Queen to consent to her removal from Bolton Castle, where she was lodged, to some stronghold in the firmly Protestant Midlands. But Elizabeth was reluctant; she wanted to preserve Mary's royal dignity and not

give the impression that she was a prisoner to be hustled unceremoniously from one place of detention to another. In the privacy of
her chambers Robert tried his persuasions, as he reported to Cecil:
'I . . . dealt with her . . . for the removing of the Queen of Scots from
Bolton . . . She did not fully resolve [the issue] with me . . .'[25]

Perhaps it was as well: even from Bolton Mary was able to influence the leaders of Elizabeth's court and government. Thomas
Howard was the first man to come under her spell. He was no
longer under the influence of Sussex, who was serving as President
of the Council of the North. It might have been better for him if he
had been (Sussex said as much in a letter to Cecil) for the Earl,
though bellicose, had a shrewd sense of political realities. His
mentor now was the aged and cynical Arundel. His enemies had
also changed: William Cecil, his erstwhile ally, was now the object of
his wrath. Perhaps it was the collapse of the Austrian alliance or a
difference of opinion over Mary Stuart which gave rise to this
volte-face. Resentment of the Secretary's influence in foreign affairs
and opposition to the drastic policies he seemed to be pursuing
were the reasons Norfolk and Arundel gave for the vendetta they
pursued in the winter of 1568-9. It was a vendetta which, briefly,
Leicester abetted.

The trouble began in November when storms and French pirates
forced a number of Spanish ships to take refuge in Plymouth and
Southampton. They were carrying about £85,000 to pay Alva's
troops in the Netherlands. On the shallowest of pretexts the
English government decided to seize the money. There can be no
doubt that the initiative in this was Cecil's and that the motive for
his uncharacteristically bold action was his desire to replenish the
government's sadly depleted coffers. The Spanish ambassador,
Gueran de Spes, was, understandably, furious. So was Alva, who
retaliated by seizing the goods and ships of Elizabeth's subjects in
the Netherlands and closing the markets to English merchants.
Now it was the turn of the London mercantile community to be
upset. The diplomatic row came at a bad time for the capital. The
country was in the grip of an exceptionally hard winter. Both
Puritans and Catholics were under attack. Some people were critical of English money recently spent on aid to Protestant rebels in
France and the Low Countries. And, to crown all, an official lottery
recently launched in London had been badly mismanaged, giving
rise to accusations of corruption. Elizabeth's government had never
been so unpopular. Many members of the Council resented having
to share the blame for policies largely conceived and executed by
the Secretary. They were alarmed at the sudden lurch of foreign

policy which, according to some diplomatic circles, had carried England to the brink of war with Spain and had certainly done serious damage to the nation's trade. They complained that they had not been consulted and that Cecil was almost entirely responsible for the decision to seize the cargoes. Urged on by de Spes, Norfolk and Arundel set about recruiting support for the overthrow of the Secretary. The first man they had to recruit was Leicester. That was not easy, and Robert only joined them after several weeks of persuasion. They presented their argument in terms of the necessity of restoring true conciliar government and preventing overpowerful individuals controlling affairs of state. Dudley certainly supported some action against his old rival though he did not want to see Cecil sent to the Tower, the destination the conspirators had in mind. He agreed that Sir William had overstepped the bounds of his authority and that it would be good for him to be taken down a peg or two. Apart from anything else he was the major obstacle to the policy which Leicester, together with a group of councillors and noblemen, had decided to adopt towards Mary Stuart. This plan, conceived by Throckmorton, involved marrying Mary to the Duke of Norfolk and restoring her to her throne on condition that the Protestant religion was maintained north of the border and a permanent alliance entered into between the two nations. There is no evidence to suggest that Elizabeth was in any way privy to these schemes. If that is so, Leicester, whose name was appended to a letter explaining the plan to Mary Stuart, was taking an extremely independent line and must have known that the Queen would be indignant when she came to hear about it. On the other hand, it is just possible that Robert told her what was afoot at the outset and that she permitted the unofficial approach to be made in order to see what would happen. If it looked like being successful, she could adopt it as her own policy. If not, all the blame would fall on others. Elizabeth's behaviour towards Norfolk the following summer suggests that she knew more than she was supposed to know, and this type of stratagem was a favourite item in her political repertoire.

Unfortunately for Leicester, the chief conspirators had only told him as much as they wanted him to know. The real plans of Norfolk and Arundel were much more sweeping. They involved a purging of 'heretics' from the Council, the reintroduction of Catholicism with Spanish (and perhaps French) help, and the speedy restoration of Mary Stuart to her throne without conditions. According to the French ambassador, the scheme had the backing of Pembroke (which is a surprise, if true), Lumley and several northern magnates, led by Northumberland, Shrewsbury and Derby.

The first part of it – the attempt to overthrow Cecil – fizzled out very quickly. This was because the Queen got to hear about it. She summoned a Council meeting in order to confront the conspirators. All of them (including Leicester) made excuses, and it was not until 22 February that Elizabeth had the opportunity to raise the issue with some of them in her Privy Chamber. The French ambassador gave a graphic account of the exchange which took place, just before supper. Cecil, Norfolk and Northampton were already present when Leicester entered. The Queen immediately took him to task for the absences from the Council chamber which had prevented business being dealt with effectively. Respectfully but firmly, Robert pointed out the depths to which the government had sunk in popular esteem. Most of the policies currently being pursued, he said, were disastrously wrong and could only have the direst consequences for the country. The man largely responsible was Cecil, whom many people believed to be the one in control of all affairs of state. Elizabeth responded with one of her theatrical rages, defending Mr Secretary and turning the attack upon Leicester and his colleagues. Considering that Norfolk had urged him to make a stand against Cecil, it might have been expected that at this point the Duke would have stood firmly by his ally. All he could do was mutter some comment to the effect that if Leicester went to the Tower he would not go alone. If the Queen heard him she did not respond.[26]

Howard's irresolution was typical and was one of the main reasons for the plot's failure. After that episode Dudley's enthusiasm for the intrigue understandably waned. According to de Spes, a conciliar majority was prepared on three separate occasions in April to press home its attack on the Secretary, but Leicester refused his support. He realised that he was being used by the conspirators, who were only interested in him because of his intimacy with the Queen. By the spring of 1569 Dudley had probably received from his network of private agents some inkling of what lay behind the Norfolk-Arundel schemes. Certainly he began to grow cold on the marriage idea. It had been canvassed in Scotland and among the English nobility with very little success. By midsummer, Cecil was also in the 'secret', and it was scarcely conceivable that the Queen did not know what was going on. But she had not been informed officially and she declined to broach the matter herself, willing the conspirators either to have the courage of their convictions or to drop the plan entirely. In July Leicester and Norfolk were both with the court for the summer progress. During the following weeks their behaviour resembled that of naughty children nudging and prodding each other to confess to some piece of mischief. Time and again the opportunity to speak presented itself. Time and again the two noblemen funked it. Sometimes the Queen deliberately dropped hints about 'a marriage' but they were not taken up.[27]

During these lost weeks the chances of the plot's success crumbled through lack of support on either side of the border. This enabled Elizabeth to decide what her attitude should be. It also gave Dudley the chance to extricate himself entirely from the futile scheme. By 6 September he had decided how best to do this. The court was at the Earl of Southampton's house at Titchfield, Hampshire, and there Robert took to his bed with a diplomatic illness. He implored the Queen to come and comfort him – a plea he knew she would not ignore. As she sat at his bedside he poured out the whole story, assuring Elizabeth that he had been a reluctant conspirator (this was true of his attitude in recent weeks though not of his initial involvement in the marriage plan), had only supported Norfolk because he knew of his mistress's concern for Mary Stuart's restoration (there was certainly some truth in that) and had never deviated from his loyalty to her majesty. Of course, Elizabeth forgave him and vented all her spleen on Norfolk that very day.

The old intimacy returned, and the whole Dudley family continued to enjoy royal favour and friendship. By January Robert was able to write from Kenilworth in his customary bantering style:

If it lay in the power of so unable creatures to yield you what our will would, you should feel the fruits of our wishes, as well as the continual offerings of our hearty prayers. We two here, your poor thralls, your *ursus major* and *minor* [greater and lesser bear – i.e. Leicester and Warwick], tied to your stake, shall for ever remain in the bond-chain of dutiful servitude, fastened above all others by benefits past, and daily goodness continually showed, the last nor the least, where to our stake there stands so sure a staff as defends curs from biting behind: and then so long as you muzzle not your beasts, nor suffer the match over hard, spare them not: I trust you shall find they fear not who come before.[28]

Norfolk's behaviour continued to be unsatisfactory and he was taken to the Tower. This was the signal for his friends in the North, who had hitherto been lukewarm supporters, to rise in revolt. They tried, unsuccessfully, to free Mary Stuart, currently in the charge of the Earl of Shrewsbury at Tutbury. Elizabeth sent Huntingdon to help Talbot and the two peers removed Mary to the greater security of Coventry. Sussex resisted the northern earls in the field and an army was sent north under Warwick and Clinton. The rising collapsed rapidly and by the beginning of 1570 its leaders were either in prison or in exile. Norfolk remained in the Tower through the winter and spring and it was partly due to Leicester's supplications that he was released from the plague-infested prison in August 1570. (He had also helped to get Arundel freed from house arrest in March.) The Duke's bitter experience had taught him nothing: he was soon involved in the machinations of Roberto Ridolfi, an Italian banker who drew Norfolk, Mary Stuart, de Spes and Catholics at home and abroad into a plot of change, by force, the government and religion of England. Howard went back to the Tower on 5 September and it was Leicester who wrote to break the news to Arundel. The old Earl professed profound shock at the news and prayed Leicester to use his good offices once more.*[29] But Howard was now beyond the help of even the Queen's favourite. Leicester was among the peers before whom the Duke of Norfolk was tried and indicted for high treason in January 1572. But Elizabeth was reluctant to sign the warrant for his execution and Norfolk was still alive four months later. It was the clamour of the Commons for the Duke's head which finally moved her. Popular agitation for the removal of this danger to the state was strong. On the very day that parliament met (8 May) Robert received a long letter from Richard Farmer, who was employed at the Tower of London. Farmer descanted upon the suspicious activities of the Duke and other prisoners. There were, if he is to be believed, clandestine visits to inmates at which the Lieutenant connived, horsemen posting back and forth to East Anglia with letters in cipher, illicit conversations and notes between the ex-conspirators. There were also disrespectful comments about Dudley:

> . . . Powell, late pensioner, the 2nd day of this instant month or thereabouts, said unto Bannister, the late duke's man,† 'How say you, you shall see shortly a horse keeper made Lord Steward of England', and did speak the same with so loud a voice that these words were heard of such as stood without the Tower upon the wharf and, as they say that heard it, [it] might easily have been heard to the further side of the Thames.[30]

Farmer piously hoped that Powell 'and all other traitors may have

---

*It was not only Arundel who looked to Leicester for clemency. The Bishop of Ross, Mary's secretary, wrote to ask him to obtain his release from confinement to Ely Place (D.P., II, f.23.)

†Howard's title had been forfeit on his attainder.

straight justice according to their just deserts'.[31] The Duke of Norfolk went to the block on 2 June.

These traumatic years brought about changes in the personnel of the Council and the court. As well as Norfolk, Arundel was also removed from political life – not by death but by disgrace. He was not able to clear himself satisfactorily of involvement in the Ridolfi Plot and he was obliged to spend his remaining years in retirement. The Earl of Pembroke died in 1570. Sir Nicholas Throckmorton died on 12 February 1571. Sir Nicholas's demise was a severe blow for Leicester who had valued the older man's advice and found great use for his talents as go-between and administrator. But Dudley soon found another ally who shared his own political and religious views and whose talents were even more formidable than Throckmorton's. Francis Walsingham was the specialist in espionage and intelligence who had uncovered Ridolfi's activities. Between 1570 and 1573 he was employed as a diplomat in France, and in December 1573 he became Secretary of State in succession to Cecil. Walsingham was staunchly Puritan and anti-Spanish. He strongly supported an alliance with France and advocated firm measures to counter the growth of Hapsburg power. There was scarcely an area of policy in which his sympathies did not lie in the same direction as Robert's and it is not surprising that they were corresponding confidentially from early in Walsingham's political career. Another personality who now emerged from the shadows of the court into the sunlight was Christopher Hatton. Like Dudley his skills were those of the courtier. He excelled in the tilt-yard and court entertainments. Like Dudley he was a member of the Inner Temple and had been considerably enriched by the Queen. He too knew how important it was to maintain Elizabeth's favour by seeming ever attentive and by making extravagant protestations of love. Such tactics had brought him, by 1572, to the position of Gentleman of the Privy Chamber, and Captain of the Guard.

But while others came and went, the two men closest to Queen Elizabeth remained. If anything, their positions were stronger in 1572 than they had ever been. Both Cecil and Dudley had come under attack since 1568. In their hour of need the Queen had supported them. They had clashed often, had sought to undermine each other's position. They would continue to do so, but by 1572 they had reached an unspoken understanding. Beneath the surface civilities and the protestations of friendship one senses an unconscious realisation in the two men that they needed each other. The Queen needed and used them in different, complementary capacities. If either had destroyed the other, he would have upset the delicate balance at the centre of English political life. It was this 'sixth sense' surely which prevented Dudley falling in enthusiastically with his Council colleagues in the spring of 1569 when they had the Secretary at their mercy. It is significant that we rely for knowledge of their rivalry and feuds on the statements of others – primarily foreign ambassadors. Were we to have only the letters of Cecil and Dudley themselves on which to base an assessment of their relationship we should have to conclude that they were much more kindly disposed to each other. In November 1568 the Secretary could inform Sir Henry Sidney: 'At the writing hereof my Lord of Leicester is in my house at dice and merry, where he hath taken pains to be evil lodged these two nights. And tomorrow we return both to the court.'[32] In February 1573 Leicester was using his influence on Cecil's behalf when the latter had incurred Elizabeth's temporary disfavour.

> For your own matter I assure you I found her majesty as well disposed as ever at any time . . . and so, I trust, it shall always continue. God be thanked, her blasts be not the storms of other princes, though they be very sharp sometimes to those she loves best. Every man must render to her their due and the most bounden the most of all. You and I come in that rank, and I am witness hitherto [to] your honest zeal to perform as much as man can. And it cannot be but [that] it will work satisfaction, which shall be a recompense to your toiling body and a great quieting of your careful mind . . . Hold [your principles] and you can never fail.[33]

When, in later years, their relationship went through periods of strain, Leicester was wont to remind Cecil of their 'thirty years friendship',[34] to insist that his colleague had 'not found a more ready friend for you and yours than I have ever been', and to remind him that his obligation to the house of Dudley went back to the days when Northumberland first employed a young, ambitious lawyer.[35] There is a symbolism in a sombre tableau which might have been witnessed in the candlelit Queen's Bedchamber at Westminster on three consecutive nights at the end of March 1572. Elizabeth lay still, pale and, her doctors feared, close to death. The two men who watched with her during those sleepless nights were Robert Dudley and William Cecil.

In the midst of the recent troubles the Queen had demonstrated her confidence in Cecil by elevating him to the peerage as Lord Burghley (February 1571) and Leicester had stood at the new baron's right hand during the ennobling ceremony. In April of the following year Dudley deputised for the Queen at Windsor when Burghley was among the new knights appointed to receive the Order of the Garter. That Cecil fully deserved these marks of royal gratitude there can be no doubt but Elizabeth may have been partly motivated by signs of the Secretary's failing health. He suffered terribly from gout and, in the spring of 1572, a severe seizure brought the Queen to his bedside in fear for his life. About this time he laid down the arduous burden of his secretaryship. Within a few weeks he was appointed to the position of Lord Treasurer, made vacant by the death of the octogenarian Marquess of Winchester. This office was first offered to Leicester but he declined it, recognising that it really demanded a greater degree of 'learning and knowledge' than he possessed and that Cecil was a much more suitable candidate.[36] Once again Robert was using his influence to preserve the status quo. It would have been relatively simple to ease Burghley out of his dominant role in national affairs and, in so doing, to have achieved more power for himself, but he did not do so.

There is a possibility that Leicester hoped for another court appointment. In the general reshuffling of offices which followed the Marquess of Winchester's death it was rumoured that Dudley would receive his father's old post of Great Master of the Household. This probably lay behind Powell's comment about a horse-keeper becoming Lord Steward of England (in 1553 the title of the Great Master's office had reverted to 'Lord Steward of the Household). Dudley would eventually enjoy this highly prestigious post, vacant since Pembroke's death in 1570. For the time being, however, Elizabeth decided to leave it unfilled.[37]

One other achievement of Robert's during these years remains to be recorded. In 1554 he had been attainted of high treason. Though he had been subsequently pardoned, the crime still stood against his name. He felt it keenly and sought an opportunity to wipe the slate clean. That chance came in 1571. In the Trinity term of that year he brought an action for trespass against Sir Christopher Heydon in the Queen's Bench. The claim concerned the Dudley lands in and around Syderstone, which Heydon rented from Queen Mary after their confiscation as a result of the attainder. It was, in fact, only a means of calling in question and re-examining the legal processes by which Robert had been found guilty of treason. The case created a great deal of public interest and Westminster Hall was filled with lawyers, students and gentlemen of the court come to hear the verbal tussle between John Ives (an Inner Temple friend of Dudley), appearing for the plaintiff, and

Richard Best, appearing for the defendant. Ives contended that his client's trial at Guildhall before Thomas White on 19 January 1554 was invalid on two grounds: the court had not been properly convened according to the commission, and the indictment had been incorrectly worded so that the court was not competent to try it. The judges accepted these technical arguments and declared that, as Dudley's trial had been defective *modo et forma*, his conviction for high treason was void.[38] Coming, as it did, at a time when the loyalty of other prominent subjects was being called in question, this clearing of Dudley's name was doubly valuable to him. From 1571 he could defy anyone to challenge his fidelity to the crown. Whatever they might say about his father and grandfather, no one would be able to call Robert Dudley traitor.

CHAPTER TWELVE

'NEVER WIGHT FELT PERFECT BLISS, BUT SUCH AS WEDDED BEEN'

Elizabeth's visit to Kenilworth Castle in July 1575 was the social event not only of the year, but of the decade; perhaps even of the reign. She had been there twice before in 1565 and 1572, but Dudley made her last visit so memorable by the incredible extravagance of the entertainment he provided that it became a talking point for years afterwards.

On 9 July the Earl of Leicester rode out from his fine castle, having satisfied himself that all the last minute preparations for the Queen's coming were in hand. He met the royal party at Long Itchington and dined them sumptuously in an enormous pavilion. By the time he had brought Elizabeth and her court back to Kenilworth it was eight o'clock in the evening, and the castle, twinkling with the light from thousands of candles and torches, looked like a fairy palace rising from the lake. To heighten the illusion, as the visitors approached the outer gate, 'appeared a floating island on the large pool there, bright blazing with torches, on which were clad in silks the Lady of the Lake and two nymphs waiting on her, who made a speech to the Queen in metre of the antiquity and owners of that castle . . .'[1]

Thenceforth, for the next eighteen days, the worlds of actuality and myth completely overlapped. When Elizabeth went hunting, a savage man and satyrs appeared to recite flattering verses. Returning on another day to the castle, she was 'surprised' by Triton who emerged from the lake, dripping weeds and water, to make another oration. Even at her departing she found Sylvanus running at her stirrup and urging her to stay for ever. There were masques and pageants in plenty, banqueting and bear-baiting. There was a rustic wedding and games arranged for the townsfolk in the tilt-yard. There were mummers and a troupe of actors from Coventry who came to present traditional plays. There were tumblers and jugglers, and firework displays. There were picnics and minstrelsy on the lake. And everywhere 'magic' surprises – bushes that burst into song, pillars that grew fruit and gushed wine, trees decked with costly gifts. To achieve this effect Dudley and an army of servants bustled behind the scenes, ready to change the programme at a moment's notice in accordance with the whim of the Queen or the weather. One must hope that Elizabeth was appreciative and impressed, although it is unlikely that she was as overwhelmed as one visitor:

Since of delicates, that any way might serve or delight; as of wine, spice, dainty viands, plate, music, ornaments of house, rich arras and silk (to say nothing of the meaner things), the mass by provision was heaped so huge, which the bounty in spending did after betray. The conceit [was] so deep in casting the [plate] at first: such a wisdom and cunning in acquiring things so rich, so rare, and in such abundance: by so immense and profuse a charge of expense, which, by so honourable service, and exquisite order, courtesy of officers, and humanity of all, were after so bountifully bestowed and spent. What may this express, what may this set out unto us, but only a magnific mind, a singular wisdom, a princely purse, and an heroical heart?[2]

The writer could afford to be enthusiastic and to look no further than the lavish pleasures laid on for the visitors' delectation. Elizabeth, on the other hand, was only too well aware of the serious purposes behind all the play-acting and buffoonery. As in Inns of Court plays and masques presented at Whitehall, the allegory at Kenilworth concealed personal messages and political statements. Did the local couple whose nuptials were celebrated in the midst of all this grandeur realise that they were present as ambassadors of the wedded state? Marriage was the constant theme. The Lady of the Lake was a maiden imprisoned by Sir Bruce sans Pitié who tried to force her to marry and who had the support of the gods. Diana's nymph, Zabeta, had stubbornly maintained her virgin state and transformed her suitors into fishes, fowls, rocks and mountains. Dudley's playwrights were basically saying two things: the Queen should marry or the Queen should release her suitors from their bondage. Most interesting of all the Kenilworth entertainments was the one which was not performed. George Gascoigne's diversion about the contest of Diana (goddess of chastity) and Juno (goddess of marriage) for the allegiance of a nymph was probably set aside because the allegory was too threadbare. In it one of the characters advised Elizabeth:

> . . . give consent, O Queen,
>   to Juno's just desire,
> Who for your wealth would have you wed . . .

Whom should she wed? The answer was more than hinted at:

> . . . where you now in princely port
>   have past one pleasant day:
> A world of wealth at will
>   you henceforth shall enjoy
> In wedded state . . .

> O Queen, O worthy Queen,
> Yet never wight felt perfect bliss,
> but such as wedded been.[3]

Dudley's noble descent and manly virtues were lauded often by his players. Yet it would be a mistake to see this exorbitant Kenilworth display as a last, desperate gamble for the Queen's hand. Robert's affections had strayed elsewhere and his formal courtship of Elizabeth was now nothing more than that. As he grew older his desire for lawful progeny grew stronger. What Robert wanted above all was for Elizabeth to make a decision, to release him from the cords which had bound him for seventeen years – cords plaited from the threads of her love and his ambition.

The possibility of Elizabeth committing herself to a political marriage was not entirely dead. In 1570 Catherine de Medici had revived the idea of uniting one of her sons to the English Queen, and Elizabeth had not closed the door on the notion of a French alliance. There was no marriage, but Dudley and Walsingham earnestly canvassed the establishment of a treaty of friendship, and this, the Treaty of Blois, was concluded in 1572. The Duke de Montmorency, the leading French negotiator, acknowledged Leicester's part in achieving agreement in a personal letter.[4] When, in July, Montmorency came to England for the ratification, he and his suite were royally entertained, Leicester acting as principal host:

> The Duke with all his train, to the number of forty, have been entertained here for their meat and drink, each in their degrees, as it is to be affirmed that the like hath not been seen in any man's memory. The honour also done to him hath been such, as surely her majesty could do no more, I mean in her courteous usage of him, in appointing sundry sorts of the nobility of the highest sort to attend on him . . . no other lord but my Lord of Leicester did feast him . . .[5]

From the beginning the new concord was placed in jeopardy by the mercurial shifts and changes of French internal politics. In August 1572 Protestant Europe was appalled to hear of the Massacre of St Bartholomew, which made England's new ally look like a principal agent of the counter-reformation. The pro-French party suffered a serious setback and Burghley once more championed a policy of *rapprochement* with Spain. For months diplomats and diplomatic messages passed to and fro between London, Paris, Madrid and Brussels. By the time Elizabeth arrived at Kenilworth in the summer of 1575 she could feel well satisfied that all this activity had produced at least a temporary stability. All the uncertain elements in the European situation were, for the time being, held in equilibrium. The outstanding differences with Spain had been resolved and Philip once again had an ambassador at the English court. Trade with the Netherlands had been restored. The Treaty of Blois was reconfirmed.

Yet the issue of a French marriage never died and Elizabeth actually came close to marrying Francis, Duke of Alençon, a 'weak, graceless and marvellously ugly'[6] prince half her age. The attraction – or seeming attraction – between Elizabeth of England and her 'Frog', which baffled observers, can only be properly understood in the light of the changing relationship between Elizabeth and Robert. In its early stages the official courtship followed a by now familiar pattern. Elizabeth said neither 'yea' nor 'nay' and matters drifted on in this indecisive fashion until 1576. Elizabeth was, of course, using the Alençon courtship as a political stratagem. The important issues for England were the maintenance of peace between France and Spain, and the prevention of the Netherlands' conflict growing into a major war. Leicester knew exactly what game Elizabeth was playing. While men like Walsingham took the Queen at face value and complained 'no one thing hath procured her so much hatred abroad as these wooing matters',[7] he warmly supported the Alençon courtship, appreciating its diplomatic importance and knowing that nothing would ever come of it. By the middle of 1576 the project had, predictably, died. Two years later it was suddenly resurrected and both parties applied themselves vigorously to its restoration to full health. This time Robert opposed the match passionately, while the Earl of Sussex and Lord Burghley once more combined to counter his influence and to encourage the Queen to marry her grotesque Frog.

When we probe these bewildering twists and turns of love and state policy to discover what lay behind them, the most notable fact is the edginess of everyone concerned throughout much of this period. Whatever the pressures upon the principal personalities of the court, they were such as to lead at times to an almost complete breakdown of working relationships. Elizabeth was impossible. She refused to make decisions herself and frequently silenced those who urged her to action. At length, only Leicester and Hatton were permitted to broach affairs of state to her. Then she forbade even them to present suits.[8] On at least one occasion Robert had to resort to his old stratagem of begging the Queen to come to his sick-bed in order to have a few hours of serious discussion with her.[9] Council members began squabbling among themselves. The delicate relationship between Dudley and Cecil was endangered. In September

1578 Robert wrote a tetchy letter to the Lord Treasurer:

> . . . we began our service with our sovereign together and have long continued hitherto together. And, touching your fortune, I am sure yourself cannot have a thought that ever I was enemy to it . . . How often and how far I have offered myself always in good dealing towards you . . . [and] what friends have slipped from me and I have shaked from also, chiefly in respect of your Lordship I know best myself . . . [Yet] if I have not both long since and of late perceived your opinion . . . better settled in others than in me, I could little perceive anything. Yet this may I say and boldly think, that all them never deserved so well at your hands as myself, except in such secret friendship as the world cannot judge of . . .
>
> You may suppose this to be a strange humour in me to write thus and in this sort to you, having never done the like before, although I must confess I have had more cause of unkindness (as I have thought) than by this trifling occasion . . .[10]

The 'trifling occasion' which called forth this rebuke was Dudley's supposed slight at not being fully consulted on some proposed changes in the coinage, but, clearly, more lay behind it.

The European situation, which fluctuated almost from week to week, placed the English government machine under severe strain, but it was Dudley whose actions disrupted its inner harmonies. The established principles upon which it worked were few and simple: the Council handled day-to-day matters and made recommendations. Leicester was the main link with the Queen. By and large he represented her wishes at the board, and he liaised with her, particularly on sensitive matters. His colleagues might resent Robert's hold on the Queen's affections but they relied on him when there were unpleasant facts or uncongenial decisions to be placed before Her Majesty. By 1578 two important changes had taken place: Dudley had become the most powerful member of the Council and begun to pursue independent policies; as a result of his other amours he ran the danger of forfeiting the Queen's love. Since Walsingham had taken over as Secretary, Burghley had been less in control of Council business – and Walsingham was Dudley's man. The new Spanish ambassador, Bernardino de Mendoza, gauged the situation fairly accurately in March 1578:

> Although there are seventeen councillors, with the two secretaries, Hatton and the new ones, the bulk of the business depends upon the Queen, Leicester, Walsingham and Cecil, the latter of whom, though he takes part in the resolution of them by virtue of his

office, absents himself on many occasions, as he is opposed to the Queen's helping the rebels [i.e. in the Netherlands] so effectively and thus weakening her own position. He does not wish to break with Leicester and Walsingham on the matter, they being very much wedded to the States . . . They urge the business under cloak of preserving their religion, which Cecil cannot well oppose, nor can he afford to make enemies of them as they are well supported. Some of the councillors are well disposed towards your Majesty, but Leicester, whose spirit is Walsingham, is so highly favoured by the Queen, notwithstanding his bad character, that he centres in his hands and those of his friends most of the business of the country and his creatures hold most of the ports on the coast.[11]

Nothing illustrates more clearly Burghley's exclusion from important affairs than the preparations for Francis Drake's 1577 expedition. Total secrecy surrounded *El Draco*'s real intentions. The official story was that he was bound for Alexandria, like some of Leicester's other ships, to take on a cargo of currants. Only his backers, the Queen, Leicester, Hatton, Clinton, Walsingham, John Hawkins and Sir William Winter, knew that the real objective was the Pacific coast of South America and the silver bullion route from Peru to Panama. That the start of this celebrated voyage should have been curtained in secrecy was an obvious precaution to prevent Philip's agents getting wind of the venture. But it was not for that reason that Cecil was excluded from the plans, which were only finalised while the Lord Treasurer was taking the waters at Buxton. (Drake would state, during the voyage, that Elizabeth had specifically instructed that 'of all men my Lord Treasurer should not know' of it.)[12]

But there was no consistency in the Queen's reaction to Leicester's policies. As often as she supported them, she resisted them. Even more often she did neither. There was a coolness in her attitude towards her ō ō now that had seldom been present before. Certainly there were times when they seemed as close as ever. In October 1578, for example, it was Robert who sat up all night with her when she had toothache.[13] Certainly none of the handsome young men, like Hatton, who seemed to be following in Leicester's footsteps, were ever admitted to the same degree of intimacy. Yet the estrangements were more frequent. Leicester more often felt the sharp edge of Elizabeth's tongue or had some suit refused. They did not now share secret laughter or send each other messages couched in terms of cheerful, intimate banter. The root cause of all this was Robert's infidelity.

His love life had become an open scandal. While his secret wife and 'base son' were kept in seclusion, his eyes were roving elsewhere. At the end of 1575 de Guaras could report: 'As the thing is publicly talked about in the streets there is no objection to my writing openly about the great enmity which exists between the Earl of Leicester and the Earl of Essex in consequence, it is said, of the fact that while Essex was in Ireland his wife had two children by Leicester . . . great discord is expected in consequence.'[14]

Lettice, Countess of Essex, was thirty-five years of age in 1575; no flighty young Maid of Honour on the look-out for amorous adventure. Her magnificent portrait at Longleat (painted some ten years later) reveals a lady with even, pretty features, auburn curls and a determined set to the mouth. She was the daughter of Sir Francis Knollys, Leicester's colleague and supporter on the Council. She was married to Walter Devereux, Viscount Hereford (later Earl of Essex) when they were both about twenty. For some years the couple lived quietly in the country, but it seems there was little domestic harmony and it may well have been a relief to Lettice when Walter volunteered to lead a colonising force to Ireland in 1573. With other local notables he was invited to Kenilworth for the Queen's visit in 1575, and later, during the same progress, she acted as hostess to the court at Chartley, Devereux's principal manor. Meanwhile her husband was conducting himself in Ireland with immense personal bravery and total ruthlessness. He was obviously more at home in his campaign tent than in his parlour at Chartley. He was in England from November 1575 until the following July and it was then, according to the Spanish ambassador, that he fell out with Dudley. Devereux spent most of those months arguing with the Council about the terms of his reappointment, and selling a large part of his English estates to pay his debts. Two months after his return to Ireland he died of dysentery. Rumour concerning Leicester's relationship with Lettice was sufficiently well-established for there to be gossip about poison. Sir Henry Sidney, the Lord Deputy, immediately ordered a post-mortem. His detailed report to the Council intimated that nothing during Devereux's last days nor in the subsequent examination suggested foul play. This was supported by a private account written by the late Earl's secretary.

That Robert and Lettice had an intimate, probably adulterous, though sporadic relationship during those years can scarcely be doubted. In all probability it did not begin before Essex's departure in 1573. Early in 1578 the inevitable happened: Lettice told her lover that she was pregnant. Robert's immediate reaction was the stratagem that had succeeded with Douglas. In the spring he married Lettice in a secret ceremony at Kenilworth. She was not satisfied. The role of deserted wife was one she had played before and had no intention of playing again. Leicester made another concession: he bought the house and manor of Wanstead, Essex, and the neighbouring manor of Stonehall and set up Lettice on this pleasant estate near the capital.

Wanstead Hall was a modest residence for a nobleman of Leicester's standing. It had been built in the 1550s by Richard Lord Rich in the traditional style round an enclosed quadrangle, its front flanked by projecting wings and low towers. It boasted a hall, great chamber and gallery, a chapel, a little gallery and some twenty bedrooms. The outbuildings included stabling for fifty-eight horses. The purchase placed an enormous burden on Dudley's over-stretched finances. Within two years, indeed, he was obliged to mortgage Wanstead for £4,000.

But still Lettice was not satisfied: her position was essentially no better than Douglas Sheffield's. Her husband was free to decide which, if either, of his two marriages he would acknowledge. Neither she nor the child in her womb had any security. She insisted that Robert disembarrass himself of the 'other woman'. His visits to Douglas had already become infrequent and he had probably grown tired of a lady who had little to commend her save her youth and her beauty. It was at a meeting in the gardens of Greenwich Palace that Dudley told his secret wife that she was freed from her obligations to him. He took with him two friends to witness the transaction. There, among the hedges and spring flowers, Robert offered his discarded mistress £700 a year to disavow their marriage and yield up custody of their son. According to Douglas's account, given many years later, she rejected his offer tearfully and he began to shout at her angrily. Then, after mature reflection, she decided to bow to the inevitable because no practical purpose would have been served by doing otherwise and she was afraid of the reprisals Dudley might take if she resisted his will.

Leicester's behaviour throughout this sordid matrimonial muddle was shabby, but we must recall that Douglas's account of events, which is almost all we have to go on, was given more than a quarter of a century later, long after all who could support or contradict her testimony were dead. There is, moreover, some evidence which suggests that Robert's actions were not entirely selfish and insensitive. Gilbert Talbot's report of 1573 and Robert's letter to Douglas indicate that it was the lady who made all the running and that it was weakness or kindheartedness, rather than passion, which made Robert agree to marriage. When Leicester had tried to terminate their relationship he had suggested that Lady Sheffield should look for a husband. In 1578 he helped his unwanted mistress to do precisely that. There was, just emerging into prominence, a young man of the same age as Douglas. His name was Edward Stafford, he was a distant relation of the Dukes of Buckingham and the Barons Stafford, and his mother was Elizabeth's Mistress of the Robes. Edward had recently become a widower, his wife, Robserta Robsart, having just died. The exact relationship of this lady to Dudley's first wife is not known but it was certainly close. She was born Robserta Chapman of Rainthorpe Hall, Tasburgh, some three or four miles from Amy's childhood home at Stanfield. Her own Christian name suggests a strong link with the neighbouring family. So does that of her brother, who had inherited Rainthorpe by 1570: his name was Dudley Chapman. Robserta, in due course, married a Robsart and on his death she became the wife of Edward Stafford. No other link than Robert Dudley can be found between the scion of an ancient Staffordshire family and the daughter of an obscure Norfolk gentleman, and it was this Edward Stafford who married Douglas Sheffield in 1579.[15]

Lettice's triumph was almost complete, but not quite. Both she and her Puritan father wanted from Leicester an irreversible commitment. Thus, a second marriage ceremony took place at Wanstead on 21 September 1578. There, in the presence of Sir Francis Knollys, Ambrose Dudley and the Earl of Pembroke, Robert and Lettice were joined in matrimony by Humphrey Tindall B.D. This seems to have satisfied the bride's family for the time being but, on 18 February 1580, Tindall was required to make a sworn deposition to the fact that he had performed the rite and copies of this statement were kept by all parties concerned.[16] This must have been to safeguard the legitimacy of the couple's child. Lettice's first baby by Robert did not long survive birth, but at the end of 1579 she was delivered of a boy who was christened Robert and known affectionately by his parents as the 'Noble Imp'. Leicester now had the heir he had longed for. His life possessed a new purpose. Any glory and possessions he henceforth acquired, he acquired for the benefit of his posterity.

How much did the Queen know about her ōō's double and treble dealing? Quite incredibly there is no satisfactory answer to this question. For years Robert's relationship with Elizabeth had been the subject of widespread scandal and gossip. It had been the despair of ministers and rival courtiers. The one thing they had feared more than anything else was that the Queen would so far forget herself as to marry her Master of the Horse. Now Leicester had made that impossible. One would have expected the letters and

reports of ambassadors and councillors to have been full of the news
of Dudley's marriage and Elizabeth's reaction. Yet there is complete
silence on the matter. It is as though the happening, so earnestly
desired by so many for so long, had turned out to be a non-event.
The only contemporary document to mention it is a letter of the
Queen of Scots dated 4 July 1579 which speaks of Elizabeth's anger
at learning that both Leicester and Hatton were secretly married.[17]
The fact that her information was only half correct must cast some
doubt upon the value of her sources. Not until 1615 was the
commonly accepted account of the disclosure to the Queen of
Leicester's infidelity published.[18] According to this, the news of
Leicester's marriage was broken to Elizabeth in July 1579 by
Alençon's agent, Jean de Simier. The Queen wept and fumed. She
talked of sending Dudley to the Tower but was persuaded to content
herself with imprisoning Leicester in rooms at Greenwich Palace.
The offender's intermediary in this exchange was the Earl of Sussex
who told the Queen curtly that no man should be 'molested for
lawful marriage'. Such is the story. Its inherent improbabilities, not
least the role assigned to Sussex, are self-evident. Throughout the
summer Leicester and Sussex led the rival factions which, for weeks,
argued bitterly over the Alençon marriage. Radcliffe would, surely,
have been delighted to get his opponent out of the way and would
hardly have pleaded for him to the Queen. It is when we try to place
the story in its allotted position in history that we find that it simply
does not fit. The events it records are dramatic, yet no official or
private correspondent found them worthy of record. There is no
evidence of Dudley being dismissed from court nor of his disgrace.
He continued to attend Council meetings where his influence was
sufficiently strong to cause anxiety to Burghley, Sussex and other
advocates of the French marriage. Robert spoke firmly to the Queen
more than once about her projected union with Alençon. He could
scarcely have done that if he had been in her bad graces, or if
marriage was a sore point between them.

What then is the truth? That Elizabeth was distressed by her
favourite's marriage there can be no doubt. Sufficient proof is her
attitude towards Lettice, who was banished from court and never
readmitted to the Queen's favour, despite Dudley's frequent pleadings. It marked the end of an epoch in her life. The man she had
regarded as a husband in almost all but name she could no longer
look upon in that way. The only great romance of her life was over.
She was desolate. She threw herself with fervour into the negotiations for a match with the ugly Frenchman partly out of pique. But
there was no great scene, no public disgrace, no angry retaliation.

The reason can only be that Robert had made his peace with Elizabeth in private. Her grief was very real and certainly had an impact upon her conduct of state affairs, but it was in essence, a secret grief and any demonstration of displeasure that she made, she made to Leicester alone. My guess, and it can only be a guess, is that Robert made his confession to the Queen as early as 28 April 1578 at Leicester House. Something of great importance passed between them on that day; something which called for secrecy and tact; something which affected Elizabeth so much that she had to cancel her engagements. It is Mendoza who gives us the clue:

> The Queen had fixed the 28th for my audience with her, but as she was walking in the garden that morning she found a letter which had been thrown into the doorway, which she took and read, and immediately came secretly to the house of the Earl of Leicester who is ill here. She stayed here until 10 o'clock at night and sent word that she could not see me that day as she was unwell. I have not been able to learn the contents of the letter and only know that it caused her to go to Leicester's at once.[19]

This secret meeting occurred at the very time that Robert was unravelling his tangled relationships with Douglas and Lettice. Perhaps he already realised that the Knollys family would not be satisfied with a clandestine marriage. Perhaps matters had become so complex that he knew they could not be kept secret. So he decided to tell Elizabeth the truth before she heard a garbled report from someone else, and he used a stratagem which had succeeded before – the confession from the sick-bed.

A few days after this interview Leicester travelled to Buxton to take the waters. He was away an unusually long time, not returning to court until late July. He missed much of the summer progress and had to ask Philip Sidney, his nephew, to deputise for him when the Queen visited Wanstead. This unprecedentedly long absence may well have been engineered in order to make Elizabeth's heart grow fonder. An exchange of letters between Leicester and Hatton certainly suggests some such design, and that it was successful. Sir Christopher reported on 18 June that Her Majesty had fallen to brooding about matrimony:

> Since your Lordship's departure the Queen is found in continual great melancholy. The cause thereof I can but guess at, notwithstanding that I bear and suffer the whole brunt of her mislike in generality. She dreameth of marriage that might seem injurious to her, making myself to be either the man or a pattern of him. I defend that no man can tie himself or be tied to such inconve-

nience as not to marry by law of God or man, except by mutual
consents, as both parties, the man and woman, vow to marry each
to other, which I know she hath not done to any man and therefore by any man's marriage she can receive no wrong.[20]

It is little wonder that Hatton was bewildered: the 'marriage that
might seem injurious to her' was, surely, not one that she herself was
thinking of contracting but one already entered into by another. Ten
days later Sir Christopher was writing again to say how delighted
Elizabeth had been to receive Dudley's letters 'because they chiefly
recorded the testimony of your most loyal disposition from the beginning to this present time.' The Queen was impatient for his return.

> Her majesty thinketh your absence much drawn in too [great]
> length, and especially in that place, supposing, indeed, that a
> shorter time would work as good effect with you, but yet chargeth
> that you now go through according to your physician's opinion.
> For if now these waters work not a full, good effect, her highness
> will never consent that you cumber yourself and her with such
> long journey again.

Dudley's professional skills were also being missed: the progress was
running into difficulties for want of horses, and the life of the household had become drab: 'This court wanteth your presence. Her
majesty is unaccompanied and, I assure you, the chambers are
almost empty.'[21] By the time Robert returned Elizabeth can have
entertained no doubt about how much she still needed him.

As for the Simier story, there appears to be no truth whatever in it.
Dudley certainly was absent from court for a few days in July 1579,
but not under a cloud, as the Spanish ambassador's report makes
clear: 'The passport [for Alençon] was given against Leicester's wish
and he is so much offended that he has retired to a house of his five
miles away [Wanstead] where the queen has been to see him and
where she remained two days because he feigned illness. She afterward returned secretly to London . . .'[22]

This voluntary absence from court seems to be the only foundation on which the story of Leicester's disgrace and banishment was
based. Robert perhaps believed that he had handled the situation
rather well and that his relationship with the Queen was basically
unimpaired. Time proved him wrong. Elizabeth behaved with
unremitting vindictiveness towards Lettice, while her attitude
towards Robert became one of destructive possessiveness. She could
not, would not be without him. To banish him would have been to
punish herself and was therefore pointless. Married he might be,
but Elizabeth would see to it that he derived as little satisfaction as

possible from that state. Robert's wife would never be admitted to the court, and Robert would seldom be allowed to go anywhere but the court. It would be a lingering revenge.

Alençon also fitted neatly into her vendetta. There were sound political reasons for resuming marriage negotiations in the summer of 1578. Monsieur had blundered into the Netherlands' situation as a friend and champion of the rebels. Unchecked, he might initiate a Franco-Spanish conflict which could only end in one or other of the major European powers gaining control of the Low Countries. To prevent this, Leicester, Walsingham and their supporters urged Elizabeth to give active financial and military support to the rebels. Burghley and the more cautious spirits were at a loss to know what course to recommend. As for the Queen, no one knew what her intentions were: 'For matters of state I will write as soon as I can have any access to her majesty, the which, as it was when your Lordship was here, sometimes so, sometimes no, and at all times, uncertain and ready to stays and revocations . . . This irresolution doth weary and kill her ministers, destroy her actions, and overcome all good designs and counsels . . .'23 So matters remained until the spring of 1578. In mid-May (some two or three weeks after Leicester's private confession, if my surmise is correct) Elizabeth sent an envoy to Paris to further the marriage negotiations with Alençon. The man she chose for this personal mission, which had not been discussed in Council, was Edward Stafford. It can hardly be a coincidence that this young man, chosen by Leicester to play a significant role in extricating him from the morass of his love life, now received his first royal employment in a cause Leicester opposed.

During the following weeks messengers passed back and forth between Alençon and Elizabeth. The substance of these exchanges remained completely unknown; the Queen confided in no one. Robert felt keenly the lack of trust which left him, like other councillors, groping for an understanding of her true intentions. Like all her councillors, he had to handle the Alençon affair with kid gloves, as he advised Walsingham:

> You know her disposition as well as I, and yet can I not use but frankness with you . . . I would have you, as much as you may, avoid the suspicion of her majesty that you doubt Monsieur's love to her too much, or that you lack devotion enough in you to further her marriage, albeit I promise I think she hath little enough herself to it. But yet, what she would others think and do therein you partly have cause to know . . . You have as much as I can learn, for our conference with her majesty about affairs is but seldom and slender . . . For this matter in hand for her marriage,

there is no man can tell what to say. As yet she hath imparted with
no man, at least not with me nor, for ought I can learn, with any
other.[24]

In January 1579 Alençon sent Jean de Simier, a close friend and
accomplished ladies' man, to conduct his wooing. From the beginning the elegant Frenchman was a total success with the Queen. He
thrilled her with an audacious style of wooing she had not experienced for many years. He gained access to her private apartments at
all hours, showered her with flattery and love tokens and 'stole'
items such as handkerchiefs and nightcaps for his master to keep
among his dearest treasures. Elizabeth admitted Simier to the exclu-
sive circle of friends to whom she granted nicknames: he became
her 'Monkey'. For six months she had eyes for no one else. She
luxuriated in his company and flaunted her affection for him before
the court, just as she had openly revelled in Robert's attentions
twenty years before. Part of this display was for Robert's benefit:
Elizabeth was demonstrating that he was not indispensable. Other
men were just as accomplished as he in the courtly arts, and if
Simier's master was anything like Simier he would make a very
acceptable husband.

If the Queen aimed to upset Dudley, she certainly succeeded. He
had to go through the diplomatic motions of entertaining
Monsieur's envoy and playing host to him at court functions. But he
was alarmed at Simier's success and devoted all his energies to
opposing the French match in Council. He was supported firmly by
Walsingham, while Sussex declared for the match and was seconded
by Burghley. The reasons Leicester gave for advising against the
marriage were twofold: the majority of Englishmen would be
violently opposed to having a Catholic on, or beside, the throne.
The issue of producing an heir no longer applied since the Queen
was past the age of safe child-bearing; a royal pregnancy now was
much more likely to have a disastrous outcome than a happy one.
Even Burghley, in his private memoranda, acknowledged these
objections. His volte-face in foreign policy is difficult to understand
in any terms save those of domestic power struggle. Once more he
was supporting Dudley's sworn enemy, Sussex, at a time when the
favourite appeared to be in a weak position. The Spanish ambassador's assessment was doubtless sound when he commented that
Sussex 'led the dance [i.e. Alençon's courtship] in order,' as he says,
'to upset Leicester and deprive him of French support.'[25] It is significant of Elizabeth's real intentions that the four man committee she
appointed to work out the details of a marriage treaty consisted of
Leicester, Sussex, Burghley and Walsingham.

In the summer Alençon begged to be allowed to come in person. Casting caution and diplomacy aside, Robert pleaded with Elizabeth day after day not to see the Frenchman. He urged all the obvious objections. He prostrated himself at her feet.[26] Not, apparently, without some effect: 'She hath deferred three whole days with an extreme regret and many tears before she would subscribe the passport, being induced thereunto and almost forced by those that have led this negotiation in despite of the said Leicester'.[27]

Alençon came and stayed for twelve August days. It was a private visit, kept secret from a hostile populace. Those who were obliged to be about the court apparently shared Leicester's embarrassment and revulsion at the dalliance between the ill-matched lovers:

> The councillors themselves deny that Alençon is here and, in order not to offend the Queen, they shut their eyes and avoid going to court, so as not to appear to stand in the way of interviews with him, only attending the Council when they are obliged. It is said that if she marries without consulting her people she may repent it. Leicester is much put out and all the councillors are disgusted except Sussex.[28]

The same reporter stated a few days later: 'A close friend of Leicester's tells me he is cursing the French and is greatly incensed against Sussex, as are all of Leicester's dependents'.[29] Two of his 'dependents' certainly demonstrated their loyalty. When, in July, Robert withdrew from court, his sister Mary, still a great favourite with the Queen, also left.[30] Her son, Philip Sidney, addressed to Elizabeth a long letter advising against the marriage and calling to mind such proofs of French treachery as the St Bartholomew massacre. He suffered a severe scolding for his pains.

At twenty-four years of age Philip Sidney had already begun to show promise of remarkable genius as soldier, courtier, diplomat and poet. Robert took a keen interest in his nephew and did all he could to forward the young man's career. Sidney's first visit to the Continent, in 1572, was undertaken under Robert's patronage and he did all he could to further Leicester's interests there. It was not always easy:

> There being nothing of which I am so desirous, right honourable and my singular good Lord and uncle, as to have continual and certain knowledge what your pleasure is by which I may govern my little actions, I cannot be without some grief, that neither since I came into Germany I could by any means understand it. Wherefore, I have most humbly to beseech your lordship that if in

any of my proceedings I have erred you will vouchsafe to impute it to the not knowing your Lordship's and their [i.e. the Council's] pleasure, by whose commandment I am likewise to be directed.[31]

By 1577 Philip had become his uncle's principal personal representative abroad. In that year he toured the major Protestant states of Europe, officially conveying greetings from his Queen, but really canvassing the policy of the Dudley-Dee circle for a new alliance in the face of mounting Catholic and Ottoman Muslim pressure.

On the Alençon issue the political instincts of Leicester and Sidney were sound. Protestant England would not tolerate a Catholic foreigner on the throne. Robert never deviated from his opposition to Monsieur. Even Alençon's courtesy and his parting gift of 'a cord for his cap', consisting of precious stones worth 3,000 crowns,[33] did not change his mind. In October Elizabeth referred the marriage question to the whole Council for debate. When a majority followed Leicester in rejecting Alençon's suit she flew into a rage, but it was her last protest. The negotiations continued for another two years but they were played in a different key. The love affair had been transformed into a political courtship of the sort at which Elizabeth was adept.

CHAPTER THIRTEEN

PUBLIC DUTY, PRIVATE GRIEF

The impatience felt by many Englishmen, inside and outside politics, at the futile Alençon negotiations urged them towards supporting the foreign policy Dudley had for years advocated. The national temper was now opposed to Burghley's subtle diplomacy and in favour of positive measures: a definite commitment to the Huguenot cause; a policy of non-appeasement towards Spain; and rigorous reprisals against Catholic fifth-columnists. Leicester now clearly emerged as the leader of those who favoured the assertion of England as an adventurous, progressive, Protestant island state, the implacable enemy of tyranny and popery.

As time passed, the options open to the *politiques* among English statesmen steadily diminished. September 1580 may be seen as a crucial month in this process. Two events occurred which pushed England and Spain much closer towards the inevitable conflict: Spanish troops under the Duke of Alva overran Portugal; Drake came home. Alva's success gave the Spanish King the entire Iberian peninsula, the port of Lisbon, command of the Straits of Gibraltar, a large military and mercantile fleet and a colonial empire in the East to be added to his own in the West. Philip now claimed naval supremacy over all the shipping lanes from the Narrow Seas to Magellan's Strait, from the Main to the Moluccas. Yet the *Golden Hind*'s arrival in Plymouth, laden to the gunwales with Peruvian silver and Indonesian spices, raised a large question-mark over any such claim. Francis Drake had rifled Philip's supposedly secure treasure houses, sailed across his supposedly private lake – the Pacific Ocean – and traded in his supposedly reserved markets. He returned with breathtaking wealth. After paying himself and his crew and making lavish presents to the Queen and chosen courtiers he was able to pay his backers £47 for every £1 invested. When accounts were settled Robert Dudley was the richer by many thousands of pounds.[1]

The reaction of Elizabeth's government to these two incidents was a clear pointer to the future trend of events. Mendoza protested at Drake's piracy in the strongest possible terms, demanding punishment and restitution. The Queen was more impressed by the wealth Drake had brought back and the enormous popularity he now enjoyed. She, therefore, welcomed her corsair to court, had his ship

placed on public exhibition and, upon its deck, she knighted him.
Subtly she involved France by having Alençon's representative,
Marchaumont, perform the ceremony. A few months later the
Portuguese pretender, Don Antonio, was also welcomed to England.
At Leicester's instigation he was installed in Baynard's Castle, which
belonged to the Earl of Pembroke.[2] Dudley was much in the company
of both Drake and Don Antonio. He had the mariner elected to the
Inner Temple[3] and he helped to plan an expedition to be led by
Drake to seize the Azores in the name of Don Antonio. Preparations
for the proposed attack were put in hand: men and ships were
mustered, backers were found, but, in August 1581, Burghley
managed to sway the majority of the Council and the Queen against
the enterprise. The voice of caution was not yet entirely silent.

Leicester's attitude towards the Netherlands had always been
consistent. He wanted England to be seen as the ally of the Dutch
Protestants, to send military aid to help drive the Spaniards out, and
he wanted to lead the expeditionary force in person. Since 1572
bands of English volunteers had crossed the North Sea to serve under
William of Orange. In the early days of the Netherlands' revolt there
was some talk of sending Ambrose Dudley at the head of an army, but
Elizabeth firmly rejected the existence of a formal English presence.
It was at this time that Walsingham was in Paris, liaising with various
Protestant princes for a joint invasion of the Spanish Netherlands and
insisting to Leicester that 'upon the good success or evil success of this
[venture depends] the common cause of religion'.[4] Robert sent Philip
Sidney to stay with the ambassador during his tour of the Continent
and the young man became an important link between Dudley and
the leaders of the Dutch revolt. In Frankfurt he met Orange's brother,
Louis of Nassau, 'whose honourable usage was such towards me, and
such goodwill he seems to bear unto your Lordship, that . . . I can but
wish him a prosperous success to such noble enterprises as I doubt
not he will shortly (with the help of God) put in execution'.[5] Nothing
came of this venture, but Leicester established a close link with
William of Orange's circle and messages passed frequently back and
forth between them.[6] Robert's principal agent was the long-serving
Dudley protégé, Thomas Wilson, who went over to the Low
Countries as Elizabeth's representative in November 1574 and whose
anti-Spanish activities were so vigorous that he was suspected of insti-
gating a plot to kidnap the Regent. The selection of such a man as
official representative between 1574 and 1577 was a major triumph
for the radicals and prevented the adoption of any accommodation
between England and Spain over the Netherlands. Wilson was
rewarded with a Council seat in 1579.

The first notable result of this liaison was the offer, in January 1575, of the crown of Holland and Zeeland to Elizabeth. Faced with the dilemma of supporting rebels against a divinely-ordained king or maintaining Philip II's already too-great power, Elizabeth prevaricated. The ambassadors had many meetings with the Council and even more with the Leicester-Walsingham faction, but all they could extract from the English Queen was her consent not to hinder the sending of private men and money to the Netherlands. Elizabeth's coolness did nothing to endear her to the Orange faction and their English supporters. In the summer of 1576 something happened which forced Elizabeth's hand. Philip's Spanish garrisons mutinied over arrears of pay and went on the rampage. This had the effect of uniting Protestant and Catholic Netherlanders against the Spaniards. William took his opportunity; in November the Pacification of Ghent brought all the provinces together under an elected assembly pledged to independence. Philip II was equally swift in his reaction: he appointed a new Regent. Don John of Austria was Europe's most celebrated soldier, the hero of Lepanto, that great Christian victory over the Turks. Elizabeth opened negotiations with both sides, and from her governmental acts it is evident that Leicester and Walsingham were largely dictating policy. The Queen dipped into her treasury to send £20,000 to the rebels and promised a loan of £100,000. The man sent to enter discussions with Don John was Edward Horsey, Dudley's intimate. Officially he was to offer Elizabeth's mediation between the Spaniards and the Dutch and, if necessary, to threaten England's energetic aid for the rebels if the Regent refused to come to terms. Unofficially he was to gauge Don John's strength and intentions. Meanwhile Wilson tried to bring the rebels to the conference table. He too had secret instructions – from Leicester (just how much the Queen knew about his undercover activities is not clear). He proposed to William of Orange that Dudley should come over at the head of an English army. In January Wilson reported that the offer of mediation had been rejected by the Dutch assembly, the States General, but that they were not averse to the sending of 'a general over an army of our nation . . . which I wish were my Lord of Leicester'.[7] In the event Don John won the diplomatic battle, offering the States terms which they found acceptable. They wrote to Dudley declining his offer of military aid.

Though nothing came of this exchange it is of considerable significance. It shows that the idea of taking an army to the Netherlands was Robert's own and that it originated many years before his appointment in 1585. In 1576 he had not seen military service for twenty years. Yet he was prepared to back his foreign policy on the

battlefield. Such action would also fulfil several personal needs. At
forty-three Robert was growing fat and had long since ceased
displaying his prowess in the tilt-yard. He wanted to break away
from the court, to prove to his Queen, his Protestant supporters and
himself that he was a dedicated champion of the reformed faith –
that he was, indeed, Northumberland's son.

When the States' message arrived Leicester decided to send a
more impressive envoy back to them. Philip Sidney was returning
from a diplomatic mission in Germany when he received fresh
instructions: he was to stand proxy for Leicester at the christening
of William of Orange's daughter. In May, therefore, Sidney met the
Dutch leader at Gertruidenberg. The two men evidently took to
each other immediately and afterwards kept up a lively correspondence. Philip was particularly impressed by the depth of William's
religion and the way it permeated all his political actions. The
Prince thought equally well of his guest and was disposed to a
greater affection for his guest's uncle. There was even a rumour in
diplomatic circles that Sidney would marry William's sister.

Philip had scarcely returned to make his favourable report before
the erratic course of Netherlands politics took another violent turn.
In July Don John seized the fortress of Namur and, using it as a
rallying point, summoned King Philip's subjects to join him in battle
against William of Orange and his supporters. This summons was a
tactical blunder: it reunited the Dutch against him and reopened
negotiations between the States General and the English court. Now
it was the Netherlanders who wanted Leicester to cross the Narrow
Sea with an army. The Marquis of Havrech, who headed the delegation, told the Queen that he knew Leicester to be a great leader
of men. In fact, he had another reason for favouring Dudley's
generalship: 'If he is in command the Queen will take care to
provide him with all that may be needful'.[8] Dudley feted Havrech
during his weeks in England and made detailed plans for the
proposed campaign. He was much encouraged by news from
William Davison, who had succeeded Wilson in Antwerp:

> Your Lordship can perceive what a gap is here opened to the great
> advancing of your honour and credit, which, if you enter and go
> through the good offices, as I doubt it not, shall gain you as many
> faithful servants here as in any part of the world. You have made a
> good beginning with the Prince and States of Holland, where, by
> the report of all men, your name is as well known and yourself as
> much honoured as in your own country. The same effect cannot but
> follow here, if you list to march with the like zeal.[9]

During these months several hopeful young men offered their services to Dudley in the forthcoming campaign. One was Thomas Digges, a scholar rather than a soldier, who offered Leicester *An Arithmetical Military Treatise Named Stratioticos*.[10] It was a book which combined a simple mathematics manual with the application of mathematical rules to such matters as ballistics and cavalry formations and which devoted many pages to the administration and discipline of 'every well governed camp and army'.

Despite all this goodwill and eager activity the scheme grounded on the shifting sands of Elizabeth's caution and the States General's hesitation. In October Leicester complained to Davison that the solemn burghers of Brussels had undermined the cordial agreement he had reached with Havrech. Then, when the States declared their reawakened interest in receiving an English army, Elizabeth poured cold water on it. She decided instead to finance a German force led by John Casimir.

The final collapse of his plan early in 1578 plunged Robert into a pit of despair, frustration and embarrassment. As he confided to Davison, 'I have almost neither face nor countenance to write to the Prince, his expectation being so greatly deceived'.[11] To a Dutch colleague he wrote, 'I am melancholy and I wish full oft that you were here'.[12] This dashing of all his political plans, coming on top of his personal problems, broke Dudley's spirit and undermined his health. It was while in this state of depression that Robert married Lettice Devereux and finally ended his courtship of the Queen. It was in the aftermath of these taxing events that he took his weary body for a prolonged cure at Buxton. In the seclusion of this newly-fashionable spa he received news from court and from overseas. In July he had not given up hope of engaging in the Netherlanders' struggle by proxy, as he indicated to Hatton:

> I have sent you a letter which I received yesterday from Casimir. It is of no new date. You may see what he writes and how earnestly. Since my hap is not to be in so honourable a voyage . . . I would be most glad that my nephew [Sidney] might go to Casimir, and if he may not as from her majesty, yet after the other sort you say her majesty could like of [i.e. as a private adventurer]. I beseech you further it and I shall be most glad it may be obtained.[13]

During the ensuing months Robert watched gloomily as all his worst fears were realised. John Casimir's expedition swallowed up English money and achieved nothing. Alençon, with Elizabeth's encouragement, cavorted ineffectually in the Netherlands. Philip sent a new army under the Duke of Parma which swiftly overran the southern part of the country, restricting William's support to Holland, Zeeland and the northern lordships (constituted as the United Provinces in 1579). The situation of the rebels was desperate but Elizabeth steadfastly refused direct aid. Tangled in the web of the Alençon marriage which she had herself woven, she affected to repose complete confidence in the military competence of her French lover. Robert had no alternative but grudgingly to fall in with her plans. Alençon visited his bride-to-be again in the winter of 1581-2, anxious to make whatever concessions were demanded in order to win her. Thoroughly alarmed, Elizabeth now agreed to finance the Duke's Netherlands activities in order to divert him. Persistent to the last, Sussex continued to argue in favour of the marriage until he and Leicester almost came to blows in the Council chamber. At last, however, Alençon departed from Sandwich on 7 February 1582.

Alençon was conveyed over the seas with full honours. His escort of a hundred gentlemen was led by Leicester and Hunsdon. At Flushing the Duke was met by Orange and a large number of dignitaries who received him with rejoicing. William was scarcely less pleased to come face to face for the first time with Robert Dudley. The two men spent many hours together, and undoubtedly Philip Sidney was present at some of their discussions. On 19 February Orange and Leicester rode side by side in the magnificent procession which brought Alençon into Antwerp. When the Prince's chaplain published an account of the festivities later that year it was to Dudley that he dedicated it. The Queen was clearly anxious about Leicester's direct association with the Dutch leaders. He had only been gone a week when she instructed Walsingham to order his return, 'since your abode there is to no greater purpose either to the Duke himself or for any cause that may concern the benefit of the country'.[14]

As long as the fiction of Alençon's rule could be maintained Elizabeth could resist the inevitability of Leicester's Netherlands policy. In January 1583 the Duke departed, discredited, from his principality. Eighteen months later he was dead. In the south Parma's strength steadily increased and the United Provinces looked once more to William of Orange as their saviour. Then, on 10 July 1584, William was shot down in the Prinsenhof in Delft by a fanatical Catholic. The inevitable had arrived and Leicester was ready to welcome it.

The obverse side of Dudley's Dutch policy was his support for firm anti-Catholic measures at home. By 1575 there were a number of Puritan and anti-papal works in circulation which bore the bear and ragged staff on their title pages and dedications eulogising Leicester's piety. As early as 1572 his leadership of the religious radicals had been tacitly accepted by the establishment of church and state when the official counterblast to Elizabeth's excommunication was dedicated to him. This was Arthur Golding's translation of a Latin treatise by the Swiss theologian, Heinrich Bullinger, called, in English, *A Confutation of the Pope's Bull . . . against Elizabeth* . . . As the work admirably indicates, the struggle in which the translator's patron was involved was not just a local one:

> Now, albeit that the brunt of that abominable bull were bent directly at our most gracious sovereign lady Queen Elizabeth and at her majesty's realm and faithful subjects, yet . . . the matter doth implyingly concern the whole state of Christ's Church, which the Romish Antichrist laboureth to draw away from the obedience and love of her true husband, Christ, to the adulterous embracing of Satan.[15]

This was how Leicester, Walsingham, Sidney, William of Orange and all the Protestant champions saw their situation and their responsibility.

In England there were hundreds of seminary priests working by the mid-1570s. Trained in France and Rome, they were smuggled into England and established themselves in manor houses up and down the country saying masses, stiffening the resistance of the Catholic gentry and spreading their faith. In 1580 they were joined by the Jesuit mission, led by Edmund Campion and Robert Parsons. At the same time small bands of Catholic adventurers were making their way to Ireland to foment trouble with the blessing of Pope Gregory XIII.

The focus of all Catholic hopes was, of course, still the Queen of Scots. She constituted a constant problem for Elizabeth and scarcely less of a problem for her councillors. It was by now obvious to all realists that the Stuart line would provide the next occupant of the English throne. Elizabeth steadfastly refused to acknowledge this but her ministers had to take it into consideration in planning the nation's future and their own. The young Scottish King, James, was safely in Protestant hands, but the faction struggle north of the border continued as fiercely as ever and the threat of French influence was always present. This made it difficult to maintain friendly relations with James. The ceaseless intrigues of his mother presented another obstacle. In 1583 a certain Francis Throckmorton was, by chance, detected in a Catholic intrigue. Under torture he confessed to the existence of an elaborate network of secret agents linking Mary, Bernardino de Mendoza and Catholic activists at home and abroad. Throckmorton was executed, others were imprisoned and the Spanish ambassador was expelled. There was now a growing body of support represented in parliament and the Council for a firm and 'final' policy towards Mary Stuart. For the time being Elizabeth firmly resisted this. So did Leicester. He favoured the continued imprisonment of Mary by his old friend, the Earl of Shrewsbury, in conditions of comfort and honour. He wanted her friends to have custody of James so that the most cordial relations could be maintained with the Stuarts.

It was not only the national interest which dictated his policy. Like other councillors, Dudley was busy securing his own and his family's future in the event of a change of regime.[16] Leicester's ambitions for a marriage alliance with the house of Stuart seem to have begun about 1577. In the summer of that year he went to Buxton to take the waters. While in the Midlands Robert took the opportunity of calling upon the Earl of Shrewsbury. For many years there had existed a warm friendship between Shrewsbury, Leicester and the Queen. George Talbot was older by some five years and had proved himself utterly trustworthy in office and congenial in companionship. He had guarded Mary since 1569 with consideration and firmness. In 1572 he had been appointed Earl Marshal. Such a man enjoyed the respect of a wide circle of friends. He also had their sympathy, for he was married to the most notorious harridan of the age, Bess of Hardwick. An undated letter to Robert in Talbot's appalling scrawl tells us much about his close relationship to Leicester, his jovial good humour and his strained domestic situation:

My Lord, although I perceive by your letter you cannot content yourself with your goods but you call us 'doggry'* which [obligeth] us to seek revenge . . . be you assured, although for a time we must content ourselves, yet shall you not rest with all unchallenged, defend you if you dare. And, rather than fail, our heartburning is such [that] we will come to Kenilworth gates this time twelve month, God and the Queen's majesty giving us leave, to perform our challenge then, if your heart faint not afore the time. And in the meanwhile I shall pray for your Lordship's health and all happiness as I would desire for myself.

Sheffield, this Friday morning.
   Your Lordship's most faithful cousin
   and friend
      G. Shrewsbury.

P.S. Notwithstanding I lost at the court, leaving £23, my purse bearer . . . coming to give me [my purse] before my wife, she, by

*This is the closest I can get to making sense of a word which is almost illegible in the original.

force, took it from me, which was £42. Thus is simple men used and spoiled of their goods.[17]

The Queen entered fully into this spirit of friendly badinage. In June 1577 she wrote to Bess Talbot, playfully advising her on the most suitable diet for Leicester, whose appetite was prodigious.

Right Trusty,
Being given to understand from our cousin, the Earl of Leicester, how honourably he was lately received and used by you, our cousin the Countess of Chatsworth, and how his diet is by you both discharged at Buxton . . . we think it meet to prescribe unto you a proportion of diet which we mean in no case you shall exceed, and that is, to allow him by the day for his meat two ounces of flesh, referring the quality, to yourselves, so as you exceed not the quantity, and for his drink the twentieth part of a pint of wine to comfort his stomach, and as much of St. Anne's sacred water as he listeth to drink. On festival days, as is meet for a man of his quality, we can be content you shall enlarge his diet by allowing unto him for his dinner the shoulder of a wren, and for his supper a leg of the same, besides his ordinary ounces . . .[18]

During this visit Robert Dudley met Mary Stuart. The interview, which took place at Chatsworth, Sheffield or Buxton, must have been an interesting one. Both were past their prime but still celebrated charmers, capable of captivating the opposite sex. Robert was courteous, even sympathetic to Mary's complaints at her confinement and he made a good impression. He probed for information about a rumoured marriage proposal from Don John of Austria but the Scottish Queen was too wily to give anything away.[19] Little of great importance passed between them but the meeting itself was sufficient to make Burghley request permission to visit the royal prisoner a few weeks later: the request was denied.

It was, however, the negotiations with Bess Talbot that were of great personal significance to Leicester. The Countess had a 22-year-old daughter by a former marriage. This girl, Elizabeth, had, to the Queen's great displeasure, been married to Charles Stuart, Earl of Lennox, brother of the murdered Lord Darnley. Lennox had subsequently died (December 1576) but not before siring a daughter, Arabella Stuart, now in the care of her domineering grandmother. This little girl, a great-granddaughter of Henry VII, stood high in the succession to the English throne and was of the Scottish blood royal. Bess of Hardwick hoped to persuade Elizabeth that Arabella's claim was better than Mary Stuart's. Robert Dudley proposed to marry Arabella to his 'base son'. The matchmakers were committed to their scheme. Perhaps they believed that the Queen would be better disposed to Arabella's claim if she were married to the heir of her favourite. Bess and Robert were, for a time, as thick as thieves. The Countess went to considerable trouble over Leicester's visits to Chatsworth and Buxton. Dudley, for his part, used his influence on behalf of Bess's children. He sought a new husband for Elizabeth Cavendish, obtained court preferment for Charles Cavendish and gave his brother Henry letters of introduction to William Davison when he crossed to the Low Countries with 500 men to aid the rebels.[20] The alliance remained in being until the end of 1579. Then Lettice presented her husband with a son who was officially legitimate. A couple of years later this other Robert Dudley, Baron Denbigh, was substituted for the 'bastard'. In the spring of 1584 Mary Stuart wrote to the French ambassador indicating that the Countess's ambitious scheme was proceeding smoothly.

> I would wish you to mention privately to the Queen that nothing has alienated the Countess of Shrewsbury from me but the vain hope which she has conceived of settling the crown of England on the head of her little girl, Arabella, and this by means of marrying her to a son of the Earl of Leicester. These children are also educated in this idea, and their portraits have been sent to each other.[21]

Leicester's enemies were not slow to draw the parallel between Arabella Stuart and Jane Grey and to ascribe to Dudley the most intricate scheming, but Leicester himself relied much more on friendly relations with the young Scottish king than on the slender lives and alliances of two infants.

Just how slender they were was cruelly brought home to Robert and Lettice in the following July. The Noble Imp suddenly ill at Wanstead and died within a few days. Child mortality was commonplace in the sixteenth century but the loss was, nevertheless, keenly felt by both parents. Leicester's legitimate son, born to him in middle age after he had risked everything in marrying Lettice Devereux, had been the focus of all his plans and hopes. Now he was dead. Leicester was on progress with the court when the news arrived. Without waiting for royal permission he left Nonsuch suddenly in order to be with Lettice. He asked Hatton to make his excuses to Elizabeth. The Queen immediately sent Sir Henry Killigrew with a message of sympathy and the following day Sir Christopher wrote a consoling letter. This, and Robert's reply, are worth quoting at some length. They reveal to us a broken man contemplating leaving public life. The loss of his son was the last in a sequence of misfortunes which came near to destroying him. The Queen continued to be estranged from Lettice; his religious policy was being overthrown; his influence was waning; and he had recently become the object of a particularly vicious libel. Well might he despair of human aid and pray for 'patience in all these worldly things'. The genuine solicitude of Hatton shows us that men could be court rivals and political opponents without being personal enemies:

My singular good Lord . . . When in the meditation of your religious conceits it shall please you to weigh the singular blessings and benefits which God hath conferred on you in this world, I nothing doubt you will be joyfully thankful; and accept this cross as the sign of His holy love, whereby you shall become happy and blessed for ever. Unto the Gospel of Christ His poor flock do find you a most faithful and mighty supporter; in the State and Government of this Realm, a grave and faithful Councillor; a pillar of our long-continued peace; a happy nourisher of our most happy Commonwealth; flourishing in the stirp of true Nobility abundantly in all virtuous actions towards God and men; all which are the high gifts of the High God. Leave not yourself, therefore, my dear Lord, for God's sake and ours. Go on in your high and noble labours in the comfort of Christ, which no man can diminish nor take from you; cherish yourself while it shall please God to let you dwell on earth; call joy to dwell in your heart, and know for certain, that if the love of a child be dear, which is now taken from you, the love of God is ten thousand times more dear, which you can never lack nor lose. Of men's hearts you enjoy more than millions, which, on my soul, do love you no less than children or brethren. Leave sorrow, therefore, my good Lord, and be glad with us, which much rejoice in you . . .

Robert replied immediately:

Mr Vice-Chamberlain, I do most heartily thank you for your careful and most godly advice at this time. Your good friendship never wanteth. I must confess I have received many afflictions within these few years, but not a greater, next her Majesty's displeasure: and, if it pleased God, I would the sacrifice of this poor innocent might satisfy; I mean not towards God . . . but for the world. The afflictions I have suffered may satisfy such as are offended, at least appease their long hard conceits . . . I beseech . . . God to grant me patience in all these worldly things, and to forgive me the negligences of my former time, that have not been more careful to please Him, but have run the race of the world. In the same sort I commend you, and pray for His grace for you as for myself; and, before all this world, to preserve her Majesty for ever, whom on

my knees I most humbly thank for her gracious visitation by Killigrew. She shall never comfort a more true and faithful man to her, for I have lived and so will die only hers. 23rd July 1584.
Your poor but assured friend,
     Robt. Leicester.[22]

Lettice and Robert had no more children. Ironically, therefore, the heir to the earldoms of Leicester and Warwick was a boy who could never claim his inheritance. It was an irony in more senses than one. Leicester's action in casting aside Douglas Sheffield had deprived the Dudley line of its only heir in the male line. Northumberland's rich crop of sons, six of whom grew to maturity and married, produced no children except Leicester's 'base son'. The irony is heavily underlined by the fact that this boy was destined to be the most able and talented of all the Dudleys – sailor, soldier, explorer, scholar, mathematician, engineer, shipbuilder and author. As a direct result of his supposed illegitimacy Sir Robert Dudley left England in 1605 to place his gifts and the remainder of his long life at the service of a foreign prince.

It was certainly not the case that Leicester neglected his 'base son'. As a child the boy was brought up by his father's kinsman and agent, John Dudley of Stoke Newington. Every care was taken over his education, and there were not wanting among Leicester's many protégés able tutors to inculcate Latin grammar, philosophy, theology and the new sciences. He was provided with a physician, personal attendants and servants, and his father visited him as often as he could. Later he was sent on long visits to Robert's friends in order to acquire the etiquette and social graces which could only be learned in a noble household. An undated letter from the Countess of Pembroke tells of a stay the boy made at Wilton House and indicates how concerned Leicester was for his welfare:

> My most honoured Lord, I perceive by your letters you are offended with me for not sending you word of your son's amendment from a great sickness . . . Indeed, when your manikin was here he was not very well, as I wrote to your Lordship, with some pain in his head and, I think, [for] a little [while] till he had wits all, I was desirous to have him send for his physician. Before he came, my Lord, he was so well as he had but little need of his help and since that time hath been so as I never saw him better since I was acquainted with him . . .[23]

In 1587 the boy was entered at Christ Church, Oxford, and placed in the care of the outstanding scholar, Thomas Chaloner. By this time Leicester's son was moving freely in exalted circles, fully acknowledged as a young man of honoured parentage and a desirable dinner guest for the socially ambitious:

> You were expected yesterday [wrote a London merchant to a friend]. We had many Lords and Lordings at dinner who spent all the day in music, and you might have done well to come among them. Here was Sir Harry Grey, Mr. Vavasour, and young Sir Dudley, the great lord's son, men well known to you.[24]

Leicester's relationship with Lettice seems to have been all that he could have wished. They were both mature people when they married. Childlessness, the loss of the Noble Imp and the implacable opposition of Elizabeth to their union drove them closer together. In his will, Robert affirmed that he had always found Lettice 'a faithful, loving, and a very obedient, careful wife'. In 1584, four days before the death of their son, Leicester gave tangible expression to his feelings when he made a jointure for Lettice of considerable estates in various counties.[25]

Many of Robert's letters reveal how keenly he felt the Queen's antagonism towards Lettice and how he sought the aid of friends and colleagues in assuaging it. After their son's funeral Robert and Lettice spent a few days at Burghley's house, Theobalds. Apparently even a mother's grief had not softened Elizabeth's heart. Leicester wrote to thank his absent host: '. . . that it pleased you so friendly and honourably to deal in the behalf of my poor wife. For truly, my Lord, in all reason she is hardly dealt with. God must only help it with her majesty . . . for which, my Lord, you shall be assured to find us most thankful to the uttermost of our powers . . .'[26]

It was to check the erosion of his influence that Leicester now advanced his stepson, Robert Devereux, to royal favour. The eighteen-year-old Earl of Essex was all that Dudley had been at his age – athletic, vigorous and flamboyant. Leicester now brought him to court to be a leader of the coterie of young gallants supporting his own vigorous radical policies, and also to be one of Elizabeth's 'lovers'. For the Queen was not allowed to grow old. While advancing age took its obvious toll of her attendants, cosmetics and determined vigour maintained for Elizabeth an aura of eternal youth. Still she commanded the attentions of beardless, smooth-cheeked men young enough to be her own sons. Unable himself to compete any longer, Robert had no alternative but to put forward his own champion.

Only those in the innermost circle of royal intimates could be aware how profoundly, if subtly, the relationship between Elizabeth and Robert was changing. To most men Leicester must have seemed as secure as ever. By 1584, if not before, he was officially designated as Lord Steward, thereby enjoying *in nomine* as well as *de facto* the central place at the court. He continued to be Elizabeth's closest adviser and to convey messages to and from the Council. He was still permitted to advocate policies and courses of which the Queen did not approve. Indeed, he did so more energetically as the years passed. Now, however, Robert was not so much a romantic consort as an old friend. His letters, though still expressing devotion, breathed no sighs of love – they were full of advice, admonition and even religious counsel.

> Thanks for your gracious remembrance sent by Mr Cotton. Your poor ō ō has no other way but by prayer to offer for recompense and that is that God will long safely, healthfully and most happily preserve you here among us . . . This is the goodness of God, my sweet lady, that hath thus saved you against so many devils. You may see what it is to cleave unto him. He rewardeth beyond all deserts, and [al]so is it daily seen how he payeth those that be dissemblers with him. Who ever of any prince stood so nakedly assisted of worldly help as your Majesty has done these many years? Who has had more enemies in show, and yet who ever received less harm? This it is when a just cause is simply and inno-cently defended. Your Majesty only has been the maintainer and setter forth of . . . his true religion against all policy and counsel of man. Yet you see how he has served, and kept you thereby.
> God grant you ever to cleave fast thereto . . .[27]

Like most established friendships, that of Elizabeth and Robert was punctuated by quarrels and disagreements which caused distress for a time but could not destroy the mutual affection built up over the years. In an undated letter to Hatton, Leicester excused himself from attending a Council meeting: 'I am not unwilling, God knows, to serve her majesty wherein I may, to the uttermost of my life, but [am] most unfit at this time to make repair to that place where so many eyes are witnesses of my open and great disgraces delivered from her majesty's mouth.'[28] In July 1580 he wrote to Burghley apologising for his recent tetchiness, caused, he explained, by the removal of 'her majesty's wonted favour' and a disagreement between them over some lands Dudley had wanted.[29] The renewal of hostilities between Leicester and Sussex brought a further display of royal displeasure in 1581. The two old enemies found themselves opposed to each other on a variety of issues: Radcliffe championed the Alençon match and resisted direct inter-vention in the Netherlands; his grant of a licence to breed horses

was taken as a personal affront by Dudley; finally they fell out over
a parcel of disputed land at Havering. Matters came to a head in
July 1581 when the Queen confined the two earls to their chambers
at court and rejected their requests to be allowed to return to their
homes.[30] Two years later Sussex was dead, implacable to the last in
his hatred of Leicester: 'I am now passing into another world [he is
supposed to have said on his deathbed] and must leave you to your
fortunes and to the Queen's graces, but beware of the gypsy, for he
will be too hard for you all. You know not the beast so well as I do.'[31]
Radcliffe's death was an important event in the development of
court politics, removing, as it did, the most effective counterweight
to Dudley's influence. The party opposed to Leicester now had no
leadership in the Council and the household. It is no coincidence
that from this time malcontents consorted with friends abroad and
found other ways of attacking Leicester and his supporters.

CHAPTER FOURTEEN

'LEICESTER'S COMMONWEALTH'

. . . I beseech your Lordship in Christ Jesus to build with both hands the Church of God in England, to the rooting out of all tyranny which as yet (most lamentable is our state) lurketh, [waiting] the like opportunity to show its fury. For [there is] no doubt [that] the papist is false when he is cautious: while he is under, humble, but when he reigneth tyrannous. There is not one nobleman that then [they will not pull down], no, not even your Honour. The Lord God send curses to bind such horned creatures and preserve your Honour long to this Church. God be merciful unto us and the blessing of the Almighty light upon your Lordship. From Frankfurt, the 20th of March 1573.
Your Lordship's wholly to command in the Lord,
William Rose[1]

It is unlikely that Dudley needed this warning from a Puritan protégé. Throughout the reign he attracted hostile comment and was pursued by rumours, slanders, plots and even assassination attempts. In 1559 Captain Drury was arrested for a projected attack. A year later Mother Dowe was spreading her poisonous tales about the Queen's pregnancy.[2] In 1572 a Cambridge student was arrested in Norwich for slanderous words against Leicester and Burghley.[3] It was the young man's opinion that the whole county would rise if the Duke of Norfolk was executed. We must however, be careful not to get Leicester's unpopularity out of proportion; he was by no means singled out for demonstrations of ill will. All the leading members of the government – Cecil, Bacon, Walsingham, Hatton and others – attracted threats, slanders and assassination rumours. The Queen, of course, was hardly ever free from plots and talk of plots. In a land where social injustice abounded and religious differences ran deep it could scarcely be otherwise.

Calumny was an established weapon in the armoury of religious and political pamphleteers. As the Puritan-Catholic war of words intensified throughout the 1570s and 1580s more and more libellous attacks were made upon prominent Englishmen. Catholic propaganda had to be published abroad, mostly in Paris. In 1580 William Parry, a spy, reported on a current best-seller in France which was entertaining papists and all who loved salacious gossip with revelations about Leicester and Hatton. At the beginning of 1588 another agent sent over to Dudley a French placard calumniating the Queen.[4] And there were many others.

However, the book which achieved the greatest notoriety and the one which was to blacken Dudley's name for posterity was *The Copy of a Letter Written by a Master of Arts at Cambridge*, commonly known as *Leicester's Commonwealth*.[5] This anonymous work was printed, probably in Antwerp or Paris, in the summer of 1584. Within a year French and Latin versions were circulating on the Continent. Their titles indicate much more clearly the pamphlet's true intent: *A Discourse on the abominable life, plots, treasons, murders, falsehoods, poisonings, lusts, incitements and evil stratagems employed by Lord Leicester;* and *Calvinist Blossoms plucked from the life of Robert Dudley, Earl of Leicester*. The choice of the English title was an obvious ploy of the author to conceal his real intent under an innocent-sounding title and the work has the appearance of a typical sixteenth-century political tract. It uses the traditional form of a dialogue, the form employed by Thomas More in *Utopia*, by Thomas Starkey in his *Dialogue between Cardinal Pole and Thomas Lupset* and by many other controversialists. The disputants are a Cambridge teacher, a London gentleman and a Catholic lawyer. The characters are cleverly chosen: they represent 'middle England', the loyal, educated subjects who do not support religious extremists of the right or left. The university man comes from Cambridge – the academic centre of the English Reformation. He has been tutor to the gentleman's son who is about to enter one of the Inns of Court – those other centres of radical opinion. The London gentleman represents both the landed and mercantile communities, unquestionably loyal and level-headed. The lawyer stands for that (by no means small) group of Catholics who rejected the fanaticism of Jesuit missionaries: 'For albeit, this lawyer was inclined to be a papist, yet was it with such moderation and reservation of his duty towards his prince and country and proceedings of the same as he seemed always to give full satisfaction to us that were of contrary opinion'.[6]

These three worthy Englishmen begin to debate the issue of treason as applied to papists and soon agree that extreme Puritans are just as much potential enemies of the state as those of a contrary persuasion, for in their words and actions they, too, defy the just laws of the realm because of their allegiance to a higher authority. Yet the moderates on both sides could scarcely be called traitors: could there be any doubt that in a national crisis they would willingly combine their efforts in the service of the Queen? This leads naturally to a plea for toleration and co-operation among all men of goodwill: 'I could wish with all my heart that either these differences were not among us at all, or else that they were so temperately on all parts pursued as the common state of our country, the blessed reign of her majesty and the common cause of true religion were not endangered thereby'.[7] These sentiments, as well as appealing, in all probability, to many moderate Englishmen, were in full accord with current establishment policy. John Whitgift, not yet one year into his long archiepiscopate, had already declared war upon all extremists and announced his intention of enforcing an outward uniformity. In this he had the full backing of the Queen. Thus far, therefore, *Leicester's Commonwealth* may well have appeared to be a wholly admirable book. From this point its tone changes completely.

The gentleman, lawyer and scholar readily agree that the one thing above all others which prevents harmony and peace settling over the land is the voracious appetite of the 'great falcons of the field', the court favourites who set up discord for their own ends. Foremost among these is the Earl of Leicester, 'the greatest enemy that the land doth nourish'.[8] Having made this weak transition from his introduction to his main subject, the author now devotes the remaining eleven-twelfths of his treatise to a vituperative denunciation of his chosen scapegoat. The book is an unbelievable catalogue of monstrous crimes and evil plots cobbled together from every fragment of gossip and invention its author could gather. As Sir Philip Sidney commented, *Leicester's Commonwealth* is 'so full of horrible villainies as no good heart will think possible to enter into any creature, much less to be likely in so noble and well known a man as he is'. Perhaps the libeller's motive was to 'backbite boldly so that, though the bite were healed, yet the scar would remain'.[9] It is extremely unlikely that the author, who was clearly a shrewd and cunning fellow, believed all the malicious tales which went into his witch's brew. Like Don Basilio, in Rossini's *Barber of Seville*, he knew well and savoured the power of *La Calumnia*: suspicion is enough to destroy reputation; there needs no proof.

Leicester's Commonwealth was a remarkable book written for what its author believed to be a time of crisis. Many men on both sides of the religious divide sensed that the years of cautious, tightrope diplomacy were coming to an end: the Protestant-Catholic Armageddon was almost upon them. The succession of conspiracies against Elizabeth's throne; the activities of defiant Puritan ministers and Catholic priests; the persistent rumours of Guise plots to invade Scotland; the severance of diplomatic relations with Spain; the assassination of William of Orange; the progress of the seemingly irresistible Parma in the Low Countries; the papal excommunication; the plans maturing in Madrid for an invasion of England; all these were signs of imminent conflicts. Zealots on both sides were determined to be ready for that conflict. Robert stood at the head of the Protestant activists. In May 1584 he wrote urging Elizabeth to forswear foreign alliances and rely on 'the mighty and assured strength you have at home'.[10] He had already begun to formulate a plan giving tangible expression to this 'mighty and assured strength'. His established protégé, Thomas Digges, wrote a pamphlet entitled *Humble Motives for Association to Maintain Religion Established*. It was a plan for a formal bond to be entered into by all English Protestants for the protection of their Queen. It was one of a number of pieces of propaganda put out by the Dudley circle and espoused by the Council the following autumn.[11] As a result, 'many men of all degrees and conditions throughout England by Leicester's means and out of their own public care and love . . . bound themselves in an Association by mutual vows, subscriptions and seals to prosecute to the death, as far as lay in their power, all those that should attempt anything against the Queen'.[12]

The Bond of Association, promulgated by the Council in the winter of 1584-5, provided for a body of twenty-four Councillors and peers who should enquire into all plots against the Queen and prosecute not only those responsible but those in whose name they were devised. In the event of a successful attempt on Elizabeth's life they were to assume control and to ensure that the claimant in whose interests the assassination had been carried out did not succeed to the crown. The Bond was ratified by parliament and copies circulated to all parts of the country where, as Camden states, thousands flocked to sign them. It was a warning to Mary Stuart and all at home and abroad who might be tempted to take up her cause that she would never benefit from any such attempt. It was accompanied by new and more stringent laws against Catholics.

Catholic extremists were driven to desperate measures in their attempts to undermine the Protestant consensus and prepare the way for foreign-aided revival. Francis Throckmorton's revelations in 1583 had led to a purge of Catholic elements throughout the realm and a closing of English ranks behind the Queen and Council. Never had the programme of Protestant imperialism which Dudley represented appeared more attractive to many of his countrymen.

Leicester's Commonwealth was published by Catholic propagandists specifically to destroy this solidarity by turning popular anger away from the Queen of Scots and her supporters and directing it upon Dudley and his 'faction'. To achieve this the author concocted an elaborate 'plot', supposedly devised by Leicester and directed against Elizabeth. According to the anonymous propagandist, the security of the realm lay not in executing Mary – that was precisely what the 'conspirators' wanted:

> It hath been a point of great wisdom . . . and of great safety to her highness' person, state and dignity to preserve hitherto the line of the next inheritors by the house of Scotland (I mean both the mother and the son) whose deaths have been most diligently sought by the other competitors, and had been long ere this, achieved if her majesty's own royal wisdom and clemency . . . had not placed special eye upon the conservation thereof, from time to time. Which princely providence, so long as it shall endure, must needs be a great safety and fortress to her majesty . . . against [the] practices of domestic aspirers . . .[13]

Dudley's supposed objective was to remove all rightful claimants to the throne until Elizabeth stood alone, and then to assassinate her. He would then back the Yorkist claim of brother-in-law Huntingdon, but only as a step to his own ultimate assumption of supreme power. Stated thus baldly, the scheme seems too absurdly far-fetched to attract any credence and had it been declared in such simple terms few contemporaries would have paid it any attention. The author's skill was shown in the way he dressed up his central argument with titillating gossip, half-truths, innuendoes and fearful suspicions.

He played upon the common fear shared by all Englishmen whose eyes were not blinded by religious fanaticism: 'If her majesty should die tomorrow . . . (whose life God long preserve and bless) but if she should be taken from us (as by condition of nature and human frailty she may) what would you do? Which way would you look? What [leader] knew any good subject in the realm to follow?'[14] It was the awful problem that had haunted councillors, members of parliament and men of substance for a quarter of a century and which became more acute as the childless Queen grew older. If the succession to the throne were not clear, that would be a bad enough calamity but it would lead directly to a worse, for Dudley and his cronies 'under colour of restraining the claims and titles of true successors . . . make unto themselves a means to foster and set forth their own conspiracy'.[15] The author was careful not to canvass unequivocally the claim of Mary Stuart of her young son. To have done so would have been clear treason under prevailing law and would have spoiled his case. It was subtler and wiser to leave men to draw for themselves the moral that safety lay in supporting the Scottish claim. What he did do was to argue away all the common objections to Mary's title. This was the central core of the book. Around it he packed the 'Dudley conspiracy' and all the garish libels about the favourite.

His personal attack on Robert had three elements: he impugned Dudley's ancestry, his morals and his policies. In reminding the reader of the treasons of Edmund and John the author was on safe ground. Both men had been unpopular. Both had ended their lives on the scaffold. It was easy to draw attention to their cunning, deceitfulness, disloyalty and manipulation of the sovereign and to suggest that these traits had been inherited by the third generation of their accursed house.

When he shifted his aim to Dudley's private life the author had an even more substantial target to hit. Leicester's failings were well-known, commonly exaggerated, an embarrassment to his friends and a comfort to his enemies. *Leicester's Commonwealth* now added hugely to the old stock-in-trade of gossip. It credited Dudley with an impressive list of assassinations, murders and attempted murders. Thus, he killed his first wife, the husbands of his mistresses, Douglas Sheffield and the Countess of Essex, Cardinal de Chatillon, Sir Nicholas Throckmorton, the Earl of Sussex and Lady Lennox, and made an unsuccessful attempt to dispose of Jean de Simier, Alençon's agent. On his orders William Killigrew tried to murder Lord Ormonde. He employed 'cunning men' to keep him supplied with 'secret poisons', and his patronage of Italian scholars was regarded as being particularly sinister in this connection. As far as women were concerned, the book asserted that 'no man's wife can be free from him whom his fiery lust liketh to abuse . . . kinswoman, ally, friend's wife or daughter, or whatsoever female sort besides doth please his eye . . . must yield to his desire . . . There are not (by report) two noblewomen about her majesty . . . whom he hath not solicited',[16] As unlikely is the allegation that he paid £300 for a night with one of the Queen's ladies.[17] The writer relates with relish Dudley's shabby treatment of Douglas Sheffield. *Leicester's Common-wealth* is the only source which mentions the clandestine birth of a daughter to Robert and Douglas at Dudley Castle. It could be true; ladies of the court often had to absent themselves mysteriously for a few weeks at a time in order to conceal from the Queen the results of their indiscretions. The comical story of the subterfuge at Dudley, on the other hand, sounds like alehouse invention.

> For the better covering of the harvest and secret delivery of the Lady Sheffield, the good wife of the castle also (whereby Leicester's appointed gossips might without other suspicion have access to the place) should feign herself to be with child, and, after long and sore travail (God wot) to be delivered of a cushion (as she was, indeed) . . . A little after a fair coffin was buried with a bundle of cloths in show of a child, and the minister [was] caused to use all

accustomed prayers and ceremonies for the solemn interring thereof.[18]

Avarice is another of the deadly sins here laid to Dudley's charge. Stories are told of his ruthless exploitation of his estates and heartless pursuance of poor men for payment of debts. The author mentions several names. Unfortunately, they are mostly the names of obscure men (supposing they lived at all) of whom we can now find no trace. If there was any truth in these allegations, Leicester's guilt was shared by almost every substantial landowner who tried to administer his estates efficiently in a time of inflation.

The author made much of Leicester's supposed wealth: 'he is better furnished at this day than ever any subject of our land either hath been heretofore or lightly may be hereafter, both for banks without the realm and stuffed coffers within . . . [his] treasure must needs . . . be greater than that of her majesty, for that he layeth up whatsoever he getteth, and his expenses he casteth upon the purse of his princess'.[19] Robert may well have wished that these particular libels were true. They were, in fact, very wide of the mark. To maintain his own state and to serve his Queen the favourite was constantly borrowing money – from Elizabeth, from friends, from merchants and bankers. William Byrd, London mercer, was a frequent money-lender. For example, between December 1559 and April 1561, £3,726. 13s. 4d. was repaid to Byrd.[20] And at the end, when the auditors went in to assess the dead Earl's effects they concluded that he died 'in debt to the value of £20,000 more than his goods and chattels are worth'.[21]

Dudley was, according to the author, an implacable enemy. Archbishop Grindal and Sir John Throckmorton are among the prominent men whom Leicester is supposed to have pursued remorselessly. There is no documentary support for any of these claims. Grindal provoked Elizabeth's personal displeasure and it was she who tenaciously opposed him for more than five years while Leicester's voice was added to those of others on the old man's behalf. Yet the libeller would have us believe that the Puritan champion hounded the Archbishop to death for refusing his Italian physician, Borgarucci, a dispensation for a bigamous marriage. He neglects to remind us that Borgarucci was also physician to the Queen.[22] Sir John Throckmorton was 'brought pitifully to his grave before his time by continual vexations',[23] according to *Leicester's Commonwealth*. A modern historian of the family tells a different story. According to Dr Rowse,[24] Sir John was a disagreeable man, a harsh landlord, an indifferent royal servant, a papist, and something of a rogue. In 1576 he fell foul of the Council, was stripped of his offices and was confined for a spell in the Fleet prison. He died soon after. There is no indication that Dudley, more than any other Councillor, was responsible for Throckmorton's disgrace. Whether he was or not, the man's fate seems to have been deserved.

So great was the favourite's supposed power and audacity that he thought he could even manipulate parliament for his own ends:

> My lord of Leicester was very careful and diligent . . . to have such a law to pass against talkers, hoping (belike) that his lordship under that general restraint might lie the more quietly in harbour from the tempest of men's tongues, which tattled busily at that time of divers his lordship's actions and affairs, which perhaps himself would have wished to pass with more secrecy, [such as] his discontentment and preparation to rebellion upon Monsieur's first coming into the land . . . his disgrace and checks received in court . . . the fresh death of the Earl of Essex and . . . [his] hasty snatching up the widow . . .[25]

The proposed legislation here referred to was a Lord's motion introduced in the 1581 session. Parliament was drafting a new sedition Bill to place some check upon the religious pamphlet war. This involved repealing the existing Marian statue which included slander against noblemen and bishops among punishable offences. The upper House sought, tentatively, to retain the 1554 Act or to replace it with a new one continuing the protection of spiritual and temporal lords. It was, thus, not a new measure invented to protect the *status quo* of the previous reign. The Commons rejected the proposal, not because they detected in it the subtle wiles of Robert Dudley, but because they realised that the suggested legislation might be used against Puritan propagandists who were critical of Anglican bishops.[26]

These and other aspersions of Dudley's character and lineage are only supporting elements of the author's main argument that the favourite has become an over-mighty subject and, like many historical villains before him, is aiming at supreme power. This fact, he asserts, is already well-known abroad: has not some stranger but recently published a book entitled '*Leicestrensem rempublicam*, a Leicestrian Commonwealth', which indicates quite clearly that it is the Earl who is the real power in the land? Indeed, ordinary Englishmen have some inkling of the truth: 'The common speech of many wanteth not reason, I perceive, which calleth him the heart and life of the court'.[27] His command of patronage has given him an unassailable position in the royal household:

It cannot be but prejudicial and exceeding dangerous unto our noble prince and realm that any one man whatsoever (especially such a one as the world taketh this man to be) should grow to so absolute commandry in the court as to place about the prince's person (the head, the heart, the life of the land) whatsoever people liketh him best, and . . . by their means, casting indeed but nets and chains and invisible bands about that person, whom most of all he pretendeth to serve, he shutteth up his prince in a prison most sure, though sweet and senseless.[28]

His money and influence have not only bought him friends and supporters at the centre of power but throughout the country.

What meaneth his so diligent besieging of the prince's person? His taking up the ways and passages about her? His insolency in court? His singularity in Council? His violent preparation of strength abroad? His enriching of his accomplices? The banding [together] of his faction, with the abundance of friends everywhere? What do these things signify . . . but only his intent and purpose of supremacy? What did the same things portend in times past in his father but even that which now they portend in the son?[29]

Leicester's climb to the heights of power where he now stood, ready to attack the summit, had not been easy. Elizabeth's proposed marriages had threatened his position and he had worked hard to overthrow all her suitors. Had Alençon succeeded there was no doubt that Dudley would have raised the standard of revolt.[30] It was, therefore, Dudley's fault that England had no heir to the throne and had been able to forge no foreign alliance which would have undergirded the security of the realm. For the favourite cared for no one but himself and nursed a secret hatred of the Queen:

such is the nature of wicked ingratitude that where it oweth most and disdaineth to be bound, there, upon every little discontentment, it turneth double obligation into hatred . . . [by sundry words and actions he has made clear] what her majesty may expect if, by offending him, she should once fall within the compass of his furious paws, seeing such a smoke of disdain could not proceed but from a fiery furnace of hatred within.[31]

As to the future, the author, supporting his disclosures largely with snippets of court gossip, stated that Leicester intended to strike at the throne with the declared objective of placing upon it the Protestant champion, Huntingdon: 'Yet it is not unlikely but that he will play the bear when he cometh to dividing of the prey and will snatch the best part to himself.'[32] And now (1584) the plans of the conspirators were all complete and ready for immediate execution. They needed only to persuade Elizabeth to dispose of her prisoner, Mary, and then the Queen herself would be at their mercy.[33]

Central to this elaborate accusation are Robert's alleged hatred of the Queen and the seriousness of the Huntingdon succession claim. Whatever the relationship was between Elizabeth and her ō ō, hatred and disdain played no part in it. Even if we refuse to allow Robert genuine feelings of love and loyalty for his sovereign we must concede that self-interest would prevent him plotting against her. So far from providing a pattern of conspiracy, the fate of his father must have been a constant warning to Leicester. He was totally dependent on the Queen for everything: wealth, lands, titles – all were the result of her bounty, a bounty motivated by her love for him. If he forsook that love, he forsook all, and if Elizabeth should die, he would have to work hard to win the favour of her successor.

As to Huntingdon, that unfortunate peer's Yorkist descent (from Richard, Duke of York, on his mother's side) was a constant source of embarrassment to him, annoyance to the Queen, and had for many years excluded him from high office. As early as 1563, the ardent Puritan Earl had poured out his heart in a letter to Dudley:

My honourable good Lord, I am sorry that my present disease is such that there are left me but these two remedies, either to swallow up those bitter pills lately received or to make you a partner to my griefs, thereby something to ease a wounded heart. At my wife's last being at court to do her duty as became her, it pleased her majesty to give her a privy nip, especially concerning myself, whereby I perceive she hath some jealous conceit of me and, as I can imagine, of late digested. How far I have been always from conceiting any greatness of myself, nay, how ready I have been always to shun applauses both by my continual low sail and my carriage I do assure myself is best known to your lordship and the rest of my nearest friends. If not, mine own conscience shall best clear me from any such folly. Alas! What could I hope to effect in the greatest hopes I might imagine to have in the obtaining of the least likelihood of that height? Will a whole commonwealth deprive themselves of so many blessings presently enjoyed for a future uncertainty? . . . of great hopes of an inestimable blessing by her princely issue in reason of her youth for a poor subject in years and without any great hope of issue? No, no, I cannot be persuaded they would, if I should be foolishly wicked to desire it, or [if] my mind were so ambitiously inclined. I hope her majesty will be persuaded of better things in

me, and cast this conceit behind her . . . What grief it hath
congealed within my poor heart (but ever true) let your lordship
judge, whose prince's favour was always more dear unto me than all
other worldly felicities whatsoever.[34]

Gradually men stopped thinking of Huntingdon as a potential
pretender. Gradually the Queen thawed towards him. In 1569 he
was nominated one of the guardians of the Queen of Scots. In 1572
he achieved major political importance as Lord President of the
Council of the North.

Robert's attitude towards his brother-in-law was one of cordiality.
Hastings and his wife, especially in the early years, joined the chorus
of relatives and friends who looked to the favourite for advancement. Catherine wrote to her brother in 1559:

> I am glad you court my lord your lord, which by your letter I
> perceive. I pray you, good brother, make of him as you will of me
> to do and esteem him as, I am sure, he giveth you cause, though
> peradventure he useth not such flattering behaviour as many will
> do unto prosperity. Brother, I would you would help to make him
> better able to wait [upon the Queen] which, I assure you, he
> desireth but necessity will drive him away unless you do help
> him.[35]

Two years later the couple's want of ready cash still created problems when the Earl had to attend court, and Catherine was obliged
to appeal to Robert again:

> I assure you when he shall go he shall not be able to carry £40 in
> his purse to bear his charges the whole journey, but if he spend
> more I am sure he must borrow it there, and that he needeth not,
> for I trow he oweth five or six thousand pounds at the least, and
> may not spend a year past five or six hundred. Good brother,
> consider his state and help that he may not spend more than he
> hath.[36]

For many years Robert was not able to do all he might have wished
for his brother-in-law. Elizabeth was very sensitive on all issues
touching the succession and even Dudley's pleading could only
acquire for Huntingdon a number of minor offices and grants.
Huntingdon was obliged to appeal to other powerful courtiers, and
his eventual emergence into the sunshine of royal favour probably
owed as much to Burghley as it did to Leicester.

Of course men discussed the succession issue and of course
members of the Council and their dependants made vague contingency plans for a situation which might arise suddenly at any time.

That crisis loomed largest in October 1562 when Elizabeth was stricken with smallpox. Then the Council split into factions and Dudley was probably among those who backed Huntingdon. He was in good company: Cecil, Norfolk, Pembroke and Bedford also favoured Hastings' claim.

But much water had flowed under the bridge in the intervening twenty-two years. Elizabeth's councillors had reluctantly accepted the fact that she would not marry, would not have children and would not name her heir. They had thrown their resources into and staked their own careers upon the preservation of the existing regime. So had men of the second rank, like Huntingdon. He served diligently in his various offices in the North and Midlands. He used every opportunity to advance the Puritan cause. And, as far as we know, no rebellious thought ever entered his head.

Having established Leicester as the monster responsible for all the nation's ills, the author urges the Queen to bring him to book:

> I know and am very well assured that no one act which her majesty hath done since her coming to the crown . . . nor any that lightly her majesty may do hereafter can be of more utility to herself and to the realm or more [gratifying] unto her faithful and zealous subjects than this noble act of justice would be for trial of this man's deserts towards his country.
>
> I say it would be profitable to her majesty and to the realm, not only in respect of the many dangers before mentioned . . . but also for that her majesty shall by this deliver herself from that general grudge and grief of mind, with great dislike, which many subjects, otherwise most faithful, have conceived against the excessive favour showed to this man so many years, without desert or reason.[37]

The author can scarcely have believed that Elizabeth would act on his advice but no doubt he hoped that his pamphlet, widely circulated by his network of agents, would spread discord throughout the realm and within the government. If it could play upon existing divisions in court and Council, it might cause the Queen to remove Dudley from his pedestal. After all, Elizabeth's father had never hesitated to set aside an able servant who had become an embarrassment to him. But in this regard Elizabeth was not Henry VIII's daughter. Most of her close advisers served her for years, survived periods of disgrace, experienced forgiveness and restitution. When, as in the case of the Duke of Norfolk, she had to dispense with a servant turned traitor, it was only with the utmost reluctance and usually after a display of intense emotion. She once boasted: '[I] never, to my knowledge, preferred for favour what I thought not fit for worth, nor bent mine ears to credit a tale that first was told me, nor was so rash [as] to corrupt my judgement with my censure, ere I heard the cause . . . this dare I boldly affirm: my verdict went with the truth of my knowledge.'[38]

Nor did the Council disintegrate into squabbling pro- and anti-Leicester factions. There might be differences among Elizabeth's statesmen. They might at times combine to disgrace and ruin one of their own number. But when an attack upon one of them came from outside, their natural reaction was to close ranks. If one councillor was vulnerable, all were vulnerable. Queen and Council were thus unanimous in denouncing Leicester's Commonwealth and in trying to prevent its circulation:

> Her majesty [testifieth] in her conscience, before God, unto you, that her Highness not only knoweth in assured certainty, the libels and books against the said Earl, to be most malicious, false and slanderous, and such as none but the devil himself could deem to be true; but also thinketh the same to have proceeded of the fullness of malice, subtly contrived to the note and discredit of her princely government over this realm, as though her Majesty should have failed in good judgement and discretion in the choice of so principal a counsellor about her, or be without taste or care of all justice and conscience in suffering such heinous and monstrous crimes (as by the said libels and books be infamously imputed) to have passed unpunished. Or finally, at the least, to want either goodwill, ability, or courage (if she knew these enormities were true) to call any subject of hers whatsoever, to render sharp account for them, according to the force and effect of her laws . . . her Highness of her certain knowledge, and we, to do his Lordship but right, of our sincere consciences must needs affirm these strange and abominable crimes to be raised of a wicked and venomous malice against the said Earl, of whose good service, sincerity of religion, and all other faithful dealings towards her Majesty, and the realm, we have had long and true experience. Which things considered and withall knowing it an usual trade of traitorous minds, when they would render the prince's government odious, to detract and bring out of credit the principal persons about them, her Highness taking the abuse to be offered to her own self, hath commanded us to notify the same unto you, to the end that knowing her good pleasure you may proceed therein, as in a matter highly touching her own estate and honour.[39]

The first copies of the book seem to have come before official eyes in the late summer of 1584. Then someone seized and sent to the

Council a pamphlet called *A Letter of Estate sent to his friend H. R. in Gratious Street, where is laid open the pract[ices and d]evices of Robert Sutton alias D[udley, Earl of L]eicester*.[40] The Queen immediately ordered a search to be made for copies and colporteurs and, at the same time, issued a new proclamation against seditious books. On 29 September Walsingham reported to Dudley the arrest of a man who was distributing the pamphlet.[41] This led to the discovery and arrest of Ralph Emerson, one of the main agents. At the counter in Poultry Emerson was examined and part, at least, of the story was extracted from him. He and John Weston, a Jesuit, had been sent over from France by the arch-propagandist, Robert Parsons, on 5 September with instructions to circulate copies of *Leicester's Common-wealth*. Emerson was left in prison and only emerged, a dying paralytic, at the beginning of the next reign.

The Council followed up the leads obtained from their interrogation and were soon interviewing known Catholics in and around London. Some were men whom they had had their eyes on for some time. One of them was Sylvanus Scory, the Bishop of Hereford's son – a 'notorious papist'.[42] He had been under surveillance for at least a year and was known to frequent the French ambassador's house along with other malcontents. Scory was taken into custody in February and closely questioned about his association with Thomas Morgan, Thomas Throckmorton and the late Spanish ambassador.[43] The names indicate the extent of the Catholic conspiracy, or, at least, the extent of conciliar suspicion about the conspiracy. The ambassador was Mendoza, recently dismissed for espionage activities. Throckmorton, kinsman of Francis, who had suffered imprisonment, torture and death for plotting against the Queen, was a recusant who had already been examined by the Bishop of London because of his unsatisfactory religious beliefs. Though a marked Catholic, he ostensibly lived most of his life quietly on his Cotswold estates. Morgan was Mary, Queen of Scots' principal agent in Paris. He had been imprisoned in 1572 on suspicion of involvement in the Ridolfi plot and on his release ten months later had taken up residence in France from where he kept up a clandestine correspondence with Mary and her sympathisers at home and abroad. He had been party to an assassination attempt on Elizabeth in 1583.

For the time being, Scory managed to satisfy his examiners. He told them that, though he knew about *Leicester's Commonwealth*, he had not seen a copy. Walsingham was convinced by what he learned from all the suspects he interviewed that Morgan was the author of this latest libel. He seems to have dismissed the opinion of Sir Edward Stafford who wrote from Paris to say that Dr William Allen

(Principal and founder of the English college at Douai) and Dr William Nicholson[44] were the authors. News reached the Queen of Scots that Dudley also shared this view and she wrote to tell her agent so.[45] The wording of her letter suggests that Leicester and Walsingham were mistaken. The most popular contemporary opinion about the authorship ascribed the book to Robert Parsons, and because of the colour of its binding it was known as 'Father Parsons' Greencoat'. The reasons for this identification seem to have been that Parsons was a leader of the Jesuit mission to England, that he was the principal propagandist of the Catholic crusade, and that during his stay in this country he had printed several tracts on a hidden press. This theory is now generally rejected.[46]

Parson's involvement in the work was probably limited to organising publication and distribution. *Leicester's Commonwealth* certainly originated from the group of English exiles living in French or Spanish territory who supported the claims of Mary Stuart. The book proclaims its author to be a man with an intense hatred of Dudley, a far from negligible literary style and a detailed knowledge of the personalities of Elizabeth's court. A possible contender is Charles Arundell, Gentleman of the Privy Chamber. He was a member of a group of secret Catholic courtiers which included the Earl of Oxford, Lord Henry Howard and Francis Southwell. Arundell had been involved in the Throckmorton plot and had fled to Paris at the end of 1583 where he became a member of Parsons' congregation of exiles. A series of events which occurred in the winter of 1581-2 throws considerable light on Arundell's character. The Queen learned of Oxford's conversion to the Roman faith and began to enquire closely into his activities and those of his friends. The group immediately disintegrated in mutual recriminations. As the mud began to fly Arundell proved himself far the most accomplished calumniator. Under examination, he accused the Earl of a panoply of sins and crimes – treason, bribery, atheism, homosexuality and the attempted murder of Leicester and Sir Philip Sidney. The relish with which he narrated Oxford's enormities and the fluency of his written style are strongly reminiscent of *Leicester's Commonwealth*:

> . . . we met in the evening at the Maids Chamber Door and after long speech between him and my cousin Vavasour (who was the means of our meeting) we departed thence to have gone to the garden but the door being double-locked or bolted we could not get in. Then we returned to the terrace and there, in the farthest part of the low gallery, the said Earl ... unfolded to me all his treachery . . . using many cunning persuasions to make me an

instrument of dishonest practice against my Lord Harry and Francis Southwell with the proffer of one thousand pounds to affirm that they were reconciled by one Stevens, a priest . . .[47]

I have seen this boy many a time in his chamber, doors close-locked, together with him, maybe at Whitehall and at his house in Broad Street, and finding it so, I have gone to the backdoor to satisfy myself, at the which the boy hath come out all in a sweat, and I have gone in and found the beast in the same plight.[48]

Oxford defended himself with a series of counter-allegations against his erstwhile friends. He gained Leicester's ear and Arundell attributed his subsequent disgrace to a conspiracy between the two noblemen. Though restored to his position, the Gentleman of the Privy Chamber now nursed a grudge and we can easily imagine him fleeing the country months later, seeking out Parsons and offering to the Catholic cause his gifts – an intimate knowledge of the court and a fertile imagination.[49]

The venom of *Leicester's Commonwealth* certainly suggests an author with a personal axe to grind. Yet there were some Catholic activists whose hatred of Dudley, for purely religious reasons, was so intense that they were prepared to use any means whatsoever to bring him down. It was clear to all contestants that Leicester was far more than just a figurehead of the Puritan party. He was, in Catholic eyes, the arch-heretic, the firmest and most influential advocate of the Protestant faith. This view persisted for a long time. In 1602 Thomas Bluet, a Catholic priest, said under examination, 'Unless God had interfered by the death of the Earl of Leicester [the Queen would have] destroyed all [Catholics] in the Kingdom'.[50]

The short term effect of *Leicester's Commonwealth* was probably very slight. The Council ordered a thorough search for copies of the offending book. Suppression seems to have been very successful. While a number of hand-written versions have survived there are very few extant printed copies of the original edition, and the eighteenth to nineteenth-century book collector, Thomas Grenville, wrote, 'I never heard of more than one copy having been in print of this first edition, so carefully was it suppressed.'[51] For a few years the illicit volumes circulated secretly among members of the Catholic community and scribes copied them out before passing them on to other avid readers. But then events overtook the book. In 1587 Mary Stuart was executed and in the following year Dudley died. Another factor which restricted its effectiveness was the rapid drift towards open war with Spain. Men of all shades of opinion rallied behind the Queen and Council to face the common enemy.

Whatever they felt about Leicester, his influence and his behaviour, these matters now seemed irrelevant. There is very little evidence that *Leicester's Commonwealth* had any great impact upon public opinion at the time or added appreciably to the fund of popular rumour concerning the favourite.

The absence of any official or semi-official counterblast to *Leicester's Commonwealth* suggests that, on mature reflection, the government decided that the book was not sufficiently important. Replies were, indeed, drafted – some, at least, with the backing of the Council – but they were never printed. Thomas Lupton, the popular Puritan propagandist, wrote a short tract in praise of Dudley, entitled *Of Virtuous Life*.* He sent it to his patron, begging him to obtain the Queen's permission for publication, for, 'thereby your kindled fame will give such a light that many shall see themselves much deceived, your enemies amazed and also ashamed, your lovers and friends thereby much rejoiced, and slanderers' reports . . . be clean banished.' Leicester apparently made no attempt to further the work. It was probably the recent libel that prompted Alberto Gentili, the celebrated legist and protégé of Dudley, to write glowingly of his patron in July 1585 in the dedication of his *De Legationibus Libri Tres*. In this scholarly Latin treatise, designed only for an academic audience, Gentili extolled Dudley's virtues, suggested that an attack on him was really an attack on the Queen and deplored the 'infamous howling against a good, loyal man'. He promised to expand his comments into a longer defence of Leicester, but the proposed work never appeared.

A far more distinguished writer who came to Dudley's support was Sir Philip Sidney. His *Defence* was certainly intended for publication. It was designed to be a public gauntlet thrown to the anonymous adversary in which Sidney called him a liar and offered to meet him in single combat, anywhere in Europe, within three months. Like Gentili, Sidney insists that Leicester is not the libeller's real target: 'The old tale testifieth that the wolves that mean to destroy the flock hate most the truest and valiantest dogs. Therefore, the more the filthy imposture of their wolfish malice breaks forth, the more undoubtedly doth it raise this well deserved glory to the Earl, that who hated England and the Queen, must also withal hate the Earl of Leicester.'[52] He dismisses the 'Huntingdon plot' on the grounds that if Dudley's faction included all those named by the author (many of whom are Sidney's own friends and relatives) it would be impossible for Sidney to know nothing about it. In fact, 'I could never find in the Earl of Leicester any one motion of inclination

*See Appendix 1.

towards any such pretended conceit in the Earl of Huntingdon'.[53] He dismisses all the accusations of *Leicester's Commonwealth* as unworthy of serious consideration, stemming, as they do, from one so false as to pretend to be a Protestant whereas 'any man with half an eye may easily see he is of the other party'.[54] Instead, he devotes the greater part of his tract to a declaration of Dudley's noble lineage and equally noble character. It has been suggested that similarities between the works of Gentili and Sidney and official statements argue for a concerted conciliar counter-propaganda campaign which was projected but never materialised.[55] Whether or not this is the case, the facts which emerge clearly from the available evidence are that Dudley did not rise personally to the libellous attack and that, after some months of energetic activity, the government decided that *Leicester's Commonwealth* constituted little real danger. We must remind ourselves that this book was only one of the hydra heads of Catholic activity menacing the realm in the mid-1580s. As reports constantly came in from the English shires and from abroad of plots and rumours of plots, Walsingham, Burghley and the others were kept busy obtaining information, issuing commissions of musters, ensuring that the levies were in a state of readiness, clamping down on recusants, examining prisoners, instructing ambassadors and checking coastal defences. By the summer of 1585 they thankfully concluded that *Leicester's Commonwealth* had been safely defused. The fact that they found it necessary in June to send out instructions for the suppression of the book would, at first sight, seem to indicate that there was a very real continuing concern about its effectiveness. However, the realisation that these orders were only sent to the leaders in London (where all sorts and conditions of men gathered) and in Lancashire and Cheshire (a staunchly Catholic area) suggest that we should put a contrary interpretation on the Council's action. Within a year of its first appearing, the effects of *Leicester's Commonwealth* had been all but completely negated.

Its subsequent history was very different. In 1641, long after the issues it had sought to influence had been forgotten, the book was republished. Yet it was certainly reprinted with an eye to contemporary events. Another royal favourite, another earl, was on trial for his life. Thomas Wentworth, Earl of Strafford, stood impeached by parliament for high treason, and England watched to see whether Charles I would allow his friend to die. In this situation *Leicester's Commonwealth* was a powerful piece of propaganda, pointing out, as it ostensibly did, the danger of an overmighty subject. Circulated widely in England for the first time, the book enjoyed a popularity which it had in an earlier generation only enjoyed on the Continent. It was soon reprinted. Further editions came out in 1706, 1708 and 1721. From then on *Leicester's Commonwealth* was a standard source book for biographers and historians. Gossip is always more entertaining than fact, slander than truth, and so a monstrous legend was created. It was reinforced by Sir Walter Scott in *Kenilworth*, and though more critical historians in the last hundred years have exposed *Leicester's Commonwealth* for what it is, they have been unable fully to undo the work of four centuries of calumny.

CHAPTER FIFTEEN

'HIGHEST AND SUPREME COMMANDMENT'

Archbishop Grindal died on 6 July 1583, and on 23 October John Whitgift was enthroned as his successor. His appointment was a tragedy for the Puritan movement and an annoyance to Leicester.

The 53-year-old unyielding prelate strove to restore the dignity and power of all grades of the ordained clergy and ruthlessly stamped out nonconformity. He became a close friend of the Queen who fully supported his campaign for the restoration of order and uniformity. Leicester and the majority of the Council had worked for ecclesiastical unity rather than uniformity. By stressing continually the threat posed by international Catholicism and by employing their influence to contain the excesses of the Presbyterians, they had helped to create a national church which, while possessing a Calvinist doctrinal basis, was comprehensive in worship and practice. Only self-confessed and detected papists were excluded. It was an important achievement, especially as England drifted into diplomatic isolation. This achievement Whitgift now set out to dismantle.

Influential opponents of Dudley could always be sure of finding friends at court. The Archbishop was no exception. His patron, Sir Christopher Hatton, had never been an ally of religious radicals. Indeed, in 1573 a fanatical Puritan had tried to assassinate him as an 'enemy of the Gospel'. Hatton, therefore, genuinely welcomed Whitgift's initiative. Until now he had not dared to oppose Leicester in ecclesiastical or other matters. As late as 30 January 1584 we have evidence of Dudley's dominance in a letter from Walsingham to Sir Christopher about the examination of a suspected Roman priest: 'Though for my own part I do very well allow of the course you were entered into touching the examining of Keeper, yet, seeing the Earl of Leicester doth not hold it best, I think it best forborne until we may confer with him tomorrow what way he shall think meet to be taken with the said party'.[1]

Yet Hatton had already taken the initiative, warning the Archbishop of projected motions against him in the Commons and assuring him of support at court.[2] Whitgift soon found himself obliged to take up this offer. When he required all clergy to subscribe to certain articles concerning belief and practice, some refused and appealed over his head to friends at court. Whitgift turned to his patron: 'I heartily

beseech your honour to foresee (as much as in you lieth) that these
men receive no encouragement from thence, and (if need require)
to signify this my petition to her majesty . . . Unless such contentious
persons were some way animated and backed they would not stand
out as they do.'[3]

Dudley, who had for years been urging his Puritan friends to
accept the prevailing pattern of church leadership and to work
within the existing framework, now found himself caught up in the
crossfire between entrenched episcopal and nonconformist positions. The radicals wanted him to stand up to Whitgift and, if
necessary, to the Queen. The Archbishop asked him to support
practically that lawfully constituted church authority to which he
had given verbal allegiance. Robert once more essayed the role of
peacemaker. He summoned representatives of the two sides to meet
at Lambeth in December 1584. For two days the disputants argued
before Leicester, Burghley, Walsingham and Lord Grey of Pirgo.
Despite claims made by Whitgift and his sympathisers that the arbi-
trators were completely won over to his point of view, the results
were inconclusive. Dudley and the Archbishop continued to be at
loggerheads, and in March 1585 Leicester delivered a blistering
attack on Whitgift's policies in the House of Lords.[4] He had powerful support: Burghley, Walsingham, Knollys and other prominent
men were equally opposed to the Archbishop. With the nation
poised for war against the forces of militant Catholicism within and
without, they were convinced that Whitgift had chosen to fight the
wrong enemy upon an irrelevant battleground. As Cecil protested,
'I desire the peace of the Church. I desire concord and unity in the
exercise of our religion. But I conclude that . . . this kind of
proceeding is too much savouring of the Roman Inquisition and is
rather a device to seek offenders than to reform any'.[5]

The Archbishop's intransigence and the Queen's support largely
and permanently checked Leicester's ecclesiastical patronage. For
the first time in years he lost control of an important area of government policy. His appointees were not presented to benefices.
Puritan sympathisers on the episcopal bench were replaced, on
death or retirement, by Whitgift's men. Some radicals were driven
into separatism, though the majority resentfully conformed. Early
in 1586 Whitgift was appointed to the Council and he was joined
there by Lord Buckhurst, both of whom were enemies of Dudley.
Another unfriendly influence was Sir Walter Raleigh who had
engaged Elizabeth's fancy in 1581 and was soon well established as
one of her favourite gallants.

With his prestige in the court and the country generally waning, and with the Queen pursuing policies he could only regard as disastrous, Leicester might well have concluded that the time had come to withdraw from public life. It might have been better for his reputation had he done so. Instead, he plunged himself with renewed vigour into the affairs of the Netherlands because he believed passionately that the security of the United Provinces was inextricably bound up with the safety of England, and because the constant pleadings of his Protestant friends across the water encouraged him to believe that he could demonstrate there his political and military talents more fully than at home. He at last persuaded the Queen to allow him to take an army to the Low Countries and to be her personal representative there. It was to be the crowning achievement of his life. Unfortunately, he overestimated his own abilities and underestimated the complexities of Netherlands diplomacy.

His enthusiasm, industry and will-power were undiminished, but Robert Dudley was not the man he had once been. He was heavy of build and had the high colour which suggests soaring blood pressure. In addition, he suffered from an intestinal disorder which brought frequent bouts of pain. He was obliged to diet often and to take the Buxton waters whenever he could. The complaint, gleefully described in *Leicester's Commonwealth* as 'a broken belly on both sides of his bowels whereby misery and putrefaction is threatened to him daily',[6] may have been severe stomach ulcers or the beginnings of a malignant growth. Whatever his ailment, it combined with Leicester's frustrations and anxieties to change his character. The easy-going extrovert now became prey to bouts of bad temper. He resented anything that appeared like criticism, could not tolerate opposition, saw enemies and back-stabbers everywhere and pursued those who offended him with quite uncharacteristic persistence and spite. The change was noticed by one of his old friends, John Aylmer, in November 1583. Writing to patch up a quarrel, he remarked:

> I have ever observed in you such a mild, courteous and amiable nature, that you never kept as graven in marble, but written in sand, the greatest displeasure that ever you conceived against any man. I fear not, therefore, my good Lord, in this strait that I am in to appeal from this Lord of Leicester . . . unto mine old Lord of Leicester, who in his virtue of mildness and of softness . . . hath carried away the praise of all men.[7]

The problems of the Netherlands vastly overtaxed him, but then they would have overtaxed a much more talented man, and it is certain that Dudley did not possess the necessary gifts. He had not seen active military service for thirty years and during those years the art of warfare had changed considerably. He did not know the country over which he was campaigning. He was opposed by the finest military commander in Europe, who had already spent eight years in the Netherlands and had subdued the southern part of the country. He led an army of Englishmen and Dutchmen whose interests differed and who needed a general of clear vision and iron will to hold them together. The political situation called for a man who combined the traditional attributes of Solomon and Job. The United Provinces were so in name only: they were a snake-pit of conflicting interests and factions. There were the zealous Reformers, particularly strong among the urban working class and led by firebrand Calvinist ministers, many of whom had fled from the south and had all the enthusiasm of religious exiles; there were the burgher oligarchies of the towns of Holland whose guiding principle was the maintenance of trade and municipal prosperity; there was the small, but by no means irrelevant, Catholic minority, quite capable of betraying a walled city to the besiegers, and the noble class which provided the traditional leaders of Netherlands society, whose leaders shared a common concern for national and territorial integrity but could not agree on how to achieve it. All these sections of society were represented among the members of the States General, but this body was split into factions along political lines also: some were pro-French, some pro-English, some looked to Prince Maurice of Nassau for leadership, others mistrusted the nobility. As Burghley once remarked, 'The States of the Low Countries are so divided that how trust may be reposed in them when one trusteth not another, I see not.'[8] All political groups and individuals looked to Leicester for different reasons. This might not have led to chaos had Dudley had the backing of his own government for the pursuance of a clearly defined policy. In fact, Elizabeth, reluctant as ever to commit herself, refused to endow her representative with the authority to achieve anything. It is doubtful whether England could have produced a statesman-general sufficiently gifted to emerge with credit and success from what was a virtually impossible situation.

It was in the summer of 1585 that Elizabeth agreed to send an army to the Netherlands. The death of William of Orange, the refusal of the French King, Henry III, to succour the rebels, Parma's conquest of the south with Spanish steel and Spanish gold, and finally the capitulation of Antwerp in August lent increasing urgency to the sporadic negotiations between Westminster and the Hague. Leicester left Walsingham to argue the case for intervention. He spent part of the summer on his Midlands estates, keeping in touch with the shifting political situation through Walsingham. At the end of August, just as he was preparing to return to court, he injured his ankle in a fall from his horse and was confined to bed for several days. This did not prevent him affirming his desire to head the force to be sent to the Netherlands. Messengers rode almost daily through the gatehouse at Kenilworth bearing news from Queen and Council. It was seldom that two pieces of information agreed. Now plans were being made for Leicester's expedition; then the leadership was to be given to John Norreys; now the covenant for the aid of the Netherlands was signed and sealed; then the Queen had stayed its despatch.[9] In mid-September Robert returned to court. He found Elizabeth ill and possessive. He sat up with her through several sleepless nights and she told him over and over again that she could not bear to be parted from him. Once, such an appeal would have moved Robert greatly. Now he found it tedious and frustrating. He wanted to know whether he was to be sent to the Netherlands or not; wanted to make his preparations. By 24 September Elizabeth was resigned to his departure but could not bring herself to issue the necessary orders.[10] That day Robert left for London. At Leicester House he dictated letters to 200 friends and dependants asking them to meet him with men and harness ready for embarkation at the end of October. He raised a loan from a consortium of London merchants, then went with Ambrose to the Tower to requisition armour and weapons. Two days were thus filled with hectic activity. He had scarcely tumbled into bed around midnight on 26/27 September when his servants admitted a messenger bearing a depressing letter from Walsingham: 'My very good Lord, her majesty sent me word . . . that her pleasure is you forbear to proceed in your preparations until you speak with her. How this cometh about I know not. The matter is to be kept secret. These changes here may work some such changes in the Low Countries as may prove irreparable. God give her majesty another mind and resolution.'[11]

Robert's official reply, 'scribbled in my bed this Monday morning almost 2 o'clock', declared his willing submission to the Queen's will. The private letter which accompanied it was couched in a different style:

This is one of the strangest dealings in the world. I find if any little stay be longer, the alteration on the other side [i.e. the Dutch] will be past remedy. They are so importunate upon me as I was fain to promise them to be ready myself to go within fifteen days . . . What must be thought of such an alteration! For my part, I am weary of life and all. I pray you let me hear with speed. I will go this morning to Wanstead to see some horses I have there, where I will tarry till 3 o'clock and then return hither again . . . If the matter alter I can have no heart to come at court or look upon any man, for it will be thought some misliking in me doth stay the matter. Send Philip [Sidney] to me, and God keep you, and, if you can possible, learn out the cause of this change.[12]

It was not an auspicious beginning to the great crusade.

Nor were the instructions he received early in December such as he had hoped to receive. Here was no schema for a war of liberation fought beneath the banner of Protestant truth; penny-pinching caution breathed through ever article. The Lieutenant General was to fight a purely defensive campaign and not to 'hazard a battle without great advantage'. English captains must not be allowed to misappropriate funds. Leicester must ensure that the Dutch contributions to the war effort were efficiently collected. He must establish and enforce a favourable currency exchange rate. As a guarantee in return for her expenditure Elizabeth had claimed the 'cautionary towns' of Flushing, Brill and Rammakens, and much of Dudley's instructions was taken up with the garrisoning and administration of these places. Towards the States General he was to act in a purely advisory capacity. The Queen had been offered the sovereignty of the United Provinces. Leicester's instructions stated that,

although she would not take as much upon her as to command them in such absolute sort, yet unless they should show themselves forward to use the advice of her majesty to be delivered unto them by her Lieutenant, to work amongst them a fair unity and concurrence for their own defence, in liberal taxations and good husbanding of their contributions for the more speedy attaining of a peace, her majesty would think her favours unworthily bestowed upon them.[13]

Robert was to create a new assembly with full powers to act, without having to refer every important decision back to the provincial governments.

The schedule set down for Leicester's guidance by the Dutch treaty commissioners was very different in tone. This spoke of wars, 'as well offensive as defensive, by sea and land'. It urged his excellency to 'keep his court' at Middelburg and to 'declare himself unto all and every unto whom it shall appertain chief head and governor general'. Above all else Dudley was urged to attend to 'the churches and the reformed evangelical religion, and by all due means to advance, confirm and to cause the same increase so much as is possible, not admitting or suffering any of contrary or papistical religion to any offices or charges of importance'.[14]

As Leicester rode out of London on 4 December at the head of his troops he had these and other problems on his mind. At his first lodging on the road he wrote a long letter to Burghley expressing his doubts and fears:

> Her majesty I see, my Lord, often times doth fall into mislike of this cause . . . but I trust in the Lord, seeing her highness hath thus far resolved and grown also to this for execution as she hath and that mine and other men's poor lives and substances are adventured for her sake and by her commandment, that she will fortify and maintain her own action to the full performance of that she hath agreed upon . . . I beseech your Lordship have this cause even to your heart . . . for this I must say to you, if her majesty fail with such supply and maintenance as shall be fit, all she hath done hitherto will be utterly lost and cast away and we her poor subjects no better than abjects. And, good my Lord, for my last [appeal], have me thus far only in your care that in these things which her majesty and you all have agreed and confirmed for me to do, that I be not made a metamorphosis, [so] that I shall not know what to do . . . no men have so much need of relief and comfort as those that go in these doubtful services. I pray you, my Lord, help us to be kept in comfort, for we will hazard our lives for it.[15]

Thus, constantly, as it were, looking over his shoulder, the Lieutenant General made his way to the east coast.

His was a princely cavalcade. The bulk of the army of 1,000 cavalry and 6,000 foot soldiers sailed from the Thames. Dudley's party comprised the cream of the English force, the mobility and gentry who had hurried eagerly to answer his call to arms. At the centre of it was Leicester's personal retinue of ninety-nine gentlemen and yeomen officers, together with their servants (ranging from his steward, secretary and chaplains to his cooks, grooms and farrier), his musicians and his troupe of actors, and his companions – twenty-two lords, knights and gentlemen with their fifty retainers.[16]

Robert's uneasiness showed itself as soon as he reached Harwich on 8 December when he had an argument with his admiral, the redoubtable Stephen Borough. The Lieutenant General told Borough that the fleet was to land at Brill. The seasoned mariner

remonstrated – Flushing was a better anchorage for such a large
fleet and he had not enough pilots for a landing at Brill. Angrily
Leicester asserted himself and cursed Borough as an inefficient
sailor. The admiral bustled about finding more pilots and sending
news of the changed plans to the other fleet in the Thames estuary.
After twenty-four hours Leicester at last gave way, acknowledging
the superior judgement of his mariners. By then conflicting
messages had spread confusion among ships of the Thames fleet, so
that some set course for Flushing and some for Brill.[17]

The welcome given by the Dutch to their liberators was ecstatic
and sumptuous. Leicester landed at Flushing on 10 December to
the booming of guns from ships and shore batteries. That night
there were banquets and fireworks. Over the next two and a half
weeks the Lieutenant General made a triumphant progress
through Middelburg, Dordrecht, Rotterdam and Delft to the
Hague. Every town competed with its neighbour to put on the most
magnificent displays of welcome and the most lavish entertainments. There were torch-lit processions, concourses of gaily-decked
barges on the canals, triumphal arches, speeches and poems
extolling Elizabeth and Leicester, banquets, plays and masques. At
Delft the citizenry spent £5,000 on their greeting. As in English
pageantry, all this display had a heavily pointed political moral.
When the feasting at Delft was presided over by a castle of crystal
and pearl topped by the figure of a protecting maiden, Elizabeth's
sovereignty was more than hinted at. When the arms of Orange
and Dudley were displayed together, Leicester's princely position
and authority was clearly suggested. When the series of pageants at
the Hague culminated in one portraying the Earl as a second
Arthur, it was clear that the Dutch did not regard Leicester merely
as a military leader. They were, for the moment, united in welcom-
ing him as their saviour. On New Year's Day a deputation of solemn
dignitaries, preceded by a herald and trumpeters, came to his
lodgings. Robert took the leaders of the delegation into his
bedchamber and there one of them made a long speech urging
Leicester to assume the mantle of government in all matters, civil as
well as military. Leicester, if he is to believed, returned, through
Davison, a non-committal answer, insisting that the authority laid
on him by the Queen was more 'than so weak shoulders were able
to bear'. But the Dutchmen were vigorous in their insistence and
repeated their offer on a number of subsequent occasions. Robert
could not delay much longer the making of a decision which must
make him unpopular either with the Queen or the States General.
Common sense urged acceptance of the proffered sovereignty,

even though it would make Elizabeth furious. The Dutch relied on him, as did the English garrisons sent over months before and still waiting for pay. The timing also appeared to be critical. Many towns and large areas of country were about to come under Parma's control, either by falling to his armies or coming to terms with his agents:

> These provinces, their estate, and the people of them did the Earl of Leicester at this his first arrival and acceptance of the government find in great confusion: the common people without obedience; the soldiers in misery and disorder for want of pay; the governors weary and tired for lack of good assistance and due obedience; the provinces themselves staggering in their union; and every town next danger [i.e. close to the enemy] ready to seek new means for their safety, such was their fear of the enemy, triumphant now with continual victories and especially with the late recovery of Antwerp; so little was their hope of their own ability to resist and so many were the enemy's deep and secret practices, even in the very bowels of them.[18]

Only a strong, able leader and a striking figurehead would, as the Netherlanders' leaders knew and as Robert now acknowledged, stand any chance of uniting the quarrelsome provinces. A man who came only as a general at the head of a relieving army was, in the view of some delegates, the worst possible kind of saviour. He had no permanent commitment and might be withdrawn at short notice, leaving the United Provinces to face, unaided, the wrath of Spain.

On 14 and 15 January, Leicester wrote to Burghley and Walsingham describing the importunate appeals of the States General and his reasons for believing that their request should be granted. He waited in vain for a reply. Ever since his arrival the winds had been in the north and east, preventing any ships leaving England for the Continent. This meant that news of Dudley's proceedings, his urgent requests for funds to pay the discontented garrison soldiers, and his appeals for advice on the constitutional issue all reached London safely but that he received not one word or penny in reply. Robert wrote to Walsingham again, on 22 January, a long, impassioned letter stressing the ecstatic reception he had received and urging the Queen to delay no longer:

> from the beginning of these troubles the people were never hotter against the enemy than at this day, nor better devoted to her, insomuch [that] she may now dispose of all and direct all, that otherwise had lost all, both countries and credit, yea with a mortal

hate for ever to our nation. And, if the case be thus for her
majesty, for God's sake let her comfort all here, and let her be sure
the enemy was never so doubtful, nor so perplexed, as he is at this
day.[19]

Still no word came from London. Leicester could wait no longer.
On 25 January, at a solemn ceremony at the Hague, he was
invested with 'highest and supreme commandment' within the
United Provinces.[20] Six days later Davison was despatched to
England to explain and excuse Leicester's action to the Queen. He
was too late.

Elizabeth heard of her favourite's new dignity not through some
carefully prepared speech by Walsingham or Burghley but from one
of her women, who had the news in a private letter from the Hague.
It was embellished with malicious rumour: Lettice Dudley was about
to go to her husband 'with such a train of ladies and gentlewomen,
and such rich coaches, litters and side-saddles as her majesty had
none such' and she would establish 'such a court of ladies as should
far pass her majesty's court'.[21] It is little wonder that Elizabeth flew
into a rage or that she resisted for months the efforts of councillors
and courtiers to bring her to a dispassionate view of the situation.
Her Robin had deceived her. That was bad enough but it seemed
that all her chief advisers were privy to his dealings and that none of
them had the courage to tell her. She wrote immediately to
Leicester. The letter bore no affectionate greeting and no tender
enquiry about his health:

> How contemptuously we conceive ourself to have been used by
> you, you shall by this bearer understand, whom we have expressly
> sent unto you to charge you withal. We could never have imagined
> had we not seen it fall out in experience that a man raised up by
> ourself and extraordinarily favoured by us above any other
> subject of this land, would have in so contemptible a sort broken
> our commandment, in a cause that so greatly toucheth us in
> honour; whereof, although you have showed yourself to make but
> little accompt, in most undutiful a sort, you may not therefore
> think that we have so little care of the reparation thereof as we
> mind to pass so great a wrong in silence unredressed: and, there-
> fore, our express pleasure and commandment is, that all delays
> and excused laid apart, you do presently, upon the duty of your
> allegiance, obey and fulfil whatsoever the bearer hereof shall
> direct you to do in our name: whereof fail you not, as you will
> answer the contrary at your uttermost peril.[22]

The bearer, Sir Thomas Henneage, was to demand that Leicester renounce his new title immediately.

It was at this stage that Davison reached court. He went first to Walsingham and was shaken to discover how downcast the Secretary appeared. The Queen received him, but only to harangue him on the subject of Dudley's ingratitude and disobedience. Davison persisted and was granted two more interviews, by the end of which he had persuaded Elizabeth to modify her instructions to Henneage and to peruse carefully Leicester's own account of his negotiations with the States General. Supported as he was by all the Queen's principal advisers, Davison was yet able to make little impression. Ambrose wrote frankly to his brother on 6 March:

> Our mistress's extreme rage doth increase rather than any way diminish and [she] giveth out great, threatening words against you. Therefore make the best assurance you can for yourself and trust not her oath, for that her malice is great and unquenchable, in the wisest of their opinions here, and as for other friendship, as far as I can learn, [it] is as doubtful as the other. Wherefore, my good brother, repose your whole trust in God and he will defend you in despite of all your enemies. And let this be a great comfort to you, and so it is likewise to myself and all your assured friends, and that is [that] you were never so honoured and loved in your life amongst all good people as you are at this day, only for dealing so nobly and wisely in this action as you have done, so that whatsoever cometh of it, you have done your part . . . Once again, have great care of yourself, I mean for your safety, and if she will needs revoke you to the overthrowing of the cause, if I were as you, if I could not be assured there, I would go to the farthest part of Christendom rather than ever come into England again.[23]

As a further measure of her disapproval Elizabeth deliberately delayed payment of the funds Dudley needed so desperately to pay his soldiers.

If Robert had shown the same resolution and fortitude as those friends and Council colleagues who stood by him in this hour of trial, he would have emerged from the episode as a figure of political stature and independence. In fact, Elizabeth's anger threw him into a panic. He cast rapidly about for scapegoats. The one who came most readily to hand was William Davison. It was he, Leicester insisted, who had urged him to accept the title first and seek permission after.

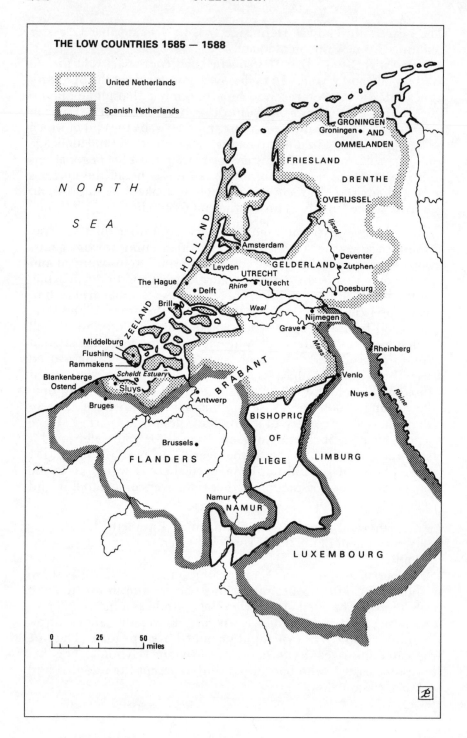

THE LOW COUNTRIES 1585 — 1588

United Netherlands

Spanish Netherlands

NORTH

SEA

GRONINGEN
Groningen • AND
OMMELANDEN

FRIESLAND

DRENTHE

OVERIJSSEL

HOLLAND

IJssel

• Amsterdam

Leyden

Deventer •
Zutphen

GELDERLAND

UTRECHT

The Hague

Rhine • Utrecht

• Delft

Doesburg •

Brill •

Waal

ZEELAND

Nijmegen •

Grave •

Maas

Rheinberg •

Middelburg

Flushing

Rammakens

Scheldt Estuary

Venlo •

Blankenberge

Ostend

• Sluys

BRABANT

Nuys •

Rhine

Bruges •

• Antwerp

BISHOPRIC

Brussels •

OF

LIÈGE

LIMBURG

FLANDERS

Namur •

NAMUR

LUXEMBOURG

0   25   50
|_._._._._|_._._._._| miles

Fortunately, Davison did not suffer as a result of Leicester's ingratitude. In fact, he was admitted to the Council in July. By this time the storm had subsided, thanks largely to Sir Thomas Shirley and Thomas Vavasour, whom Leicester sent over in March. Shirley, an old friend and protégé, employed one of his master's favourite devices to enlist the Queen's sympathy: he told her that Leicester was sick and needed the ministrations of a certain Dr Goodrowse.[24] Elizabeth was moved and promised that the physician should be despatched immediately. By the end of the month Sir Walter Raleigh could report that Dudley was once again her majesty's Sweet Robin.[25] On 1 April Elizabeth wrote to tell Robert that his offence, if not forgiven, would be forgotten:

We are persuaded that you who have so long known us, cannot think that ever we could have been drawn to have taken so hard a course herein, had we not been provoked by an extraordinary cause. But, for that your grieved and wounded mind hath more need of comfort than reproof, whom we are persuaded, though the act in respect of the contempt can no way be excused, had no other meaning and intent than to advance our service, we think meet to forbear to dwell upon a matter wherein we ourselves do find so little comfort, assuring you that whosoever professeth to love you best taketh not more comfort of your well doing or discomfort of your evil doing than ourself.[26]

At length a formula was found which enabled Elizabeth to accept Leicester's Governor Generalship: it was urged that the sovereignty he wielded was one granted to him by the people of the United Provinces and not one usurped from his monarch. In all matters affecting the crown he remained the Queen's Lieutenant General, and he was careful to see that his subordinate position was made clear on public and ceremonial occasions. For example, when he kept the St George's Day feast at Utrecht, a chair of state was set for the absent Elizabeth in the place of honour while Dudley sat at one end of the high table on a stool. Throughout the banquet the fiction of the Queen's presence was maintained, food and drink being proffered to the vacant chair. By July the old, familiar note had crept back into Elizabeth's letters: 'Now will I end, that do imagine I talk still with you, and, therefore, loathely say "Farewell ō ō", though ever I pray God bless you from all harm and save you from all foes, with my million and legion of thanks for all your pains and cares. As you know, ever the same. E.R.'[27]

In fact, Leicester's sovereignty was completely hollow. Real power lay with the people who held the purse-strings. Both Elizabeth and the States General were supposed to be contributing to Dudley's campaign costs. Both were slow and niggardly about making payments. Both used their financial levers to move political events. Caught in the middle, with soldiers deserting and companies on the point of mutiny, Leicester had no alternative but to meet expenses, as far as possible, out of his own pocket. By July 1586, when he at last received money from England, he had already spent more than £11,000. Even this was counter-productive in that it enabled the Dutch to delay their contributions still further. When military funds were available most of them were appropriated by the officers: little cash found its way to the poor soldiers. The end result was an under-paid and demoralized army, making its resentment known by indiscipline, desertion and pillaging of the local citizenry.[28] Robert did not mince words in his reports to the Council:

> I do swear to you by the living God that if it had not been for the money which I borrowed . . . we had had the foulest and most reproachful revolt and mutiny among our people that ever had been seen, and at this day [we would have been] forced to feed them with fair words and promises: 'Tomorrow, tomorrow they shall have'. Oh Lord, who would think it possible for any men sent as we are and in action for that realm chiefly, and all Christendom also, to be so carelessly and overwillingly overthrown for ordinary wants. Wishing cannot serve me to be at home, nor that I had never come here, but shame and dishonour will make me weary of my life . . . What opportunities we have lately lost. We are ready to eat our own flesh for anger but that cannot help.[29]

The campaign itself had degenerated rapidly after a striking initial success. This was the relief of Grave, a heavily-fortified town, commanding the Mass and one of the principal routes into the northern provinces. It had been besieged all winter by the Duke of Parma. At the end of March, Leicester sent a strong detachment under John Norreys and Count Hohenlohe to force their way in with reinforcements and supplies. The principal engagement occurred on 6 April when the Anglo-Dutch force put to rout a much larger body of the enemy, leaving 500 Spanish dead on the battlefield. After this, Leicester's men dismantled three of Parma's fortifications and brought fresh troops into the town, together with victuals for nine months. It was a brave and well-managed attack and a much needed boost for the allies.

But while they were rejoicing Parma was taking stock of the situation and planning his next move. During the next months he sent detachments of troops in various directions to confuse his opponents.

Having forced Leicester to divide his forces, he drew together his entire army of 12,000 foot and 4,000 cavalry and marched upon Grave at the beginning of May. He had also, by then, infiltrated his own agents into the town and satisfied himself that 'the match for the town was fully concluded before he would set out'[30] Confident that the citizens and garrison of Grave were now nerved and equipped to continue their resistance (a confidence boosted by the boasts of the governor, Baron Hemart), Dudley applied himself to diversionary tactics with a raid on Nijmegen and neighbouring Spanish forts. But Parma's show of strength before Grave and his fifth column within the walls unnerved the defenders. After receiving only a token battering from the Duke's artillery, the town surrendered. The news of this disaster, which 'seemed so strange that it was not at the first believed',[31] reached Leicester just as he had secured the immediate hinterland and was assembling his troops for the relief of Grave. Its effect upon morale was catastrophic. All the Governor General's problems were intensified as soldiers and civilians alike lost heart.

Faced with the choice between pressing home his advantage by advancing northwards and consolidating his hold on the region already penetrated, Parma elected the latter. He thus denied Leicester the opportunity of confronting him on the march, played on the timidity of burgher-dominated towns, deployed his troops and artillery over a smaller area and forced his opponent to fight a campaign of siege warfare for which he was ill-equipped. Leicester made urgent appeals to England for sappers and pioneers – apparently to little effect. Venlo and Nuys fell in fairly swift succession in much the same manner as Grave.

In addition to these military humiliations, Dudley had to face a political situation which was equally unsatisfactory. His honeymoon with the States General passed rapidly. He discovered that body to be 'a monstrous government where so many heads do rule',[32] peopled by men for whom he had nothing but contempt. They were, he said, mere 'churls and tinkers'.[33] They refused to meet their financial obligations.[34] They opposed his policies and appealed behind his back to the Queen.[35] Yet, instead of being able to dominate them as their sovereign, he was obliged 'to use flattery to those that ought to have sought me'.[36]

Unable to enforce or engineer cohesion among the ruling elements, Leicester entered the faction struggle. His natural allies were the Calvinists, who sought to set up a Protestant theocracy and to exclude from office all who were not zealous in the Reformed faith. They wished to establish a national government which would overawe the town oligarchies. It was this faction which dominated the council of state appointed by the Governor General and which supplied his principal advisers. Utrecht, the major Calvinist stronghold, became Leicester's centre of action. In other towns where the radicals enjoyed or were struggling for power, they had Dudley's support. Other groups came together to oppose this powerful Calvinist alliance. They were led by those who have been called the 'libertinists' – men who were anti-confessional, secularist and latitudinarian. The 'libertinists' were strongest in Holland and their main centre was Leyden. Holland and Zeeland had also sound economic reasons for opposing extremist policies. They were the richest states of the union. Their wealth derived from trade, much of it with Spain. From their bases in the inland states the politico-religious extremists criticised this commerce with the enemy on both moral and tactical grounds. The burghers of Holland and Zeeland countered the argument that a trade embargo would cripple the enemy, by asserting that Spain would easily find other markets and that the income from Spanish deals was helping to finance the war effort. It was this very issue that became the first trial of strength between Leicester and his political opponents. In April he issued an edict prohibiting all commerce with Spain. The merchants of the coastal states reacted with vociferous protests in public and a complete defiance of the ban in private. The Governor General established an audit office to seek out and fine smugglers. In the States General he rounded on the foremost spokesman for Holland, Paul Buys, and had him imprisoned, even though Buys had been one of his earliest and staunchest supporters. Having antagonised the middle-class oligarchs of Holland and Zeeland, Leicester now went on to alarm the aristocracy by his treatment of Baron Hemart, who had surrendered Grave. Convinced of the man's treachery, Leicester put him on trial for his life. Protests poured in: Hemart was a nobleman of an ancient house; he was well-connected; not even the Prince of Orange had dared to call such exalted people to account. No plea, no veiled threat, nor even the protests of Sir John Norreys moved Dudley; Hemart was condemned, sentenced and, on 18 June, beheaded.

Within months, Leicester had thus accumulated a powerful coterie of enemies. This would have mattered less had he possessed the power to enforce his policies and had he not been obliged to rely on all sections of the United Provinces for support in the military struggle. Just how far self-interest and lack of confidence could undermine the war effort is shown by the events accompanying the garrisoning of Deventer. The burghers, fearing that the presence of an English garrison would commit them to an uncomfortably stiff resistance, refused to allow the entry of foreign troops. Sir Henry Killigrew, therefore, kept the town council busy with protracted discussions for the space of two days while Edward Stanley sent his men into the town in groups disguised as citizens. When some 300 soldiers were concealed within the walls, Leicester's personal representative, Sir William Pelham, addressed the council with a final demand for the new garrison to be installed. He requested an answer by eight o'clock the following morning. The panic-stricken burghers immediately made preparations to resist their allies: they trebled the watch and threw chains across the streets. But long before the appointed hour Stanley's troops were assembled in the marketplace, and at 7.00 a.m. Pelham burst in upon the council. One of the Dutchmen tried to slip away to raise the alarm. At this Pelham unleashed his fury. 'Do you think,' he shouted, 'you have a people that are come over to spend their lives, their goods, and leave all they have, to be thus used of you and to be betrayed amongst you?'[37] He ordered the guard to be disbanded and the gates of the town surrendered. 'This done, he sent them to prison, appointed new officers, and brought this stubborn town in one day to a good safety'.[38]

The fresh military initiative, of which the garrisoning of Deventer was part, began in August. At last Dudley was provided with more men and money. He was also spurred on by Elizabeth's personal taunts: in one of her letters she said she had supposed her general was another Northumberland but now discovered that she had been mistaken. She told him she was tired of his grumblings and accusations and ordered him to expend his energies more constructively.

Having secured most of the territory between the Maas and the Waal, Parma began, in late summer, to move northwards along the line of the Rhine and Ijssel. By this means he hoped to neutralize Overijssel and Groningen, whose support for the United Provinces was patchy. Having achieved that, he could turn westwards at leisure into the heartland of the confederation. He began with the siege of Rheinberg. Sir Martin Schenck, the commander of the town, was a man who combined shrewdness and skill with reckless bravery. He had already played a prominent part in a number of dramatic incidents during the campaign and Leicester had knighted him as an example of courage to his fellow countrymen. Under Schenck, Rheinberg held out valiantly for several weeks, giving Leicester time to take counter-measures. The Governor General now mustered his entire force for an attack upon Doesburg, one of Parma's important outposts. After a show of force by the allies the people of Doesburg surrendered. During the action Leicester displayed some of that generalship that had endeared his father to his soldiers. He constantly moved among his men, encouraging them and inspiring them to greater effort. Regardless of personal danger, he went close to the walls to supervise the work of the pioneers in the trenches. It was while thus engaged that Sir William Pelham, standing in front of Leicester, was shot in the stomach. Fortunately the wound did not prove fatal and the marshal was carried from the field, praising God that he had protected his commander-in-chief. The town was an important gain for the allies and its capture forced Parma to lift the siege of Rheinberg.

Leicester now moved northwards to attack Zutphen, which, with its two forts, straddled the Ijssel. These places were considered almost impregnable: two years previously a Dutch army of 14,000 had besieged them for ten months without result. Parma, however, could not trust to their reputation and was obliged to come to their aid. He made his camp nearby and, on 22 September, he sent a relief column with supplies for Zutphen. Leicester despatched a force under Essex, Sidney, Lord Willoughby and John Norreys to confront the enemy. They had to contend with a heavy fog, and when it lifted they found themselves within range of Parma's arquebuses. The order was given to charge. Braving the fusillade of shots, the English cavalry rode straight at their opponents and, after several sallies, put them to rout. English losses were few but Sir Philip Sidney was shot in the thigh. Throughout the action he had fought with reckless bravery. One horse was shot under him but he remounted and rode deep into the enemy ranks. It was while turning to rejoin his companions that he received his wound. Normally his armour would have protected him but, with characteristic chivalry, he had removed his cuisses when he noticed that Sir William Pelham, only just recovered from his recent injury, was not wearing his. Sidney managed to reach the camp, and it was there that the celebrated incident of the water-bottle occurred. Sir Philip called for a drink and was just setting the flask to his lips when a dying soldier was carried past. He let the other man drink first. 'Thy necessity is greater than mine,' he said. Sidney was carried to Arnehem where he was nursed by his wife and friends. But the wound would not heal and, on 17 October, he died. Robert was heartbroken:

> Sir, [he wrote to Walsingham] the grief I have taken for the loss of my dear son and yours [Sidney had been married to Walsingham's daughter] would not suffer me to write sooner of those ill news unto you, especially being in so good hope so very little time before of his good recovery. But he is with the Lord and his will must be done. If he had lived, I doubt not but he would have been a comfort to us both, and an ornament to his house. What perfec-

tion he was grown unto and how able to serve her majesty and his country all men here almost wondered at. For mine own part, I have lost, beside the comfort of my life, a most principal stay and help in my service here and, if I may say it, I think none of all hath a greater loss than the Queen's majesty herself.[39]

The death of Sidney masked the success of the Zutphen operation, which Leicester prosecuted with determination and vigour against the advice of his officers:

The hope of our leaders, both English and others, was small for the obtaining of these forts; they were so strong and well provided every way and our means scant sufficient for so great an exploit. But his excellency's own self, contrary to all and every their advices, persisted in his intent most constantly and would not hear anything that might tend to dissuade him from this purpose . . . he most diligently and dangerously attended always in person, both early and late, and put his own hand almost to every particular service of it.[40]

But, when it came to the point, Dudley's captains gave him of their best. Edward Stanley was particularly valiant. First in at the breach of one of the forts, he fought alone 'first with his pike, then with the stumps of his pike, and afterward his sword'.[41] Robert was not slow in recognising such conspicuous bravery. Immediately after the stronghold had been won, he knighted Stanley 'in the trenches, gave him forty pounds sterling in gold, and sent him the next day a patent of one hundred marks sterling by year'.[42] The defenders of the other fort did not wait to receive the same fate as their comrades, but fled by night, leaving all their ordnance behind. During the next few days a number of smaller fortifications in the area were overthrown and Deventer was garrisoned, leaving Zutphen itself isolated and obliging its garrison to face the winter with dwindling supplies and little possibility of relief. In fact, the governor was soon obliged to reduce his garrison and expel some of the townsfolk in order to eke out his meagre victuals. Parma displayed little concern for their plight. Contenting himself with his gains farther south, he withdrew his men into winter quarters and retired to Brussels.

Leicester now renewed his request for a temporary recall. He was exhausted by his exertions and difficulties. He needed to discuss with his Council colleagues a political situation which was steadily worsening. Word had reached the Dutch leaders that Elizabeth had reopened negotiations with Spain (which was true) and this convinced many of Leicester's friends that their new ally was about to desert them. The opposition to Dudley had also now found a formidable champion in the figure of Johan van Oldenbarneveldt, Advocate of Holland. He began to unite burghers and aristocrats in a movement for national recovery without outside aid. For her part, Elizabeth was now also anxious for Robert's return to England. According to Burghley, she wanted his company and was concerned for his health. She also needed his advice in facing the greatest crisis of her reign.

In July the Babington Plot, clearly involving Mary, Queen of Scots in a scheme to assassinate Elizabeth and take her place on the throne, was uncovered. All the councillors clamoured for Mary to be put on trial and executed. From across the North Sea Leicester added his entreaty to theirs. He urged his colleagues to brook no delay in the matter:

> I do assure myself of a new, more desperate attempt if you shall fall to such temporizing solemnities [i.e. the summoning of parliament], and her majesty cannot but mislike you all for it. For who can warrant these villains from her if that person live, or shall live, any time? God forbid: And be you all stout and resolute in this speedy execution or be condemned of all the world forever. It is most certain if you will have her majesty safe it must be done, for justice doth crave it besides policy.[43]

Elizabeth procrastinated. Robert was anxious to return and appeal to the Queen in person. As soon as Lord Grey de Wilton arrived to relieve him, Leicester left the Netherlands on 23 November. He returned to discover that his political influence had weakened considerably in his absence. Not only had members of the Whitgift-Hatton group been brought into the Council but some of his own supporters had grown cool. The main reason for this lies in their new experience of easier access to the Queen. So often in the past royal approval for a policy or a decision had rested upon the prior agreement of the favourite. Now, Dudley's intermediary role had been suspended for a year. No one had stepped into his place and this meant that councillors, individually and corporately, had closer contact with their sovereign. Leicester's quarrels in the Netherlands with various of his subordinates, such as Davison and Norreys, had also won him enemies at home, for there were no senior members of his entourage who did not have friends and sympathisers at court. Leicester had even fallen out with his staunchest supporter, Walsingham. The issue between them was Sir Philip Sidney's debts. The gallant knight's disposable goods would not 'suffice to answer a third part of his debts already known'[44] and legal difficulties had been raised concerning the provisions of his will for the selling of lands to satisfy creditors.

The results of this were that Walsingham, as executor, was under considerable pressure, and Sidney's body remained unburied for lack of funds to provide a suitably lavish funeral. Sir Francis paid £6,000 out of his own pocket and appealed to Dudley to share his burden. Unfortunately, Leicester's own finances were in such disarray that he could do nothing immediately. Walsingham clearly believed that it was the will and not the ability to help that his old friend lacked. The situation was exacerbated when Leicester refused to support Walsingham's application for the Chancellorship of Duchy of Lancaster and put forward instead a candidate of his own. Within the Council and the court the rising star was Sir Christopher Hatton. In April 1587 he was appointed Lord Chancellor, despite the opposition of the legal fraternity to a man who had no professional training. To many men Hatton seemed destined to fill the role that had been Leicester's. Inevitably their rivalry increased though, for the moment, no political issues divided them.

If Leicester's dominance in the Council had been weakened, his standing with the Queen had not. She had been angry at his demands for exorbitant sums of money and attributed the high cost of the Netherlands venture to his mismanagement. But her indignation was swept aside by her need for her old friend's aid with the terrifying problems and decisions confronting her. By late November Elizabeth was desperate to see her ō ō, to have him beside her, to confide in him her secret fears, to seek his advice. Never had she been more alone that she was in that autumn of 1586. Political England clamoured for her to shed Mary's blood – a thing utterly repugnant to her. Catholic Europe and the Scottish king urged her to resist her people – a course of action she could not take. The Netherlands campaign was draining the treasury and making havoc of her careful finances. The international peace she had worked so hard to preserve was on the point of being shattered: Philip was known to be mustering his fleet for an invasion of England. As she tried to turn back the tide of the inevitable, no one stood beside her or sympathized with her predicament. As she wrestled with her doubts, fears and moral dilemmas and possibly came close to a breakdown,[45] Elizabeth had advisers in plenty – preachers reminding her of her duty; parliamentarians urging her to be revenged on her enemies; councillors steeling her arm for battle – but there was no one who understood her or realised that the policy she was being urged to pursue represented for her a deep personal failure. She lingered at Richmond, refusing to come to Westminster, 'being loath to hear so many foul and grievous matters revealed and ripped up'[46] by parliament. By 12 November Lords and Commons had ratified the death sentence which had, ultimately, been passed upon the Queen of Scots. On the 24th a parliamentary deputation urged Elizabeth to issue a proclamation concerning the execution of Mary. She returned them an 'answer-answerless' and with that they had to be content. Then Dudley arrived. What passed between the two old friends as they supped alone that evening we do not know. But we do know that Elizabeth's doubts were overborne. She scrawled a note to the Lord Chancellor ordering him to make the proclamation. Her resolve, however, did not survive the withdrawal of Robert and the ensuing sleepless night. Before dawn another message was on its way to Westminster rescinding her order and adjourning parliament for a week. During that week, Leicester, firmly reinstalled in his favoured place, used all his powers to bring Elizabeth to the point of no return, while Burghley and other councillors passed back and forth between Richmond and the capital with messages and draft proclamations. On 4 December the Queen's determination to execute her cousin was made known to her subjects.

Now all that was needed was the signed warrant for Mary's death, and Elizabeth's advisers expected that it would follow rapidly upon the proclamation. They should have known better. The Queen resisted every attempt to urge her to immediate action. The air was thick with rumours of fresh Catholic conspiracies, protests from foreign courts, and bloodthirsty thunderings from Protestant pulpits. Early in January an embryonic plot was either unearthed or fabricated by the Council. Leicester spent long hours with Hatton, Burghley and Davison questioning Chateauneuf, the French ambassador, about the activities of his servant, Des Trappes, and William Stafford, brother of Chateauneuf's counterpart in Paris. Little came of it all and the main objective of the councillors was to alarm the Queen. They were not strikingly successful and Mary lived for another month. The activities of that month – the issuing of the warrant to Davison, the Queen's frequent changes of mind, the despair of the Council, the eventual execution of the warrant, Elizabeth's angry denial of responsibility, Davison's disgrace – are too well-known to bear repetition. Leicester was closely involved in all of them, either by virtue of his attendance at Council meetings or his waiting upon the Queen.

Apart from occasional visits to Wanstead, Robert slipped back into the old routine life at court and government. He presided at ceremonial occasions. For example, it was he and Burghley who escorted Hatton in state from Ely Place to Westminster for his swearing in as Lord Chancellor. And he attended the elaborate funeral of Sir Philip Sidney at St Paul's in February. He also returned to the ever-present bickering of the royal household. The main source of grievance was, as usual with Elizabeth, money. She required full accounts from Leicester of his use of government funds in the Netherlands. This reasonable request was relayed to the favourite via Burghley. Leicester took umbrage at being required to do work 'more the province of an auditor or clerk, than one in high position'. He complained that, in this matter of accounts, Cecil, one of the staunchest supporters of the Netherlands venture, had on several occasions taken a contrary stance in front of the Queen. Burghley replied that his criticisms were only of the treasurers responsible for accounting for the funds and not of the Governor General. 'I protest before God,' he wrote, 'I have had and always desire to have your Lordship's favour and good liking'.[47] To the casual observer it was very much the same mixture as before.

Meanwhile the situation in the Netherlands was worsening rapidly. In January the military gains of the previous season were wiped out at a stroke. Sir William Stanley, whom Leicester had left in command of Deventer, was a Catholic and a man with a grievance (he believed that his long service in Ireland had not been adequately recompensed). Perhaps the sentencing of Mary Stuart impelled him to desperate action; perhaps he had already resolved on the course he was going to take. Whatever the reason, Stanley conspired with Sir Rowland York, captain of the Zutphen fort, to yield their positions to the enemy. The two traitors surrendered to the Spanish governor of Zutphen and took most of their men into King Philip's service. Parma accurately assessed the impact of this defection in a letter to his master: 'The Zutphen fort . . . and Deventer which was the real objective of last summer's campaign and is the key to Groningen and all these provinces are thus Your Majesty's at a trifling cost. But what is better, the effect of this treason must be to sow great suspicion between the English and the rebels, so that hereafter no one will know whom to trust.'[48]

He was right – Oldenbarneveldt now had no difficulty in getting Maurice of Nassau recognised as military leader. The Prince was appointed Stadholder and Captain-General in Holland, Zeeland and Friesland. Elizabeth sent Lord Buckhurst to deliver a strong protest. Oldenbarneveldt assured the envoy that Maurice's appointment was but temporary and did not 'touch the honour, either of the Earl of Leicester, or the English nation, or to prejudice the authority of his lordship, whose speedy return they so earnestly desired'.[49] But at the same time the 'libertinists' tried to persuade Buckhurst (known to be no friend of Leicester) to support their attempt to limit the Governor General's powers. Buckhurst did not respond but Dudley's Calvinist

friends did. They informed Leicester of the schemes afoot. They
thundered from the pulpits against their own politicians. The
Friesland synod and the leaders of several towns wrote urging
Elizabeth to assume unrestricted sovereignty in their land.

With Netherlands politics more chaotic than ever and with Philip
and Parma triumphant it was obvious that Elizabeth would have to
continue her aid to the States General. Buckhurst was soon writing
letters very similar in tone to Leicester's of a year before:

> I have so often and so earnestly written for money to relieve the
> poor soldiers here and so plainly signified the great poverty and
> penury that they endure, with the fearful danger that seemeth to
> approach us all, by means of this woeful want of pay . . . so long
> have I upheld these provinces with the painted pillars of hope and
> expectation (whom I found in a manner desperate and, as it were,
> believing certainly her majesty would abandon them) as if neither
> mean be established how to govern their estate, nor men trans-
> ported to defend the enemy, nor money sent wherewith to pay the
> soldiers.[50]

Leicester received no less importunate letters from his friends in the
Low Countries. He and the Queen both appreciated fully the urgency
of the situation but neither was prepared to endure a repetition of the
previous year's events. Elizabeth demanded, through Buckhurst, that
the United Provinces put an army of 14,000 in the field and pay for
it themselves. Robert, for his part, insisted that he would not return
before all arrears of army pay had been made up and a royal loan of
£10,000 guaranteed to meet his personal expenses.

Meanwhile a fateful change of policy had been decided upon in
Madrid. Parma was ordered to arrest the conquest of the northern
provinces and concentrate on securing as much of the coast as
possible, for his King had decided to launch the Enterprise of
England without further delay. In the spring of 1587 Parma assembled half his available troops at Bruges for an attack upon Sluys, a
fortified harbour at the mouth of the Scheldt defended by the local
militia. Parma was hampered by famine as well as by Sluys's impressive system of defensive waterways. His conquered province was
almost barren and the siege went slowly. He was, however,
constantly urged on by Philip.

Madrid's eagerness was not matched in London. May passed and
June dragged sluggishly on. Elizabeth could not decide whether to
send Leicester or Norreys to the Netherlands. Robert waited impatiently, unable to reply to his friends across the water. Walsingham
was at his wits' end with the Queen. It was midsummer before

Elizabeth could be prevailed upon to agree the terms of Leicester's renewed commission. Robert now wrote to his supporters in the United Provinces, urging them to a last effort to gain control of the various state and town councils. The political conflict was thus destined to continue exactly as before.

Leicester sailed on 25 June with 3,000 fresh troops and an impressive flotilla of warships under the command of Lord Admiral Howard. When they arrived off Sluys, the town, surrounded on all landward sides, had been under siege for three weeks. Sir Roger Williams, a Welsh veteran, had fought his way in with an English detachment and, thus strengthened, the garrison was putting up a courageous resistance that drew the admiration of the professional Parma. Leicester anchored at Flushing and immediately took council with his allies and his own officers about the best means of raising the siege. They could not agree. The General's misfortune was that he was reliant upon the support of the Zeeland navy, led by Justin of Nassau, and the Dutch pilots who were familiar with the channels and sandbars of the Scheldt estuary. These men were all cautious to a fault and refused to commit themselves to an assault from the sea until tide and weather conditions were ideal. Had Leicester asserted his authority, a ship-borne attack in force might well have smashed its way through Parma's tenuous system of batteries, barriers and bridges. In the event, he allowed himself to be diverted from this. His next plan was to lead an assault upon the Spanish headquarters on the island of Cadzand. This involved the use of flat-bottomed boats to carry the troops. Justin of Nassau calmly informed Leicester that he could not release the necessary vessels without written permission from the States General. Without the enthusiastic support of his allies, direct intervention to aid Sluys was impossible. Leicester had to fall back on a diversionary manoeuvre: he landed Sir William Pelham at Ostend with 4,000 foot and 400 horse and orders to take Blankenberge. This small fort, further up the coast, was important to Parma because it guarded his rear and his supply lines from Bruges. He was forced to send a large detachment of Spanish veterans to meet the English army. Pelham was fearful of pitting his raw levies against these crack troops and he withdrew to Ostend without firing a shot.

Now Dudley really did assert himself over the allied commanders. He insisted on a frontal assault by water on the following day. The plan was for a fireship to go ahead and destroy the floating bridge Parma had thrown across the channel. Justin's small warships would then bear through with Leicester, who would personally lead the attack, and the troops. They would make an entry for the supplies and reinforcements, carried by flyboats and barges. It was an exacting

manoeuvre, demanding fine timing and accurate manipulation of
many vessels through the shallows of the estuary. There was very
little room for error or mishap. On the evening tide the fireboat was
steered towards its target. It was a fearsome sight. Against inexperi-
enced troops and timorous commanders it would probably have
been very effective. Parma simply gave the order for part of the
bridge to be unfastened and swung out of the way, allowing the
'hellburner' to pass through and exhaust itself harmlessly in the
inner basin. The attacking fleet was, necessarily, coming up at some
distance from the fireship. Seeing the failure of his stratagem,
Leicester went from ship to ship in his barge, ignoring small arms
fire from the Spanish positions, ordering more sail and full speed so
as to reach the bridge before the enemy had time to close the gap.
The Dutch captains and pilots simply refused to co-operate. They,
too, had observed Parma's cunning, and were afraid of running
their ships into a narrow, closed channel where they would have no
room to manoeuvre. While his allies argued and Leicester fumed,
Parma repaired his breach, the tide slackened, the wind changed
direction and the opportunity was lost.

No further serious effort was made to relieve Sluys. The town held
out bravely until 26 July when the governor asked for a parley and
surrendered on honourable terms. The siege had been scarcely less
exhausting for Parma than for the garrison and townsfolk. He had
lost 700 men and many more had been wounded. The greater part
of the campaign season was past and he had insufficient strength to
attempt the capture of Flushing or any other coast town. He was
only too pleased to win a breathing space by entering peace negotiations with the Queen of England. The finance-conscious Elizabeth
was not altogether sorry that active hostilities were over for a while.
She was, apparently, under no illusion as to where the blame lay for
the loss of Sluys. She reposed no trust in her Dutch allies or their
ability to maintain their independence, as she wrote to Robert:

> We have thought good considering the broken state of things
> therewith do threaten nothing but the ruin of those countries, the
> great touch of honour we have received by the loss of Sluys
> through the malice or other foul error of the States, and such as
> ought to have succoured it and the little hope we have of better
> success in times to come, to yield to the said treaty. And for that by
> the contract between us and the States of those countries, it is
> agreed that we shall not treat of anything with the King of Spain
> that may concern them without their privity. We think very [well]
> you should acquaint the States General with this our disposition

and the urgent reasons leading us thereto . . . We cannot but advise them to concur with us in taking profit of this overture made unto us by the said Duke, for that otherwise we do not see how they shall be able to hold out but shall by the neglecting of the same obstinately persevere in a course that will work their open ruin though through their unthankfulness, and sundry indignities offered unto us, the contempt of our government under yourself and misusage of our subjects, with daily loss of our subjects, for their price we have no great reason to be so careful as we have been and yet are.[51]

The breach between the allies was now too wide to be bridged. Each side blamed the other for the Sluys fiasco. The Dutch believed that Elizabeth had all along intended to make a separate peace treaty with Spain. Dudley, charged with the task of bringing the States General to the conference table, found it impossible to overcome the hostility of the Dutch leaders. A popular cartoon depicted the United Provinces as a cow which Leicester milked until he drew blood. The States General refused to continue to recognise his authority. Yet Dudley still enjoyed considerable support, particularly among the religious extremists, and he made one last effort to consolidate his followers into a party. When that failed he informed the Queen that he could do her no more service in the Netherlands and on 10 November Elizabeth recalled him. Leicester had a medal struck to commemorate his departure. It was distributed to his many Dutch friends to reassure them as to the reason for his going. The head side displayed Dudley's bust and titles. The reverse showed a guard dog walking away from a flock of sheep. Some watched him sorrowfully; others had their heads buried in the grass. The legend ran *non gregem sed ingratos invitus desero*: 'I reluctantly leave not the flock, but the ungrateful ones.'

CHAPTER SIXTEEN

'A GLASS UPON THE WATER'

When Robert returned finally from the Netherlands at the beginning of December 1587 he found the Queen not unnaturally displeased at his failure to effect her policy. She received him warmly in public but would not readmit him to his old intimacy with herself. He spent most of his time at Wanstead and it was from there, a month after his return, that he wrote beseeching Elizabeth 'to behold with the eyes of your princely clemency my wretched and depressed estate'.[1] Noting this estrangement, Lord Buckhurst thought the time propitious for an attempt to topple the favourite. He should have known better. Whatever their private relations might be, Elizabeth had always been unswervingly loyal to her Sweet Robin in public. She remained so to the end. Buckhurst's attempt to call Leicester to account for his mismanagement of Netherlands' affairs in open Council was scotched as soon as the Queen heard of it.[2]

Despite his pleas to be restored 'to some degree of Your Majesty's grace and favour',[3] it seems that Dudley was tiring of public life. His service in the Low Countries had brought nothing but anxiety, frustration and disillusionment and had further affected his health. Within days of his return to England he relinquished the Mastership of the Horse in favour of his stepson, the Earl of Essex. It was no sudden decision: young Devereux, who had already won a firm place in the Queen's affections and had used it loyally in Leicester's interests during the latter's absence, was discussing the possibility of his becoming Master of the Horse as early as the previous May. The placing of Essex close to the Queen to further Leicester's interests had worked extremely well. During Leicester's prolonged absence in the Low Countries he continued to enjoy Elizabeth's affection, as it were, by proxy. His protégé was her constant companion. It was he who sat late into the night with her playing cards; it was he who rode with her in Windsor Great Park; it was he who delivered private, intimate messages from his stepfather and effectively negated the activities of Dudley's opponents.

Now, it seemed, the time had come to make the experiment permanent. As Master of the Horse, Essex would be the Queen's constant companion and able to further Dudley's policies without Dudley himself having to be always at court. When, in April 1588,

Essex was admitted to the Order of the Garter, it seemed that his career was following Leicester's own remarkably closely.

There was, of course, always the risk that the arrangement might work too well: that the protégé might become a rival. The fact that this danger never materialised is due not to Elizabeth's love for Leicester but Essex's profound loyalty. He was bound to his stepfather by those strong bonds of affection which, as we have seen, held so many of Dudley's friends, both young and old. Nothing illustrates this more clearly than a perplexed letter young Devereux wrote to Leicester the following August:

> Sir, Since your Lordship's departure her majesty hath been earnest with me to lie in the court and this morning she sent to me that I might lie in your Lordship's lodging, which I will forbear till I know your Lordship's pleasure, except the Queen force me to it. So offering to you my best service now as at any time else, I humbly take my leave . . . Your son to do you service, Essex[4]

The Queen certainly looked to Leicester to play a major part in the defence of England when Philip's Armada finally set sail. Through the winter of 1587-8 Robert was a frequent attender at Council meetings, urging with Walsingham and others that more reliance should be placed on the navy and army than on diplomats talking peace with the treacherous Spaniards. On at least one occasion he was a member of a sub-committee which met to discuss naval reorganization. Against the usual odds – the Queen's dislike of martial solutions, the shortage of money, lack of civilian enthusiasm to take up arms – the Council struggled to put the realm in a state of readiness for the conflict which was now so obviously almost upon them. Through the local musters they were sure of an army numbering, on paper, 50,000 foot and 10,000 horse. In fact, the total of men reporting for duty fell far short of those figures. To knock the recruits into some semblance of soldiers, several veterans of the Netherlands' and Irish campaigns were engaged – men like Sir Roger Williams and Black Jack Norreys. There never seems to have been any doubt about the general who was to be in overall command of the land forces. Robert Dudley enjoyed the position and title he had held in the Low Countries 'Lieutenant and Captain General of the Queen's armies and companies'. The appointment was not formally ratified until 24 July but before that date he was already busy issuing commands, ordering supplies, enquiring into the state of coastal defences and tackling a hundred and one other tasks with his usual enthusiasm.

By early June it was known that the Armada had set sail. Fears and rumours ran around the country. The southern sea-board counties mustered their levies. But Medina Sidonia's ships made slow progress: not till 19 July did they pass the Lizard and start beating up the Channel. Leicester's pre-occupation was the establishment of the camp at Tilbury where the main English army was to be stationed to guard the approaches to London, which would be Parma's first objective if he landed his invasion force successfully. It was neither an easy task nor an enviable responsibility. On 22 July he was complaining to Walsingham that the absence of his commission made it impossible for him to assume command of the troops.[5] The same day he travelled down river to examine the fortifications at Tilbury and Gravesend. He found them sadly lacking in powder, ordnance, implements and provisions and doubted whether either could be rendered impregnable.[6] He supervised the construction of a boom across the Thames but (correctly, as it turned out) doubted its adequacy.[7] When it came to mustering the members of his army, Dudley ran into many difficulties. All the men of substance and their retainers were heading for London to serve under Hudson in the army designated to defend the Queen and the capital.[8] The men of Essex and the surrounding country, who might be presumed to be most interested in repelling the invader, were slow to come in. By 25 July he had only 4,000 men in camp[9] and the Spanish fleet was already off the Isle of Wight. He still had inadequate Officers to train his soldiers and was annoyed because the Council had sent Norreys to Dover. The following day it was shortage of victuals that exercised his mind. He had personally had to order 100 tuns of beer and had instructed 1,000 reinforcements from London to stay where they were unless they were bringing their own provisions with them. He had had town criers out in all the surrounding boroughs appealing for food for the troops but found East Anglian farmers and victuallers reluctant to trust the royal quartermasters. Leicester hurried back and forth between Tilbury, Gravesend, Chelmsford, Harwich and other towns in an effort to stir up patriotism or, failing that, self-interest and could, with some justification, claim that he was expected to 'cook, carter and hunt' for his army.[10] It was the normal pattern of sixteenth-century military administration.

Gradually order emerged from chaos. On 27 July Robert felt that he could urge the Queen to pay a personal visit to Tilbury. Elizabeth had written to ask his advice. He responded by suggesting that the Queen should keep about her a small army of picked men and that she should establish her headquarters at Havering, some ten miles distant from the main camp at Tilbury. From there, he hoped, Elizabeth would come to spend two or three days 'in your poor lieutenant's cabin' to inspire her troops. Elizabeth did not leave

Westminster for Havering but she did, on 8 August, travel to Tilbury by water and there made one of the most famous speeches in English history.

By then the immediate danger of invasion was past. Lord Admiral Howard and his fleet had harried the Spaniards all along the Channel like terriers. Laggard vessels had been picked off one by one. Then the 'hell burners', the sand-banks and the tempest had reduced the proud Armada to a fleeing rabble of battered ships. Now the true value of Leicester's inglorious Netherlands campaign could be appreciated. Scant as had been the military achievements, the Anglo-Dutch forces had inhibited Parma's progress. He had failed to overrun the United Provinces. He had not gained command of the ports of Holland and Zeeland. He had not neutralized the United Provinces' navy. As a result, his invasion barges remained pinned down in Nieuport and Dunkirk and Medina Sidonia's harassed ships could find no haven in which to repair, revictual and regroup.

The army at Tilbury eventually numbered about 11,500. Of these Robert despatched a contingent of 500 to Harwich. This involved a confrontation with the Earl of Oxford who categorically refused so insignificant a command, despite Leicester's insistence that it was a position of 'great trust and danger'.[11] The commander was still dissatisfied with the equipment: 'Some burgonets have come from the Tower but not a man will buy one, being ashamed to wear it. Armoury must be better looked to.'[12] On 5 August Robert received a personal message from the Queen signifying her intention to come to Tilbury. He was apparently confident now that the camp was in a fit state to be visited and urged Elizabeth to maintain her resolve: 'Good sweet Queen, alter not your purpose if God give you good health. The lodging prepared for Your Majesty is a proper, sweet, cleanly house, the camp within a little mile of it and your person as sure as at St James'.[13] By the morning of the 8th Robert's energy and organising ability had created what may have been little more than an illusion of military might and bold defiance. Within neat palisades and ditches the tents and pavilions stood in orderly rows, those of the officers gay with heraldic flags and bunting. The foot soldiers were drawn up in their squadrons, breastplates gleaming and a semblance of uniformity about their dress and weapons. The mounted troops made a more impressive display with their nodding plumes and proudly caparisoned chargers. It was Robert's last and greatest piece of stage-management, the apotheosis of all the court tournaments he had organised over the years. Everything was ready for the appearance of the principal performer.

And Elizabeth knew exactly how to respond. Leaving all her body-guard before Tilbury fort, she went among her loyal subjects with an escort of six men. The Earl of Ormonde walked ahead with the Sword of State. He was followed by a page leading the Queen's charger and another bearing her silver helmet on a cushion. Then came Elizabeth herself, all in white with a silver cuirass, and mounted on a grey gelding. She was flanked by the two men who represented her past and her future: on her right Robert Dudley, portly and bareheaded but still an impressive figure on horseback; on her left the intensely handsome Earl of Essex. Sir John Norreys brought up the rear. It had all been arranged to perfection, just as the Queen's speech had been carefully prepared and rehearsed. The spectacle did not fail to achieve its effect. The cheering soldiers saw their sovereign come among them as 'your general, judge and rewarder' and believed that she would 'lay down for my God and my kingdom and for my people, my honour and my blood'. Those who had eyes to see might also discern that the Dudley interest was still paramount in the circles closest to the Queen.

Camden relates that, some time during those summer months when the country was gripped by the fear of foreign domination, Elizabeth once more contemplated elevating her old friend to a position of unprecedented power in the state. The chronicler states that letters patent were drawn up naming Dudley Lieutenant Governor of England and Ireland, and that the Queen was only dissuaded from signing them by the fervent arguments of Burghley and Hatton.[14] There is no reason to disbelieve the story and the delay over the issue of Leicester's commission may well lend it some support. It signifies only that the Queen, as in 1562, when confronted by the possibility that some peril might overtake her, named the man she trusted most as her deputy. Despite her annoyance over the Netherlands campaign, Elizabeth's confidence in her Sweet Robin remained firm to the end.

The Queen dined with Leicester and her officers and slept that night in the lodging Robert had requisitioned for her. The next day she was back at Tilbury again, enjoying the bustle of camp life and watching the troops at their drill. But news arrived that Parma, despite the earlier setback, was now ready to cross the Channel. Dudley, who had urged Elizabeth to come down river, was now among those who begged a reluctant Queen to remove herself from possible danger. On the evening of Friday, 9 August, Robert handed Elizabeth into her barge and watched as she was rowed towards London.

Reports from the coast, from returning English captains and from diplomats overseas, were confused. The Armada, or what was left of it, was still heading north but no one knew whether Medina Sidonia would attempt a leading or whether the ingenious Parma would find some way of getting his troops across the Narrow Seas. In addition, there was always the possibility of trouble at home caused by groups of determined Catholics. Clearly the army could not be disbanded. Dudley had to keep his soldiers trained and victualled. He was also responsible for the defence of other parts of the realm. On 9 August there came a report of a rumoured Spanish landing at Dungeness. Robert had to write to Sir Thomas Scott, commanding a force at Norborne, about precautions and reinforcements.[15] The Earl of Sussex wrote to inform Leicester of the death of Captain Highfield at Portsmouth and asked that the vacant office be bestowed on his cousin or someone 'with whom I can live quietly and orderly'.[16] On 12 August, the Earl of Huntingdon wrote from Newcastle deploring the lack of preparedness in the north: 'If there be doubt of the enemy looking this way, I trust the defences will soon be repaired. If I thought otherwise my mislike of my case here would be greater than yet it is, though, in truth, it is such as, happily, your Lordship would not think it to be.'[17]

He even received appeals from the Netherlands. Although his Governor-Generalship had been revoked in March, English officers and Dutch Calvinists still looked to him for aid. Henry Killigrew, the ambassador, found his position intolerable: the States General would not commit themselves fully to the war effort and unsavoury slanders about the Queen were being spread. He begged Dudley to obtain his recall.[18] Sir William Russell, Governor of Flushing, was also unhappy:

> Understanding the States mind to work all the means they may to have the forces of this garrison to be weakened, I thought it very necessary not only to advertise your Lordship thereof but withal humbly to entreat your Lordship's honourable favour and assistance by all means to frustrate their purposes. If this is not possible I beg your Lordship that I may be replaced by someone more plausible and more agreeable unto their honours.[19]

These were just a few of the many wider concerns to which Robert had to give his attention while also supervising his army at Tilbury.

By the middle of the month it was clear that the immediate danger was past. Leicester, under growing pressure from the money-conscious politicians, broke up the camp and sent the levies back to their districts. He cannot have been less than thankful to lay down the responsibility. The efforts of the last few weeks had further weakened him. He was in considerable discomfort from his stomach ailment and had begun to run a temperature (a 'continual fever' in contemporary parlance). This did not prevent him taking what was virtually a triumphant entry to the capital. He returned with a considerable escort of gentlemen, followed by a picked contingent of soldiers. None of them had fired a shot in anger but in the prevailing euphoria of relief and victory they were welcomed as heroes by a cheering citizenry. He stayed at court a day or two and was present at a special troop review staged by Essex, but his health would not allow him to remain for the other celebrations. He excused himself from the Queen, who was, as always, concerned for his well-being and now readily gave permission for her Robin to take the waters at Buxton. She gave him also some medicine prescribed by her own physicians: Robert and Lettice left Wanstead on 26 August to make their way by easy stages to the Midlands spa. On the 28th they were guests of Lady Norreys at Rycote and from there, the following morning, Dudley wrote one of those many inconsequential letters to Elizabeth, enquiring after her health, assuring her of his loyalty, thanking her for a 'token' just received. Whatever this 'token' was, it was yet further proof that even in the press of affairs following on the defeat of Spain, Sweet Robin was not far from the Queen's thoughts.[20]

He was now very ill. He managed to travel another twenty-five miles, perhaps with an overnight stay in Oxford, and reached his lodge at Cornbury. There he took to his bed. After several days and nights of pain he died on 4 September.

Almost as a matter of course the rumour was soon circulating that Leicester had been poisoned. The culprit was supposedly his wife, who wanted Dudley out of the way in order to marry her lover. William Haynes, one of the Earl's pages, had, it was said, witnessed the administration of the fatal cup. The story gained some credence later when Lettice married Christopher Blount, Leicester's Gentleman of the Horse. The post-mortem, however, produced no evidence of foul play, and it is quite clear that Robert Dudley's massive physique was undermined by a chronic intestinal complaint aggravated by overwork in the service of Queen and country.

The news was soon conveyed to Elizabeth and she was grief-stricken. In the midst of all the rejoicing over her great victory she had suffered a loss which robbed her of all happiness. According to the only contemporary account, 'she was so grieved that for some days she shut herself in her chamber alone and refused to speak to anyone, until the Treasurer and other councillors had the doors broken open and entered to see her'.[21] It was characteristic of her and it was fitting. Her relationship with her ō ō over so many years had been essentially a private one and now she mourned him in private. Within a month, however, she had sufficiently recovered to instigate a minute examination of the late Earl's estate with a view to recovering every last part owed to her. This should not be seen as evidence that she no longer cherished tender memories of her old friend: Elizabeth had always been able to keep financial and emotional matters quite separate. Furthermore, in seizing some of Dudley's lands, Elizabeth's insensitivity was turned not against Leicester, but Leicester's widow.

No one ever replaced Robert in the Queen's affections. The favourites of Elizabeth's later years – Hatton, Raleigh, Essex – did not occupy the same position in her court or her heart. The ageing Queen engaged in wild flirtations and, perhaps, with Essex tried to recreate something of the love she had experienced with Sweet Robin, but if she did, she was unsuccessful. She could never hear Dudley's name or reputation besmirched. For example, in 1596, when her godson and friend, John Harington, published a book containing some slightly disparaging remarks about Leicester,[22] Elizabeth was furious and banished the offender from court 'till he had grown sober'. After her own death on 24 March 1603, an old letter was found in the small casket at her bedside which contained her personal treasures. It contained no information of importance, no passionate declaration of love. Its message was commonplace – even trivial:

> I most humbly beseech your Majesty to pardon your poor old servant to be thus bold in sending to know how my gracious lady doth, and what ease of her late pain she finds, being the chiefest thing in the world I do pray for, for her to have good health and long life. For my own poor case, I continue still your medicine and find that [it] amends much better than any other thing that hath been given me. Thus hoping to find perfect cure at the bath, with the continuance of my wonted prayer for your Majesty's most happy preservation, I humbly kiss your foot. From your old lodging at Rycote, this Thursday morning, ready to take on my journey, by Your Majesty's most faithful and obedient servant,
>
> R. Leicester
>
> Even as I had writ thus much, I received Your Majesty's token by Young Tracey.[23]

But the hasty note was very special to Elizabeth because it was, as she wrote upon it, 'his last letter'.

According to some observers, the Queen's grief at Robert's death was unique to her. The Spanish agent who recorded Elizabeth's reaction boldly affirmed that 'no other person in the country' shared the Queen's sense of loss. The poet Edmund Spenser seemed to be of much the same opinion three years later:

> He now is dead and all his glories gone
> And all his greatness vapoured to naught
> That as a glass upon the water shone
> Which vanished quite, as soon as it was sought.
> His name is worn already out of thought.
> Ne any poet seeks him to revive.
> Yet many poets honoured him alive.[24]

Most historians have also been content to consign Dudley to oblivion with little more than a passing word of disapproval: 'England, indeed was well rid of him'; 'Leicester represented all that was worst in the politics and culture of the English Renaissance'; 'Robert Dudley stood for no one except Robert Dudley.'[25] Some, ever since the time of William Camden, have paused to puzzle over the problem of how an otherwise admirable Queen could become so deeply involved with 'a handsome, vigorous man with very little sense'[26] or to reflect that, 'one of the most amazing things about this amazing woman was her blind faith in Leicester'[27]

Elizabeth I has always been regarded as one of the shrewdest and most successful of English sovereigns. Yet, if the majority opinion is to be believed, she took into her confidence for the greater part of her reign a man who had nothing more to commend him than a handsome face and an athletic figure. She gave considerable power and influence in the state to one who was an unprincipled, political incompetent. Her passion and devotion for this man were so great that, denied him as her husband, she forsook all thought of matrimony and 'lived and died a virgin'.

It is not difficult to see why Robert Dudley has had such a bad press. His grandfather and father before him were unpopular men who died as traitors. He was a royal favourite, and such men always stir up jealousies and resentments. Even if we dismiss from our minds all the unsavoury stories of adulteries, murders and intrigues, the fact remains that Dudley's private life furnished plenty of fuel for the fires of gossip, and his enemies made very effective use of that fuel. His failures were impressive; his accomplishments less obvious. His greatest opportunity to write a dramatic chapter in the history of Europe was his leadership of the Netherlands – and that ended in apparent disaster. Alongside this, we can set the facts that he was the most accomplished courtier of his age and among its most energetic politicians; that he was one of the finest Masters of the Horse in the long history of that office, and

was personally accomplished in all the martial arts; that he was the leading Renaissance patron of artists, writers and philosophers.

Yet there are two more important reasons why Robert Dudley's name deserves to be remembered. The first is his leadership of the imperial-Protestant crusade. This programme, to which, like so many of his friends and protégés, he was committed, was based on personal devotion to the Queen and dedication to Puritanism. He championed it throughout his political career, gradually gaining more and more adherents, and ultimately seeing his endeavours bear fruit in the Netherlands venture and the defeat of the Armada.

Because he was not a 'pure' politician his role in government has been underestimated – the more so because of the excellent studies of Burghley and Walsingham, readily available to students of the Tudor age. It was the secretaries who wrote the letters, the reports and the memoranda that were the preparations for, and results of, Council meetings. This does not necessarily mean that they were the major creative forces in English politics. Dudley was almost as assiduous as they in his attendance at Council meetings. He valued highly his membership of this unique and remarkably successful institution[28] because it was the best legitimate medium for the exercise of that political power he believed to be a part of his birthright; because it was a means of serving the Queen in a wholly serious capacity; and because it provided him with a platform to urge his belief in the expansion of Elizabeth's Protestant empire.

Nor was it only in the political arena that he pursued this ideal. Through John Dee and his circle he promoted it in the realm of ideas. Through preachers and pamphleteers he made it the subject of vigorous propaganda. Through merchants, sailors and soldiers he put it into practical effect. As long as Leicester lived, radical and adventurous spirits had an obvious champion – one who was close to the throne, involved in every area of national life and committed to aggressive, interventionist policies.

The other reason qualifying Dudley for a special place in the history of the sixteenth century was his relationship with Elizabeth. He was, in effect, the royal consort. He fulfilled many regal functions, especially ones which Elizabeth, as a woman, could not perform. He was the host, as well as the organiser and principal participant, in tilts and tourneys and related ceremonials. He presided with the Queen over banquets and dances at the court. All aspirants for royal favour, from Burghley and the lords of the Council down to poor scholars and artists, saw Dudley as the supreme mediator with Her Majesty. Little could be achieved on a personal or political level which did not have the approval of

Elizabeth's ō ō. Councillors and courtiers determined to pursue policies contrary to the Dudley interest were usually obliged to proceed by intrigue. Ambivalent as Robert's position was, it was one which Elizabeth found vital in the maintenance of her court and government. She needed a close male companion whose loyalty she could rely upon implicitly; who would give honest advice; whose company she enjoyed; who would support her in crises; who would amuse her when she needed diversions from affairs of state.

She also needed someone who could be a bridge between herself and the Council. Over and again Robert conveyed the royal veto to his colleagues, or persuaded the Queen to accept sound advice, or brought to his royal mistress recommendations which the councillors knew would be unpalatable to her and which no one else dared convey. Elizabeth allowed Dudley considerable political latitude, even in issues over which they differed (such as the religious question). Of course, she always remained firmly in command, and even Robert was not immune from her sudden changes of opinion, her outbursts of wrath or her frustrating indecision. So complete was the Queen's trust in her Sweet Robin that on at least two occasions she contemplated his formal appointment as regent or deputy.

It must follow that Elizabeth saw in her favourite, or thought she saw, qualities that eluded most other observers. What those qualities were we can only guess, but the one which counted for most is obvious: devotion. 'I have lived and so will die only hers',[29] Dudley once protested to Hatton. It was a sentiment he reiterated in every letter to Elizabeth. And it was true. True, not merely because he stood to gain from royal favour. True because he and Elizabeth had been life-long friends. True because total loyalty to the crown had been instilled into him from his childhood. This loyalty was the dominant factor in Robert's life. He strove to please the Queen by personal attention and by diligent performance of all his duties. His time, his talents, his wealth were all at her disposal. For years he denied himself the delights of family life because Elizabeth would not tolerate the thought of her Sweet Robin marrying another woman. He rarely initiated policies behind the Queen's back or pursued a course of action to the point where it would incur her wrath. Even when Leicester was in the Netherlands, his career pledged to the independence struggle, he wrote to assure Elizabeth that he would support her peace overtures to Spain if she had decided on a change of policy.[30]

The Queen forgave Robert his failures, his presumption, even his union with Lettice, because she knew that he was motivated by deep personal dedication. And because she loved him. Robert was the only man she ever wanted to marry or ever seriously contemplated marrying. Love, trust and devotion – these were the bonds that bound together these two very different people. They were strong enough for Elizabeth to cherish Robert's memory to the end of her days.

It is difficult to understand how a man who occupied such a prominent place in the life of the nation can have passed so rapidly into obscurity. Can it really be true that none of the Queen's subjects mourned his passing; that none continued to cherish the ideals Dudley had striven for and regretted the loss of so dedicated a champion? The answer must be a firm 'no'. Several authors printed poems and prose works in defence of Leicester and in reverence of his memory.

A collection of poems, published in 1593 by an anonymous 'R.S.', a gentleman of the Inner Temple, opened with a prose eulogy of Leicester called 'The Dead Man's Right'. The piece decried the libels of Dudley which had come from the presses. It denied that Leicester had been ambitious and claimed that all his offices and rewards had been fairly won and were a recognition of his undoubted qualities:

... of his valour and affection to his country's peace, no honest mind but is satisfied. Whereof what greater testimony can we require than the travels his aged body undertook and [the] dangers the same was subject unto in the wars of the Low Countries, where he voluntarily offered his person in combat against the devoted enemies of this state and her majesty; leaving his wife, possessions and home, not regarding his safety, riches and ease, in respect of the godly, honourable and loving care he bare the common quiet.[31]

Chief among Dudley's virtues, according to the anonymous author, was his steadfastness in the Protestant faith. Puritan authors took up the same theme. Thomas Digges, writing in 1601, looked back on a 'golden age' of faith: 'When the Earl of Leicester lived, it went for current that all papists were traitors in action or affection. He was no sooner dead, but . . . Puritans were trounced and traduced as troublers of the state.'[32]

A decade earlier one of Leicester's Italian protégés, John Florio, had risen to his ex-patron's defence:

The maidenhead of my industry I yielded to a noble Maecenas (renowned Leicester), the honour of England, whom though, like Hector, every miscreant mirmidon dare strike, being dead, yet . . . that Hector must have his desert: the general of his prince, the paragon of his peers, the watchman of our peace . . . the supporter of his friends, the terror of his foes, and the . . . patron of the muses.[33]

In the same year the more famous John Lyly wrote a play called *Endimion, the Man in the Moon* for performance before the court on New Year's Day. Its allusions were thickly wrapped in classical allegory but for those trained to read between the lines, as Elizabeth undoubtedly was, it told the story of Robert's devoted love for the unattainable object of his desire.

Yet the inescapable fact remains that Dudley made little lasting impact on the direction of English policy. The triumph over the Armada, which might have been expected to launch an era of Elizabethan expansionism, only led to a period of nervous warfare with Spain, prosecuted without much enthusiasm by a finance-conscious Queen and Council. There were not wanting bold spirits, such as the Earl of Essex, who carried out several daring raids by land and sea, but many of these adventures turned out to be costly failures and all of them lacked the crusading spirit which had marked the enterprises of earlier years. Those influences against which Dudley and his supporters had always struggled – cautious statesmen and religious moderates – now gained the upper hand. The process had begun some years before with the Whitgift-Hatton initiative against Puritanism. The Dudley circle had been weakened by death and desertion during the 1580s. Leicester himself was absent in the Netherlands at a vital stage. Sidney's loss was a great blow to the movement. John Dee spent the years 1583-9 in travel on the Continent and on his return he never regained his favoured place at court.[34] Within two years of Robert's death both Walsingham and the Earl of Warwick had followed him to the grave. Without vigorous leadership the campaign that Leicester had led languished. In the 1590s, when England laboured under the financial burden of the war and also sustained a series of economic crises, even Robert Dudley would have found it difficult to counter the widespread reaction against national expansionism.

If carved stone and engraved epitaph were a true indication of a man's worth, we should have to conclude that Robert Dudley was a great man indeed. His remains repose now beneath a sumptuous tomb in the magnificent Beauchamp Chapel of St Mary's Church, Warwick. His armed effigy wears a coronet; and his virtues are proclaimed in elegant Latin. Such visual eulogising is as false as the calumnies of *Leicester's Commonwealth*. The testimony of a scholar and martyr who had little in common with Dudley is more reliable.

It was the Jesuit, Edmund Campion, who once wrote of Leicester:

> Thirteen years to have lived in the eye and special credit of a
> prince, yet never during all that space to have abused this ability
> to any man's harm; to be enriched with no man's overthrow; to be
> kindled neither with grudge nor emulation; to benefit an infinite
> resort of daily suitors, to let down your calling to the need of mean
> subjects; to retain so lowly a stomach, such a facility, so mild a
> nature in so high a vocation . . . this is the substance which maketh
> you worthy of these ornaments wherewith you are attired.[35]

Robert Dudley was in large measure careless of his own reputation. He had his sovereign's love and that was all that mattered to
him. Soon after his emergence as the Queen's favourite, when jealous tongues were recounting again the treasons of Edmund and
John, a certain Thomas Trollope offered to publish a vindication of
Robert's progenitors. If only Lord Robert would permit the offering
to be printed, the author affirmed, it would 'win unto your lordship
of all the nobility and commons of this realm the honour' they had
grudged him hitherto.[36] Lord Robert did not permit and the treatise is now lost. Following the appearance of *Leicester's Commonwealth*
in 1584, clients, friends, relatives and even the government came to
the Earl's aid with counter-propaganda but none was ever
published. Edmund Spenser wrote a long poem entitled *Stemmata
Dudlieana* in praise of his patron's family. Leicester did not allow its
production and it vanished without trace. Yet another pamphlet
designed to counter anti-Dudley slander was Thomas Lupton's *Of
Virtuous Life* which was offered to Leicester some time in the 1580s.
This, too, went unpublished and remains among the *Dudley Papers* at
Longleat in manuscript form only (see Appendix 1). Robert was,
therefore, in some measure to blame for the predominantly
unfavourable verdict of posterity.

Dudley was easy-going, generous, passionate. He was a good
friend and patron, but one whose vices often caused his more pious
adherents to despair. He was not a vindictive enemy, not, at least,
until the pressures of his latter years took their toll of his health and
his character. He was enthusiastic and dedicated, though he lacked
the subtlety, intellectual depth and mental stamina to overcome all
obstacles. He confined his activities willingly and deliberately within
the limits of royal approval. Like his father and grandfather before
him, he was a dedicated supporter of the Tudors and wore himself
out in their service. And therein lies Robert Dudley's greatest contribution to the history of England. More important than his
succouring of the Puritans; more important than his patronage of

Renaissance poetry and drama; more important than his champi-
oning of political and mercantile expansionism was his giving to
Elizabeth Tudor that devotion, strength, companionship and love
which helped her to survive the early part of her reign, surmount
the plots of her enemies and the wrong-headed endeavours of her
friends. By 1588 Elizabeth of England was able to stand alone, to
endure the strains of office, sift the advice of councillors, form her
own opinions, pursue her own policies, assess the strengths and
weaknesses of herself and her state. All that was not true of the
young woman who had mounted the throne in 1558. It was Robert
Dudley, above all others, who sustained her throughout the long,
hard process of self-tutelage and enabled her to emerge as the
Gloriana of legend.

> O happy Queen of fairies, that hath found,
> Mongest many, one that with his prowess may
> Defend thine honour, and thy foes confound.
> True loves are often sown, but seldom grow on ground.[37]

NOTES

Abbreviations

A.P.C.   = *Acts of the Privy Council*
D.N.B.   = *Dictionary of National Biography*
D.P.   = Dudley Papers at Longleat
Cal. Pat. Rolls = *Calendar of Patent Rolls Elizabeth I, V, 1569-1572*
Cal. S.P. Dom. = *Calendar of State Papers, Domestic, Edward VI, Mary, Elizabeth I and James I*
Cal. S.O. For. = *Calendar of State Papers, Foreign, Elizabeth I*
Cal. S.P. Scot. = *Calendar of State Papers relating to Scotland, 1509-1589*
Cal. S.P. Mil. = *State Papers and Manuscripts existing in the Archives and Collection of Milan, I, 1385-1618*
Cal. S.P. Span. = *Letters and State Papers relating to English Affairs, preserved principally in the Archives of Simancas*
Cal. S.P. Ven. = *State Papers and Manuscripts relating to English Affairs, existing in the Archives and Collections of Venice, VII, VIII, 1558-1591*

Chapter 1: 'Droit et Loyal'

1. A. Collins, ed., *Letters and Memorials of State*, I, p.64.
2. M. Waldman, *Elizabeth and Leicester*, p.171.
3. Harleian MSS, Vol. 807. Cf. Also G. Adlard, *The Sutton-Dudleys of England*, p.1.
4. Harleian MSS, Vol. 1042.
5. D.N.B.
6. D.M. Brodie, 'Edmund Dudley, Minister of Henry VII', *Transactions of the Royal Historical Society*, Fourth Series XV, 1932, pp.133-61.
7. J. Stow, *Annales*, p.810.
8. D.N.B.
9. *Baga de Secretis*, Pouch IV.
10. E. Dudley, *The Tree of Commonwealth*, BM Add. MS. 32091.
11. *Letters and Papers . . .*, iii, 3516.
12. R. Morison, *A discourse . . . shewing the godly and vertuous resolution . . .* in *Literary Remains of England VI*, ed. J.G. Nichols, I, ccxxiv.
13. *Letters and Papers . . .*, v, 1727; 1834.
14. No proof of Robert's birth exists, though he is known to have been born in 1532 or 1533. It was assumed by many contemporaries that he and Elizabeth were of an age. 1533 fits better with the known birth dates of Robert's brothers and sisters.

Chapter 2: Childhood

1. P.F. Tytler, *England Under the Reigns of Edward VI and Mary*, II, p.155.
2. Public Records Office, S.P. 15/4, No. 8.
3. Historical MSS Commission, *Report on MSS at Magdalene College Cambridge*, II, No. 729, pp.1-2.
4. J. Stow (ed. C.L. Kingsford), *A Survey of London*, II, p.36.
5. Thomas Hatcher, *G. Haddoni Legum Doctoris, S. Reginae Elizabethae a supplicum libellis, lucubrationes passim collectae*, pp.419-20. I am indebted to the Rev. Ian Watson for assistance with the translation.
6. Two eminent scholars dedicated works to this young man and offered fulsome praise for his gifts: Walter Haddon's *Cantabrigienses: sive Exhortatio ad Literas*, 1552, and Thomas Wilson's *Arte of Rhetorike*, 1553, were the books in question.
7. Cf. C. Cross, *The Puritan Earl.*
8. J.L. Vives (trans. F. Watson), *On Education*, p.204-5.
9. Cf. E. Rosenberg, *Leicester, Patron of Letters*, pp.30-1.
10. D.N.B.
11. Perhaps in July 1544 when the Prince's household was reorganised on the occasion of Henry's departure for the French campaign. 'His Majesty wills that my lord Prince shall on Wednesday next remove to Hampton Court and that the Lord Chancellor and the Earl of Hertford shall repair thither on Thursday and there discharge all the ladies and gentlemen out of the house and also admit and swear Sir Richard Page Chamberlain to my Lord Prince, Mr. Sydney to be advanced to the office of Steward, Jasper Horsey to be Chief Gentleman of his Privy Chamber, and Mr Cox to be his Almoner, and he that is now Almoner to be Dean, and Mr Cheke as a supplement to Mr Cox, both for the better instruction of the Prince and the diligent teaching of such children as be appointed to attend upon him.' *State Papers of Henry VIII*, I, 199.
12. *State Papers*, I, Pt.II, cxciii.
13. R.B. Wernham, *Before the Armada*, pp.204-7; W.K. Jordan, *Edward VI: The Threshold of Power*, pp.490-3.
14. *State Papers*, V, ccccxciii.
15. *Hamilton Papers*, (ed. J. Bain), I, 286-7.
16. *Hamilton Papers*, II, pp.159, 161, 7. B.L. Beer, *Northumberland*, p.29.
17. Cal. S.P. Span., XXI, i, p.289.
18. Cal. S.P. Span., VIII, p.557.
19. Cf. J.G. Nichols, *Literary Remains of Edward VI*, pp.lxxv ff. Nichols suggests that the two groups were quite distinct and enumerates the various officers appointed to look after the henchmen but any attempt to distinguish the personnel of the two groups is beset with obstacles: extant records are incomplete; composition of the Prince's household changed frequently as young men left or were promoted to other offices; the henchmen and the young lords, if, indeed, they were distinct, seem to have shared many functions. Nichols gives one scrap of information which might suggest that the henchmen and the young lords were one and the same. Early in 1550 some of the latter were sent to France as hostages as part of the negotiations of a peace treaty. The official 'appointed by the King's majesty to attend upon the young lords sent over the sea' was Sir George Howard who was currently the Master of the Henchmen (*Ibid*, p.lxxvi).
20. J.G. Nichols, *Literary Remains*, p.lvi.
21. Ibid., p.lxxvii.
22. H. Robinson, *Original letters Relative to the English Reformation*, I, p.321.

23. J. Knox, ed. D. Laing, *Works*, III, p.176.
24. C. Heresback, *De Educandis Erudiendisque Principum Liberis*, p.56 .

Chapter 3: Man's Estate

1. This is not the place to refute in detail the old myth of John Dudley as 'the subtlest intriguer in English history' (A.F. Pollard, *England Under Protector Somerset*, p.244) who planned over a long period of time the overthrow of the Seymours and set his sights firmly on the crown. Professor G.R. Elton has recently affirmed, 'it is not easy to reconcile the picture of a wicked, amoral, wildly ambitious intriguer with the evidence of many of his actions and most of his surviving letters' (*Reform and Reformation, England 1509-1558*, p.353). The work of rehabilitation has yet to be completed, but for detailed and more responsible consideration of Dudley's character, motives and actions see B.L. Beer, *Northumberland*, and D.E. Hoak, *The King's Council in the reign of Edward VI*.

2. The earldom had passed by marriage to the Nevilles in 1449 and subsequently to George, Duke of Clarence. Clarence's son, Edward, spent most of his life in the Tower and was executed by Henry VII in 1499 as part of that monarch's drastic pruning of the Yorkist tree.

3. B.L. Beer, *Northumberland*, pp.177-9.

4. From a contemporary MS in the College of Arms quoted by J.G. Nichols, *Literary Remains*, pp.cclxxviii-ccciii.

5. Ibid., p.xcci.

6. A. Neville, *De Furoribus Norfolciensium Ketto Duce*, 1575, trans, by R. Wood as *Norfolk's Furies*, 1615.

7. Thynne Papers, Longleat, ff.24-5.

8. Apart from the original documents cited I am indebted for much of the information about Amy Robsart and her family to an MS and notes deposited in the Norfolk Record Office by the Rev N. Fourdrinier, sometime Rector of Syderstone. The MS is entitled *Amy Robsart, the Wife of Lord Robert Dudley the favourite of Queen Elizabeth I. Her life, ancestry, and the true cause of her tragic death*. The catalogue number is MC5/29.

9. The King entered in his journal the figures 6,000 foot soldiers and 1,500 horsemen. Nicholas Sotherton, an eye witness, estimated the total at around 12,000. Alexander Neville, writing in the 1570s, raised the number to 14,000. Julian Cornwall, in a recent careful study of the campaign, concluded from documentary evidence that Warwick commanded some 10,000 to 10,500 troops. Cf. W.K. Jordan, ed., *The Chronicle and Political Papers of Edward VI*, p.15; Nicholas Sotherton, *The Commoyson in NO[rfolk]*, Harleian MS. 1576, ff. 251-7; A. Neville, *Norfolk's Furies*; Julian Cornwall, *Revolt of the Peasantry 1549*, pp.212-4.

10. Yelverton MS. 141 (BM Add. MS. 48126), printed by A.J.A. Malkiewicz, 'An Eye-Witness's Account of the Coup d'Etat of October 1549' in *English Historical Review*, 70, 1955, p.601.

11. Harleian MS. 1576, p.8208.

12. Ibid. The bear and ragged staff, the badge of the earls of Warwick, was adopted by all members of the Dudley family after John's elevation to the earldom. It was an outward and visible sign of their claim to descent from the once-powerful Beauchamps, for the badge originated with that family. The Dudley device was the double-tailed lion but both heraldic beasts were frequently combined on seals, banners and in decorative motifs. The ragged

staff sometimes appeared by itself as part of Robert's insignia. For example, in the magnificent portrait of Lettice Knollys at Longleat, Leicester's third wife is depicted wearing a gown whose border is embroidered with roses for her father's house and ragged staffs for her husband's.

13.   A. Neville, *Norfolk's Furies*, pp. 18-19.

14.   Yelverton MS. 141 (BM Add. MS. 48126); cf. A.J.A. Malkiewicz, 'An Eye-Witness's Account of the Coup d'Etat of October 1549'.

15.   This is not the place to argue forcefully for the dismissal of the myth of the 'Good Duke' of Somerset and the blacker-than-black Earl of Warwick. Cf. C.R. Elton, *Reform and Reformation*, pp.334-5.
      The most detailed exposé of Seymour's acquisitiveness is M.L. Bush, *The Rise to Power of Edward Seymour, Protector Somerset, 1500-1547*, Cambridge Ph.D. thesis, 1965. See also M.L. Bush's *The Government Policy of Protector Somerset*, D.R. Hoak, *The King's Council in the Reign of Edward VI* and B.L. Beer, *Northumberland*.

16.   'There was no request that Warwick made after his return but he had a repulse and went without it; in so much that he was quite in despair for ever having any lawful favour at the Duke of Somerset's hands', Yelverton MS. 141 (BM Add. MS. 48126).

17.   Opinions differ on the exact sequence of events between September 1549 and February 1550 and on the motives of the main participants. See A.J.A. Malkiewicz, 'The Coup d'Etat of October 1549', pp.600-9; D.E. Hoak, *The King's Council in the Reign of Edward VI*, pp.239-58; B.L. Beer, *Northumberland*, pp.85-95; C.J. Adams, *Tudor Minister: Sir Thomas Wriothesley*, Manchester M.A. thesis, 1970, pp.115-32. The very brief outline of events as I have set it forth follows none of the above in all points but is based on a close study of the evidence and arguments brought forward by all the authors mentioned.

18.   J.G. Nichols, *Literary Remains*, II, p.237.

19.   A.J.A. Malkiewicz, 'The Coup d'Etat of October 1549', p.605.

20.   Ibid.

21.   Paget and Wingfield to the Council. Cal. S.P. Dom. Edward VI, III, 149.

22.   J.G. Nichols, *Literary Remains*, pp.cxxxii-cxiii.

23.   BM, Add, MS. 48126, fo. 16a.

24.   D.E. Hoak, *The King's Council in the Reign of Edward VI*, p.266.

25.   Cal. S.P. Edward VI, Span. X, 435-8.

26.   Cf. D. MacCulloch, *Thomas Cranmer*, p.495.

27.   G.R. Elton, *England under the Tudors*, p.209.

28.   In later years Robert became a leading patron of actors but he was following his father's lead, for John Dudley obtained the Council's licence for a group of players including Edmund Strodwick, John Smyth, Hugh Barnesby, Thomas Hillie and Miles Rolfe to perform 'within all the King's dominions such matters, interludes and plays as tend not to exceed in any wise the limits and bounds of honest meaning'. Cf. B.L. Beer, *Northumberland*, p.127.

29.   W.K. Jordan, *The Chronicle . . . of King Edward VI*, pp.31-2.

30.   Wheat which had stood at 8s. 1³/4d. a quarter in 1548 was 16s. 4d. in 1549 and 18s. in 1550. Cf. R.B. Outhwaite, *Inflation in Tudor and Early Stuart England*, pp.9-15; J.M. Stratton, *Agricultural Records A.D. 220-1977*, pp.40-1, 248.

31.   Robert found himself with interests in East Rudham, West Rudham, Broomsthorpe, Barmer, Burnham Market, Tittleshall, Syderstone, Thorpe Market, Bradfield, Hapton, Foulsham, Wood Norton, Hillington, East Barsham, Broughton, Tattersett, Tatterford, Oxwick, Guestwick and King's Lynn.

32.   D.P., Box II, 1 – an indenture drawn up by Warwick and Sir John Robsart,

24 May 1550, being a settlement by them upon Robert Dudley and Amy Robsart. The Coxford lands had gone at the Dissolution to Thomas Howard, Duke of Norfolk. On Howard's attainder they were granted to Warwick.

33. It comprised 'the manor, 30 messuages, 14 cottages, 1,000 acres of land, 200 of meadow, 1,000 of pasture, 80 of wood, 1,000 of furze and heath, with the advowson of the vicarage', F. Blomefield & C. Parkin, *An Essay towards a Topographical History of the Country of Norfolk*, XI, pp.166-7.
34. Ibid., IX, p.435.
35. W.K. Jordan, *The Chronicle . . . of King Edward VI*, pp.32-3.
36. Cal. Pat. Rolls, 27 February 1553.
37. But it was returned briefly to the crown in 1549-50 as part of a complex of land deals, see C. Sturge, *Life and Times of John Dudley*, London Ph.D. thesis, 1927.
38. P. Clark, *English Provincial Society from the Reformation to the Revolution*, p.83.
39. B.L. Beer, *Northumberland*, p.181.

Chapter 4: Prisoner

1. Letter to William Cecil, 7 Dec. 1552 quoted in P.F. Tytler, *England Under the Reigns of Edward VI and Mary*, II, p.148.
2. In Professor Elton's view it was Dudley and Paget who 'rescued Cromwell's Council reform' from its total neglect by Somerset 'and preserved the institution for its Elizabethan heyday', *Reform and Reformation*, p.354. For a full assessment of the methods and success of Northumberland's government see D.E. Hoak, *The King's Council in the Reign of Edward VI*.
3. P.F. Tytler, *England Under the Reigns of Edward VI and Mary*, II, p.155.
4. S.P. Dom. Edward VI, XV, 68.
5. J.G. Nichols, ed., *The Diary of Henry Machyn 1550-1563*, pp.13-14.
6. Ibid., p.103.
7. The best modern summaries of the situation are: S.T. Bindoff, 'A Kingdom At Stake', *History Today*, III, 1953, pp.642-8; W.K. Jordan, *Edward VI, The Threshold of Power*, pp.510-32; B.L. Beer, *Northumberland*, pp.147-60. One factor seems to emerge clearly from all these: historians who have cast John Dudley in the role of a consummate intriguer have always been at a loss to understand how he bungled so completely the plot to debar Mary Tudor and set Lady Jane Grey on the throne. The answer must surely be that he was not a master schemer but a man confused by conflicting interests and loyalties.
8. Giulio Raviglio Rosso, *Historia delle cose occorse nel regno d'Inghilterra*.
9. Etienne Perlin, *Description d'Angleterre et d'Ecosse*.
10. Sir Nicholas Throckmorton, 'Poetical Autobiography' in *Chronicle of Queen Jane and of Two Years of Queen Mary*, ed. J.G. Nichols, 2, xi, 272.
11. Cal. S.P. Edward VI and Mary, Span. XI, 46.
12. J.G. Nichols, *Literary Remains*, I, p.ccliv.
13. Cal. S.P. Dom. Edward VI. Addenda. IV, 24.
14. Cal. S.P. Edward VI and Mary, XI, Span. 17 Mar. 1553.
15. *Le Report de un Judgement done en Banke du Roi.*
16. J.G. Nichols, *Chronicle of Queen Jane*, p.111.
17. Ibid., p.81.
18. J.G. Nichols, *Greyfriars Chronicle*, p.83.
19. Harleian MS. 2342.
20. R. Brooke, *Catalogue of Nobility*, p.150.
21. *Le Report de un Judgement done en Banke du Roi.*

22.   Ibid.
23.   J.G. Nichols, *Chronicle of Queen Jane*, p.39.
24.   Ibid., p.55.
25.   Ibid., p.59.
26.   Ibid., p.58.
27.   Cf. PRO E. 154/2/39, L.R. 2/118/f.93 and B.L. Beer, *Northumberland*, p.197.
28.   A Collins, *Letters and Memorials of State* I, p.35.
29.   Ibid., I, p.81.
30.   Ibid., I, p.34.
31.   Cal. Pat. Rolls, 22 Jan. 1555. Some confusion over the date of Robert's release seems to have arisen. Stow's Annales gives 18 October 1554 as the day when all the brothers were set at liberty but only John left the Tower on that day. Most historians seem to have accepted Stow's account, but B.L. Beer stated that the three remaining brothers were released four days before their mother's death though he gave no evidence (cf. B.L. Beer, *Northumberland*, p.165). The official document seems to clinch the matter and receives some support from Jane's own will in which she states that at the time of writing her sons had not been pardoned: '. . . my three sons and my brother Sir Andrew Dudley stand presently attainted of high treason . . . my said will cannot take place according to my meaning in all things if I should be called out of this life before my said sons and brother have obtained the King's and the Queen's most gracious pardon . . .' (A. Collins, *Letters and Memorials of State*, I, p.35).
32.   D.P., Box III, f.66.
33.   A. Collins, *Letters and Memorials of State*, I, p.33.
34.   D.M. Loades, *Two Tudor Conspiracies*; C. Garrett, *The Marian Exiles*, pp.147-9.
35.   Cal. S.P. Ven. VI, i, 137.
36.   Documents relating to Robert: D.P., Box I, A; PRO, E. 371/389 Originalia Roll, 3 and 4 Philip and Mary, pt. 1, rot. 18; 4 and 5 Philip and Mary, c12, 7, III, 1558. The lifting of the attainder was ratified by the next parliament which met from 20 January to 7 March 1558.
37.   J.G. Nichols, *Diary of Henry Machyn*, p.128.
38.   PRO, C.P., 26(1), (Common Pleas, Notes of Fines) 94, Cf. also N. Fourdrinier, *Amy Robsart, the Wife of Lord Robert Dudley . . .*, MS. MC5/29, Norfolk Record Office.
39.   Society of Antiquaries MS. 139, ff. 129, 131; Lyttelton MSS (in Birmingham Reference Library), 351613; PRO, c54/546, m.16 con.
40.   A. Collins, *Letters and Memorials of State*, I, p.30.
41.   D.P., III, f.67.
42.   G. Adlard, *Amye Robsart and the Earl of Leicester*, pp.263-4.
43.   Quoted by F. Chamberlin, *Elizabeth and Leicester*, App. IX, pp.92-3.
44.   *La Vie d'Elizabeth, reine d'Angleterre de l'Italien*, pp.444- 5.
45.   Cotton MSS, Vespasian F III, f.27; quoted in J.E. Neale. 'The Accession of Queen Elizabeth', *History Today*, May, 1953.
46.   Cf. E. Rosenberg, *Leicester*, pp.56-7 Castiglione was among Dudley's Italian protégés from very early in Elizabeth's reign and it seems unlikely that their acquaintance did not begin before 1558.
47.   Bedford to Cecil; P.F. Tytler, *England under the Reigns of Edward VI and Mary*, II, p.493.
48.   R. Holinshed (ed. H. Ellis), *Chronicles of England, Scotland and Ireland*.
49.   Lyttelton MSS, 351624, 351627, 351632, 351634; Society of antiquaries MS. 139, ff.129-31. For a full discussion of these transactions see N. Fourdrinier, *Amy Robsart*, pp.134-8.

50. Harleian MS. 4721. Printed in G. Adlard, *Amye Robsart*, pp.16-17.
51. Ibid.
52. Cal. S.P. For. Elizabeth, I,3.

Chapter 5: Master of the Horse

1. Cal. S.P. Dom. Addenda, XIX, 73.
2. D.P., Box I, f.14.
3. Leicester to William Davison at Antwerp, 25 April 1579. Cal. S.P. Dom. Addenda, XXVI,9.
4. D.P., V, XI.
5. D.P., XIII.
6. D.P., III, f.31. The total value is given as £5,070.
7. D.P., I, f.172.
8. The D.N.B. and records in the Armoury Library at the Tower of London give April 1560 as the date of Ambrose's appointment to the Ordnance Office but it was unlikely that the Queen would leave so important a post in the hands of a man she had dismissed from the Council. In fact, de Feria, the Spanish Ambassador, reported on 21 November that Ambrose was now 'Master of Artillery' in succession to Southwell (Cal. S.P. Span., I, 1). In March 1560, hearing a rumour of Ambrose's death, the Duke of Norfolk sought the Ordnance Office for his cousin, George Howard (Cal. S.P. For., II, 855).
9. Cal. S.P. Span., I, 4.
10. D.P., Box III, f.19.
11. D.P., II, f.6.
12. M.M. Reese, *The Royal Office of Master of the Horse*, pp.138-9, 158.
13. Cal. S.P. Ven. VII, 10.
14. M.M. Reese, *The Royal Office of Master of the Horse*, p.155.
15. S. Anglo, *Spectacle, Pageantry and Early Tudor Policy*, p.346.
16. R. Tottel, *The Passage of our Most Dread Sovereign . . .*, sig. A.iir.
17. S. Anglo, *Spectacle, Pageantry and Early Tudor Policy*, pp.344-59.
18. The royal studs were at Eltham, Hampton Court, Tutbury, Malmesbury, Ripon, Jervaux and the Duchy of Lancaster estates in Staffordshire.
19. R. Holinshed, *Chronicles*.
20. D.P., I, ff.50, 72.
21. Cal. S.P. For. II, 104.
22. Cal. S.P. For. II, 223, 240.
23. Cal. S.P. For. II, 314.
24. Cal. S.P. For. II, 319.
25. Cal. S.P. For. II, 462, 554, 564, 608.
26. M.M. Reese, *The Royal Office of Master of the Horse*, p.159.
27. The works is presented in full in C.M. Prior, *The Royal Studs of the Sixteenth and Seventeenth Centuries*, pp.11-38.
28. D.P., III, 57.
29. BM. Additional MSS, 15891, F. 58b; H. Nicolas, ed., *Memoirs of . . . Christopher Hatton* pp.269-70.
30. Cal. S.P. Span., I, 314.
31. From a list of items requisitioned from the Clerk of the Stables, 4 June 1567 –18 April 1568; D.P., III, f.43.
32. Ibid.
33. Cf. G. Adlard, *Amye Robsart*, pp.16 ff.; N. Fourdrinier, *Amy Robsart*, MS. MC5/29, Norfolk Record Office, pp.143 ff; J.E. Jackson, 'Amye Robsart' in

Wilts. Archaeological Magazine, XVII, pp.61 ff. All these accounts are based on extracts from the Dudley Papers which are cited hereinafter. The house at Denchworth still stands, though it is much altered since Tudor times.

34. D.P. XIV and XV, account books of Dudley's stewards, William Chaucy and Richard Ellis, *passim*.
35. Ibid.
36. Ibid.
37. Among the papers at Longleat is an extensive and detailed account from William Edney, a London tailor, for gowns, petticoats, bodices, kirtles, sleeves, ruffs, collars, lace, trimmings and materials covering a period of several months (D.P., IV, f.7).
38. Harleian MS. No. 4712.
39. Cal. S.P. Span., 1,27.
40. Cal. S.P. Ven., VII, 69.
41. Cal. S.P. Ven., VII, 71.
42. Cal. S.P. Ven., VII, p.28.
43. BM. Lansdowne MS. 94, f.29.
44. D.P., II, f.15.
45. D.P., I, f.13.
46. Ibid., I, f.25.
47. Ibid., I, f.48.
48. Ibid., I, f.139.
49. Ibid., I, f.46.
50. E. Rosenberg, *Leicester*, p.69.
51. D.P., I, f.56.
52. Cal. S.P. Span., I, 114.
53. Cal. S.P. Span. I, 118; Cal. S.P. For., III, 350. It was Robert who eventually obtained the Drurys' release and to whom William later appealed to intercede on his behalf with the Queen. He regretted that her majesty 'hath taken with displeasure those rash words which only I meant and spoke of your Lordship' – D.P., I, f.204.
54. Cal. S.P. For., II, 387.
55. Cal. S.P. Span., I, pp.113-14.
56. N. Williams, *Thomas Howard, Fourth Duke of Norfolk*, pp.49-51; A. Hassell Smith, *County and Court, Government and Politics in Norfolk 1558-1603*, pp.39-41. Both authors suggest that Howard and Dudley began the reign as friends, united by their Norfolk contacts and the marriage of the Duke to Henry Dudley's widow (1558). Such a suggestion relies largely on the assumption that Lord Robert was not wielding political influence until much later. This was not the case, as I have tried to show in Chapter 6. It is clear from de Quadra's reports that the two men were at daggers drawn by November 1559. Dudley's challenge at court and in the shire began in the early days of the reign and Howard had been goaded by many annoyances before making the outbursts reported by the Spanish ambassador towards the end of the year.
57. D.P., III, f.23.
58. D.P., II, ff.4, 7, 8.

Chapter 6: 'Careful for the Quiet of the State'

1. I beg leave here to differ with Professor MacCaffrey who states that at this time Dudley 'had taken up no ideological stance or policy position' (*The Shaping of the Elizabethan Regime*, p.85). From the evidence herein cited it should be clear

that from the beginning of the reign men were associating Lord Robert with specific attitudes on political and religious matters. It is important to establish the continuity of Dudley's thoughts from his youth up, in order to refute, as I do, that he was little more than a cynical opportunist favouring whatever policies and factions best suited his own ends. MacCaffrey, while not whole-heartedly following this traditional line, does suggest that Robert only developed a political scheme of his own about 1564 after relinquishing all hope of marrying the Queen. This involved 'deliberate patronage' of the Puritan party 'calculated to give him a prominent and a strong position in the kingdom' and also a wholly new diligence in 'every major piece of public business' (p.305). The Dudley papers and the State Papers furnish many letters and references which indicate Lord Robert's lively interest in many aspects of national and international affairs. Certainly he was recognised as a supporter of the proto-Puritan cause from the very early days of the reign.

2.   *A Harbour for Faithful and True Subjects*, dedicatory epistle. Cf. E. Rosenberg, *Leicester*, p.27.

3.   Leicester to Thomas Wood, 19 Aug. 1576. P. Collinson, ed., *Letters of Thomas Wood*, pp.13-14.

4.   Magdalene College, Cambridge, Pepysian Library, MS. 'Papers of State', II, 701.

5.   Cal. S.P. Span., I, 2.

6.   Cal. S.P. Span., I, 4.

7.   D.P., I, f.11.

8.   Vergerio was one of the most notable converts to the Reformed cause. He became a Lutheran while serving as Bishop of Capodistria and was subsequently deprived by the Pope in 1549. He was a leading politico-religious activist in Protestant Germany.

9.   Cal. S.P. For., I, 304. The document is tentatively ascribed to Cecil on the grounds that one of the many amendments, in various hands was made by the Secretary. But the whole tone of the letter is uncharacteristic of the cautious Cecil. The writer confesses to being 'far inferior in learning to others'. That certainly would not apply to Cecil but was true of Bedford, Pembroke and Dudley, any one of whom might have originated the letter. Such an important communication, though ostensibly personal in nature, would have to be scrutinised by the Council, which explains the many amendments.

10. Cal. S.P. For., II, p.76.

11. Cal. S.P. Span., I, 62.

12. M. Aston, *The King's Bedpost*, pp.106-7.

13. P. Collinson, *Letters of Thomas Wood*, pp.xxi-xxiii.

14. Cal. S.P. For., I, 826, 867, 987, 998, 1405.

15. S. Haynes & W. Murdin, eds., *Collection of State Papers . . . Left by William Cecil*, p.444.

16. W. Camden, ed. W.T. MacCaffrey, *The History of . . . Princes Elizabeth*, p.53.

17. P.F. Tytler, *England Under the Reign of Edward VI and Mary*, II, p.436-7.

18. Ibid., p.475.

19. J.G. Nichols, *Diary of Henry Machyn*, p.203.

20. Cal. S.P. For., II, p.96.

21. P. Forbes, ed., *A Full View of the Public Transactions in the Reign of Queen Elizabeth*, I, p.455.

22. Ibid., p.494.

23. J.G. Nichols, *Diary of Henry Machyn*, pp.238-41.

24. Cal. S.P. For., II, p.385.

25. PRO, S.P. 12/13/21, 21(1).
26. Cal. S.P. Dom. Add., XI, 86; Cal. S.P. Span., I, 408.
27. D.P., I, f.146.
28. BM. Stow MSS, f.180 b.
29. PRO, S.P., 70-71, 27 August.
30. Cal. S.P. I, pp.174-5; J.A. Froude, *History of England*, VII, pp.283-5.

Chapter 7: 'So Pitifully Slain'?

1. Thomas Blount was a distant relative of Robert and a lifelong servant of the Dudleys, having attended Northumberland for some years before his fall. His fine tomb effigy may still be seen in Kidderminster Church. Proudly it wears the chain of office and the family insignia appropriate to a Dudley retainer.
2. Quoted in G. Adlard, *Amye Robsart*, p.32. This book prints all the correspondence between Dudley and Blount and a considerable amount of other relevant material. Important articles on Amy's death are: J.E. Jackson, 'Amye Robsart' in *Wilts. Archaeological Magazine*, XVII, pp. 58-93; I. Aird, 'The Death of Amy Robsart', in *English Historical Review*, LXXI, pp.69-79. N. Fourdrinier in *Amy Robsart*, MS. MC5/29, Norfolk Record Office, goes over all the known evidence in detail.
3. G. Adlard, *Amye Robsart*, pp.34-6.
4. Ibid., p.37.
5. Ibid.
6. Ibid., p.36.
7. Ibid., pp.36-7.
8. Ibid.
9. S. Haynes & W. Murdin, *Collection of State Papers . . . Left by William Cecil*, I, pp.361-2.
10. G. Adlard, *Amye Robsart*, p.41.
11. A friend writing from Hampton Court to the Earl of Sussex in Ireland complained that it was 'stuffed with mourners', Cotton MSS, Vesp., F. XII, f.151.
12. J.G. Nichols, *Diary of Henry Machyn*, pp.242-3; another account of the funeral is in Dugdale, MSS, T.2, f.77, reprinted in G. Adlard, Amye Robsart, pp.52-5.
13. G. Adlard, *Amye Robsart*, p.43.
14. J.E. Jackson, 'Amye Robsart' in *Wilts. Archaeological Magazine*, XVII, pp.89-90.
15. D.P., Box IV, f.25.
16. Cal. S.P. Span., I, 27.
17. Cal. S.P. Span., I, 104.
18. Cal. S.P. Span., I, 123.
19. This theory was put forward by I. Aird in 'The Death of Amy Robsart', *English Historical Review*, LXXI, pp.69-79.
20. This theory is canvassed by Fourdrinier, *Amy Robsart*, pp.255-6.
21. C. Read, *Mr. Secretary Cecil and Queen Elizabeth*, p.201.
22. D.P., I, f.115.
23. J.G. Nichols, *Diary of Henry Machyn*, p.245.
24. P. Yorke, ed., *Miscellaneous State Papers*, I, p.167.
25. Ibid.
26. Cal. S.P. For., III, 19.
27. Cal. S.P. For., III, 834.
28. C. Read, *Mr Secretary Cecil and Queen Elizabeth*, pp.206-7.
29. P. Yorke, *Miscellaneous State Papers*, I, pp.163-9.

30. Cal. S.P. Span., I, 178, 180, 181-3.
31. BM. Additional MSS, 35830, 74.
32. F.A. Inderwick, *Calendar of the Inner Temple Records*, I, pp.216-18.
33. J.G. Nichols, *The Diary of Henry Machyn*, pp.273-4.
34. G. Legh, *Accedens of Armory*, p.224.
35. D.P., Box II, f.9.

Chapter 8: 'Worthy to Marry the Greatest Queen'

1. Cal. S.P. Dom. Addenda, XII, 54.
2. Cal. S.P. Dom., CLIX, I.
3. Cal. S.P. Span., I, pp.262-4.
4. Cal. S.P. Dom., XXIX, 54.
5. D.P., Box II, f.11. With Kenilworth went sundry parcels of land in Lancashire and the Marcher Lordships of Mortimer and Denbigh.
6. Cal. S.P. Ven., VI 1077.
7. D.P., III, f.37.
8. Ibid., ff.33, 37.
9. G. R. Elton, *The Parliament of England, 1559-1581*, pp.360-3.
10. J.E. Neale, *Elizabeth I and Her Parliaments*, 1559-1581, p.109.
11. Ibid., p.127.
12. Cal. S.P. Span., I, 304.
13. PRO, S.P., 52-9-385.
14. Cal. S.P. Scottish, 1563-69, p.233.
15. C. Read, *Mr Secretary Cecil and Queen Elizabeth*, p.315.
16. Ibid., pp.314-15.
17. G.R. Elton, *The Parliament of England*, p.363.

Chapter 9: 'I have lived always above any living I had'

1. D.P., Box III, f.52.
2. D.P. XIV, f.26.
3. D.P. XIV, f.32.
4. Ibid.
5. D.P., IV, 18.
6. John Barthlet, *Pedigree of Heretics* . . .
7. John Lupton, *Of Virtuous Life*.
8. P. Collinson, *Letters of Thomas Wood*, p.19.
9. John Tomkyns, *A Sermon Preached the 26 Day of May 1584*.
10. Cal. S.P. Dom., XXXVI, 73, 81, 82, 83; XL, 17, 21, 30.
11. Ibid., XXXIX, 57.
12. Ibid., XLII, 18, 25, 26, 27, 31, 32, 33, 35, 37, 39, 40, 61; XLIII, 56; XLIV, 14, 15, 16.
13. Cf, C.T. Carr, ed., *Select Charters of Trading Companies, 1530-1707*, XXVIII, pp.14-15.
14. Cal. Pat. Rolls, 1569-72, 3357.
15. R. Laneham, *A Letter, wherein part of the entertainment unto the Queen's majesty at Kenilworth Castle in Warwickshire in this summer's progress – 1575 – is signified*, reprinted in G. Adlard, Amye Robsart, p.124.
16. D.P., II, f.321.
17. D.P., IV, f.13.
18. D.P., XIV, f.28; XV, f.20.

19. *Colin Clouts Come Home Again*, 1591.
20. F. Yates, *Astraea: The Imperial Theme in the Sixteenth Century*.
21. R.C. Strong & J.A. Van Dorsten, *Leicester's Triumph*, pp.83-7.
22. Vagrancy Act of 1572; 16 Eliz. c.5.
23. E.K. Chambers, *The Elizabethan Stage*, II, p.86.
24. T. Fuller, *History of the Worthies of England*, II, p.311.
25. J. Stow, *Annales*, p.697.
26. Quoted in R.C. Strong & J.A. Van Dorsten, *Leicester's Triumph*, p.83.
27. Cal. S.P. Span. 1558-67, pp.404-5.
28. *English Literature in the Sixteenth Century, excluding Drama*, p.270.
29. E. Rosenberg, *Leicester*, pp.166-72; C.S. Lewis, *English Literature in the Sixteenth Century*, pp.269-71; M. Axton, *The Queen's Two Bodies: Drama and the Elizabethan Succession*, pp.64-6.
30. Following the building of the Theatre in 1576 there was a gradual shift in theatrical initiative from the Inns of Court to the public stage. Patrons such as Leicester were an obvious link between occasional and professional drama; common players could reach a much wider audience. The interests of a powerful patron may well have thrust both coterie and professional play texts into print for reasons which were not primarily theatrical. In any case, texts such as *Damon and Pithias, Tancred and Gismund* and *Horestes* survive to suggest ways in which coterie themes and conventions could be adapted 'for six to play' and made available to the public in the provinces and regularly, after 1576, in London. M. Axton, *The Queen's Two Bodies*, p.73.
31. H.N. Hillebrand, *The Child Actors*, p.91.
32. Letter of John Field (1581). Cotton MS. Titus B.VII, f.22 r.
33. Robert Crowley, *The Way to Wealth; Select Works*, p.163.
34. For a full discussion of the problem see E. Rosenberg, *Leicester*, pp.335-44.
35. *A Summary of the Chronicles of England* (1604 ed.).
36. *Renaissance Man*, p.90.
37. J.Stow, *A Summary of the Chronicles of England*, Dedication, 1565 ed.
38. *Two Histories of Ireland: the one written by Edmund Campion, the other by Meredith Hanmer*, 1633, passage from Campion's dedication.
39. Cal. S.P. Milan, I, 1012.
40. R. Simpson, *Edmund Campion* p.296.
41. Cf. R. Forster, *Ephemerides Meteorographicae*.
42. BM. Add. MS. 18035.
43. Cal. S.P. Dom., XXXVIII, 2; XXVII, 61.
44. D.P., Box V, f.150.
45. Cal. S.P. Span, III, 2.
46. D.P., VI, VIII.
47. E. Lodge, *Illustrations of British History*, II, p.125.
48. T.S. Willan, *Studies in Elizabethan Foreign Trade*, 1959, pp.164-242.
49. D.P., I, f.237.
50. D.P., II, f.154.
51. J.T. Ben, ed., *Early Voyages and Travels in the Levant*, vii.
52. D.P., I, f.202.
53. D.P., III, 36, 40, 34, 43.
54. W.T. MacCaffrey, 'Elizabethan Politics: the First Decade, 1558-1568', in Past and Present, April 1963, p.34.
55. F.A. Inderwick, *Calendar of the Inner Temple Records*, I, pp.289, 290, 311, 318, 328, 335-6, 343.
56. D.P., II, 1; F. Blomefield & C. Parkin, *An Essay . . . of Norfolk*, pp.166-7.

57.   Cf. L. Stone, *The Crisis of the Aristocracy (1558-1641)*.

58.   Quoted in J. Williams, *Ancient and Modern Denbigh*, I, p.94.

59.   For much of the information about Dudley's Welsh interests I am indebted to documents in the Clwyd County Record Office, Ruthin, and articles in the *Denbighshire Historical Society Transactions* (hereinafter referred to as D.H.S.T.). The older standard works on the period are T. Pennant, A Tour in Wales (1778-81), and J. Williams, *Ancient and Modern Denbigh*. Both works are heavily biased against Dudley and reproduce uncritically much of the libellous material written about him. Some modern works have, to a certain extent, redressed the balance: D. Williams, *A History of Modern Wales*; A.J. Roderick, ed., *Wales Through the Ages*; G.D. Owen, *Elizabethan Wales*.

60.   Enid Roberts, 'Teulu Plas Iolyn' in D.H.S.T., 13(1964), pp.38-110; E. Gwynne Jones, *Exchequer Proceedings (Equity) Concerning Wales*, 1952, pp.228-9. S.L. Adams, 'The Composition of 1564 and the Earl of Leicester's Tenurial Reformation in the Lordship of Denbigh', *Bulletin of the Board of Celtic Studies*, XXVII(1976), Pt.4, pp.492-5.

61.   Cf. E.T. MacDermot, *A History of the Forest of Exmoor*, p.225. The writer of *Leicester's Commonwealth* built up the feud between Dudley and Bulkeley into a highly colourful affair of attempted poisonings and hired assassins, culminating in a plot to drown Bulkeley in the Thames. Robert must have found his opponent a considerable irritant but not sufficient to murder him.

62.   C.A. Gresham, 'The Forest of Snowdon in its Relation to Eifionydd', *Transactions of the Caernarvonshire Historical Society*, XXI(1960) p.54. S.L. Adams, *op.cit.*

63.   E. Gwynne Jones, 'An Inventory of the Goods and Chattels of Edward Jones Esq.', in D.H.S.T., VI, 1957, p.11.

64.   J. Williams, *Ancient and Modern Denbigh*, p.97.

65.   Enid Roberts, 'William Cynwal', D.H.S.T., XII, 1963, p.66.

66.   G. Penrhyn Jones, 'Some Aspects of the Medical History of Denbighshire', *D.H.S.T.*, VIII, 1959, pp.53-4.

67.   S.L. Adams, 'The Gentry of North Wales and the Earl of Leicester's Expedition to the Netherlands 1585-6', *Welsh History Review*, 1974-5, p.145.

68.   J. Williams, *Ancient and Modern Denbigh*, pp.98-9.

69.   J.H.E. Bennett, 'Two Elizabethan Chamberlains of the Palatinate of Chester', *Journal of the Architectural, Archaeological and Historical Society of Chester and North Wales*, New Series XX, 1914, p.196.

Chapter 10: 'Her Majesty Mislikes'

1.   W.T. MacCaffrey, *The Shaping of the Elizabethan Regime*, pp.128-9; P. Clark, *English Provincial Society . . .*, pp.136-8.

2.   Cf. T. Wright, *Queen Elizabeth and Her Times*, I, p.209.

3.   PRO, S.P., 52/10, f.68.

4.   Lansdowne MS, CII, f.121.

5.   As Cecil recorded in his diary, Hatfield MS. 39.

6.   Cal. S.P. Dom. Addenda, XII, 87.

7.   Cal. S.P. Ven., VII, 359.

8.   Some modern writers have too readily assumed that Robert opposed all marriage plans for the Queen because he knew they would result in his own downfall – e.g. W.T. MacCaffrey, *The Shaping of the Elizabethan Regime*, pp.161-2. In fact, the relationship between them was too close for that to have ever been a likely contingency. Elizabeth's union with a well-disposed spouse would have

had one very real advantage for Leicester: it would have freed him to marry. As time passed he grew increasingly concerned about his lack of an heir who could be legitimately proclaimed.

9. Camden, in his *Annals*, asserts that Elizabeth was soon disillusioned about the honour done her by the French King: 'This she took for a great honour, remembering herself that no Englishman was ever honoured with this order save only Henry VIII, Edward VI and Charles Brandon, Duke of Suffolk. But when she exactly observed all things that belonged to the honour of it, she was at length much displeased to see it so vilified that it was prostituted indiffer- - ently to every man.' After the Whitehall investiture Rambouillet and Dore headed north to confer the order on Lord Darnley - not the best of omens.

10. Cal. S.P. Dom., XXXIX, 41.

11. Cal. S.P. Dom., XXXIX, 31.

12. Historical Manuscripts Commission Pepys MSS. 78.

13. Cal. S.P. Dom. Addenda, XIII, 8.

14. Ibid., XIII, 7, 8.

15 Cal. S.P. Dom. Addenda, XIII, 73. The letter bears no year or date and in the Calendar it is tentatively assigned to 1567. However, bearing in mind the mood of the letter and the known movements of Dudley and Throckmorton, it seems to fit much more easily into 1566.

16. HMC Hatfield MSS, I, 1154.

17. Thynne MSS Longleat, quoted by J.E. Jackson in 'Amye Robsart', *Wilts. Archaeological Magazine*, XVII, p.78.

18. A.P.C., VIII, 248.

19. The principal documents in the Appleyard case are HMC Hatfield MSS, I, 1131, 1136, 1137, 1150-55; HMC Pepys MSS in Magdalene College, Cambridge, pp.103 ff. The story has been pieced together by N. Fourdrinier, *Amy Robsart*, MS, MC5/29 Norfolk Record Office, pp.211 ff.

20. Cal. S.P. Span., I, 415.

21. Ibid.

22. Cal. S.P. Span., I, 422.

23. PRO, S.P., 63/18-19.

24. A.L. Rowse, *Ralegh and the Throckmortons*, pp.50-1.

25. Cambridge University Library MS. Gg. III, 34, ff.208, et seq.

26. PRO, S.P. Dom. Eliz., XL, 91.

27. HMC Hatfield MSS, 1883-1940.

28. S. Haynes & W. Murdin, *Collection of State Papers . . . Left by William Cecil*, p.444.

29. PRO, Baschet Transcripts, 16, 17 Feb., 10 May 1565, W.T. MacCaffrey. *The Shaping of the Elizabethan Regime* p.135. Professor MacCaffrey's surmise that Leicester inaugurated these discussions is unwarranted: Catherine had had the possibility of an English alliance in mind for five years and had opened serious negotiations with Elizabeth in July 1564. Cf. H. de la Ferrière, *Les Projets de Marriage de la Reine Elizabeth*, 1881, pp.60-1.

30. H. de la Ferrière, *Le XVI Siècle et les Valois*, 1877, pp.184-5.

31. Cal. S.P. Span., I, 304.

32. Ibid., I, 434.

33. W.T. MacCaffrey, *The Shaping of the Elizabethan Regime*, p.135.

34. N. Williams, *Thomas Howard, Fourth Duke of Norfolk*, p.94.

35. BM. Cotton MSS, Titus B ii, 330.

36. Cal. S.P. Span., I, 520.

37. Cal. S.P. Span., I, 580.

38. M. Levine, *The Early Elizabethan Succession Question 1558-1568*, pp.89-162.

39.   Ibid., p.172.
40.   J.E. Neale, *Elizabeth I and Her Parliaments 1559-1581*, pp. 142-3.
41.   D.P., III, f.39.
42.   Cf. G. Mattingly, *Renaissance Diplomacy*, pp.191-3.
43.   Cal. S.P. Span., I, 415.
44.   A.P.C. passim.

Chapter 11: 'I May Fall Many Ways'

1.   P. Wiburn, *A Check or Reproof of Mr Howlet's Untimely Screeching*, 1581.
2.   E.g. W.T. MacCaffrey, 'Elizabethan Politics; the First Decade, 1558-1568', *Past and Present*, April 1963, pp.31-3; F. Chamberlin, *Elizabeth and Leycester*; M.M. Knappen, *Tudor Puritanism*: 'there is no evidence that he ever had a sincere religious thought', p.191; A.F. Scott Pearson, *Thomas Cartwright and Elizabethan Puritanism*, pp.266-7.
3.   PRO, Baschet Transcripts 31/3/26, f.207. See P. Collinson, *The Elizabethan Puritan Movement*, p.53 and note.
4.   Dedication of his translation of Theodore Beza's *A Brief and Pithy Sum of the Christian Faith*, 1563.
5.   Cal. S.P. Dom., XLIV, 72.
6.   P. Collinson, *Letters of Thomas Wood*, p.xx.
7.   J. Strype, *Annals of the Reformation*, p.103.
8.   John Harington, *A Brief View of the State of the Church of England*, p.8; A.F. Scott Pearson, *Thomas Cartwright and Elizabethan Puritanism*, pp.227-33, 290-4.
9.   Lansdowne MS., 17, f.55.
10.   D.P., II, f.60.
11.   Leicester to Robert Beale, 7 July 1572, BM. Egerton MS., 1693, ff.9-10. P. Collinson, *Letters of Thomas Wood*, pp.xxix-xxx.
12.   H. Robinson, ed., *Zurich Letters*, pp.220-1; P. Collinson, *Letters of Thomas Wood*, p.xxx.
13.   P. Collinson, *Letters of Thomas Wood*, p.10.
14.   Ibid., pp.11-12.
15.   Ibid., p.15.
16.   D.P., II, f.177. For a full treatment of the Archbishop's disgrace see P. Collinson, *Archbishop Grindal*, pp.233-65.
17.   P. Collinson, *Letters of Thomas Wood*, pp.10-11.
18.   Ibid., p.12.
19.   Ibid., p.14.
20.   Ellesmere MSS in Huntington Library, USA; C. Read, 'A Letter from Robert, Earl of Leicester, to a Lady', *Huntington Library Quarterly*, April 1936, p.25.
21.   E. Lodge, *Illustrations of British History, Biography and Manners . . .*, II, p.17.
22.   According to one rumour, Douglas became pregnant in 1571 or 1572 and hastened to Dudley Castle (her sister, Mary, was married to the Baron) to give birth to a girl who died almost immediately. Lady Sheffield denied this in later years but it is hard to decide whether to attach more weight to the rumour or the denial.
23.   C. Read, 'A Letter from Robert, Earl of Leicester . . .', p.24. No name or date appear on this letter but Dr Read argues a cogent case for Lady Sheffield as its recipient and places it tentatively in the spring of 1573. With the first deduction I cannot argue: I know of no other lady in Robert's life whose circumstances fit the facts as well as those of Douglas Sheffield. The date, however, depends on Dr. Read's rejection of any suggestion that the lovers

were ever married. This, on balance of evidence, I do not accept (see note 24 below). If, as I assert, they did go through a clandestine marriage in May, 1573, the letter must pre-date that event by weeks at least, and probably months.

24. The validity of this marriage has always been questioned. Both partners later set it aside and formed other unions. The issue was put to the legal test in 1604 when Sir Robert Dudley, the son of Leicester and Lady Sheffield, attempted to establish his legitimacy. Unfortunately, Sir Robert found himself up against the Sidneys, who had inherited the titles of Leicester and Warwick in default of legitimate heirs, and they had the ear of the new King, James I. In a celebrated Star Chamber trial, remarkable for its flagrant flouting of justice, the legality of the Esher ceremony was never decided. Rather it was brushed aside and Dudley condemned for the very attempt to prove his legitimacy. His witnesses were discredited and all his evidence impounded. The case, therefore, never established whether or not Leicester and Lady Sheffield were married and its handling by the crown lawyers leads one to suspect that they could not successfully have set aside the 1573 ceremony. Early in the nineteenth century the legal issue was opened again when Sir John Shelley-Sidney laid claim to the barony of Lisle and Dudley. The only bar to his claim lay in the possible legitimacy of Sir Robert Dudley, which might have resulted in some other direct heir being alive. The Committee of Privileges of the House of Lords concluded that Sir John had not established his claim, thereby again suggesting that the Esher wedding might, indeed, be valid. Copies and abstracts of most of the documents presented to Star Chamber and the preliminary hearings are preserved in D.P., Boxes VI-VIII. Also to be borne in mind is Leicester's subsequent treatment of his 'base son'. He could not openly acknowledge him as legitimate, particularly after his marriage to Lettice Knollys. Yet in his will he did treat Robert as his virtual heir, leaving him the bulk of his estate, instead of just a substantial legacy which would have been the appropriate portion for a bastard.

25. BM. Harleian MS. 6990, 37, f.78.
26. Quoted from Fénélon's correspondence by C. Read in *Mr. Secretary Cecil and Queen Elizabeth*, pp.442-3.
27. S. Haynes & W. Murdin, *Collections of State Papers . . . Left by William Cecil*, pp.521-7.
28. Cal. S.P. Dom. Addenda, XVII, 31.
29. D.P., II, f.55.
30. D.P., II, f.101.
31. Ibid.
32. PRO, S.P. 63/26/14.
33. BM. Harleian MS. 6991, f.27.
34. Cal. S.P. Dom., CXXV, 73.
35. BM. Lansdowne MSS, 45, 34.
36. BM. Lansdowne MSS, 20, 38.
37. This matter is one which would repay detailed research. Some of Leicester's protégés, when using all his titles, sometimes included the Lord Stewardship; e.g. Prospero d'Osma dedicated his *Report on the Royal Studs* (1576) to Dudley and called him 'Grand Master to her Majesty'. The editor of the Calendar of State Papers Domestic suggested that the appointment was made on 1 November 1584 (Cal. S.P. Dom., CLXXIII, 94). The first reference in the Lords' Journal to Robert holding this office is on 26 November 1584. A letter from Robert to Hatton of 27 September 1581 (quoted in H. Nicolas, *Memoirs*

of . . . Christopher Hatton, p.204) refers to Leicester's filling certain household vacancies 'as all other predecessors in this office have done'. R. Beatson and J. Haydn in *Book of Dignities* (1851) state that Dudley became Lord Steward in 1570. Whatever the truth of the matter, it is clear that Robert occupied a unique position as leader of the royal household, a position which gave him wider powers than any Lord Steward. His appointment, whenever it came, was simply recognition of an authority he had long enjoyed.

38. *Le Reporte de un Judgement done en Banke du Roi.* From a copy of the plea among the Dudley Papers at Longleat we learn that the assessment of damages was referred to a jury on 4 July 1571 (Box A, 1). Cf. also J. Bellamy, *The Tudor Law of Treason*, p.54, where the author suggests another technical reason for considering Dudley's sentence invalid.

Chapter 12: 'Never Wight felt Perfect Bliss, but such as Wedded Been'

1. A. Collins, ed., *Letters and Memorials of State*, I, p.48. This book contains a very abbreviated account of the entertainments. Two full length accounts exist: R. Laneham's *Letter*, and George Gascoigne's *The Princely Pleasures at . . . Kenilworth Castle*. An interesting commentary upon the entertainments is in M. Axton, *The Queen's Two Bodies: Drama and the Elizabethan Succession*, pp.61-6.
2. R. Laneham, *A Letter*, p.162.
3. G. Gascoigne, *The Princely Pleasures . . . at Kenilworth Castle*, pp.203-4.
4. D.P., II, f.7.
5. D. Digges, ed., *The Complete Ambassador*, p.218.
6. I. Mahoney, *Madame Catherine*, p.174.
7. Quoted in J.E. Neale, *Queen Elizabeth*, p.238.
8. BM. Harleian MSS, 6991/216.
9. Cal. S.P. Span., I, 493.
10. PRO, S.P., XII/125/73.
11. Cal. S.P. Span., I, 486.
12. D. Wilson, *The World Encompassed*, pp.19-24, 88.
13. PRO, S.P., 12/126/10.
14. Cal. S.P. Span., I. 431.
15. F. Blomefield & C. Parkin, *An Essay Towards a Topographical History of the County of Norfolk*, V, p.217. Douglas Sheffield's testimony is among the many papers dealing with the court case in D.P., VI. It is also described in G.F. Warner, ed., *The Voyage of Robert Dudley . . . to the West Indies*, 1594-5, p.xii et seq. Cf. also A.G. Lee, *The Son of Leicester*, pp.27-34, 110-115.
16. D.P., III, f.61.
17. A. Labanoff, ed., *Lettres, Instructions et Memoires de Marie Stuart*, V, p.94.
18. W. Camden, *History of . . . Queen Elizabeth*, pp.204-5.
19. Cal. S.P. Span., I, 493.
20. D.P., III, f.190.
21. D.P., III, f.191; for Leicester to Hatton, 9 July 1578, cf. H. Nicolas, *Memoirs of . . . Christopher Hatton*, pp.68-70.
22. Ibid, I, 583. Despatch dated 6 July 1579.
23. BM. Harleian MSS, 6991/216; letter of Sir Thomas Smith to Burghley.
24. J.B. de Lettenhove, *Relations Politiques des Pays Bas et de l'Angleterre*, X, p.678.
25. Cal. S.P. Span., I, 592.
26. Cal. S.P. Ven., I, 768.
27. A. Labanoff, *Lettres . . . de Marie Stuart*, V, p.94.
28. Cal. S.P., I, 592.

29.   Ibid., I, 594.
30.   Ibid., I, 583.
31.   D.P., II, f.65.
32.   Cal. S.P. Span., I, 596.

Chapter 13: Public Duty, Private Grief

1.   D. Wilson, *The World Encompassed*, pp.191-204.
2.   C. Read, *Lord Burghley and Queen Elizabeth*, p.261.
3.   F.A. Inderwick, ed., *Calendar of the Inner Temple Records*, I, p.318.
4.   D. Digges ed., *The Complete Ambassador*, p.212.
5.   D.P., II, f.65.
6.   Cf. R.C. Strong & J.A. Van Dorsten, *Leicester's Triumph*, pp.4-17.
7.   J.B. de Lettenhove, *Relations Politiques* . . . IX, p.159.
8.   Cal. S.P. Span., II, 465.
9.   J.B. de Lettenhove, Relations Politiques . . . , IX, p.486.
10.   It was eventually published in 1576 with a fulsome dedication to Leicester. It was reprinted in 1590. Digges was another devoted Dudley protégé. He accompanied his patron to the Netherlands in 1585 and is probably the 'T.D.' who wrote the pamphlet, *A Brief Report of the Military Services done in the Low Countries by the Earl of Leicester, Written by one that Served in a Good Place there*, cf. E. Rosenberg, Leicester, pp.282-6.
11.   R.C. Strong & J.A. Van Dorsten, *Leicester's Triumph*, p.13.
12.   Ibid.
13.   Dudley to Hatton, 9 July 1578. H. Nicholas, *Memoirs of . . . Christopher Hatton*, p.69.
14.   D.P., II, f.222.
15.   Quoted in E. Rosenberg, *Leicester*, pp.215-16.
16.   Hunsdon hoped to marry either his niece or daughter to King James. Burghley was establishing good relations with James on behalf of himself and his son, Robert, Cf. C. Read, *Lord Burghley and Queen Elizabeth*, pp.289-91. Evidently there was considerable personal rivalry among leading councillors to make a good impression.
17.   D.P., II, f.317.
18.   G.B. Harrison, ed., *Letters of Queen Elizabeth*, pp.125-6.
19.   A. Labanoff, *Lettres . . . de Marie Stuart*, IV, p.369.
20.   D.P., II, f.175; Cal. S.P. Dom. Addenda, XXV, 85. Cf. also E.C. Williams, *Bess of Hardwick*, pp.120-50.
21.   Quoted in A.G. Lee, *The Son of Leicester*, p.34.
22.   H. Nicolas, *Memoirs of . . . Christopher Hatton*, pp.381-3.
23.   D.P., II, f.187.
24.   Cal. S.P. Dom. Addenda, XXX, 58.
25.   These comprised 'all his manors, lands, etc. in Long Itchington, Hampton-in-Arden, Rudfen, Balsall, Knowle and Astell Grove, County Warwick; Cleobury Mortimer, Cleobury Borrow, Cleobury Liberty and Ernewood, County Salop; Wooton-Under-Edge, Symondshall, Wooton Farrer, Wooton Nibley and Cromehill, County Gloucester; and St. Clements without Temple Bar, with Leicester House', D.P., Box III, 60.
26.   PRO, S.P. XII/180/45; Cal. S.P. Dom., CLXXII, 37.
27.   Cal. S.P. Dom. Addenda, XXVIII, 29; Leicester to the Queen, 20 September 1583.
28.   H. Nicolas, *Memoirs of . . . Christopher Hatton*, p.97.

29. Cal. S.P. Dom., CXL, 23.
30. Cal. S.P. Dom., CXLIX, 67, 69, 71.
31. D.N.B.

Chapter 14: 'Leicester's Commonwealth'

1. D.P., II, f.154.
2. Cal. S.P. Dom., XIII, 21.
3. Cal. S.P. Dom., LXXXV, 34.
4. D.P., II, f.243.
5. This title was first used for the edition of 1641.
6. All quotations are from the 1904 edition of *Leicester's Commonwealth*, printed under the title *History of Queen Elizabeth, Amy Robsart and the Earl of Leicester* by F.J. Burgoyne and hereafter referred to as 'Burgoyne, *History*'. Burgoyne, *History*, p.6.
7. Ibid., pp.18-19.
8. Ibid., p.21.
9. A. Collins, *Letters and Memorials of State*, I, p.63.
10. Cal. S.P. Dom., CLXX, 88.
11. Cf. E. Rosenberg, Leicester, pp.x, 286; C. Read, *Lord Burghley and Queen Elizabeth*, p.293 ff. Professor Read suggests that the Bond of Association was originated by Burghley and Walsingham but quite clearly it emanated from the Dudley circle, a fact confirmed by Camden, who was certainly not well-disposed towards Leicester.
12. W. Camden, *History of . . . Princess Elizabeth*, p.178.
13. Burgoyne, *History*, p.211.
14. Ibid., p.143.
15. Ibid.
16. Ibid., p.49.
17. Ibid.,
18. Ibid., p.52.
19. Ibid., p.84-5.
20. D.P., XV, f.5.
21. D.P., III, ff.91-102.
22. Burgoyne, *History*, p.111.
23. Ibid.
24. *Ralegh and the Throckmortons*, pp.73-4.
25. Burgoyne, *History*, p.26.
26. J.E. Neale, *Elizabeth I and Her Parliaments 1559-1581*, p.398.
27. Burgoyne, *History*, p.66.
28. Ibid., p.58.
29. Ibid., pp.155-6.
30. Ibid., pp.27-33.
31. Ibid., pp.134-5.
32. Ibid., p.119.
33. Ibid., pp.166-7.
34. BM. Harleian MS. 767, 16. Cf. also C. Cross, *The Puritan Earl*, pp.142-58.
35. D.P., I, f.14.
36. D.P., I, f.183.
37. Burgoyne, *History*, pp.226-7.
38. J.E. Neale, *Elizabeth I and Her Parliaments 1559-1581*, p.116.
39. Letter under the royal sign manual to the Lord Mayor of London, quoted in

G. Adlard, *Amye Robsart*, pp.56-7.

40.   Cal. S.P. Dom, CLXXV, 101.
41.   Cotton MSS, Titus B.VII.
42.   Cal. S.P. Dom., CCIII, 61.
43.   Cal. S.P. Dom., CLXXVI, 53.
44.   Cal. S.P. For., IV, p.33.
45.   A. Labanoff, *Lettres . . . de Marie Stuart*, VI, p.300.
46.   Parsons made his position quite clear: 'Certain it is that, unto me and my conscience, he which in any point believeth otherwise than I do and standeth wilfully in the same is an infidel . . . I affirm and hold that for any man to give his help, consent or assistance towards the making of a king, whom he judgeth or believeth to be faulty in religion . . . is a most grievous and damnable sin to him that doth it of what side soever the truth may be'. *A Conference About the Next Succession to the Crown of England*, 1594, p.216. This is far removed from the religious tolerance urged in *Leicester's Commonwealth*.
47.   D.P., III, f.202.
48.   PRO, S.P. 12/151, 45. Cf. also Cal. S.P. Dom., CLI, 42-57.
49.   For a discussion of the authorship of *Leicester's Commonwealth* see Catholic Record Society, XXI, pp.57-9; XXXIX, pp.248; P. Caraman, *An Autobiography from the Jesuit Underground*.
50.   Cal. S.P. Dom., CCLXXXIII, 70.
51.   BM. Add. MS. 33739.
52.   A. Collins, *Letters and Memorials of State*, I, p.62.
53.   Ibid., I, p.64.
54.   Ibid., I, p.62.
55.   E. Rosenberg, *Leicester, Patron of Letters*, pp.291-3.

Chapter 15: 'Highest and Supreme Commandment'

1.   H. Nicolas, *Memoirs of . . . Christopher Hatton*, p.361.
2.   J. Strype, *Annals*, III, p.333.
3.   H. Nicolas, *Memoirs of . . . Christopher Hatton*, pp.371-2.
4.   P. Collinson, *The Elizabethan Puritan Movement*, pp.269-70.
5.   Quoted by C. Read in *Lord Burghley and Queen Elizabeth*, p.295.
6.   Burgoyne, *History*, p.50.
7.   H. Nicolas, *Memoirs of . . . Christopher Hatton*, pp.348-9.
8.   J.B. de Lettenhove, *Relations Politiques des Pays Bas et de l'Angleterre*, IX, mmmdlix.
9.   Cal. S.P. Dom., CLXXXI, 68; CLXXXII, 1, 6.
10.   Ibid., CLXXXII, 24, 32.
11.   J. Bruce, ed., *Correspondence of Robert Dudley, Earl of Leicester during his Government of the Low Countries . . . 1585-6* (hereafter called *Leicester's Correspondence*), p.4.
12.   Ibid., pp.7-8.
13.   Ibid., pp.12-15.
14.   Ibid., pp.15-19.
15.   Ibid., pp.21-24.
16.   D.P., III, f.63.
17.   Stephen Borough's 'Journal' in *Leicester's Correspondence*, pp.461-2.
18.   The only detailed eye-witness account of the Sluys campaign is T. Digges, *A brief report of the proceedings of the Earl of Leicester for the relief of the town of Sluys from his arrival at Flushing about the end of June 1587 until the surrender thereof*

26 July next ensuing. Whereby it shall plainly appear his excellency was not in any fault for the loss of that town. This is attached as an appendix to the 1590 edition of Digges' *Stratioticos*.

19. *Leicester's Correspondence*, p.69.
20. J. Stow, *Annales*, p.715.
21. Ibid., p.112.
22. G.B. Harrison, *Letters of Queen Elizabeth*, pp.174-5.
23. *Leicester's Correspondence*, p.151.
24. Ibid., p.174.
25. Ibid., p.194.
26. Ibid., p.209.
27. G.B. Harrison, *Letters of Queen Elizabeth*, p.179.
28. This was by no means a new situation, peculiar to Leicester's campaign; corruption and exploitation had been features of military finance for decades. Indeed, Sir John Fortescue, the historian of the British army, could comment, 'There have been many sovereigns and many ministers in England who have neglected and betrayed their soldiers, but none more wantonly, wilfully and scandalously than Elizabeth'. (J.W. Fortescue, *History of the British Army*, i, p.128). Robert did, in fact, make recommendations for the reform of some administrative abuses but they were not taken up by the Council (C.G. Cruickshank, *Elizabeth's Army*, p.155).
29. *Leicester's Correspondence*, pp.365-6. For a full discussion of this subject see J.E. Neale, 'Elizabeth and the Netherlands, 1586-7', in *English Historical Review*, xlv, p.373. Neale seeks to exonerate Elizabeth from blame and points out that she paid all and more than she had promised. That is true, but how realistically had the expenses of the war been calculated in the first instance and how far might ultimate costs have been reduced if the instalments had been paid promptly? The charge of incompetence on Dudley's part cannot be totally refuted but it does under-estimate the Governor General's difficulties. A.M. van de Woude, writing in the *Tijdschrift voor Geschiednis* (1961), examined the finances of the Netherlands' Campaign and concluded that both allies lacked the necessary funds. Leicester was merely the unfortunate man in the middle.
30. T. Digges, *A Brief Report*.
31. Ibid.
32. *Leicester's Correspondence*, p.367.
33. Ibid., p.312.
34. Ibid., p.426.
35. Ibid., pp.378, 394.
36. Ibid., p.312.
37. Letter of Henry Archer to Sir Thomas Heneage, 23 October 1586; Harleian MS., 285, f.264, printed in *Leicester's Correspondence*, pp.478-80.
38. Ibid., p.480.
39. *Leicester's Correspondence*, pp.445-6.
40. T. Digges, *A Brief Report*.
41. Leicester to Walsingham, 6 October 1586; *Leicester's Correspondence*, p.428.
42. T. Digges, *A Brief Report*.
43. Leicester to Walsingham, 10 October 1586; *Leicester's Correspondence*, p.431.
44. Ibid., p.457.
45. P. Johnson, *Elizabeth*, p.289.
46. Ibid.
47. Cal. S.P. Dom., CXCVIII, 19; B. M. Lansdowne MSS, 55, No. 33; Cotton MSS.

Calba C, xi, f.229.
48. Quoted by G. Mattingly, *The Defeat of the Spanish Armada*, p.60.
49. Buckhurst to Walsingham, quoted in A. Collins, *Letters and Memorials of State*, I, p.56.
50. Ibid., p.57.
51. G.B. Harrison, *Letters of Queen Elizabeth*, pp.189-90.

Chapter 16: 'A Glass Upon the Water'

1. Cal. S.P. Dom., CXCVIII, 19.
2. W. Camden, *History of . . . Princess Elizabeth*, p.305.
3. Cal. S.P. Dom., CXCVIII, 19.
4. D.P., II, f.265.
5. Cal. S.P. Dom., CCXIII, 9.
6. Ibid., CCXIII, 10.
7. Ibid.
8. Ibid., CCXIII, 22.
9. Ibid., CCXIII, 27.
10. Ibid., CCXIII, 38.
11. Ibid., CCXIV, 1.
12. Ibid.
13. Ibid., CCXIV, 34.
14. W. Camden, *History of . . . Princess Elizabeth*, p.330.
15. Cal. S.P. Dom., CCXIV, 52.
16. D.P., II, f.225.
17. D.P., II, f.249.
18. D.P., II, f.251.
19. D.P., II, f.257.
20. Cal. S.P. 12/215/65.
21. Cal. S.P. Span., IV, p.431.
22. *A New Discourse on a State Subject called the Metamorphosis of Ajax.*
23. PRO, S.P. 12/215/65.
24. E. Spenser, *The Ruines of Times.*
25. C. Read, *Lord Burghley and Queen Elizabeth*, p.436; C. Wilson, *Queen Elizabeth and the Revolt of the Netherlands*, p.102; W.T. MacCaffrey, *The Shaping of the Elizabethan Regime*, p.85.
26. G.R. Elton, *England under the Tudors*, p.282.
27. C. Read, *Lord Burghley and Queen Elizabeth*, p.435.
28. Cf. M.B. Pulman, *The Elizabethan Privy Council*, pp.235-50.
29. H. Nicolas, *Memoirs of . . . Christopher Hatton*, p.383.
30. P. Geyl, *The Revolt of the Netherlands*, p.212.
31. 'The Dead Man's Right', in 'R.S.', *The Phoenix Nest.*
32. T. Digges, *Humble Motives for Association to Maintain Religion Established.*
33. J. Florio, *Second Fruits*, dedicatory epistle.
34. F. Yates, *The Occult Philosophy in the Elizabethan Age*, p.87.
35. *History of Ireland*, dedication.
36. D.P., I, f.207.
37. Edmund Spenser, *The Faerie Queen*, Book I, Canto IX.

APPENDIX I

Extracts from 'Of Vertuous Life' by Thomas Lupton. Dedicated to Robert Dudley, Earl of Leicester (D.P., III, f.209)

'To the right honourable Sir Robert Dudley knight of the honourable order of the garter Baron of Denbigh Earle of Leicestre, master of the Quenes majesties horse and one of her highnes most noble privie Councellors. Though the Ethnÿckes (Right Honourable) thought there were but twoe kindes of fame, that is to say, good and evell, yet we may instlie say that there is a third called godlie fame, whereto for them to attayne is ympossible, and for us very hard (the fourth I make no accompt of which is false fame favord of fooles, set forward by flatterars, and blasde abrode by Buffardes, whereby the wicked are mysnamd and counted good, and the godlie defamed and called wicked, meanyng, here only of those that by dedes are desserved) The fyrst whereof we are apt to embrace, the second now not much prac-tized, and the third smallie followed, yet the worthy Grecians and Romaynes thorough their stout stomakes, captaynelike corage, and honest hartes, did such doughtie dedes for the gettyng of good fame, whereat we will shrynke for a great gayne. And as eche frute either good or evell hath his tree stump or roote from whence he doth spryng, Even so these thre fames have every one of them their sprynge from whence they doth flowe. For wickednes, mischief, crueltie, and tyranny, doe noorish evell fame, evell fame engendreth hate, and hate hastes allwaies to hurt. Activitie, liberalitie, faithfull frendship, good pollecye and affabili-tie, which such lyke are guydes to good fame, and good fame bringes foorth parfit love, and parfit love gettes ayde quietnes and saffetie, And farvent faith burnyng charitie, and hevenlie hope procures christian constancy, unfayned amitie, merciful liberalitie, and judgement with equitie, which doe brede and bring foorth godlie fame, and godlie fame achiveth the poore mans prayer, and the poore mans prayer purchaseth and obteyneth gode favour . . .

This godlie game is she that we ought to rune after, for the other twoe bringe foorth no such frute as this, for evell fame springes out of wickednes and bringes foorth mischief, the other which the heathen counted and the best fame, though it procede from honest hartes, yet after death gettes nothing but vayne praises. But this godlie fame springes from such vertuous dedes which in this lief please both god and man and after death bringes everlasting ioye and fame. Then seyng godlie fame is such a pretious thing, how happy are they that may embrace the same. But as none can be an Arithmetycian unles he fyrst learne numeracion addicion and subtraction with other principles thereof, nor yet an Astronomer except first he understand the rules, centers, arguments, and the meane motions of the planettes, nor yet a profound musition unless he learne fyrst both to tune and to tyme, the length and shortenes of every note, the measures, proporcions and the distaunce of one note from another, with other thinges very necessary. Even so none can attayne to this godlie fame but such as treade fyrst in the path that leades to the same, that is he must be gentle, affable, patient, redy to forgeve, mercifull, a procurer of good thinges, a helper of many, a hurter of none, a noorisher of the nedie, a feder of the fatherles and a faithfull christian. Which godlie fame, your honour seeks dailie to acquyre, as it semes by the way you walke yn, if truth may trye it, if the act may affirme it, if practize may prove it, or if right may report it, for to say truth (Beseching your honour not to suspect me of flattery, for as god knoweth my thought, I meane nothing lesse) it semes to me you doe degresse nothing from the forenamed way that leads to this fame. And to prove it more playnelie whereby all suspition of flatery may be quenched, (for trewe praise can not be rightlie counted adulacion) what good thing hath bene graunted (meanyng since you might) but you have bene guide to get it, what good publique sute but your honour hath set forwarde, what comon proffit but you have procured, what poore frendles sewter hath your lordship reiected and have not many learned men by you bene preferred what redynes is in you to ayde and helpe many, and who can approve that you have hurt any, which well wayed in equall ballaunce, you desserve to be loved of all and hated of none. But as Cayn did envie his brother Abell, because he was better beloved of god then he was (although he knewe no fault by hym), and as Jozeph was hated of his brethren because they thought he should come to promocion, Even so if your honour be not estemed as you have desserved, neither yet loved, as you have merited, assure your self it is onelie of such as are of cancred Caynes broode, which can not abide the prosperitie of such as are contrary to their wicked conditions. And for that your honourable lordship hath such a zeale to proffit the poore, to set forward good sewtes, to comforte the carefull, to helpe the nedye, and to mynde the miserable, I offer unto your honour a woork to such an ende and purpose framed, a comoditie to my contrie, (though rudelie yet well ment) that you may peruse viewe and consider the same thinking my self happie that I have found out such a mediator for such a matter, such an advocate for such a cause, and such a worthie sollicitor for such a godlie sute. Beseching your lordship (if I may be so bolde to crave it) not onelie thoroughlie to read it, but also to further the same to the Quenes majestie, whereby her grace may the better embrace it, more allured to allowe it, the gladder to graunt it, and the willinger to aucthorise it. Which being allowed graunted and aucthorised, the rather by your lordshippes good menes and thereby the comendable dedes therein performed, yt will not onlie be a marveylous prayse to the Quenes majestie with many other comodities as to her highnes I have sufficientlie described, but also it will make the poore to pray for you, the commons to commend you, poore prisoners to loove you, maymed soldiars to honour you, poore scollers to reverence you, poore captives to extoll you, and all england to favour you. And thereby your kindled fame will geve such a light that many shall see them selves much deceived, your enemyes amased and alsoe shamed, your lovers and frendes thereby much reioysed and, slaunderors reportes of force be clene banished. Thus leaving further to troble your honour, doe pray god as well to styrre and move you to favour this my rare sute and practize, as also to guide you in goodnes to fence you from foes, to encrease you in honour, to lend you long lif and to bring you to blisse.

Your honours most obedient

THOMAS LUPTON

APPENDIX II

Extracts from Robert Dudley's Will, written at Middelburg on 1 August, 1587, proved 6 September 1588.

THIS IS THE LAST WILL AND TESTAMENT of me Robert Earl of Leicester, her Majeftys Lievtenant General of all her Forces in the Low-Countries, and Captain-General of all the United Provinces, written with his own Hand the Firft of Auguft in Middleborough. Firft I take it to be the Part of every true Chriftian, to make a true Teftimony of his Faith at all Times, and efpecially in fuch a Cafe and fuch a Time as this is. And, therefore, I do mean here faithfully to make a fhort Declaration to teftify in what Faith I do live, and depart from this World, through the Grace of my Lord and Saviour to continue me in the fame till the Seperation of this Life and Body. And fo I do acknowledge my Creation and Being, to be had and continued by the Providence of our Almighty God, the Creator of all Things both in Heaven and Earth, and do confefs, that above all Deeds, that his divine Majefty hath done for Mankind, is the Gift of his bleffed Son, Chrift Jefus, to be the Redeemer and Saviour of his People that be faithfull, by whofe only Merits and Paffion, I verily believe, and am moft affured of the Forgivenefs of all my Sinnes, be they never fo great or infinite, and that he only is the fufficient Sacrafice that hath appeafed the Wrath of his Father, and that bleffed Lamb, which innocently fuffered all Torments, to bear the bitter Burden due to us miferable Wretches, for his moft tender Compaffion over all that have Grace to believe in him. All which his Graces Goodnefs and Mercy I moft faithfully take hold on, being fo promifed by himself, who is the only Truth itfelf, that I am the Child of Salvation; and to be the Inheritour of his ever-lafting Kingdom, and to meet with him at the joyfull Day of Refurrection, with all the faithfull Children, and Saints of God. In this Faith I now live and in this Faith I truft to change this Life, with continual Prayer to the Throne of Grace, to grant me, during this Pilgrimage of mine, a true, humble, and penitent Heart, for the due Recognition of all mine Offences, and the willing Amendment of the fame, and to fly inftantly to the fure Ankerholde my Lord and Saviour, Chrift Jefus, to whom with the Father, and the Holy Spirit, be all Honour, Glory and Dominion, forever, *Amen.* Thus being in perfect Health and Memory, and having fet down my Faith as a true Chriftian, and being uncertain of the Hour of Death, I think it my Part to fettle my worldly Matters in as good Eftate as I can, fpecially being haftily and fuddenly fent over, and likewife having very little Leafure, fince my Arrival, to get any Time for my private Buifinefs. But firft my Will is, to commit this wretched Body of mine, when it fhall pleafe God to feperate it from the Soul, to the Order of my dear Friends, that fhall be living as my Executors, and my Overfeers of this my laft Will and Teftament, and they to take fuch Order for the Burial of my Body, as they fhall think mete, always requiring that it may be done with as little Pomp or vain Expences of the World, as may be, being perfwaded that there is no more vain Expences than that is a convenient Tombe or Monument I wifh there fhould be. And, for the Place where my Body fhould lye, it is hard to appoint, and I know not how convenient it is to defire it; but I have always wifhed, as my dear Wife doth know, and fome of my Friends, that it might be at Warwick, where fundry of my Anceftors doe lye, either fo, or elfe where the Queens Majefty fhall command, for as it was when it had Life, a moft faithfull, true, loving Servant unto her, fo living, and fo dead, let the Body be at her gracious Determination, if it fhall fo pleafe her. Touching my Bequefts, they cannot be great, by Reafon my Ability and Power is little, for I have not diffembled with the World my Eftate, but have lived always above any Living I had (for which I am heartily forry) leaft that, thro my many Debts, from Time to Time, fome Men have taken Lofs by me. My Defire therefore is, and I do charge my Executors to have due Confideration, that if any Perfon fhall juftly after my Deceafe make fuch Complaint, that they may be fatisfied as far as it fhall be found in any Equity it is due unto them, with Advantage to them befide. I do here appoint my moft dear welbeloved Wife, the Countes of Leicefter, to be my fole Executrix of this my laft Will and Teftament; and do require her, for all Love between us, that fhe will not only be content to take it upon her, but alfo to fee it faithfully and carefully performed. And albeit there may many Imperfections be found with the Making of this Will, for that I am no Lawyer, nor have any Councel now with me to place Things in fuch Forme as fome are able, yet as my true Meaning is I truft to exprefs, that accordingly it may be interpreted, for I mean to make it as plain as I can. And firft of all, before and above all Perfons, it is my Duty to remember my moft dear, and moft gracious Sovereign, whofe Creature under God I have been, and who hath been a moft beautiful, and moft princely Miftrefs unto me, as well in advancing me to many Honours, as in maintaining me many Ways by her Goodnefs and Liberality. And as my beft Recompence to her moft excellent Majefty can be from fo mean a Man, chiefly in Prayer to God, fo whilft there was any Breath in this Body, I never failed it, even as for mine own Soul. And as it was my greateft Joy, in my Life Time, to ferve her to her Contentation, fo it is not unwelcome to me, being the Will of God to dye, and end this Life for her Service. And yet albeit I am not able to make any Piece of Recompence of her great Goodnefs, yet will I perfume to prefent unto her a Token of an humble, faithfull Heart, as the leaft that ever I can fend her, and with this Prayer withall, that it may pleafe the Almighty God, not only to make her the oldeft Prince, that ever he gave over England, but to make her the Godlieft, the Virtoueft, and the Worthieft in his Sight, that ever he gave over any Nation. That fhe may indeed be a bleffed Mother and Nurfe to this People, and Church of England, which the Almighty God grant for his Chrifts Sake. The Token I do bequeath unto her Majefty, is the Jewel with the three great Emrodes with a fair large Table Diamond in the Middeft, without a Foyle, and fet about with many Diamonds without Foyle, and a Roap of fayre white Pearl, to the Number fix Hundred, to hang the faid Jewel at; which Pearl and Jewel was once purpofed for her Majefty, againft a Coming to Wanfted, but it moft now thus be difpofed, which I do pray you, my dear Wife, fee performed, and delivered to fome of thofe whom I fhall hereafter nominate and appoint to be my Overfeers for her Majefty.

Next her Majefty I will now return to my dear Wife, and fet down that for her, which cannot be fo well as I would wifh it, but fhall be as well as I am able to make it, having always found her a faithfull, loving, and a very obedient, carefull Wife; and fo do I truft this this Will of mine fhall find her no lefs mindfull of me being gone, then I was always of her being alive . . ., and for that the faid Lands of Butlers were intended at the first, by the faid Butler, to be given to my faid bafe Son Robert, I do in Liew thereof give unto him the faid Lordfhips of Denbigbe and Chirke, & c. but after the Death of my dear Lord, and Brother, the Earl of Warwick, to whom, with all other my Lands, during his Life, I do give and bequeath; faving fuch as I have already granted to my faid dear Wife, in Joynture, or fhall grant unto her, by this my laft Will and Teftament. The Caftle of Kenelworthe, I do likewife give unto my faid Brother, with all the Parks, Chafes, and Lands, during his Life, and the Park and Padock of Rudfine only excepted, which I always gave unto my Wife, during her Life, the Timber Woods of all which I do referve from any Wafte (Reparations neceffary excepted) or it if fhall pleafe my Lord and Brother to built out the Gallery which I once intended, then to take fuch Timber as fhall be convenient for the fame. Item, I do will and give all Stuff and Implements of Houfehold, as I have heretofore ftored the faid Caftle with, all to remain to the faid Caftle and Houfe, and not to be altered or removed. I do alfo give two Garnifh of filver Veffell, to remain, as the reft, to the faid Caftle, with two Bafons and Ewers of Silver gilt, with other Plate for a Cupboard, to the Value of two hundreth Pounds, over and above the former Parcells of Veffell and Bafons and Ewers. Item, I do give and grant, by this my Will, the faid Caftle, and which I have purchafed to the fame: Alfo, after the Deceafe of my Lord and Brother, to my bafe Son Robert Dudley, as alfo the Fee Farme of Rudfyne. I do give alfo to my dear Wife my Houfe and Mannor of Langley, with all the Appurtenances, and the Ufe of all the Coppice Woods there, with the Leafe of Wbitney, until my faid bafe Son accomplifh the Years of one and twenty; both which after, I do give and grant to Robert, my bafe Son, in fuch Sort as fhall be limited unto him, with the reft of the Lands I give him. If he dye before the faid one and twenty Year, then my faid Wife to enjoy the faid Lands and Leafes during her Life. I give him alfo the Leafes of Grafton Pafture, after the Deceafe of my faid Wife. I doe alfo defire my good Lord and Brother, the Lands aforefaid coming to his Hands, that it will pleafe him to give fome reafonable Stipend to the Boy, when he comes to more Years, for his Maintenance. In the mean Time, after the Deceafe of Gabriel Bleke, and his Wife, I do give and grant to the faid Robert, all fuch Lands and Leafes, as I have conveyed unto me from the faid Gabriel forever; and the fame Lands, Houfes, and Leafes, to enjoy prefently after the Deceafe of the faid Gabriel Bleke, and his Wife, now living. I do give and grant to my faid bafe Son, alfo, after the Deceafe of my dear Wife, the Mannors of Balfoll, and Long Itebington, in the Countye of Warwicke, with all Appurtenances. I do likewife give and grant to my faid bafe Son, the Mannors of Cleobury and Eurnewood, after the Deceafe alfo of my faid dear Wife. The Moyety of fucb Lands as was recovered from the Lord Berkley, I do leave unbeftowed; but to be imploied by my Lord and Brother upon fucb our next Heirs (for that it came by Defcent) as he fhall find living with him, Sir.

And where my bafe Son is young and cafual, whether thefe my Gifts fhall come unto him or no, if he dye before he be one and twenty Years old, unmarried and without Child; then, if my Lord and Brother be living, I fhall require him to difpofe of all thofe Lands, leaving them unto him as my right and lawfull Heir. Save only, that if my faid bafe Son Robert fhould dye without Iffue, and that the Mannor of Denbigh and Chirk be redeemed, I do give and bequeath forever the Lordfhip of Chirk, to my welbeloved Son in Law the Earl of Effex, as alfo my Houfe in London, called Leicefter Houfe; if the faid Robert my bafe Son dye without Iffue, to whom I give and grant, as other the former Lands, after the Deceafe of my dear Wife, the faid Houfe, and the Remainder, if he dye without Iffue, to my faid Lord the Earl of Effex, my Son in Law, and to the Heirs of his Body lawfully begotten. And where, in one Article before touching my purchafed Lands in Wanfted, I left my faid Lands undifpofed but during the Life of my faid Wife: I do hereby, alfo, give and grant thofe purchafed Lands, not paffed unto her by Deed before, or not inclofed within the Park of Wanfted, to Robert my bafe Son during his Life, and to the Heirs of his Body, if he have any lawfully begotten; otherwife if he dye without Iffue, I do give and grant thofe Lands purchafed in Wanfted, to the Lord of Wanfted, being any of

the Heirs of the Body of my faid dear Wife, forever. And where I have erected an
Hofpital for the Relief of certain poor Men, and do think that I have fully accom-
plifhed the fame, or two hundred Pounds by Year, of fufficient Land and Rent, for
the Maintenance of the Mafter and poor Men, according to a Rate fet down; if any
Want be, either of Default of Rent, or other Affurance, I do give Authority, by this
my Will, to my Lord and Brother the Earl of Warwick, to make it up out of the
Mannor of Hampton, in Worcefterfhire, called Hampton magna. If the faid Hofpital
be fully made up to the aforefaid Summe, then, the faid Mannor to come to my
Brother, excepting any Eftate made to my Wife for Joynture, whereof I am here
uncertain. But if it be, and the Hofpital do lack of the Value, I doubt not but fhe will
be well content to fuffer my Brother to make any fuch Conveyance, which fhall not
hinder her Joynture, to the Benefit of that poor Houfe. And do hope God will fend
her Life and Ability to provide fome Means to joyn fome good Deed to that Houfe,
in finding fome Number of Poor Women, fuch as fhall not be idle, but to be fet on
Work in making Linnen Cloatb, or fuch like; a Work of good Charity it will be, and
I truft it fhall not be the lefs thought on to joyn with me, in that I have begun there:
And by this Will I do give to my Hofpitall two hundredth Pounds in money, for a
Stock to relieve their Neceffitys.

And for my Overfeers, I doe hereby appoint and heartily defire them, that they
will for the long good Will between us, take it upon them, and to help, affift, and
comfort, my dear and poor difconfolate Wife; Sir Chriftopher Hatton Lord
Chancellor of England, my loving Brother the Earl of Warwick, and my very good
Lord and Friend the Lord Howard High Admiral of England, trufting, that, as they
will not deny my Requeft, fo they will be carefull to help my poor Wife for the
Performance of this my laft Will and Teftament, who I know fhall need the good
Favours and Affiftance of my good Friends, and whom I make my fole Executrix.
Not doubting but fhall find her willing every Way to the utmoft of her Power, to do
all I have committed to her Charge, not thinking good to trouble any other of my
Friends, but herfelf, with my hard and broken Eftate, being I know not how many
Thoufand, above Twenty in Debt; and, at this prefent, not having in the World five
hundreth Pounds towards it. And the harder will her Cafe be, if I receive not fuch
Debts, as are here due to me by the States, which I much fear; but I have appointed
Lands to be fold, and fome Leafes I leave to my Wife, to fee how all, with all that I
have left her to pay my Debts, which God grant to the good Sattisfaction of my
Creditors . . .

APPENDIX III

'The Dead Man's Right'. An anonymous tribute (perhaps by Nicholas Breton) included in The Phoenix Nest, an anthology of poems published in 1593 and compiled by a member of the Inner Temple.

Written upon the death of the Right Honorable the Earle of Leicester.

IT is not vnknowne how wicked Libellors haue moft idiouflye fought the flander of our wife, graue, and Honorable fuperiours: diuulging defamatorie Libels, to full of immodeft railings and audacious lies, as no indifferent Reader but may eafily difcouer their enuie, and judge of the veritie: The Authors whereof, though in the qualitie of their offence (tending wholie of fedition) they haue woorthily deferued death, yet the fubftance of their Pamphlets haue not merited anfwere.

For want whereof fome as euill affected as themfelues, to whofe hands moftly fuch bookes haue come, are flattered with a poore aduantage, imputing the wife and filent difgefting of fuch inhoneft and fcurilous cartels to their guiltineffe: when (fimple as they are) who is elfe fo foolifh as knoweth not if all diuulged were true, how eafily Authoritie might excufe them, hauing pens and Preffes at commande-ment, and power to patronize: Much more when fo vntrue as themfelues afhamed of their falfhoodes, dare not auouch them vnder their owne names being without reach and feare of Authoritie.

Amongft others, whofe Honors thefe intemperate railors haue fought to fcandal-ize, none haue more vildly bin flandered than the late deceafed Earle, the godly, loiall, wife, and graue Earle of Leicefter. Againft whom (void of all iuft touch of difhonor) they forged millions of impieties, abufing the people by their diuelifh fictions, and wicked wrefting of his actions, all to bring his vertues & perfon in popular hatred.

Which though he during his life meekely bare as a man vntouched, without publifhing defence of his innocencie. Yet becaufe the toongs of men irritated to enuie by the inftruments of thofe libellors, being without feare of controlment, fith his death are become ouer fcandalous and at too much libertie. It fhall not be amiffe to perfwade more modeftie and pietie of fpeech.

And for as much as I perceiue the greateft and moft generall objection they haue to blemifh his honor, is but an opinion of his ambition and afpiring minde, where-with the capitall and cardinall Libellor of them all hath cunninglie infected that knew not the ftate of his honors: Let vs fee how he may juftly be touched.

Did he euer affume vnto himfelfe anie vaine or vnlawfull tytle, or was vnfatiate of rule? Did he purchafe his honors otherwife than by his vertues, or were they fo extraordinarie, as nowe or in times paft they haue not beene equaled in others infe-rior vnto him in condition of birth, and more in defart? If not I maruell the father of this peftilent inuention blufh not as red as his cap, and his children be not afhamed of his falfehood.

Admit this woorthie Earles and our moft gratious Souereigne who wifely judged of his vertues, and worthily rewarded his loialtie and paines, did honour him with titles aboue others of his time: (in humble and feemley fort, I fpeake it without comparifon) who euery way was more fit for the dignitie he bare, and more complet to accomplifh them: whereof the Libellor could not be ignoraunt, but that too much yeelding to his malice, he fought to flaunder this notable teftimonie of his Excellencie.

Such rather would I judge ambitious, as for promotions whether Ecclefiafticall or Temporall, hauing once conceiued a hope of greatneffe, without regard of confcience or Countrie, with voluntarie hazarde of all things purfue the fame, by fhamefull traiterous, and ungodlie meanes, exafparating their naturall Prince and fuperiour Magiftrates by rebellious and feditious Libels. Thefe be the true tokens of an afpiring minde, whofe nature is to hinder by malice, where it can not hurt by power.

But leauing further purfute of their malice, I will remember this Earles woorthineffe. For the firft and principall vertue of his vertues, his Religion, it fhall be needleffe to fpeake much fith all Chriftendome knows he profeffed one Faith, and worfhipped one onely God, whom he ferued in vprightness of life, and defended with hazard thereof in armes and action againft his enemies. How he fuccoured and relieued diftreffed members of the Church, I leaue to thofe that haue made proofe, who ought in dutie to make relation thereof.

Next I thinke there is none that will, dare, or can impeach his loialtie, either in fact or faith, fufficiently teftified by hir Majefties gratious loue to whom that belonged, as alfo by his dutifull and carefull feruice vnto hir. So as further narration thereof fhall not neede.

His wifedome by the grauitie of his place, the caufes he managed, and the cariage of his perfon, is approoued not onely vnto vs, but to moft nations of the world.

Laftlie of his valour and affection to his Countries peace, no honeft minde but is fatisfied: whereof what greater teftimonie can we require than the trauels his aged bodie vndertooke, the dangers the fame was fubiect vnto in the warres of the Low Countries, where he voluntarily offered his perfon in combate againft the deuoted enimies of this ftate and her Maieftie. Leauing his Wife, poffeffions, and home, not regarding his fafetie, riches, and eafe, in refpect of the godly, honourable, and louing care he bare the common quiet.

All which the vngratefull Malecontents of this time, on whome any thing is ill beftowed (much more the trauels of fo memorable a Noble) fpared not to reproch: Hyring the toongs of runawaies and roges, fuch as neither feare God nor the diuell, or are woorth a home, to proclaime hatefull and enuious lies againft him, in alehoufes, faires, markets, and fuch affemblies.

At whofe returne when his dealings were truely difcuffed, and truth ouercame their flanders, this was the refuge of their whifpering malice: His greatneffe and fmooth toong (faie they) beares it awaie: as if Honor once loft in act, could be hidden by greatnes, or recouered by grace and eloquence of fpeech. Both which taken away by his happie death, and our vnhappie loffe, he is fithence more cleared than before.

Maruell not then at their enuie, fith, *Virtutis comes inuidia*, but deteft the enuious, that thus blafpheme vertues, whom (for mine owne part) as I fee meafure their rage, fo will I judge of their affection to the ftate: for vndoubtedly none but the difcontented with the time, or fuch as he hath iuftlie punifhed for their lewdneffe, will thus calumniouflie interpret his proceedings.

If I meant to write a difcourfe of this Earles life, or an Apologie in his defence, I would proceede more orderly in repetition of his virtues, and more effectually in anfwere of their poifoned Libels: But as mine intent at firft was onelie to admonifh loofe toongs (fuch as mine eares haue glowed to heare of) and forewarne the ouer

credulous that are eafily abufed, hauing finifhed my purpose, it if effects amendment, I fhall be glad, if not, their fhames be on their owne heads.

   Befeeching God this Realme feele not the want of him alreadie dead, and greater
judgements infuse for our vnthankfulneffe.

   LEICESTER he liu'd, of all the world admir'd,
   Not as a man, though he in fhape exceld:
   But as a God, whofe heauenlie wit infpir'd,
   Wrought hie effects, yet vertues courfes held,
   His wifdome honoured his Countries name,
   His valure was the vangard of the fame.

BIBLIOGRAPHY

Manuscript Sources

The principal sources are the *Dudley Papers* (referred to as 'D.P.' in the Notes) at Longleat, Wiltshire and the *de Lisle and Dudley Papers* in the Kent County Archive Office at Maidstone.

Individual MSS and small deposits are in the Public Record Office, the British Library and other collections. Individual references to cited MSS are given in the Notes.

Printed Sources

Acts of the Privy Council of England, ed. J.R. Dasent (1890-1907)
Ascham, R., *The Schoolmaster* (ed. J.E.B. Mayer, 1863)
Aylmer, J., *A Harbour for Faithful and True Subjects* (1559)
Bain, J., (ed), *Hamilton Papers* (1890-92)
Barthlet, J., *The Pedigree of Heretics . . .* (1566)
Ben., J.T., (ed), *Early Voyages and Travels in the Levant*, Hakluyt Soc., 1st series LXXXVII, (1838)
Brooke, R., *Catalougue of Nobility* (1619)
Bruce J., (ed), *Correspondence of Robert Dudley, Earl of Leicester, during his Government of the Low Countries . . . 1585-6*, Camden Society (1844)
Burgman, H., *Correspondentie van Robert Dudley, Graaf van Leycester* (3 vols, 1931)
Burgoyne, F.J., (ed), *History of Queen Elizabeth, Amy Robsart and the Earl of Leicester* (1904)
Calendar of Patent Rolls Elizabeth I, V, 1569-1572 (1966)
Calendar of State Papers, Domestic, Edward VI, Mary, Elizabeth I and James I (ed. R. Lemon and E. Green, 1856-1872)
(Referred to in the Notes as Cal. S.P. Dom.)
Calendar of State Papers, Foreign, Elizabeth I (various editors, 1863-1950)
(Referred to in the Notes as Cal. S.P. For.)
Calendar of State Papers relating to Scotland, I *1509-1589* (ed. M.J. Thorpe 1858)
(Referred to in the Notes as Cal. S.P. Scot.)
Campion, E., *History of Ireland* (1571)
Caraman, P., *An Autobiography from the Jesuit Underground* (1955)
Carr, C.T., (ed), *Select Charters of Trading Companies 1530-1707*, Selden Soc., XXVIII, (1913)
Clowes, W., *A Proved Practice for all Young Chirurgians* (1565)
Collins, A., (ed), *Letters and Memorials of State* (2 vols 1746)
Collinson, P., *Archbishop Grindal, 1519-1583; The Struggle for a Reformed Church* (1980)
Collinson, P., (ed), *Letters of Thomas Wood, Puritan, 1566-1577* (1960)
Corte, C., *Il Cavalerizzo*, (trs. T. Bedingfield, 1584)
Crowley, R., *Select Works*, Early English Text Society edition, 1872
Cunningham, W., *The Cosmographical Glass Containing the Pleasant Principles of Cosmography, Geography, Hydrography and Navigation* (1559)

Dee, L., *General and Rare Memorials Pertaining to the Perfect Art of Navigation* (1577)

Digges, D., ed., *The Complete Ambassador* (1655)

Digges, T., *An Arithmetical Military Treatise Named Stratioticos* (1579)

Digges, T., *Humble Motives for Association to Maintain Religion Established* (1601)

Digges, T., *A Brief Report of the Proceedings of the Earl of Leicester for the Relief of Sluys . . .* (1590)

'T.D.', *A Brief Report of the Military Services done in the Low Countries by the Earl of Leicester, Written by one that served in a Good Place there* (1587)

Dudley, E., *The Tree of Commonwealth* (ed. D.M. Brodie, 1948)

Fills, R., *Laws and Statues of Geneva* (1561)

Florio, J., *Second Fruits* (1591)

Forbes, P. (ed), *A Full View of the Public Transactions in the Reign of Queen Elizabeth* (1740-41)

Forster, R., *Ephemerides Meteorographicae* (1575)

Fuller, T., *History of the Worthies of England* (1811 ed)

Gale, T., *Certain Works of Chirurgery* (1563)

Gascoigne, G., *A Hundred Sundry Flowers Bound up in One Small Posy* (1572)

Gascoigne, G., *The Princely Pleasures at the Court at Kenilworth* (1575)

Gascoigne, G., *A Discourse of a New Passage to Cathay* (1576)

Gascoigne, G., *The Spoil of Antwerp* (1576)

Gentili, A., *De Legationibus Libri Tres* (1585)

Giles, J.A., (ed) *The Whole Works of Roger Ascham* (1864)

Golding, A., *A Confutation of the Pope's Bull . . . Against Elizabeth . . .* (1572)

Grafton, R., *Abridgement of the Chronicles of England* (1563)

Haddon, W., *Cantabrigiensis: sive Exhortatis ad Literas* (1552)

Hakluyt, R., *The Principal Navigations, Voyages, and Discoveries of the English Nation . . .* (1904 ed)

Harington, J., *A Brief View of the State of the Church of England* (1653)

Harington, J., *A New Discourse on a State Subject called the Metamorphosis of Ajax* (1596)

Harison, G.B., *Letters of Queen Elizabeth* (1968)

Hatcher, T., *G Haddoni Legum Doctoris, S. Reginae Elizabethae a Supplicum Libellis Lucubrationes Passim Collectae* (1567)

Haynes, S. and Murdin, W., (eds), *Collections of State Papers . . . Left by William Cecil, Lord Burghley* (1740-1759)

Historical Manuscripts Commission:

Calendar of de Lisle and Dudley MSS

Calendar of Hatfield MSS

Calendar of Pepys MSS in Magdalene College Cambridge

Holinshed, R., *Chronicles of England, Scotland and Ireland* (ed. H. Ellis, 6 vols, 1807-8)

Hunnis, W., *A Hive of Honey* (1578)

Inderwick, F.A. (ed), *Calendar of the Inner Temple Records* (1896-1901)

Jordan, W.K. (ed), *The Chronicle and Political Papers of Edward VI* (1966)

Knox, J., *Works* (ed. D. Laing, 1846-64)

Labanoff, A., *Letters: Instructions et Memoires de Marie Stuart* (1844)

Laneham, R., *A Letter, wherein part of the entertainment unto the Queen's Majesty at Kenilworth Castle in Warwickshire in this summer's progress – 1575 – is signified.*

Legh, G., *Accedens of Armoury* (1562)

Leicester's Correspondence, see J. Bruce.

Le Report de un Judgement done en Banke du Roi (1571)

Letters and Papers Foreign and Domestic of the Reign of Henry VIII Preserved in the Public Record Office, The British Museum and Elsewhere, (ed. J.S. Brewer, J. Gairdner and R.H. Brodie 1862-1910)

Letters and State Papers relating to English Affairs, preserved principally in the Archives of Simancas (ed. M.A.S. Hume, 1892-1899)
(Referred to in the Notes as Cal. S.P. Span.)

Montgomery, J., *On the Maintenance of the Navy* (1570)

Neville, A., *De Furoribus Norfolciensium Ketto Duce* (trs. R. Wood, 1615)

J. Nichols, *Literary Remains of Edward VI* (1857)

J. Nichols, (ed), *The Diary of Henry Machyn 1550-1563*, Camden Soc., Old series XLII (1848)

J. Nichols, (ed), *Chronicle of Queen Jane and of Two Years of Queen Mary*, Camden Soc., Old series XLVIII (1850)

J. Nichols, (ed), *Greyfriars' Chronicle*, Camden Soc., Old Series XLXIV (1852)

Nicholas H., ed., *Memoirs of the Life and Times of Sir Christopher Hatton* (1847)

Osma, P.d', *Report on the Royal Studs* (1576)

Parsons, R., *A Conference About the next Succession to the Crown of England* (1594)

Perlin, E., *Description d'Angleterre et d'Ecosse* (1558)

Read, C., 'A Letter from Robert, Earl of Leicester, to a Lady', *Huntington Library Quarterly* (April 1936)

Robinson, H., (ed), *Zurich Letters*, 2nd series, (Parker Society, 1845)

Robinson, H., (ed), *Original Letters Relative to the English Reformation* (Parker Soc., 1846-7)

Rosso, G.V., *Historia delle cose occorse nel regno d'Inghilterra* . . . (1558)

'R.S.', *The Phoenix Nest* (1593)

State Papers and Manuscripts existing in the Archives and Collections of Milan, I, 1385-1618 (ed. A.B. Hinds, 1913)
(Referred to in the Notes as Cal. S.P. Mil.)

State Papers and Manuscripts relating to English Affairs, existing in the Archives and Collections of Venice . . ., VII, VIII, 1558-1591 (1890-95)
(Referred to in the Notes as Cal. S.P. Ven.)

Stow, J., *Annales, or, a general chronicle of England* (ed. E. Howes, 1631)

Stow, J., *A Survey of London* (ed. G.L. Kingsford, 1908)

Stow. J., *The Chronicles of England, from Brute unto this present year of Christ* (1580)

Strype, J., *Annals of the Reformation* (1824)

Tomkyns, J., *A Sermon Preached the 26th Day of May 1584*

Tottel, R., *The Passage of our Most Dread Sovereign Lady Queen Elizabeth through the City of London to Westminster* . . . (1960 ed.)

Veron, J., *Treatise on Free Will* (1562)

Vives, J.L., *On Education* (trs. F. Watson, 1913)

Warner, G.F. (ed), *The Voyage of Robert Dudley* . . . *to the West Indies, 1594-5*, Hakluyt Soc., 2nd series, III (1899)

Wiburn, P., *A Check or Reproof of Mr Howlet's Untimely Screeching* (1581)

Wilson, T., *A Discourse Upon Usury* (1572)

Wilson, T., *Arte of Rhetorike* (1553)

Wriothesley, C., *A Chronicle of England* (ed. W.D. Hamilton), Camden Society (1875-7)

Yorke, P. (ed), *Miscellaneous State Papers* (1778)

Secondary Works

Adams, S.L., 'The Gentry of North Wales and the Earl of Leicester's Expedition to the Netherlands', *Welsh Historical Review*, VII, (1974-5)

Adlard, G., *Amye Robsart and the Earl of Leycester* . . . (1870)

Adlard, G., *The Sutton Dudleys of England and the Dudleys of Massachusettes in New England* (1862)

Aird, I., 'The Death of Amy Robsart', *English Historical Review*, LXXI.

Anglo, S., Spectacle, *Pageantry and Early Tudor Policy* (1969)

Aston, M., *The King's Bedpost, Reformation and Iconography in a Tudor Group Portrait*, Cambridge, (1993)

Axton, M., *The Queen's Two Bodies: Drama and the Elizabethan Succession* (1977)

Bacon, F., *History of the Reign of Henry VII* (ed. J.R. Lumley, 1876)

Beatson, R. and Hayden, J., *Book of Dignities* (1851)

Beer, B.L., *Northumberland, the Political Career of John Dudley, Earl of Warwick and Duke of Northumberland* (1973)

Bellamy, J., *The Tudor Law of Treason: An Introduction* (1979)

Bindoff, S.T., 'A Kingdom at Stake', *History Today*, III (1953)

Blomefield, F. and Parkin, C., *An Essay Towards a Topographical History of the County of Norfolk* (1805-1810)

Brodie, D.M., 'Edmund Dudley, Minister of Henry VII', *Transactions of the Royal Historical Society*, 4th Series, XV (1932)

Bush, M.L., *The Government Policy of Protector Somerset* (1975)

Butler L., Leicester's Church in Denbigh: An experiment in Puritan Worship', *Journal of the British Archaeological Association*, 3rd Series, XXXVII

Camden, W., *The History of the Most Renowned . . . Princess Elizabeth*, (ed. W.T. MacCaffrey, 1970)

Chamberlin, F., *Elizabeth and Leicester* (1939)

Chambers, E.K., *The Elizabethan Stage* (2 vols, 1923)

Charlton, K., *Education in Renaissance England* (1965)

Christy, M., 'Queen Elizabeth's Visit to Tilbury in 1588', *English Historical Review*, XXXIV (1919)

Clark, P., *English Provincial Society from the Reformation to the Revolution* (1977)

Collins, A.J., 'The Progress of Queen Elizabeth to Tilbury, 1588', *British Museum Quarterly*, X (1936)

Collinson, P., *The Elizabethan Puritan Movement* (1967)

Collinson, P., *Archbishop Grindal, 1519-1583; the struggle of a Reformed Church* (1980)

Cornwall, J., *The Revolt of the Peasantry, 1549* (1977)

Cross, C., *Church and People 1450-1660: The Triumph of the Laity in the English Church* (1976)

Cross, C., *The Puritan Earl: Henry Hastings, Third Earl of Huntingdon* (1966)

Cruickshank, C.G., *Elizabeth's Army* (1966)

Cunliffe, J.W. (ed), *Early English Classical Tragedies* (1912)

Dorsten, J.A. van, and Strong, R.C., *Leicester's Triumph* (1964)

Elton, G.R., *England Under the Tudors* (1955)

Elton, G.R., *Reform and Reformation, England 1509-1558* (1977)

Elton, G.R., *The Parliament of England, 1559-1581*, Cambridge, (1986)

Erickson, C., *Bloody Mary* (1978)

Fortescue, J.W., *History of the British Army* (1899)

Garrett, C., *The Marian Exiles* (1966)

Geyl, P., *The Revolt of the Netherlands, 1555-1609* (1932)

Hassell Smith, A., *Country and Court, Government and Politics in Norfolk 1558-1603* (1974)

Heal, F. and O'Day, R., (eds), *Church and Society of England: Henry VIII to James I*, (1977)

Heller, A., *Renaissance Man* (1978)

Hillebrand, H.N., *The Child Actors* (1926)

Hoak, D.E., *The King's Council in the Reign of Edward VI* (1976)

Jackson, J.E., 'Amye Robsart' *Wilts Archaeological Magazine*, XVII (1898)

Jebb, S., *Life of Robert Earl of Leicester* (1727)

Johnson, P., *Elizabeth, A Study in Power and Intellect* (1974)

Jordan, W.K., *Edward VI, The Young King* (1968)

Jordan, W.K., *Edward VI, The Threshold of Power* (1970)

Knappen, M.M., *Tudor Puritanism* (1939)

la Ferrière, C.f.H de, *Les Projects de Marriage de la Reine Elizabeth* (1882)

la Ferrière, C.f.H. de, *Le XVI Siècle et la Valois* (1877)

Lee, A.G., *The Son of Leicester* (1964)

Leti, G., *La Vie d'Elizabeth, reine d'Angleterre traduite de l'Italian* (1696)

Lettenhove, J.B.M.C.K. de, *Relations Politiques des Pays-Bas et d'Angleterre* (1882-1900)

Levine, M., *The Early Elizabethan Succession Question 1558-1568* (1966)

Lewis, C.S., *English Literature in the Sixteenth Century, Excluding Drama* (1954)

Loades, D.M., *Two Tudor Conspiracies* (1965)

Lodge, E., *Illustrations of British History . . . in the Reigns of Henry VIII, Edward VI, Mary, Elizabeth and James I* (1838)

MacCaffrey, W.T., 'Elizabethan Politics: the First Decade, 1558-1568', in *Past and Present*, (April 1963)

MacCaffrey, W.T., *The Shaping of the Elizabeth Regime* (1969)

MacCulloch, D., *Thomas Cranmer*, Yale, (1996)

Mahoney, I., *Madame Catherine* (1975)

Malkiewicz, A.J.A., 'An Eye-witness's Account of the Coup d'Etat of October 1549' *English Historical Review*, LXX (1955)

Mattingly, G., *Renaissance Diplomacy* (1955)

Mattingly, G., *The Defeat of the Spanish Armada* (1959)

Motley, J.L., *The Rise of the Dutch Republic* (1856)

Neale, J.E., *Elizabeth I and her Parliaments, 1559-1581* (1953)

Neale, J.E., *Elizabeth I and her Parliaments, 1584-1601* (1956)

Neale, J.E., *Queen Elizabeth* (1934)

'The Accession of Queen Elizabeth', History Today (May 1953)

Outhwaite, R.B., *Inflation in Tudor and Early Stuart England* (1969)

Owen, G.D., *Elizabethan Wales: the Social Scene* (1962)

Parker, G., 'The Dutch Revolt', *Tijdschrift voor Geschiednis*, LXXX 4 (1976)

Peck, D.C., 'Government Suppression of English Catholic Books: The Case of "Leicester's Commonwealth"', *Library Quarterly*, XLII 2 (1977)

Pennant, T., *A Tour in Wales* (1778-81)

Pollard, A.F., *England Under Protector Somerset*, (1909)

Prescott, H.F.M., *Mary Tudor* (1952)

Prior, C.M., *The Royal Studs of the Sixteenth and Seventeenth Centuries* (1935)

Pulman, M.B., *The Elizabethan Privy Council in the Fifteen Seventies* (1971)

Read, C., *Lord Burghley and Queen Elizabeth* (1960)

Read, C., *Mr Secretary Cecil and Queen Elizabeth* (1955)

Reese, M.M., *The Royal Office of Master of the Horse* (1976)

Richardson, A., *The Lover of Queen Elizabeth* (1907)

Roderick, A.J., (ed), *Wales Through the Ages* (2 vols 1959-60)

Rosenberg, E., *Leicester, Patron of Letters* (1955)

Rowse, A.L., *Ralegh and the Throckmortons* (1962)

Scott Pearson, A.F., *Thomas Cartwright and Elizabethan Puritanism* (1925)

Simpson, A., *The Wealth of the Gentry 1540-1660* (1961)

Smith, A.G.R., *The Government of Elizabethan England* (1967)

Simpson, M.A., *Defender of the Faith, Etcetera* (1978)

Simpson, R., *Edmund Campion* (1867)

Simpson, R., *The Crisis of the Aristocracy (1558-1641)* (1965)

Stone, L., 'Anatomy of the Elizabethan Aristocracy', *Economic History Review*, XVIII (1948)

Stone, L., *The Crisis of the Aristocracy, 1558-1641*, Oxford, (1967)

Strong, R.C. and Van Dorsten, J.A., *Leicester's Triumph*, (1964)

Tytler, P.F., *England Under the Reigns of Edward VI and Mary* (1939)

Waldman, M., *Elizabeth and Leicester* (1944) — 1969

Wernham, R.B., *Before the Armada, The Growth of English Foreign Policy, 1485-1588* (1966)

Williams, D., A *History of Modern Wales* (1950)

Williams, E.C., *Bess of Hardwick* (1959)

Williams, J., *Ancient and Modern Denbigh: A Descriptive History of the Castle, Borough and Liberties* (2 vols. 1856)

Williams, N., *All the Queen's Men* (1972)

Williams, N., *Thomas Howard, Fourth Duke of Norfolk* (1964)

Wilson, C., *Queen Elizabeth and the Revolt of the Netherlands* (1970)

Wilson, D.A., *The World Encompassed: Drake's Great Voyage 1577-1580* (1977)

Woude van der, A.M., *Der Staten, 'Leicester en Elizabeth in Financiele Verwikkelingen'*, *Tijdschrift voor Geschidnis*, LXXIV (1961)

Wright, T., *Queen Elizabeth and Her Times* (1838)

Yates, F., Astraea: *The Imperial Theme in the Sixteenth Century* (1975)

Yates, F., *The Occult Philosophy in the Elizabethan Age* (1979)

Unpublished Works

Adams, C.J., *Tudor Minister: Sir Thomas Wriothesley*, Manchester M.A. Thesis (1970)

Bush, M.L., *The Rise to Power of Edward Seymour, Protector Somerset, 1500-1547*, Cambridge Ph.D. Thesis (1965)

Fourdrinier, N., Amy Robsart, *the Wife of Lord Robert Dudley the Favourite of Queen Elizabeth I. Her Life, Ancestry and the True Cause of Her Tragic Death*. M.S. MC5/29, Norfolk Record Office.

Hodgkinson, L.A., *The Administration of the Earl of Leicester in the United Provinces*, M.A., Liverpool, 1925

Jong de, G., *The Earl of Leicester's Administration of the Netherlands 1585-86*, Ph.D. Wisconsin, 1956

Oosterhoff, F.G., *The Earl of Leicester's Governorship of the Netherlands 1586-87*, Ph.D. London, 1967

Sturge, C., *Life and Times and John Dudley, Earl of Warwick and Duke of Northumberland, 1504(?)-1553*, London Ph.D. Thesis 1927

INDEX

Abingdon 95, 121, 122, 149, 177
Abrdgement of the Chronicles of England 165
Alençon, Duc d' 154, 163, 224, 230, 232–42, 250, 257, 260
Allen, Dr William, Principal of English College, Douai 265–6
Alva, Duke of 212, 237
Antonio, Don, Portuguese pretender 238
Antwerp 240, 242, 274
Appleyard, John 33, 113, 122, 125, 185–7, 192
Arithmetica Memorativa 18
Arithmetical Treatise Named Stratioticos, An 241
Arnhem 288
Arnold, Sir Nicholas 18
Arundell, Charles, Gent of P.C. 266–7
Ascham, Roger 16, 18
Ashley, John 130
Ashley, Kate 130
Ashridge 17, 26
Audley End 152
Augsburg Confession 111
Aylmer, John 108, 137, 273

Babington, Francis, Master of Balliol 126
Babington plot 175, 292
Bacon, Sir Francis 252
Bacon, Sir Nicholas 252
Baker, Andrew 169–70
Barbary Company 151, 169
Baxter, Edmund 118
Bear, the 170
Bedingfield, Thomas 92n
Benger, Thomas 102
Bentham, Thomas 202
Best, Richard 220
Beverley, Yorks. 105
Blois, Treaty of 224
Blount, Christopher 304
Blount, Sir Richard 125
Blount, Sir Thomas 122–5, 128, 185
Bluet, Thomas 267
Blundeville, Thomas 92
Bolton 211–12
Bond of Association, The 255
Borgarucci, Dr Giulio 210
Borough, Stephen 277–8
Bothwell, James 189
Boulogne 22
Bowes 122
Boxall, John 117
Bray, Sir Reginald 5
Brill 276, 277, 278
Bristol 151, 169
Bruges 295
Buckhurst, Lord 272, 293–4, 298
Buckley, William 18, 24
Bulkeley, Sir Richard 175
Bullinger, Heinrich 243

Burbage, James 157, 158
Burghley, 1st Baron *see* Cecil, Sir William
Burghley House 152
Burton Lazar, Leics. 105
Buxton 167, 241, 245, 246, 273, 304
Byrd, William 258

Cabot, Sebastian 20
Calais 73, 78, 85, 107, 110, 111, 118, 138, 140
Calvinism 108, 117
Cambridge 18, 58, 59, 171, 202, 203, 252, 253
Camden, William 88, 114, 255, 302, 306
Campion, Edmund 165–6, 243, 311
Carey, Henry, Lord Hunsdon 115, 134, 159, 180, 242, 300
Cartwright, Thomas 202–3
Casimir, John, Duke of Palatine 241
Cateau–Cambrésis, Treaty of 107, 109–10, 114, 116
Catholic recusancy and propaganda (*see also* Jesuits) 243, 252–70, 303
Cave, Sir Ambrose 201
Cavendish, Charles 246
Cavendish, Elizabeth, Countess of Shrewsbury 244–6
Cavendish, Richard 177
Cecil, Sir William, later Lord Burghley 47, 52, 80, 86, 106, 107, 108, 110, 113–14, 117, 118, 119–20, 124, 128, 129– 36, 137, 144–6, 150, 152, 153, 179, 180, 183, 187–95, 208, 211, 212, 213, 214–15, 230, 238, 245, 250, 252, 263, 272, 277, 279, 280, 292, 293, 302, 307; relations with Dudley 217–19, 224–6
Certain Notes of Instruction Concerning the Making of Verse 161
Certain Works of Chirurgery 167
Challoner, Thomas 91–2, 103, 118, 248
Chamberlain, Sir Ralph 111
Chamberlain, Sir Thomas 115, 126
Chapel Royal choirboys 161–2
Charles, Archduke of Austria 183, 191–7
Charles IX of France 171n, 182, 193–4
Charterhouse, London 87–8
Chatillon, Cardinal de 257
Chatsworth, Derby. 245, 246
Cheke, Sir Johhn 18, 57
Chelmsford 300
Cheshire 269
Chester 177
Chirk 174
Chowte, Sir Philip 172
Christmas 111–12, 134–5
Chronicles of England from Brute unto this Present Year of Christ 165
Chronicles of England, Scotland and Ireland 165
Clinton, Edward Fiennes de, Earl of Lincoln 110, 226
Clowes, William 167